Trade Unions and the New Industrialization of the Third World

Trade Unions and the New Industrialization of the Third World

Edited by
Roger Southall

Zed Books Ltd.
London

Trade Unions and the New Industrialization of the Third World
was first published in 1988 by:
Zed Books Ltd, 57 Caledonian Road, London N1 9BU, UK,
and
University of Ottawa Press, 603 Cumberland, Ottawa, Ontario K1N 6N5, Canada
and
University of Pittsburgh Press, Pittsburgh, Pennsylvania 15260, USA

Cover designed by Andrew Corbett
Printed and bound in the United Kingdom
by Biddles Ltd, Guildford and King's Lynn

British Library Cataloguing in Publication Data

Trade unions and the new industrialisation
of the Third World.
1. Trade-unions—Developing countries
I. Southall, Roger
331.88′09172′4 HD6940.7

ISBN 0-86232-578-1
ISBN 0-86232-579-X Pbk

Canadian Cataloguing in Publication Data

Trade unions and the new industrialisation of the
Third World

(International development)
Includes bibliographical references.
ISBN 0-7766-0192-X

1. Trade-unions—Developing countries.
2. Industrialization. 3. Developing countries—
Economic conditions. I. Southall, Roger II. Series:
International development (University of Ottawa Press).

HD6940.7.T73 1987 331.88′09712′4 C87-090322-5

Library of Congress Cataloging-in-Publication Data

Trade unions and the new industrialisation of the Third
World.

(Pitt series in social and labor history)
1. Trade-unions—Developing countries. 2. Developing
countries—Industries. 3. International division of
labor. I. Southall, Roger. II. Series.
HD6940.7.T73 1988 331.88′09172′4 87-40608
ISBN 0-8229-1152-3

Contents

Tables

List of Contributors

Manfred Bienefeld, a Fellow at the Institute of Development Studies, University of Sussex, is an economist/economic historian. He has worked at the University of Dar es Salaam, carrying out research for several ministries on wages and manpower questions, and also on licensing, urbanisation and industry. His current work has three related strands: Tanzania/East Africa; employment and industrialization; and global North-South developments. He has recently completed an EEC employment and development mission to Fiji.

Maja Bjorkman is a sociologist at Roskilde University Centre, Denmark. He has published work about US national and international labour strategies in the 1980s and about the female labour market in the Third World.

Dennis Engbarth is a doctoral student in the Department of Sociology, State University of New York, Binghamton.

Laksiri Fernando is Senior Lecturer in Political Science at the University of Peradeniya, Sri Lanka. He is a grass-roots activist and during 1984-85 was seconded to the headquarters of the World University Service in Geneva.

Jeffrey Harrod writes academic and current analysis on labour issues and international political economy. He is part-time Professor of International and Comparative Labour Studies at the Institute of Social Studies, The Hague. He has recently been publications' and research consultant for an international trade secretariat. His publications include *Trade Union Foreign Policy: Activities of British and American Unions in Jamaica* (London, Macmillan, 1972); *The Unprotected Worker: Social Relations of Subordination* (New York, Columbia University Press, 1986); and (with Vic Thorpe) *Asbestos: The Politics and Economics of a Lethal Substance* (Geneva, ICEF, 1984)

Nigel Haworth lectures in industrial relations at Strathclyde University. His research interests are in Latin American labour studies, labour and MNCs, and the electronics industry.

Rhoda Howard is Associate Professor of Sociology, McMaster University, Hamilton, Ontario, Canada. She began her studies on Africa with her *Colonialism and Underdevelopment in Ghana* (London, Croom Helm, 1978) and has published extensively in third world and Africa oriented journals. Since 1979 she has been working on refugees and human rights.

Laurids Lauridsen is a political scientist working at the International Development Studies department at Roskilde University Centre, Denmark. He has published on the new international division of labour and industrial development in Latin America and South East Asia.

Henrik Secher Marcussen is a sociologist and economist working at the International Development Studies department at Roskilde University Centre, Denmark. He is co-author of *The Internationalization of Capital: Prospects for the Third World*, (London, Zed Press, 1982) and has also published on agricultural and agri-industrial development in Africa.

Valentine Moghadam was born in Tehran and has studied in Canada and the US. Her recently completed dissertation is a sociological analysis of industrialization and the industrial labour force in Iran. She is active in Iranian left circles and currently teaches sociology in the Department of Sociology, New York University, New York.

Ronnie Munck is Senior Lecturer in Sociology at the University of Ulster. He is author of *Politics and Dependency in the Third World* (London, Zed Books, 1984) and co-author of *Argentina: From Anarchism to Peronism. Workers, Trade Unions and Politics 1855-1985*, (London, Zed Books, 1987). He is currently working on a book about democratisation in South America (Zed Books, forthcoming).

James Petras is Professor of Sociology at the State University of New York, Binghamton. He has written extensively about Latin American issues and about the influence of US imperialism on Latin America. His numerous books include *Politics and Social Structure in Latin America* (New York, Monthly Review Press, 1970), *Peasants in Revolt* (Austin, University of Texas, 1973) and other co-authored and edited works. He has also published extensively in journals such as *New Left Review* and the *Journal of Contemporary Asia*.

Harvie Ramsay lectures in industrial relations at Strathclyde University. His research interests include industrial democracy issues in both capitalist and socialist countries, international capital and labour responses, new technology and work in local government, and labour in the Third World.

Roger Southall is Lecturer in Politics at the University of Leicester, having previously researched or taught at universities in Uganda, Ghana, Lesotho and Canada. He is author of *South Africa's Transkei: The Political Economy of an 'Independent' Bantustan* (London, Heinemann, and New York, Monthly Review Press, 1982) and articles in various third world and Africa oriented journals. During 1985 he worked for the Canadian Labour Congress in Africa. He is editor of the recent special issue (November 1985) of *Labour, Capital and Society* (also an outcome of the conference on Third World Trade Unionism), and is currently continuing to work on South Africa.

Hobart Spalding is Professor of Latin American and Caribbean History at Brooklyn College of the City University of New York. He has published *Organized Labor in Latin America* (New York, New York University Press, 1977) and his numerous articles have appeared in *Latin American Perspectives*, *Science and Society*, *Latin American Research Review*, *Journal of Interdisciplinary History*, *Nueva Sociedad* and *Labour, Capital and Society*. He is currently continuing work on US labour imperialism.

Nicholas Van Hear is a freelance researcher and writer based in London. Since completing his Ph.D on 'Northern labour and the development of capitalist agriculture in Ghana', (Birmingham, 1982), he has concentrated on the impact of recession on African workers, expulsions of migrant workers from African countries, and the commercialization of agriculture in Africa and that continent's drought.

Peter Wad is a Lecturer at the Institute of Cultural Sociology, University of Copenhagen. He is co-editor of *Industrialization and the Labour Process in Southeast Asia* (Institute of Cultural Sociology, 1984), and works on trade unionism in East and South East Asia.

Arne Wangel teaches in the Department of Sociology, University of Copenhagen. He has undertaken research in Malaysia and is currently continuing to work on labour in that country's electronic industry.

Peter Waterman teaches third world politics at the Institute of Social Studies, The Hague, having previously worked for the World Federation of Trade Unions in Nigeria. He has written widely on third world labour and social movements, and is co-editor of *African Social Studies: A Radical Reader* (London, Heinemann, 1977). He is founder editor of the *Newsletter of International Labour Studies*, and is associated editorially with *Labour, Capital and Society*, *Third World Book Review* and *International Labour Reports*. He is currently working on international labour communications.

Preface

The contemporary economic crisis has given rise to varied formulations concerning a new international division of labour which – placing emphasis upon a shift of labour-intensive manufacturing to the third world – suggests an increasing global disadvantage for labour. The papers in this volume, which were all originally presented to a conference on 'Third World Trade Unionism: Equity and Democratization in the Changing International Division of Labour' (organized by the Institute of International Development and Cooperation of the University of Ottawa in October 1984), seek to address this question from a progressive perspective by examining the prospects, characteristics and capability of third world unions for protecting and promoting the interests of workers within this context. The key issues are: do third world unions possess the capacity for offensive as well as defensive activities within a changing global capitalist order? Is organized labour doomed to submission at the behest of the capital logic of the world market? What are the prospects for international labour solidarity? Whether or not the result here is entirely satisfactory is doubtful, but it is, I believe, provocative, and on that count should serve to stimulate committed consideration of the conditions and potential of third world labour in the enormously difficult circumstances it is facing.

Happy to relate, interest in the conference was widespread, and it was attended by 80 odd academics and trade unionists from some 21 countries (even though it was a matter of regret that there were fewer third world representatives of labour than had been hoped). In the course of organizing the event, many debts were incurred. In particular, generous funding was provided by the Canadian International Development Agency, the Canadian Social Sciences and Humanities Research Council, the International Development Research Centre and Labour Canada, with the Institute itself providing much material assistance, not least through the patient, skilful and willing help of its secretarial and administrative staff. A special mention is due also to Bill Paton, my assistant, whose capacity for rational-bureaucratic control over a sprawling conference far exceeded my own, and whose humour sustained us both. Finally, thanks are due to the International Department of the Canadian Labour Congress and its Director, John Harker, for not only supporting the conference by recommending it to the international trade union network but also for providing me thereafter with some practical union experience in Africa. Praxis, perhaps, will make some of us less imperfect!

Roger Southall
Department of Politics
University of Leicester

Introduction

At issue: Third World Trade Unions in the Changing International Division of Labour

Roger Southall

The enormity of the present economic crisis, which in the advanced industrialized countries of the West has entrenched an apparently permanent high rate of unemployment and thrown organized labour on to the defensive, has greatly sharpened the focus upon how changing global conditions affect conditions of employment throughout the third world. Capital accumulation and capitalist development have always occurred unevenly – spatially, sectorally and temporally – producing differential degrees of industrialization and varying modes and levels of integration into the global capitalist economy. Today, however, there is widespread recognition that a fundamental transformation is taking place in the conditions of accumulation and the expansion of capital on a world-historical scale. Emphasis upon such factors as the major shift towards the internationalization of production, the greater concentration and centralization of capital under the sway of transnational corporations (TNCs), and the enhanced mobility of capital facilitated by modern communications technology, implies something of a transition away from the classical international division of labour (whereby underdeveloped areas were incorporated into the global capitalist order principally as suppliers of minerals and agricultural commodities) towards a restructured world economy wherein the third world is increasingly providing sites for industries which manufacture goods for sale on the world market.

Such a movement towards a globalization of production and the creation of a global market threatens world labour, whose bargaining potential appears critically weakened by the existence of surplus population on a world scale. Given, first, widespread perceptions of third world trade unions as variously bureaucratic, aristocratic and externally dominated by labour imperialisms, and second, the stress put upon the inherent limitations of trade unions under capitalism by many of those who work within the Marxist tradition, the prospects for labour and unions throughout the underdeveloped world would appear, on the surface at least, to be unutterably grim. If this *is* the case then there is obviously an unprecedented urgency for posing the question of what organizational forms, if not trade unionism, can offer protection at the workplace to third world workers if, in confronting employers, they are to go beyond informal resistance and spontaneous struggles. On the other hand, if it is *not*, then it is equally urgent to call forth a new analysis of not just the weaknesses but also the strengths and progressive possibilities of trade unionism as it exists in the third world today and as it could become.

Clearly, at one level, this poses many classic questions as to what role trade unions should play in circumstances which contain the seeds of revolution (South Africa) or where revolution has already brought forth a viable socialist project (Nicaragua), whether or not the latter is under siege. Similarly, it raises the difficult issue of trade union autonomy in proclaimed workers' states where the production system, as in China, has already been very largely collectivized. On the whole, however, the major thrust of debate about third world trade unions in a changing international division of labour (CIDL) concerns itself with the potential for organization and resistance to exploitation of workers in the majority of third world countries which are directly incorporated into global capitalism, whatever their state form or popular aspirations may be. Against this, of course, certain contemporary tendencies within collectivized formations (notably China) which point to their limited re-integration into the capitalist market economy clearly indicate the dangers of making any discussion artificially discrete.

In a time of deep global recession, when governments in the major capitalist countries are launching direct attacks upon working-class living standards by cutting back on socially reproductive expenditures and when the international financial institutions are compelling debt-ridden third world regimes to do the same, trade unionism – and by implication the combined muscle of workers everywhere – is widely judged to be incontrovertibly on the decline. Worse, in a contemporary world whose economic contours are increasingly shaped by high technology, trade unions are often contemptuously written off as being hopelessly out of date.

The conference from whose proceedings the papers that follow are drawn was based on very different assumptions, for although it brought together diverse political and intellectual tendencies, these were none the less welded together by a fundamental belief that, for all their problems and many ambiguities, trade unions remain basic working-class institutions. As Peter Waterman has opined,

> unions remain the typical and universal organization of the workers, the one they cannot do without and through which they both discover and impose themselves on society. The efforts made to capitalise on them, to influence, control and smash them, are all witness to their significance for the working class.[1]

Trade unionism, in other words, should never be written off, least of all by the left, whatever dissatisfaction there may be with the condition of organized labour at any one time. 'Trade unions', asserts Perry Anderson, 'are an essential part of a capitalist society because they incarnate the *difference* between Capital and Labour',[2] an opposition and incompatibility which holds no less in peripheral capitalist countries than in economies at the core.

That said, it must be noted that widespread disillusion and disappointment, particularly amongst radicals, with the performance of trade unions in the new states, combined with discontent with the appropriateness of concentrating analysis upon organizations which cater for only a very small proportion of the workforce in still predominantly agricultural countries, has produced a shift away from traditional concerns (industrial relations, trade union structures, wage rates, employment levels and mobility of labour and so on) towards emphasis upon broader processes. Robin Cohen identified these some time ago as proletarianization and class formation, the political character of worker struggles, the role of the urban poor, the practice and potential of labour internationalism (and its polar opposite, labour imperialism), labour migration as it revolves around the parasitic reliance of capitalist production upon the reproductive capacities of pre- and non-capitalist formations and, critically, the various forms of exploitation which affect women as producers and reproducers in peripheral capitalist societies.[3] Informed by a vision of labour power – or rather its expropriation by capital and its reaction to that – as the principal motor of history, this more critical approach not only merged into the broader project of attempting to define how the exploitation of labour within peripheral societies multiplies the accumulation of capital on a world scale, but also shifted an earlier almost exclusive preoccupation with overt organization towards a more comprehensive and subtle uncovering of workers' 'hidden consciousness', informal resistances and labour activity as it extends beyond both industrial production and direct engagement with the State.

Whether or not this transition was indeed sufficiently different or theoretically coherent and uniform to constitute a 'new international labour studies', as Cohen proposed (and there are those who contribute to this collection who disagree) need not detain us here, save to observe that the explicit focus of the conference on trade unions was not an assertion that the pendulum had swung too far away from the study of workers' organizations *per se* and that hence we should return to the comforting certainties of defining easily recognizable structures. Rather, *pace* Waterman and Anderson, the design was to harness the strengths and conceptual insights of the new approach(es) to allow for a critical re-evaluation of trade unions as perhaps *the* basic organizations of workers, even in the third world, at this extended moment of crisis. The objective, therefore, was quite explicitly to question whether workers at the periphery are as helpless as a mechanical reading of the crisis might imply or whether, in fact, their collective organization does render them some effective capacity for defence and offence. Necessarily, this agenda also provided for consideration of whether a new international division of labour is more likely to undermine than to underpin potential for a new labour internationalism.

Before proceeding to such an analysis, it is necessary to set the scene.

This introduction will accordingly begin by sketching out in more detail what is meant by the CIDL and how it affects the general terrain on which workers' struggles and those of their unions are being fought. It will then set out the principal challenges which this poses to trade unions in the third world and how it impinges upon the prospects for international labour solidarity. The nature and appropriateness of organized workers' response to the CIDL will then be addressed in the introductions to the three sections into which the collection has been divided in the light of what the diverse contributors have to say.

Inevitably, the compression of a very complex debate will entail greater simplication, if not distortion and mis-statement, than the other contributors will likely approve. For that reason, the editor alone assumes responsibility for the manner in which the major concern which informs this volume is posed. However, it is hoped that the fact that each of the papers published here was written in response to an initial proposal will impart an overall coherence to a subject matter that is as controversial as it is broad.[4]

The New International Division of Labour

Theories of the internationalization of capital have in recent years posited the arrival of a New International Division of Labour (NIDL) whereby a shift of capital to world areas where labour is cheap is resulting in the industrialization of the global periphery (and the corresponding de-industrialization of the advanced capitalist core). As it has been developed by a number of theorists, but most notably as it is associated with the work of Frobel, Heinrichs and Kreye,[5] the thrust of such analysis may be summarized as follows.

The structure of the global capitalist economy in the post-Second World War period has been transformed by the growth and extending domination of global production and exchange by transnational corporations, linked to a loss of control over national economies by governments in favour of transnational financial conglomerates and international financial institutions.

NIDL theorists place great emphasis upon transnational corporations as the major instruments of global capitalism, arguing that as a result of a worldwide drive to corporate conglomeration, centralization and concentration via growth, merger and acquisition (whose tempo has increased markedly since 1970), the global market has increasingly fallen under the sway of a small number of TNCs. Clairmonte and Cavanagh calculated that there were some 18,000 TNCs by the early 1980s, yet argue that the centre of TNC power is located in far fewer hands, with 'the top 200's soaring revenues as a per cent of global GDP (minus that of the Centrally Planned Economies) moving from 18 to 29 per cent over the last two decades.'[6]

This massive extension of monopoly conditions has in no way made relations in the global market less antagonistic, for although multinational in scope, TNCs are cohesively linked to state power. Even so, such national commitments are, unsurprisingly, severely constrained by the calling to maximize profit and TNCs accordingly play one government and one labour force off against another, cross-subsidize product lines, engage in transfer pricing and so on. In sum, through such mechanisms, the major TNCs have been able to ride the tiger of the current recession and become vehicles of prodigious economic power, their dominance based not just on gargantuan size alone but also on their ability to mobilize and shift resources from one sector and one market to another in order to maximize profit and realize other corporate goals.

In tandem with the extending pre-eminence of the TNCs is the growing role of transnational financial conglomerates (TFCs) whose rapid expansion and combination of diverse activities (banking, insurance, securities broking, futures operations, credit card operations) has now made them powerful agencies in determining the fortunes of the global market. Indeed, TFCs have been critical to the extension of TNC power in many ways, including the provision of funds for mergers and takeovers, of credit for trade and foreign investments and of loans to bankrupt countries to pay for imports. Inevitably, in an era of fluctuating exchange rates and electronic technology, they are at the centre of enormous financial manipulations as they and TNCs switch funds from one country to another, a process facilitated by the trend towards government deregulation of financial services in the US and elsewhere. Their role, in turn, is complemented by a widespread array of state weaponry designed to assist national TNCs (research grants, guaranteed loans, government contracts, export financing and bail outs) to retain and expand their global market shares. However, precisely because TFCs move money across borders according to the dictates of corporate (not national) policy, the governments of the advanced capitalist countries seek to exercise power on a multilateral basis by regulating the free-for-all through the General Agreement on Trade and Tariffs, the International Monetary Fund, the World Bank and other global measures and institutions. The need for more centralized financial management has been made imperative by the disorder in world money markets caused by the collapse of the Bretton Woods system of fixed international exchange rates during the period 1968–71, the oil crisis of the early 1970s, subsequent inflation and the growth of third world indebtedness.[7]

It is through these various international financial institutions that policies deemed the most appropriate for facilitating the conditions for accumulation by the TNCs are imposed upon the third world by the conditional provision (or otherwise) of credit. Particularly significant in this context has been the shift away from the emphasis on basic needs strategy which was pushed by the World Bank in the 1970s to the contemporary stress upon the merits of export-led growth.

This shift to export-oriented industrialization (EOI) has been accomplished at the expense of the import-substitution industrialization (ISI) model which was earlier favoured as having led the first wave of third world claimants (Brazil, Argentina, South Africa, India) to semi-peripheral status in the inter- and earlier post-war years.[8] Basically, the limitations of ISI as a development strategy – notably the restricted size of internal markets, the resulting protection and high cost goods, limited possibilities for economies of scale, inability to create an export market for high priced goods, the need to import the capital equipment and technology required to produce consumer goods (and the resulting foreign exchange problems) – have meant that the model has become increasingly associated with an inflow of direct foreign investment into the third world and an industrialization that thereby serves the international strategy of the TNCs. Given, *inter alia*, that TNCs typically prefer world-oriented rather than locally-geared product choice, the resultant restructuring of ISI towards the production of globally standardized goods (together, not uncommonly, with a symbiosis induced between national and transnational capitals) encourages orientation to the world market rather than satisfaction of local needs. But notwithstanding the potential benefits to be gained from such a shift such as buoyant export earnings, increase in employment and a widening of income distribution, a multiplication of backward linkages, and the achievement of economies of scale by linking home to external markets), contemporary experience indicates that TNCs' (and local exporters') requirement for cost minimization and concession maximization by the local state results in EOI tending to take place within enclaves cut off from the developmental needs of the population and wherein labour is subjected to despotic conditions of employment.

The root cause of the restructuring of the global economy lies in the long-run tendency for the rate of profit in the advanced centres of capital to fall.

NIDL theorists base their analysis on the contradiction inherent in the capitalist mode of production, identified by Marx, whereby as the ratio of capital invested to wages in the net product rises it becomes less possible for capitalists as a whole to maintain the rate of surplus-value extraction that sustains the level of profit. Capitalists will therefore attempt to increase the rate of surplus-value extraction either by introducing new technology or reducing the cost of labour. The inevitable result is a crisis (or rather a succession of crises) of over-production caused by the inability of wages and spending (market demand) to absorb production. Increased competition on a world scale is the ultimate result as capitalists do battle to realize their profits. From this perspective, NIDL theorists identify an historic tendency for the rate of profit to fall in all the major centres of capitalism. This has coincided with a latter day challenge, particularly by Japan and the more dynamic European market economies (centred around West Germany), to the hegemony which the US earlier confirmed for itself at the end of the Second World War and the dramatic globalization of production processes and marketing by TNCs.[9]

In essence, this development is seen as threefold. Firstly, the early post-war decades were a period of rapid capitalist expansion during which the US established its global hegemony on the basis not only of the exhaustion of its major competitors by the war but also by the opening up of the world market offered by European reconstruction, the dissolution of Empire and the collapse of imperial protection. Notwithstanding the expansion of the collectivized economies under Soviet hegemony and the withdrawal of the Chinese from the capitalist system, post-war liberalization of the global market facilitated a massive expansion of US capital in both industrialized and peripheral economies. US post-war strategy in the core was to build a mass market for consumer goods which, together with massive expenditures on armaments, would sustain demand for industrial production; at the same time a high rate of economic growth, full employment and the expansion of welfare provisions would curb working-class disenchantment with capitalism and lead to the incorporation of labour into a lasting political consensus structured on capital's terms. Adopted in its broad essentials by the Western European leaderships, this strategy was implemented with only minor variations by conservative and social democratic parties alike, notwithstanding the very real struggles which labour had to undertake to secure its share of the bargain.

The second aspect of this development was the fundamental change in the conditions of accumulation wrought by the concentration and centralization of capital. At first mostly US firms, but later those of the other major capitalist centres too, were transformed into TNCs whose very logic of operation demanded that they switch investment from one location to another according to where they could maximize their profit. This meant that when the domestic market in the US became saturated and the rate of profit began to fall, there was a decline in domestic investment and an increasing flow of capital to foreign sites. Meanwhile, less burdened by defence expenditures (in contrast to the US which assumed the role of global policeman on behalf of the capitalist world), Japan and the other major European powers organized a successful assault on the US market. 'The US share of the Western market fell from 70% in 1950 to 57% in 1965 and 48% in 1973',[10] whilst the Europeans protected themselves by forming the EEC. The number of US firms in the top 200 TNCs fell (from 127 in 1960 to 91 in 1980) and there was a corresponding rise in those based in other countries, notably France (7 to 15) and Japan (5 to 20), these varying rankings being matched by similar changes in the national proportions of total sales.[11]

Meanwhile, and thirdly, the conditions of accumulation were profoundly altered not only by the rise of the TNCs but also by revolutionary advances in science and technology as each advanced capitalist state joined with private capital to devote greatly increased resources to research and development. This at first enhanced the lead of US capitalism over its rivals; whereas the latter had previously relied to some considerable extent upon the plunder of their colonial possessions and had paid rather less attention to the modernization of their domestic industries, American capital had revolutionized its production processes by the adoption of Taylorism and the methods of the assembly line. As production and production methods became increasingly transnationalized, however, the other major capitalist centres caught up, thereby undercutting the international lead of US capitalism whose export competitiveness was in any case by the late 1960s coming under heavy pressure on account of the overvaluation of the dollar caused by the administration's deficit financing of the Vietnam War. The subsequent devaluation of the dollar, its de-linking from gold and the freeing of international exchange rates thereafter enabled the US to considerably redress its competitive position in relation to its major rivals (except Japan). But the crisis into which the global system was plunged by the disorder on the world's money markets (which in turn triggered the rise in the price of oil and other fuel) also reflected a general fall in the rate of profit as TNCs steadily devoted a greater proportion of surplus value to capital goods (a trend enhanced by the shorter life-span of machinery induced by continuous innovation). Resulting balance of payments problems and accelerated inflation in the core countries led inevitably to a contraction of production, an extended credit squeeze, unemployment and a more aggressive approach to labour. These combined to reinforce a growing tendency for TNCs to relocate production to peripheral countries where a workforce could be found which was not only cheaper but more easily controlled; at the same time there were widespread hopes that a breakthrough into a new generation of technology would provide for a general increase in the rate of profit.

The conditions for the expansion and accumulation of capital on a world scale have been transformed by the development of technology which provides for the fragmentation of production and the worldwide sourcing of manufacturing.

The essence of the NIDL is postulated as the relocation of certain largely labour-intensive production processes in some industries (notably clothing, textiles, shoes and electronics) from industrialized to developing nations. Revolutionary advances in science and technology, particularly in transportation, information systems and communications, have freed production from the geographical and time constraints of the past. By providing for the rapid and inexpensive transportation of both bulk and fragile goods, modern technology facilitates not only the easier penetration of distant markets but also the integration of discrete production tasks undertaken at separate industrial sites. Telecommunications and advanced information technology mesh TNCs' global production lines and financial decision-making. Although the bulk of such world-oriented production is still concentrated in relatively few peripheral countries, the rest of the third world is now providing sites for manufacturing on a significant and increasing scale. Third world manufacturing output remains only 7–8% of the global total; but it is currently growing at a somewhat faster rate than manufacturing output in the industrtialized countries, with export production being organized and vertically integrated into the world market through the global structures of TNCs.

This relocation has been made possible by technological innovations which facilitate the decomposition of complex production processes into simpler tasks which can easily be performed by unskilled or semi-skilled labour. Such job fragmentation not only enables more expensive to be replaced by lower cost labour but encourages the relocation of industrial tasks away from higher wage to lower wage countries. 'In other words', observe Frobel, Heinrichs and Kreye,

> the imperatives of capital expansion and accumulation demand that production technology and labour organisation be developed so as to minimize the costs of production worldwide, explicitly taking into account the different wages and skills of potential labour forces throughout the world.[12]

Increasingly in evidence, therefore, is a tendency for production to be moved from low wage countries (e.g. Hong Kong, South Korea and Singapore) to ones where wages are even lower (Malaysia, Sri Lanka, Thailand and the Philippines); the implication being that as costs rise at any one site, TNC operations will move on to another, a process which will continue so long as there is a constant supply of takers clamouring for scarce investments.

As locational flexibility and transnational mobility of industrial production increase, the previous division of the world into industrial centres and non-industrialized periphery will be superseded by a division between highly sophisticated production (using advanced technologies, software and so forth) and industrial production using standard technologies. Even so, there is recognition that the low cost of labour offered by the third world may in time become less attractive to TNCs as yet further technological innovation increases the share accounted for by components and capital in the final product. So-called 'mature' or 'sunset' industries, which just a few years ago were prime candidates for relocation to the third world, are now, as technology becomes more complex, again being made viable in higher wage countries and are likely to stay or return. The watch and clock, office machinery, garment, textile, steel and automobile industries are all, to a varying extent, examples of born again industries wherein the value added by assembly operations is diminishing and the advantage of low cost labour therefore declining. A country such as South Korea, whose exports of electronic goods jumped from $177 million in 1972 to $1,396 million in 1978, may have enjoyed spectacular growth but now appears specially vulnerable to the rapid automation of the formerly highly labour-intensive assembly and testing of chips where the trend is towards 'the complete production cycle in one manufacturing location, worldwide marketing, fast market introduction and close cooperation with end user industries.'[13] Overall, therefore, prospects for LDCs appear to be 'dismal, not only by reason of their non-participation in the change but also by reason of their lack of awareness of the issues at stake.'[14] Meanwhile, within the advanced industrial economies, technological innovation leads to an overall decrease in labour requirements and an allied increase in the proportion unemployed.[15]

The conditions for the globalization of production have been similarly transformed by the development of a world market for labour.

The transition to the NIDL is proposed as having created a surplus labour force on a world scale. With the ever increasing mobility of capital, workers in the industrialized countries no longer have a quasi-monopoly of jobs in manufacturing; rather, they now have to face the challenge of relentless job seeking by the rest of the world's labouring population which, under the impact of the pressures emanating from the rapid pace of third world economies' incorporation into the global market, now constitutes an apparently inexhaustible pool of potential labour available for the accumulation process occurring under the aegis of TNCs and other agencies.

Capital is attracted to third world countries because labour there is dramatically cheaper (Frobel *et al.* suggest a differential – inclusive of social overhead costs – between traditional and newly industrializing countries of the order of 80–90%),[16] readily available, equally productive, more easily subjected to discipline, hard work and longer hours and offers an optimal selection of workers in terms of skill, age, gender and so on.

Wages are so much cheaper for two major reasons. By dint of struggle and organization, labour in the industrialized countries has been able to extract a relatively high real rate of return which, precisely because the accumulation process has entailed higher capital-intensity, has enabled capital to offset higher wages by increasing surplus value. Critical to this, historically, was the formation of nation states which, for one reason and another, imposed restrictions on labour mobility and thereby created artificial scarcities. The condition of the working class in any one industrialized country therefore bears even today a fairly strict relation to that country's place in the classical international division of labour and its particular mode of specialization within it.[17] Secondly, the expansion of capitalist production processes and market relations to incorporate most of the globe has resulted historically in the disintegration or subordination/preservation of non-capitalist forms of production. At one level, this (as in the past) now ensures the constant expulsion of population from the land (more especially to the extent that capitalist transformation of agriculture deprives an increasing proportion of rural inhabitants of access to land); and at another, it subsidizes capital by enabling it to pay wages below the cost of the social reproduction of labour.

Focus upon the emergence of a NIDL stresses three particular dimensions of the labour supply in the contemporary third world. The first is that the restructuring of the accumulation process has generated major international migrations of labour from the periphery. Reflecting a transition from the forced labour mobilizations and colonizing migrations of the classical era, a shift to *international* labour migrations has been premised upon the decolonization process which has accomplished the global expansion of capital. One aspect of the exodus of labour today is the brain drain which siphons scarce human capital investment out of the third world. More typical, however, is the increasing flow of migrant/immigrant labour from peripheral to core countries (e.g. Algeria to France, Mexico to the US) in jobs that are considered undesirable or too low paying by indigenous workers. Meanwhile, international labour migration is a growing phenomenon *within* the third world (as to Middle East oil-exporting countries after 1970 when an acute labour shortage was a major obstacle to large scale new industrialization there). Such international labour migration is particularly useful to trans-national capital in that it creates a distinct category of labour within any given national labour supply system which is generally divided (by housing, culture, sector and language) from the indigenous workforce; it separates the cost of reproduction (which is borne by the home country) from that of simple subsistence (thereby enabling capital to employ migrant labour in lower paying jobs); and it typically offers a disorganized workforce which is particularly susceptible to control.[18]

The overwhelming majority of international labour migrants are men. In contrast, women are particularly favoured by certain industries (textiles, clothing and electronics assembly) which plead the inherent virtues of female dexterity and its consequent suitability for the intricate work they require. Passing over the fact that such dexterity becomes associated with women precisely because of the socialization they receive in the course of domestic labour and not because it is gender inherent, the major advantages for capital in employing women may be identified as lower unit costs of production because wage levels for women are almost always significantly less than for men, whilst productivity for comparable jobs appears not unusually to be higher. In addition, because women are subordinated as a gender they are more manipulable and generally less organized and hence more suited to the widespread industrial requirement for standardized, repetitious (though *not* unskilled) and highly labour-intensive work. Women are more easily hired and fired only for so long as they are not tied down by family responsibilities. Their structured susceptibility to domination therefore makes their labour power a peculiarly appropriate commodity in world market factories which are acutely vulnerable to changes in the conditions of accumulation (such as demand fluctuations and protectionism) in the industrialized world.[19]

The third, related, fact about third world labour is its immiseration. As countless millions are uprooted from the countryside and swarm into the burgeoning slums of the rapidly expanding towns and cities, their presence crushes the wage aspirations of the active labour force. The 'immiserated', argues Cockcroft, referring to the urban poor in most of the countries of

Africa, Asia and Latin America, 'constitute the lower strata of the working class, in main part the relative surplus population which today is emerging as the new majority on a national and world scale.'[20] In turn, the over-employment (as opposed to the underemployment) of such elements (in multiple jobs, family labour, long hours and unregulated work) in myriad ways – as street vendors, market-sellers, message boys and massage girls, prostitutes, small workshop employers and employees, artisans and so on – provides a significant market for mass produced commodities, thereby allowing surplus to be drained off into the circuit of capital at the same time as it guarantees the reproduction of the labour force.

The global expansion of capital and the transnationalization of production requires and generates repressive political institutions and social formations in the third world whose role is to educate, discipline and mobilize the potential and actual labour force for servitude.

The logic of the globalization of production and the development of a world market for labour requires the development and maintenance of highly repressive regimes in newly industrializing countries precisely because the international mobility of capital dictates that the peripheral state maximize its attractiveness as a site for investment by minimizing the cost of labour and ensuring its quiescence and adaptability. The imposition of authoritarian controls upon labour by both capital and the state as an accompaniment to new industrialization is therefore a 'world historical phenomenon' occasioned by 'the accumulation of capital on a world scale'.[21]

James Petras has stressed that the relation of peripheral states to the global economy varies according to their class nature and their position in the old or new division of labour.[22] From this perspective, he argues, we may identify at least four different types of regimes that are still overwhelmingly primary commodity exporters. These are: (i) neo-colonial regimes, which still depend heavily upon metropolitan political and military support to sustain their ruling elements (Zaire, Thailand, Gabon); (ii) dependent developmental regimes, which rest upon internal political and military forces yet depend upon metropolitan finance and investment to fuel economic expansion even while continuing to rely upon traditional exports as they industrialize (Kenya, Ivory Coast, Colombia); (iii) state capitalist regimes (Algeria, Libya, Iran and Nigeria) where strong state ownership and the development of heavy industry has led to heavy dependence on oil exports to finance new projects which are not yet competitive on international markets; and (iv) revolutionary regimes, such as Cuba, which, while opening up new areas of production and transforming the class structure, have been unable to move out of the primary commodity supplying role.

A similar range of peripheral state regimes which do participate in the NIDL can likewise be indentified. Hence (i) colonial (Hong Kong) and settler-colonial (South Africa) regimes are found amongst the industrial exporters; (ii) *dependent development regimes*, where industrial strategy is geared to the global market, include Argentina, Sri Lanka, Malaysia, South Korea, Brazil, Taiwan and Singapore; (ii) state capitalist regimes under which state intervention and heavy industrial development have enabled world competitiveness in certain spheres would include India; and (iv) revolutionary regimes which are seeking to increase participation in the world market would today include a post-Mao China which has turned towards the West.

The possibilities of a peripheral state redefining its relation to the international division of labour relate to its capacity to channel resources towards classes willing and able to develop the forces of production. Equally, however, participation in the new international division of labour requires the availability of cheap labour and the state's preparedness to exploit it for export-orientated industrialization. Whilst on the one hand this may mean the provision of an appropriate mix of export incentives and tax concessions to induce investment by national or international capital, it may equally mean the imposition of despotic forms of labour control ranging from denial of protective legislation and basic trade union rights to outright coercion of workers on the job. The need for participants in the NIDL to continuously compete with new entrants to the world market who are attempting to undercut existing labour-intensive producers suggests the reversibility of new industrialization for those states which allow labour costs to move seriously out of line.

The NIDL: Criticisms and Modifications

All this clearly attests to a significant restructuring of the global economy. How new this is is, however, debatable for the old international division of labour was never cast in stone and has been modified throughout the 20th Century. In particular, the last major crisis of accumulation, the Great Depression of the 1930s, followed by the stimulus of wartime restrictions on trade, generated a growth of manufacturing via import substitution in such countries as Brazil, Argentina, Mexico, India and South Africa. This development continued well into the 1950s and enabled these countries to develop their industrial structures by making producer goods as well as diversifying into export markets.

That said, there can be no gainsaying the spurt of industrialization which has taken place more recently in the third world, most notably during the two decades 1960-80 (whereafter the growth momentum was, at least temporarily, halted). Between 1960 and 1978, for example, developing countries as a whole registered a modest yet significant increase in industry and manufacturing as a share of Gross Domestic Product;[23] and between 1960 and 1975 85 of them increased their proportion of world manufacturing added from 6.9 to 8.6%.[24] LDCs increased their share of world trade in manufactures from 6% in 1960 to over 10% in 1979,[25] having consistently sustained a growth rate in manufacturing output which outperformed that of the Northern countries.[26]

Whether or not this has reduced global polarization between rich and poor countries is a complex question which does not directly concern us here.[27] What should be noted, however, is that although the recent strides towards the industrialization of the third world represent an historically impressive rate of growth, these have led to a marked differentiation first, between regions (with Africa accounting for only 0.8% of world manufacturing value added in 1975, Latin America 4.8%, South and East Asia 2.5% and West Asia 0.5%, with South and South-East Asia recording the largest relative gains);[28] and second, between what are now conventionally referred to as middle income and low income developing countries. The latter were defined by the World Bank in 1984 as having per capita incomes below $400, some 34 countries thereby falling into the lower income category whilst some 60 countries above that mark were identified as middle income (these excluding the income rich developing countries – Oman, Libya, Saudi Arabia, Kuwait and the United Arab Emirates – which are now set apart as capital surplus oil-exporters).[29] Hence, as noted above in regard to the repressive essence of new industrialization, there are many third world states which remain firmly locked into the old division of labour. In fact, only two groups within the middle income category – the Latin American diversifying economies plus South Africa, and the small number of South-East Asian countries which in recent years have pursued a path of export-led industrialization – are defined by the World Bank (1979) (by virtue of manufacturing now accounting for 20% of Gross Domestic Product) as non-European newly industrializing countries (NICs), namely Argentina, Brazil, Colombia, Mexico, South Africa, Singapore, Hong Kong, Taiwan, Malaysia and the Philippines. However, other less advanced third world countries (e.g. Nigeria, Sri Lanka and Iran) are also set on a course of new industrialization, if to a less advanced degree.

If, given these developments, it is today generally accepted that dependency theory overstated the case that imperialism stunted prospects for capitalist industrialization at the periphery, then it appears equally to be the case that Bill Warren's proposition that imperialism created the conditions for the destruction of international inequality (by spreading capitalist relations and productive forces throughout the non-capitalist world) greatly exaggerated the potentiality for great leaps forward by discrete national capitalisms linked together by a non-antagonistic interdependence.[30] Indeed, certain developments during the 1970s – such as the oil crisis, the imposition of restrictions upon imports from peripheral into core countries, the debt burden – imply that the economic miracle accomplished by (especially some non-oil) NICs in previous decades may prove to be resting on somewhat shaky foundations. None the less, it must be allowed that for certain countries (most notably the NICs, but also certain others such as Kenya and Nigeria, which are following in their wake), in certain historical circumstances (featuring an accumulating bourgeoisie and a strong state) and enjoying certain economic advantages (location, a large internal market and mixed resources), industrialization–whether or not dependent on foreign capital–does allow for forms of capitalist development, even if this occurs at the expense of the majority of the population and is subject to recurrent cycles of expansion and recession as dictated largely by the condition of the world economy. Further, the expansion of the global market implied by third world industrialization has been necessary to absorb the expanded production of goods and services at the metropolitan centre as well as at the semi-periphery (via South–South trade).

Given the rise of the NICs and indications of a more widespread industrialization throughout the third world, it is not surprising that theories of the internationalization of capital should have displaced dependency theory as the predominant Marxist paradigm for the study of development in the third world. Since they provide a dynamic explanation of the trajectory of third world industrialization they offer a more convincing interpretation of a continuously changing contemporary world than an approach which views the global economy in zero-sum terms and whose suggestion of blocked capitalism has proved quite unable to account for the reality of industrial advance. That said, the conception of the NIDL undoubtedly gives cause for legitimate concern and complaint if taken to its limits.

Although third world contribution to manufacturing has increased, focus upon the emergence of a NIDL may exaggerate the extent of change that is taking place. It remains true that the large majority of third world countries are still overwhelmingly exporters of raw materials; hence, in 1980, primary commodities accounted for 70% or more of total exports of as many as 42 of 59 third world countries for which the World Bank was able to give data.[31] It is the old rather than a new international division of labour which continues to define the relationship of most peripheral countries to the global economy. This is not to deny the existence of a *trend* towards increased export manufacturing (for between 1961 and 1980 it seems that 46 of the forementioned 59 countries increased their percentage of non-primary exports), but to re-iterate that industrialization in the third world remains limited in extent and is uneven in its impact. Not only does new industrialization appear remarkably fragile in that it is centred around labour-intensive industries (textiles, clothing and electronics) for which the availability and docility of cheap labour is critical but third world manufacturing is dominated by a small group of NICs (with, in 1977, some 14 countries accounting for 90% of LDC industrial exports).[32] The real issue, as Petras remarks, is not so much the growth of the NIDL but 'the very limited opening of industrial markets in the metropole, the constraints on industrial financing, the construction of barriers to the transfer of technology'. In other words, it is 'precisely the incapacity of the Third World countries to break into new markets and the intransigence of the metropolitan countries in resisting the creation of a new international division of labour' which still features as the major conflict between North and South.[33]

Critics argue that the extent to which jobs and capital have been relocated by TNCs from the core to the periphery has been overstated. Changes have been wrought in the international division of labour more by corporations' relative reduction in *new* investment in the country of origin rather than by direct displacement of productive capital.[34] Similarly, given that TNCs typically relocate mainly assembly operations to the third world, industrial production at the periphery remains dominated by metropolitan forces; such tentative industrialization can be undermined by any combination of automation and wage reductions (e.g. in motor assembly) which may attract mobile TNCs back to the core. Similarly, there is some doubt that foreign direct investment in export processing zones plays such a crucial role as is often portrayed, that world market demand is necessarily more important to TNCs in determining their global operations than local market expansion, that minimization of labour costs is invariably the most important factor in attracting foreign investment, and so on.

In its most pristine form, the NIDL thesis rests on the projected establishment of an increasingly perfect global market wherein capital enjoys unhindered transnational mobility facilitated by the decomposition of advanced production processes made possible by advanced technology and modern communications. However, critics point out that this vision of a new world capitalist order does not conform to the reality of *political* economy in a world of competitive nation states. In other words, not only are TNCs often closely identified with home governments (and hence lack the unhindered autonomy which is often imputed to them), but the state often plays a key role in stimulating and organizing capitalist development in NICs as diverse as Brazil, India, South Korea and South Africa (a point made forcefully by Petras and Engbarth below). Conversely, to the extent that production in free enterprise zones in the periphery is dominated by TNCs rather than by governments, it can be properly described as *third world* industrialization only in a somewhat constricted sense.

The implications of NIDL theorizing are deterministic, if not fatalistic, and suggest that the global periphery is simply acted upon by the core. Just as dependency theory advocated the external dimension as the primary cause of underdevelopment, so the conception of the NIDL can devalue the internal dynamics of third world social formations as determinants of, or obstacles to, capitalist growth and industrialization. New industrializers do, however, typically have to overcome the legacy of having been incorporated into the capitalist system on unequal and unpropitous terms. These include the determination of their economic structures from outside, the external implantation of capitalism (rather than its emergence from internal political struggles), as well as the tendency for capitalism at the periphery not to destroy pre-capitalist modes of production (as under early capitalism at the core) but to depend upon and articulate with their continuing existence.

Finally, it can be argued that NIDL theorizing is so suffused with capital logic that – curiously for a Marxian approach – it denies the centrality of the struggle between capital and labour as the principal dynamo of contemporary capitalist development. Indeed, its perspective implies that labour in both the first world and the third is passive in the face of exploitation and transnational relocation of jobs. In contrast, it may be argued that not only is organized labour at national and international levels becoming increasingly sophisticated in counteracting the manoeuvres of TNCs, but also that third world workers have demonstrated time and again a willingness and capacity to struggle against the imposition of capital and the state.

Having noted such criticisms, it is only fair to point out that much of the debate surrounding the conception of a NIDL fails to differentiate between three distinct levels of argument, namely, the abstract analysis of capitalism, the analysis of the world economy as it really is, and the analysis of particular social formations located within the context of global disparities of power and wealth and external and internal class forces.[35] Even so, the partial nature of recent changes in the global economy indicates quite clearly that reference to a new international division of labour is premature, and worse, may be mistaken for heralding the arrival of a New International Economic Order providing for a fairer distribution of goods, resources and roles between North and South. Accordingly, it is preferable to see the current tendencies as comprising a *changing international division of labour* (CIDL) wherein global *continuities* should be stressed as much as *transformations* amd wherein certain *modifications* are occuring in the global marketplace.

Assuming that such a focus does indeed offer a productive working model for examining global political economy, it now becomes possible to identify the principal challenges which the CIDL issues to trade unions, and most notably those in the third world.

Third World Trade Unions and the CIDL: The Problem Posed.

There are four major (overlapping) areas of concern upon which it is most useful to focus in considering the challenges posed to trade unions in the third world by the CIDL. These are: (i) the threat posed by the emergence of a worldwide industrial reserve army of labour; (ii) the forms of segmentation of the global workforce implied by the CIDL; (iii) the fact that new industrialization tends to take place under repressive state forms; and (iv) the danger that although the internationalization of production posits an extending depth of global proletarianization, it simultaneously creates new obstacles to international labour solidarity.

Trade Unions and the World Wide Reserve Army of Labour. According to one recent source

> The number of the world's unemployed is growing faster than the world's population or its labour force. Between now and the end of the century the population is likely to increase by 31.5 per cent from 4,600 million to 6,050 million. The labour force will grow from 2,400 million to 3,630 million, a 51 per cent increase. And the number of people unable to earn a minimal living, if present economic trends continue, will grow from 900 million to 1,540 million, an increase of 71 per cent.[36]

This shift to global surplus population clearly implies an erosion of the strength of labour on a world scale. According to Frobel *et al.*, unemployment and pressure on real wages and working conditions will increase virtually everywhere, especially in the third world where, they argue, effective trade unions do not exist.

In his account of the development of corporatist state structures in advanced capitalist societies after the Second World War, Leo Panitch observes:

> Within the context of the general trend towards the structural strengthening of the working class in the monopoly capitalist era, it was the attenuation of the reserve army of labour as a result of nearly full employment in particular societies that critically further strengthened the organized working class at the industrial level.[37]

Correspondingly, the movement of capital away from the core as the rate of profit fell towards the end of the 1960s heralded the dismantling of the corporatist project during the 1970s as governments and employers sought to restore the rate of exploitation and thrust labour on the defensive – a posture it still assumes. Disconcerted by the assault on workers' post-war gains (of which Thatcher's victory over the British mineworkers in 1984-5 stands out as a key indicator of a more general trend), unions in the West have tended to shift their priorities away from higher wages towards securing their members' jobs in a situation of apparently intractable structural unemployment for an ever increasing proportion of the workforce.

The situation in third world countries undergoing new industrialization is, of course, qualitatively different; the accumulation process is generally bringing about an absolute increase in the active wage labour force. However, precisely because of the expansion of the surplus population within and *beyond* national boundaries (for the latter are generally breached if the supply of labour becomes artificially short), workers' combinations are beset by severe market limitations. The implications are critical for countries which have based their economic strategy on the supply of their surplus labour, whether this is offered to the world market for export (via migrant contracts) or in special enterprise sites at home.

'For some time now the international labour market has not been a seller's market, and it may never be so again.'[38]

How trade unions in both the first and the third world should confront the mondialization of the capitalism's industrial reserve army manifestly constitutes the principal challenge of the contemporary era. In that global full employment remains an inherently unlikely prospect in the foreseeable future, global corporatism – the incorporation under capitalist hegemenony of organized labour into the international policy-making arena – is thereby excluded as an option, except in so far as trade union international organizations come to represent the interests of only a favoured segment of the employed. Any solution to this historical dilemma clearly lies beyond economism.

Trade union leaders in the advanced capitalist countries are likely to become increasingly obsessed by the loss of jobs implied by the relocation of capital from core to third world sites. This process may be stayed by a number of factors, not least inducements offered to TNCs by the state to retain production at home. Yet whatever their protests about the unfair competition offered by sweated labour in the newly industrializing countries of the third world, there is little that trade unions can do to stabilize or even attract capital except to offer wage or benefit concessions or to agree to rationalization schemes whereby profitability is maintained by productivity agreements (usually entailing a reduction in the number and/or skill of the workforce by means of automation). Nor will an outright protectionist response (not uncommonly favoured by unions who urge political intervention to safeguard local markets for local industry and local labour) elicit long-term support from the state if, as is not unlikely, it serves to render national production steadily less competitive internationally.

Defensive measures may offer short-term returns; yet over the long haul they are unlikely to halt the drift of jobs away from the centre to the periphery; this, after all, is the very essence of the CIDL. This may, indeed, imply 'a world society in which the experiences of employment and redundancy are common to people in both rich and poor countries'.[39] Whether or not this will lead to joint defensive and even offensive labour action across the divide is, to put it mildly, extremely problematic, for, inevitably, there must be an element of conflict between workers in the industrialized countries who actually lose, or are threatened with the loss of, their jobs because of the relocation of employment to the third world. Western trade unions cannot be expected to limply release employment on the grounds that distant third world workers will gain; not only is their primary rationale to struggle to maintain and improve the livelihoods of their own members, but such a strategy would play right into the hands of the TNCs. Equally, however, western trade unions cannot deny the right to work of the globally unemployed. There is, in other words, no straightforward solution which does not point to the need for international worker solidarity to contest the modes, if not the very logic, of the internationalization of production. But–as ever–the problem is how to achieve it.

Trade Unions and the Segmentation of the Global Workforce

The emergence of a reserve army on a global scale interacts with the transition to a world market for labour to structure a new segmentation of the international workforce. Two resultant challenges which trade unions need to address are that a CIDL which encourages high-tech industry in the North and labour-intensive industry in the South may sharpen divisions between the first and third world workers and between well paid and more highly skilled workers and low paid, less skilled marginally employed and unemployed labour.

Whereas the early growth of capitalism shaped an increasingly homogeneous industrial proletariat, the development of monopoly capitalism has divided rather than unified the working class. Hence, following Edwards,[40] it is possible to identify the emergence under monopoly conditions of three fractions of the working class–the working poor, the traditional proletariat and the 'middle layers'–which, whilst continuing to share various class unities (most notably their common subjection to 'the yoke of capitalist employment'), are differentiated principally by the operation and existence of three distinct labour markets, i.e. the secondary, subordinate primary and independent primary markets respectively.

These segments are defined not by any fundamental or decisive criteria but by a cluster of characteristics. Thus whereas the secondary market is made up of jobs (spanning production and non-production work) which are typically non-unionized and offer low pay, no security and poor working conditions, both types of primary jobs are characterized by some job security, relatively stable employment, higher wages and extensive linkages between successive jobs. Subordinate primary jobs–in mass production industry, lower level sales, clerical and administrative work and production jobs elsewhere in the core economy–are further distinguished from the secondary market most fundamentally (though not invariably) by the presence of unions, but differ from independent primary jobs in that their work tasks are repetitive, routinized and subject to machine pacing. In contrast, the independent primary market–ranging from technical staff through jobs growing out of craft work (such as electricians and machinists) to the professions–typically revolves around specialized training, skill and career structures and requires standards of performance and independent initiative and self-pacing.

Whilst racial and sexual discrimination provide one set of forces leading to segmentation (reflecting the limited bargaining power of disadvantaged groups), it is the changing nature and requirements of the labour process which underlies the three market segments.

> The secondary labour market is the market expression of workplaces organised according to simple control. The subordinate primary market contains those workplaces (workers and jobs) under the 'mixed' system of technical control and

unions. And the independent primary market reflects bureaucratically controlled labour processes.[41]

It must be stressed, however, that this relationship between labour process and labour markets is an historical one, and by that token the fit between types of control and labour market segements is not perfect; rather, it is an outcome of the struggle between labour and capital on shop- and office-floor. Hence technical control–entailing machinery design and work planning to minimize the social problem of transforming labour power into labour whilst maximizing the physical possibilities of achieving efficiency–began its career living quite happily with secondary market casual labour. But the inherent tendency of the mass production methods which develop under monopoly capitalism is, by job fragmentation and de-skilling, to summon up a mass of semi-skilled operatives, thereby facilitating combination and bringing unionization in its wake. In the US , observes Edwards, the great organizing drives of the CIO in the 1930s–the success of car workers, steel workers, electrical workers and others in building industrial unions–married technical control to job security, stability and promotional prospects via firm–union agreements.. However, in the contemporary era, it is precisely the advantages of technical control and secondary casual labour which motivate 'corporations' investments in Brazil, South Korea, and other repressive countries where workers cannot establish unions or win job rights', just as some firms move production facilities to the south of the US because of that region's 'peculiar blend of anti-union law and local custom'.[42]

If it is accepted that under the CIDL the tendency is for labour-intensive work to become internationalized (both by the relocation of capital *away* from the centre and the movement of migrant labour *to* the centre), then this clearly implies a remarriage of technical control to secondary labour markets, most notably in the third world, where the massive size of the reserve army renders the establishment of a subordinate primary labour market not impossible (as the advance of industrial unionism in South Africa indicates) but, at the very least, highly problematic. This in turn echoes suggestions that the international and national structures of employment are increasingly likely to accord to the principles of global Fordism whereby the labour process–involving 'a disjuncture between conception and unskilled execution' (with skilled productive operations continuing to play a minor role)–approximates to geographical regions: 'engineering and conception in region I; skilled production in region II; unskilled assembly in region III'.[43] If such is the case, then the danger is that the structure of trade unionism, nationally and internationally, will replicate the segmentation of the global workforce, with unions entrenching rather than diminishing divisions between higher skilled and more organized (primary market) and lower skilled and less organized (secondary market) workers. For trade unions to overcome such a potential divide on an international scale will demand unprecedented political sympathies and linkages, for the defensive posture of globally advantaged workers (higher paid, more skilled, white, male and citizen) almost inevitably defines disadvantaged labour (lower paid, less skilled, non-white, female and immigrant or foreign) as competitive.

This global focus must not be allowed to obscure the extent to which segmentation of the workforce has already taken root *within* the third world. As described by Peter Lloyd, third world workers are typically divided into three segments: first, 'the privileged strata of workers employed by the large, multinational companies' (which prefer a stable labour force); second, workers employed by local or national capital in smaller operations located in labour-intensive sectors who, alongside state sector workers, are less well remunerated and experience markedly inferior working conditions; and third, workers engaged in the informal sector.[44] Clearly, the imputed privilege of being employed by TNCs (and this has been the subject of enormous controversy, as Lloyd acknowledges) corresponds to the development in such employment spheres of at least some primary market characteristics. It may be suggested, however, that any such tendency probably corresponds much more closely to ISI than EOI; whereas the former allows workers to extract an element of rent from employers (who may recoup it from customers in a protected market), the world market orientation of relocated, labour-intensive industries puts a premium on the absolute minimization of labour's cost. Thus although either model of industrialization will inevitably encourage the tendency of workers to combine, the shift away from ISI towards EOI implied by the CIDL suggests a narrowing of the space wherein trade unions may operate.

The most immediate challenge to trade unions posed by the CIDL is simply to assist the organization of workers to resist the impositions of capital. This, it must be stressed, is no easy task, and the corresponding imperfections and limited achievements of defensive combination in the third world (as elsewhere) should not be lightly mocked. Going beyond that, however, trade unions must confront the complex economic and political issues raised by labour market segmentation. In an industrializing context wherein some form of segmentation may in fact be inevitable, union activity must equally inevitably come to be associated with a struggle for conditions of employment which Edwards has characterized as establishing a primary labour market. The challenge must be (and this is an unsatisfactory formula) *not* for unions *not* to defend whatsoever privileges some workers may obtain, but to struggle continuously to extend those benefits to others, whilst avoiding a fractional or sectoral exclusivity which separates them politically (notably in regard to a broader re-ordering of market relations in a democratic and socialist direction) from the mass of labour in the secondary labour market.

Trade Unions and Repressive Industrialization in the Third World.

Forms of labour control are closely related to the requirements of the labour process; but the conditions of production are also shaped by controls imposed *outside* the workplace. Hence it is that Michael Buroway urges the notion of a politics of production which links the organization of work to that of the state, arguing that the development of advanced capitalism from the competitive to the monopoly phase has involved a transition in the regulation of production in the factory from despotic regimes (in which coercion prevails over consent) to hegemonic regimes (in which consent prevails, although never to the exclusion of coercion).[45] In the early period, the search for profit lead capital to rely upon intensive methods of exploitation; in response, workers sought protection from tyranny through combination, resistance and collective representation in production and (because they had no other means of livelihood than through the sale of their labour power for a wage) social insurance *outside* production. Simultaneously, because the success of despotism reduced the purchasing power of workers, capital faced worsening crises of over-production (because it could not realize the value it had produced). It was only the state, acting at the level of collective capital, which could resolve both issues by enforcing mechanisms for the regulation of conflict and (via social insurance) introducing a minimal social wage.

The necessity for state intervention was dictated by the logic of capitalism; the timing and mechanisms varied from country to country. Whatever the forms established, however, the transition laid the basis for a further crisis in profitability, for the cost of incorporating labour within hegemonic regimes placed such constraints on accumulation that international competition from lower wage states became increasingly threatening to capitalist production within any particular country. Hence today, the logic of capital accumulation on a world scale renders state intervention less and less able to influence the politics of production; the international mobility of capital leaves workers defenceless in face of rationalization, technological advance and the intensification of work. Within advanced capitalism, therefore, the CIDL and capital mobility are leading to a period of hegemonic despotism.

> The new despotism is founded on the basis of the hegemonic regime it is replacing. It is in fact a hegemonic despotism. The interests of capital and labor continue to be concretely coordinated, but whereas before labor was granted concessions on the basis of the expansion of profits, now labor makes concessions on the basis of the relative profitability of one capitalist vis a vis another . . . The new despotism is not simply the resurrection of the old: it is not the arbitrary tyranny of the overseer aimed at *individual* workers (although that happens too) but the 'rational' tyranny of capital mobility aimed at the *collective* worker . . . The fear of being fired is replaced by the fear of capital flight, plant closure, the transfer of operations, and disinvestment.[46]

Meanwhile, if in semi-peripheral countries such as Brazil and South Africa manufacturing industry has not yet installed hegemonic regimes but relies on a combination of economic and extra-economic means of coercion, workers in countries undergoing new industrialization (most notably in the case of those labouring within export processing zones) are subject to an autocratic despotism fostered by the state.

Autocratic despotism is therefore the politics of production which most nearly corresponds to the national level of politics of most third world states; for in both the element of coercion is paramount (even if the degree of coercion will vary according to the form of regime). If we also accept that in semi-peripheral countries – pre-eminently South Africa where organized resistance by workers is at an historically high level – faltering steps are on occasion made towards rather more hegemonic forms, then none the less it may be argued that, more generally, the production politics that prevail reflect the predominance of a secondary labour market in which a largely unskilled and unorganised workforce is subject to coercive mechanisms imposed by both capital and the state.

Trade unions are no strangers to victimization; but systematic survey indicates that reality reflects theory and that there is now a global trend (inclusive of the centrally planned economies) towards the curtailment of basic trade union rights, with violations of freedoms of association regularly occurring in all parts of the world.[47] Trade unions are variously suspended, dissolved, forced into controlled central bodies and subject to a battery of restrictive measures, whilst according to the International Confederation of Free Trade Unions (ICFTU) in 1983,

> Since 1980 more than a hundred trade unionists have been assassinated by, or with the complicity of, government authorities in at least twelve countries. Mention can be made of numerous cases of disappearances, torture, arrests of trade unions on a massive scale, prolonged detention without trial or even without charges being brought, internment in psychiatric institutions, forced exile and extremely heavy sentences for normal trade union activities.[48]

As Rhoda Howard argues below, trade union rights are inextricably linked with other basic rights to form an ensemble of human rights (material and otherwise) which are hardly likely to exist without each other. It follows that the most immediate and urgent task for trade unions in the third world is to articulate production politics with state and global politics not only in order to achieve and guarantee basic rights but also to pose the more far-reaching question of what re-ordering of society would serve to marry an expansion of such rights to a viable accumulation strategy.

Global Proletarianization and International Labour Solidarity.

Trends in the internationalization of production suggest an increasing similarity of work and life experiences for workers in core and peripheral societies while simultaneously entailing an increase in the proportion of the global population dependent upon the sale of its labour power on the market. To that extent we may point tentatively towards a process of global proletarianization, although it must equally be recognised that there is little evidence of an accompanying process of international working-class formation in the sense of coherent class activity, organization, identity or mobilization. Global unionism, a potential response to internationalized production, therefore remains a distant, even utopian prospect; too many variables intervene. *Inter alia*, as noted above, global segmentation of the workforce by wages, skill and function–not to mention divisions of race, gender, language and sector–pose major barriers to international solidarity: for instance, western trade union pressure for 'fair labour standards' are more concerned with protecting workers in the core countries against the risks of cheap imports than with protecting workers in the third world against exploitation.[49] Critically, too, although the proletarianization of the third world is occurring under the impact of international production, the uneven development and differential impact of global capitalism ensures that working-class formation and consciousmess tends to be *nationally* nurtured and structured in a world of vigorously competing states, whilst TNCs are strenuously opposed to effective international worker action.

The various inhibitions upon shop-floor based democratic trade unionism imposed by state and capital throughout the globe, as well as the oft remarked negation of democracy practised within many union organizations themselves, set enormous limitations on the realization of international worker solidarity. This, it must be stressed, is definitely *not* to deny the considerable amount of important, down to earth, nitty-gritty international labour cooperation and servicing provided by such organizations as the ICFTU and international trade secretariats (ITSs) (despite searching critiques to the contrary). For instance, despite its many deficiencies, the ICFTU may claim to have played a key role in financing the emergent trade union movement in South Africa since the early 1970s[50] and to have lent other support; constructive assistance to Black workers has also been extended by a number of ITSs.[51] But it remains true that the most concerted and genuine effort to bring about international working-class mobilization occurred before 1914, when wage labourers were much more occupationally and ethnically homogeneous, as well as being much more geographically concentrated than they are now; this effort was smashed decisively by the First World War.[52] Subsequently, to quote Connell, Internationals have been 'clandestine, or sectarian, or gutless' as a conscious attempt to organise political solidarity of an international working class has collapsed, its place taken by the much more limited apparatus of international trade union cooperation.[53]

It is, in fact, the close alignment of the world's major international labour bodies, the ICFTU and the World Federation of Trade Unions (WFTU), with the strategic concerns of the advanced capitalist powers and the Soviet Union respectively which still poses the major obstacle to labour internationalism. Even if today the Western European affiliates of the ICFTU are considerably more independent of government influence than during the years of the Cold War (in contrast to the AFL–CIO which remains as tied to the US State Department, CIA and multinational nexus as ever), the traditional international unions are still constrained by their financial dependence on government funding, their ideological commitments, the bureaucracy of their operations, the limited extent of their internal democracy and by the fact that, in the third world particularly, their network of affiliates–many of whose leadership is inactive and unrepresentative–is patched together by patronage as much as by concern with the condition of workers and the unemployed.[54]

That said, there are today new grounds for cautious optimism. 'In this period', anticipates Buroway, the working classes may begin 'to feel their collective impotence and the irreconcilability of their interests with the development of capitalism understood as an international phenomenon'. If this is perhaps just a stretch too apocalyptically utopian, it would seem none the less that the internationalization of production is laying something of a basis for a shared consciousness amongst workers in diverse parts of the globe as they become increasingly aware that struggles in each nation and on each continent are vitally linked: the recent Bhopal disaster, when a chemical gas leak devastated an entire Indian town, gives a new sense of unity based on realized mutual concerns not only to those directly employed by Union Carbide, wherever they may be, but also to those in the wider global community who might be afflicted by a similar tragedy. The flight of capital from higher to lower wage areas likewise heightens internationalism even among groups of workers without a highly developed consciousness of class.

Developments such as these–together with the formation of international shop stewards combine committees, cross-national links between workers employed by the same TNCs, a meshing of single issue concerns (peace activism, anti-racism, women's liberation, third world development) with socialist and labour struggles, together with restructured forms of organization and communication which extend the scope of the traditional union internationals–have led to recent discussion by Waterman and others about a new labour internationalism.[55] There is a growing appreciation that international trade union activity centred exclusively around production (wage and labour) concerns will be likely to merely reproduce the competition between nationally different conditions of production 'in the form of a latent national fractionalisation within the trade union movement'.[56] If international solidarity is to be facilitated by the internationalization of production, then it will therefore only be achieved (struggled for) by an international politics which deliberately develops the common political interests of an economically differentiated global workforce. Within this context, the particular challenge for third world workers and their unions is to avoid marginalization and dependence in the international labour sphere in favour of participation on an actively democratic basis.

Third World Unions and the CIDL: Shaping a Response.

How should third world trade unions respond to the CIDL and the global disadvantage it has brought to labour? Are their current strategies appropriate and are they adequately equipped for the tasks and struggles that lie ahead? Is their working-class base in newly industrializing yet still predominantly agricultural societies sufficient to provide the muscle for a concerted challenge to repressive states and both international and national capitals?

As indicated above, this introduction does not set out to provide answers but only to pose questions. How contributors view the manner in which unions are wrestling with and should address the issues raised are discussed briefly in the section editorials below. But it must be said that any answers should be clearly related to the historical specificities of the unions and formations concerned. There is not, it must be stressed, any such phenomenon as third world trade unionism *per se*: not only is the term 'third world' merely a convenient euphemism to aggregate a set of non-western states which exhibit a remarkable diversity in terms of their poverty, power and potential, but the trade unions which are located in these countries operate in, embody and reflect an enormous variety of national, industrial, cultural, ideological and other influences. Even so, precisely because the internationalization of capital is binding global workers together in an ever more intimate relation, the ultimate objective must be to comprehend labour action and its obstacles *not* as a property of world areas but rather as a world phenomenon: 'a complex totality in which "centre–periphery" relations . . . occur within as well as between (groups of) countries, and in which many of the key problems of theory and practice are universal in incidence.'[57]

Third world unions' responses to the CIDL will be shaped by factors which will include:

- the level, type, extent and intensity of industrialization and the consequent impact upon trade union structures;
- the relationship which unions enjoy (or otherwise) with the state and other forces, progressive or reactionary;
- workers' historical experiences of struggle, the level of proletarianization, the uneven development of different working-class segments, cultural variations, the impact and content of the ideology which shapes union practices;
- the strategic location of unions by industrial sector (mines, advanced or simple manufacturing, agriculture or services) and the composition and characteristics of membership (male/female; proportion of workforce organized; extent and nature of unity.)
- the internal dynamics of working-class organization, the accountability of leadership and the extent in actual practice of worker democracy;
- the commitment of unions to shop-floor struggle, progressive

political platforms, anti-imperialism and so on as evolved by theory and practice;

- the nature of unions' international labour alignments and their degree of autonomy from or dependence upon external interventions.

An economy's mode of incorporation into the classical or new international division of labour, and the historical shape of trade unions, will inevitably have a marked impact upon the working-class strategy and capability that evolves.

Specification and differentiation of unions along the lines suggested above would undoubtedly allow for assessment of union potential to respond to the various challenges posed by the CIDL; yet it is a task for which we are at present inadequately equipped (although it is hoped that this volume will itself make initial amends). To make progress, therefore, it may be helpful if, in conclusion, brief reference is made to the manner in which third world trade unions are generally viewed. This must be done at two levels: first, we must look at the classical notions of what trade unionism is and what it does, and secondly, at how these have been applied to organized labour at the periphery.

It is useful at this stage to resort to Richard Hyman's delineation of optimistic and pessimistic traditions of how unions are conceived by those who are sympathetic to working-class concerns. The optimistic tradition, deriving from Marx and Engels, sees trade unionism as preparing workers for a direct onslaught on capitalism, whose very advance provides the preconditions for collective organization by concentrating workers together and driving them into combination through awareness of their common exploitation. Precisely because trade union wage achievements under capitalism are limited by long-run economic laws, workers move on to political struggle and ultimately challenge the entire edifice of class domination.

In contrast, the pessimistic tradition – which flows from Lenin, Michels and Trotsky – suggests variously that the sectional nature of the trade union struggle along occupational lines divides rather than unites workers; that the limited and immediate objectives of trade unions, and to some extent their achievements within capitalism, blunts workers' recognition of the irreconcilable antagonism between labour and capital and leads only to trade union rather than revolutionary consciousness; that the difficulties of operating direct democracy, and the need for specialized knowledge and efficient administration, leads to oligarchical control of unions by leaders whose acquired lifestyle and aspirations cut them off from the mass; and lastly, that the rise of monopoly capitalism, if it does not entail the destruction of unions (as under fascism) leads to their incorporation by the state.[58]

These conflicting views have had a profound impact on the study of trade unions in the third world. On the whole it may be said that the pessimistic tradition has predominated. Trade unions, it has been widely maintained, have largely functioned as the self-serving organs of a labour aristocracy, the minority of more skilled, permanently employed and contextually well paid workers whose capacity for collective organization secures them a privileged status at the expense of the nation and/or differentiates them from the mass of other workers, peasants and the surplus population.[59] Restricting themselves in the main to economistic concerns, such consumptionist bodies have arrogated to themselves scarce resources which could otherwise have been devoted to increasing production, to the benefit of society as a whole.[60] Ineffective to the extent that they have been unable to resist state repression, and where they have not been split along party lines,[61] trade union leaderships – most notably in Latin America – have co-operated with populist and/or more reactionary forms of state to demobilize the working class and to manipulate and contain its militancy.[62] Co-option of leaderships has, in turn, been accompanied by the bureaucratization of union organizations, the consequent unresponsiveness of unions to rank and file demands, and the distortion of union structures into channels of upward mobility for individual members of the working class.[63] Subject often to debilitating corruption, such unrepresentative and uncaring bodies have been highly susceptible to external blandishments and have been easily drawn into the orbit of international labour imperialisms.[64]

This pessimistic perspective is close to what Jon Kraus has, in the African context, identified as an insensitive radical paradigm which has largely ignored the questions of how union leaders and workers should cope with state power in conditions which are normally non-revolutionary and when their organizational and financial resources are meagre.[65] As a consequence, more recent work – whilst not altogether optimistic – has dealt more sympathetically with the ambiguous contexts in which third world unions are located. While there is a continuing debate over the important issues of whether or not workers *are* politicized or simply have more basic economistic concerns,[66] and also whether or not union leaderships are in touch with their memberships,[67] there is now a re-assertion of the role of trade unions as the only remaining mass organizations of the labouring poor in the majority of third world countries.[68] Because so many states lack legitimacy and stability, unions commonly supersede political parties and represent the most significant bloc of social forces after the military. Precisely because workers are concentrated in a few industrial sectors and are conscious of their potential, they can have much greater impact than did similar groups in industrial countries during the period of early industrialization. In general, too, it is suggested that labour aristocratic tendencies, if they exist (for wage differentials between skilled and unskilled workers would seem to have often been exaggerated), are mitigated both by the large number of dependants such privileged workers generally support and by the fact that they have proved to be no less militant than others.[69] Furthermore, given that most trade unionists have little option but to work within economistic labour organizations, there is appreciation that mobilization of the working class may proceed beyond the structural limits established by reformist trade union leaderships to take in more radical forms of political action.[70] Astute use of international labour networks to defend trade union and basic rights is seen as providing an opportunity for developing working-class autonomy and questioning the dominance of TNCs.[71]

Hyman espouses neither the optimistic nor the pessimistic perspective on trade unionism, but rather draws out a modified synthesis which emphasizes the ambivalence inherent in the trade union function; despite its potential for stabilizing capitalism, it simultaneously embodies workers' revolt, however tentative, and may thereby lead on to a fundamental challenge by reacting against the extraction of surplus value from workers' labour and by raising issues of power and control within the workplace and beyond.[72]

This provides an appropriate vantage point from which to start to analyse the response of trade unions to the challenge posed by the CIDL. Although there has been much reason for pessimism when surveying the action and orientations of third world unions, the recent trend towards more nuanced interpretations which balance potentialities against limitations provides a basis for a more sophisticated understanding of the space which these unions inhabit and which they may enlarge by appropriate strategies, even within the considerable constraints imposed by the internationalization of capitalist production. The global surplus of labour, the segmentation of workforces, the repression of the working class in one country after another and the very considerable obstacles to labour internationalism together constitute an increasingly threatening environment for trade unions as vehicles of working-class protection and struggle. Trade union activity, if confined exclusively to wage offensives in an era of enhanced international capital mobility, will indeed become, in Rosa Luxemburg's term, a 'sort of labour of Sisyphus',[73] fulfilling all the most gloomy prognostications of NIDL theorizing. However, as the contradictions of the CIDL become ever more apparent – as, for instance, the development of industrial capacity within the third world is matched by the continuous swelling of the reserve army – it becomes steadily more possible for worker based movements in the third world to evolve a comprehensive *political* response in which the social relations which legitimate capital (national and international) are eroded and those which determine the return to labour are challenged, democratized and collectivized. If we can look forward to 'a new round of Third World labour-based social revolutions',[74] we should expect and require that third world trade unions will be at their centre.

Notes

1. Peter Waterman, 'Workers in the Third World', *Monthly Review*, vol. 29, no. 4, 1977, p.58.

2. Perry Anderson, 'The Limits and Possibilities of Trade Union Action', in Robin Blackburn and Alexander Cockburn, *The Incompatibles: Trade Union Militancy and the Consensus* (Penguin, Middlesex, England, 1967), p.264.

3. Robin Cohen, *The 'New' International Labour Studies: A Definition,* Working Paper Series No. 27, Centre for Developing Area Studies, McGill University, Montreal, 1980.

4. Roger Southall, 'Third World Trade Unionism: Equity and Democratization in the Changing International Division of Labour', *Canadian Journal of Development Studies*, vol. V, no. 1, 1984, pp.147-56.

5. F. Frobel, J. Heinrichs and O. Kreye, 'The World Market for Labor and the World Market for Industrial Sites', *Journal of Economic Issues*, vol. XII, no. 4, 1978, pp.843-58 and *The New International Division of Labour* (Cambridge University Press, London, 1980).

6. Frederick F. Clairmonte and John H. Cavanagh, 'Transnational Corporations and the Struggle for the Global Market', *Journal of Contemporary Asia*, vol. 13, no. 4, 1983, pp.446-80.

7. Frederick F. Clairmonte and John H. Cavanagh, 'Transnational Corporations and Services: the Final Frontier'. *Trade and Development: An UNCTAD Review*, no. 5, 1984, pp.215-73.

8. Andre Gunder Frank, *Crisis: In the Third World* (Holmes and Meier, London and New York, 1981).

9. F. Frobel, J. Heinrichs and O. Kreye, 'The Global Crisis and Developing Countries', *Trade and Development: An UNCTAD Review*, no. 5, 1984, pp.41-52 and Yann Fitt, Alexander Faire and Jean-Pierre Vigier, *The World Economic Crisis: US Imperialism at Bay* (Zed Press, London, 1980).

10. Fitt, Faire and Vigier, *The World Economic Crisis*, p.150.

11. Clairmonte and Cavanagh, 'Transnational Corporations and the Struggle for the Global Market'.

12. Frobel, Heinrichs and Kreye, 'The World Market for Labor', p.847.

13. J. Rada, *The Impact of Micro-electronics: A tentative appraisal of information technology* (International Labour Office, Geneva, 1980), p.92.

14. J. Rada, 'Advanced Technologies and Development: are Conventional Ideas about Comparative Advantage Obsolete?', *Trade and Development: An UNCTAD Review*, no. 5, 1984, pp.275-96.

15. Rada, *The Impact of Micro-electronics*, pp.103-9.

16. Frobel, Heinrichs and Kreye, 'The World Market for Labor', p.846.

17 Kimmo Kiljunen, 'New International Division of Labour and Adjustment Problems of a Peripheral Industrialised Economy', *Development and Change*, vol. 11, 1980, pp.517-29.

18. Saskia Sassen-Koob, 'Towards a Conceptualization of Immigrant Labor', *Social Problems*, vol 29, no. 1, 1981, pp.65-85.

19. Diane Elson and Ruth Pearson, '"Nimble Fingers make Cheap Workers": An Analysis of Women's Employment in Third World Export Manufacturing', in Peter Waterman (ed.), *For a New Labour Internationalism: a Set of Reprints and Working Papers*, (International Labour Education Research and Information Foundation (ILERI), The Hague, 1984).

20. James D. Cockcroft, 'Immiseration, Not Marginalization: The Case of Mexico', *Latin American Perspectives*, vol. X, nos. 2 and 3, pp.86-107.

21. James Petras, 'Neo-Fascism: Capital Accumulation and Class Struggle in the Third World', *Journal of Contemporary Asia*, vol. 10, nos. 1/2, 1980, pp.119-29.

22. James Petras, 'The "Peripheral State"; Continuity and Change in the International Division of Labour', *Journal of Contemporary Asia*, vol. 12, no. 4, 1982, pp.415-31.

23. For low income countries, from 17% to 24% for industry as a whole and from 11% to 13% for manufacturing; for middle income countries from 31% to 34%, and from 22% to 25% (*World Development Report 1980*,Oxford University Press, New York, 1981 Annex, Table 3).

24. United Nations Industrial Development Organization (UNIDO), *World Industry Since 1960: Progress and Prospects* (UN, New York, 1979), Table II.1, p.33.

25. Ankie M.M. Hoogvelt, *The Third World in Global Development*, (Macmillan, London, 1982), p.26.

26. 'In manufacturing output, the growth rate differential in favour of the South was even higher; 7.8 per cent for the South compared to 6.6 per cent for the North between 1963 and 1973 . . . This pattern continued after 1973 in that manufacturing output in the South grew at 5.6 per cent per annum between 1973 and 1979, a rate twice as high as that of the North.' (UNIDO, *Industry and Development: Global Report 1985* (UN, New York, 1985), p.10.

27. For a thorough discussion of the widening gap debate, see Hoogvelt, *The Third World*, pp.34-40.

28. UNIDO, *World Industry Since 1960*, p.38.

29. *World Development Report 1984*, Table 1, pp.218-19.

30. Bill Warren, 'Imperialism and Capitalist Industrialization', *New Left Review*, no. 81, 1973, pp 1-44; and *Imperialism: Pioneer of Capitalism*, (New Left Books and Verso, London, 1980).

31. Calculated by author from *World Development Report 1984*, Table 10, p.236.

32. UNCTAD, Review to *Recent Trends and Developments in Trade and Manufactures and Semi-manufactures, 1974*, TD/B/C.2/154, 11 May 1975.

33. Petras, 'The "Peripheral State"', p.425.

34. Werner Olle and Wolfgang Schoeller, 'World Market Competition and Restrictions upon International Trade Union Policies', *Capital and Class*, no. 2, 1977, pp.56-75; reprinted in Waterman, *For a New Labour Internationalism*, pp.39-58.

35. Irene Nørlund, Peter Ward and Viggo Brun (eds) *Industrialization and the Labour Process in Southeast Asia* (Institute of Cultural Sociology, University of Copenhagen, Repro-serie 1984 no.6), introduction, pp.10-32.

36. Paul Gerhardt, Stuart Howard and Pratibha Parmar, *The People Trade* (International Broadcasting Trust, London, 1985), p.54.

37. Leo Panitch, 'Trade Unions and the Capitalist State', *New Left Review*, no. 125, 1981, pp.21-43, (quote from p.20).

38. Gerhard, Howard and Parmar, *The People Trade*. p.55.

39. Ibid.

40. Richard Edwards, *Contested Terrain: The Transformation of the Workplace in the Twentieth Century* (Heinemann, London, 1979).

41. Ibid., p.178.

42. Ibid., p.181.

43. Alain Lipietz 'Towards Global Fordism?', *New Left Review*, no. 132, pp.33-47.

44. Peter Lloyd, *A Third World Proletariat?* (George Allen & Unwin, London, 1982).

45. Michael Buroway, 'Between the Labor Process and the State: The Changing Face of Factory Regimes under Advanced Capitalism', *American Sociological Review*, vol. 48, no. 5, 1983, pp.587-605.

46. Ibid., pp.602-603.

47. ICFTU, *Trade Union Rights: Survey of Violations 1983/84* (ICFTU Press, Brussels, no date).

48. ICFTU, *Trade Union Rights* (Thirteenth World Congress, Oslo, 23-30/6/1983, p.8).

49. David M. Dror, 'Aspects of Labour Law and Relations in Selected Export Processing Zones', *International Labour Review*, vol. 123, no. 6, 1984, pp.705-22.

50. Johann Maree, 'The Emergence, Struggles and Achievements of Black Trade Unions in South Africa from 1973 to 1984', *Labour, Capital and Society*, 18. 2 1985, pp.278-303.

51. Although in some cases only after Black workers had asserted themselves against paternalism and racism within the ITSs. See Eddie Webster, 'The International Metalworkers' Federation in South Africa (1974-1980)', *South African Labour Bulletin*, vol. 9, no. 6, 1984, pp.77-94 and reprinted in Waterman, *For a New Labour Internationalism*, pp.213-32.

52. R.W. Connell, 'Class Formation on a World Scale', *Review*, vol. VII, no. 3, 1984, pp.407-40 and reprinted in Waterman, pp.176-212.

53. Ibid., p.434.

54. For critical perspectives on international trade unionism see, *inter alia*, Don Thomson and Rodney Larson, *Where were you, Brother?: An Account of Trade Union Imperialism* (War on Want, London, 1978) and Ake Wedin, *International Trade Union Solidarity: ICFTU 1957-1965*, (Bokforlaget Prisma, Landsorganisationen i Sverige, 1974).

55. For example Mike Press, 'The Lost Vision: Trade Unions and Internationalism', in Walterman, *For a New Labour Internationalism*, pp.88–107.

56. Olle and Schoeller, 'World Market Competition', pp.70-71.

57. Richard Hyman, 'Third World Strikes in International Perspective', *Development and Change*, vol. 10, 1979, pp.3-14.

58. Richard Hyman, *Marxism and the Sociology of Trade Unionism* (Pluto Press, London, 1971).

59. See Peter Kilby, *Industrialization in an Open Economy: Nigeria 1945-66* (Cambridge University Press, London, 1969), p.281 and G. Arrighi and J. Saul, *Essays on the Political Economy of Africa* (Monthly Review Press, New York, 1973).

60. W. Ananaba, *The Trade Union Movement in Africa: Promise and Performance* (Hurst, London, 1979) and Victor Gerdes, 'The Social Role of African Labour', *Manpower and Unemployment Research in Africa* vol. 7, no. 2, November 1974.

61. See Robin Cohen, *Labour and Politics in Nigeria 1945–71* (Heinemann, London, 1974) for a study of party divisions within a labour movement.

62. E.g. A.M. Almeida and M. Lowy, 'Union Structure and Labor Organization in the Recent History of Brazil', *Latin American Perspectives*, vol. III, no. 1, 1976, ; E.C. Epstein, *'Control and Cooptation of the Argentine Labor Movement', Economic Development and Cultural Change*, vol. 27, no. 3, April 1979

and R. Sandbrook, *Proletarians and African Capitalism: The Kenyan Case 1960-72* (International Labour Office, Geneva, 1972).

63. For a discussion (and an attempt to go beyond) see J. Nun 'Workers' Control and the Problem of Organisation', Latin American Reseach Unit (University of Toronto) *LARU Studies*, no. 1, 1976.

64. Hobart Spalding, 'US and Latin American Labor: The Dynamics of Imperialist Control', *Latin American Perspectives*, vol. III, no. 1, 1976. (See also Spalding's paper in this collection).

65. Jon Kraus, 'African Trade Unions: Poverty of Progress?', *The African Studies Review*, vol XIX, no. 3, 1976, pp.95-108.

66. P. Konings, 'Emphasising the Importance of Trade Unions', and R. Sandbrook and J. Arn, 'Labouring Poor and Urban Class Formation: A reply', *Manpower and Unemployment Research*, vol. 11, no. 1, 1978, pp.77-81 and 86-93 respectively.

67. J. Crisp, 'The Labouring Poor, Trade Unions and Political Change in Ghana: Some Empirical and Conceptual Observations', *Manpower and Unemployment Research*, vol. 11, no. 2, 1978, pp.93-100 and P. Konings, *The Political Potential of Ghanaian Miners: A Case Study of the AGC workers at Obuasi* (African Studies Centre, Leiden, 1980).

68. Peter Waterman, 'Third World Strikes: An Invitation to Discussion', *Development and Change*, vol. 7, 1976, pp.331-44.

69. J.S. Saul, 'The Labor Aristocracy Thesis Reconsidered', in R. Sandbrook and R. Cohen, *The Development of an African Working Class* (Longman, London, 1975) and P. Waterman, 'The "Labour Aristocracy" in Africa: Introduction to a Debate', *South African Labour Bulletin*, vol. 2, no. 5, pp.10-27.

70. T.F. Harding and H.A. Spalding, 'The Struggle Sharpens: Workers, Imperialism and the State in Latin America: Common Themes and New Directions', *Latin American Perspectives*, vol. III, no. 8, 1976 and E. Sofer, 'Recent Trends in Latin American Labor Historiography', *Latin American Research Review*, vol. XV, no. 1, 1980.

71. M. Bienefeld, M. Godfrey and H. Schmitz, 'Trade Unions and the "New" Internationalization of Production', *Development and Change*, vol. 8, 1977.

72. Hyman, *Marxism and Trade Unionism*, p.38.

73. R. Luxemburg, 'Social Reform or Revolution', in *Selected Political Writings of Rosa Luxemburg*, (ed. D. Howard) (Monthly Review Press, London and New York, 1971) p.105.

74. Petras, 'The "Peripheral State"', p.426.

Part 1 Organized Labour and the Industrialization of the Contemporary Third World

Introduction

Much of the discussion about how trade unions should cope with the internationalization of capital revolves around the prolific writings of Charles Levinson, General Secretary (Emeritus) of the International Federation of Chemical, Energy and General Workers' Unions, who, in an opening address to the Ottawa conference, outlined his vision of a multinational unionism to counter multinational corporations. Elaborating upon themes which he has developed elsewhere,[1] Levinson depicted TNCs as the most creative and dynamic economic forces in the world today, engulfing the most modern sectors of capitalist and centrally planned societies alike, as well as sucking the third world into their maw. Governments are losing the ability to govern as TNCs become increasingly powerful; what the world faces today is a growth recession in which the major enterprises grow as employment declines.

Levinson's basic response to the TNCs is that if trade unions can't beat 'em, they should join 'em. The TNCs, he argues, prefer and seek out union free environments; yet at the same time limits are placed on the scope of their action, for however much they replace labour on the assembly line they need workers as consumers of their products. There is, therefore, space wherein unions may operate, and the appropriate response is for organized labour to establish multinational company councils whereby trade union representatives from the different plants of TNCs should formulate their demands and negotiate on a coordinated basis. He also advocates co-determination to enable workers to participate in decisions about global locations and forms of investment.

Whilst there is much in Levinson's analysis of TNCs with which most would agree, his critics argue that his uncomplicated advocacy of company councils and co-determination fails to address the danger that the involvement of international trade union leaders in TNC structures and strategies is likely to lead to their incorporation and the transformation of the most advantaged unionized elements into a global labour aristocracy. The inherent incompatibility and struggle between labour and capital will be replaced by the absorption of trade unions as junior partners in global management.

One such critic is Jeffrey Harrod, whose distinctive contribution to the debate concerning the changing international division of labour is to focus in the paper which follows upon the rise of a postulated international managerial class which has evolved with the internationalization of capital. The most significant development of the contemporary era, he argues, is the growth of large scale organizations, and it is those in *control* of them (rather than those who *own* them) who should be the focus of our concern. A section of this managerial class is particularly concerned with world governance. Located principally within the TNCs, it spans also governments and international organizations, and exercises its power via four major systems of labour control: agrarian coercion, employer domination, power bargaining and central planning, each of which resonates at state and factory levels. Within the third world, agrarian coercion was predominant within the early colonial period, while the later colonial period saw a transition to employer domination; the neo-colonial phase corresponded to power bargaining in key industrial sectors where labour was most advanced. During the 1970s, however, the global crisis and the shift against labour brought a widespread reversion to employer domination (matched by widespread loss of faith throughout the world in central planning). Levinsonian prescriptions of worker representatives linking up with management in co-determination of TNCs global strategies is therefore seen either as unrealistic (in that the global environment is presently less favourable to power bargaining, which involves a temporal recognition by management of labour's countervailing power) or as incompatible with trade union principles in that international union leaders will likely become engaged with the international managerial class in operating a system of labour control.

Harrod's contribution is unorthodox and challenging and rounds out theories of the internationalization of capital by focusing upon the controllers of the large scale organizations which have become, in his view, determinate at the global level. It is also highly provocative on at least two counts: first in its insistence upon global class formation when those such as Connell would argue that international economic structures are in practice as much vehicles of antagonism between the world's rich as of solidarity;[2] and secondly, I would argue, on account of its deeply disturbing outlook and its profound pessimism (which it shares with Frobel *et al.* and other proponents of the NIDL school). Harrod's international managerial class bases its lifestyle and governance upon a global surplus of labour; its coming has been accompanied by the strategic forging of a new dualism within the global labour market whereby the TNCs have set out to co-opt the support of privileged, high productivity and organized workers against the interests of unorganized, low productivity and socially disadvantaged workers; the very essence of labour control is coercive; and more generally the segmentation of the global workforce – within the industrialized countries as much as the third world – would seem to negate the possibility of effective labour riposte. The prospects of third world labour and unions upsetting the global balance of forces seems inherently limited.

The paper by Maja Bjorkman, Laurids Lauridsen and Henrik Marcussen offers a more orthodox representation of Marxist approaches to the internationalization of capital and its effect upon labour markets. They attempt to construct an abstract model of the capital–labour relation as it occurs under different types of industrialization in the third world. Their model building is a complex and scrupulously logical process which can only be impoverished by summary; but what it proposes, in essence, is that (simple and advanced) import-substitution industrialization and (simple and advanced) export-orientated industrialization frame the capital–labour relation in distinctive ways. Under both strategies, however, the transition from absolute to relative surplus-value extraction by capital is seen as providing the basis for the development of muscle by labour in terms of the relative scarcity of the skills it has to offer and – especially in the case of ISI – capital's need to expand its local market. The challenge emerging from their analysis is to move beyond the abstract to situate their models more precisely within the changing historical accumulation needs, strategies and phases of capital.

In contrast to both Levinson and Harrod, who argue – albeit from very different perspectives – that TNCs play a major role in determining the lot of the third world, and equally in contrast to the orthodoxy of Bjorkman, Lauridsen and Marcussen, Petras and Engbarth contend that uncritical focus upon the NIDL has exaggerated both the level of industrialization in the third world and the extent to which such industrialization as has taken place has been principally directed and designed by metropolitan and multinational capital. In actuality, they argue, whatever the development strategy pursued, third world industrialization has usually featured powerful and extensive state leadership and the rise of strata of domestic capitalists alongside the involvement of direct TNC investment, whilst the NIDL school has also understated the centrality of finance capital (recent years having seen a dramatic shift from direct to indirect investment fom the centre). In sum, capital accumulation in the third world has usually come very largely from domestic sources, including the earnings of local entrepreneurs from export earnings.

Such is the stress upon the dynamism of local forces in the third world that at points we may wonder whether one of the authors is the same James Petras who lacerated Bill Warren for his thesis that capitalism develops as imperialism declines.[3] Yet the paper offers an extremely rich as well as a provocative analysis which, as well as being likely to spark off a debate within and about the NIDL school, provides a searching assessment of the options available to third world unions and workers as *active* agents in their own fate. Noting that the industrialized working class is only a small proportion of the population in most countries of the third world, they stress the need for unions to forge links with the wider community (e.g. migrant miners with peasants); to develop their different strategic strengths (e.g. the politically effective leverage enjoyed by service workers); and to establish factory based democratic structures to counter danger of capture by the state. Within this context defence of jobs in stagnant industries must be balanced against the need for global competitiveness, with unions ensuring that such a pragmatically nationalist orientation does not work towards ensuring inequality between owners and workers. At the same time, with unions ever more conscious of the attack by the world market upon wages and conditions as well as the emerging dominance of finance capital, there must be a search for allies from other classes against reactionary forces and the IMF. Precisely because third world society and economy is permeated by the state, the union struggle must be extended to political terrain, even though it thereby greatly increases the chances that trade unionism will be repressed.

Petras and Engbarth thus point to the complexity and contradictory nature of third world industrialization and insist that it is a phenomenon whose origins and process cannot be reduced to the changing imperatives of metropolitan capital (even though some may feel that they swing the pendulum too far back the other way). Yet by offering a forcible warning against too narrow a reliance upon the economistic logic of the world market for labour approach, they highlight the necessity for unions to adopt situationally appropriate political strategies and thereby provide an excellent backdrop to the widely differing case studies which follow in the second section of the book.

Notes

1. Charles Levinson, *International Trade Unionism* (George Allen and Unwin, London, 1974).
2. R.W. Connell, 'Class Formation on a World Scale', *Review,* vol. VII, no. 3, 1984, pp. 407–40.
3. Philip McMichael, James Petras and Robert Rhodes, 'Imperialism and the Contradictions of Development', *New Left Review,* no. 85, 1974, pp. 83–104.

1. Social Relations of Production, Systems of Labour Control and Third World Trade Unions

J. Harrod

For some years Professor R.W. Cox and myself have been working on a typology of modes, or forms, of social relations of production which together cover the whole of the world labour force.[1] However, in this paper I wish to use a more limited concept of a system of labour control and motivation. The objective is to explore the possibilities which such a concept offer to a wide audience interested in analysing global policies and strategies which will profoundly affect the current position and future direction of third world trade unions.

Social Relations of Production and Systems of Labour Control

In the study cited above the concept of a mode, or form, of social relations of production is used to mean the technical or material way of producing things and services and the social relations, or power relations, associated with it; a form of social relations of production is then a distinct set or pattern of power relations surrounding production.[2] This means that a subsistence farmer, artisan carpenter, housewife, factory worker or casual labourer may each be within a different form of social relations of production, each with its own dynamics, contradictions and ideologies which precipitate different forms of consciousness and paths of transformation.

Twelve such forms of social relations have been identified and given labels, namely subsistence, peasant–lord, primitive labour market, enterprise labour market, bipartite, tripartite, enterprise corporatist, state corporatist, self-employment, household, central planning and communal. In each of these forms there are distinct social groups (or sometimes individuals) which are dominant and subordinate. Such groups may or may not be classes but they all engage in power relations connected with the control of production, extraction and distribution of surpluses.

*I am indebted to the editor for critical comments received on an earlier draft of this paper. I am also grateful for the financial support of the Institute of Social Studies, The Hague, in producing this paper and in enabling me to attend the Ottawa conference.

A social formation is comprised of a number of forms of social relations some of which are dominant and others subordinate. Clearly, dominant groups in dominant forms of social relations of production are likely to exercise power throughout the social formation and, in coalition, comprise a ruling class or group.

The concept of a form of social relations as defined above is an analytical tool which is initially neutral as to the focus of attention given to particular groups and classes. It is a pattern which is being analysed as well as the dynamics of changes in that pattern. Thus an engineered over-supply of unskilled labour may be the base mechanism for control and extraction from third world urban 'marginals' and could be considered as a system of labour control, even though in such a primitive labour market our approach gives equal importance to the organisations, practices and resistances of the subordinate marginals.

In contrast to the broad scope of a form of social relations of production, a system of labour control and motivation can be considered as a distinct set of ideologies, strategies and technologies used by those in control of production to extract a surplus and maintain and increase the productivity of labour.[3] The basis of such a concept is its assumption of a class or group capable of taking decisions (and seeing them implemented) which affect the extraction from, and productivity of, labour. It takes the emphasis off the broad analysis of dynamics and places it on the strategies and practices of a dominant group which may be considered as a managerial class.

A system of labour control is thus a more limited concept than a form of social relations (at least as defined above) for two reasons. First, because it excludes large numbers of producers. Thus, for example, the world's self-employed are engaged in power relations with buyers, suppliers, regulators and competitors and these relations together constitute a form of social relations of production; but it is unlikely that a central and coordinated decision can be made concerning increased productivity or extraction from the self-employed which would have any chance of securing the results intended. Thus most policies directed at the self-employed are designed to secure their elimination rather than greater extraction. Self-employment cannot therefore be considered as a system of labour control if the above definition is retained. The same applies to the social relations associated with subsistence farmers, women producing household services, the casually employed and so on.

The second important limitation of the concept of system of labour control stems from its assumption of a dominant class or group capable of controlling labour, which in turn implies a linear form of authority, domination and control. The concept tends to disguise the power flux, the contradictions and the dynamics. It directs us away from the range of possible resistance to authority as it is exercised in the control of labour. The equal weight given to resistance, reaction and dynamics in the concept of a form of social relations is the crucial emphasis which distinguishes it from the concept of a system of labour control.

Occasionally, forms of social relations may also be systems of labour control. Thus the power (and its support structures) of an employer to dismiss an employee may be a system of labour control as well as a form of social relations of production and furthermore one which in the nineteenth-century industrialization process in Europe assumed dominant proportions. Except for the differences in emphasis noted above the form of social relations designated earlier as the enterprise labour market appears also as the employer domination system of labour control. When this is the case the choice of concept must depend upon the audience and objective.

The concept of a form of social relations of production is, in conclusion, less limited and more theoretically elegant. Elsewhere I have argued that the multiple forms of social relations of production approach is a superior analytical tool for both activists as well as passive analysts.[4] It allows us to disaggregate, in terms of consciousness and material impact, otherwise blanket concepts as 'urban mass', 'labouring poor', 'informal sector' or 'peasant' which are usually applied across diverse forms of social relations of production.

Despite these limitations, for the purpose of this paper the concept of a system of labour control will be used for the following reasons. First, one of the objectives of the paper is to illustrate the international forces affecting third world labour and trade unions. For such an objective, concepts which are few in number and have easily recognizable national examples are needed for the requisite macro-global analysis. The world system of labour control concept as defined above fits this need. Second, in laying emphasis on the current and most pressing preoccupations of the various managerial classes the strategies and policies adopted by them are illuminated. Finally, that section of the world managerial classes which concerns itself with the global management of world politics, resources and production is growing in size and power and as it grows the greater the need for heuristic devices to reveal its operations more clearly.

Systems of Labour Control and Motivation

A system of labour control and motivation implies a class or group capable of organizing and exercising control. Since the middle of the last century there have been theorists concerned with the existence of such a managerial class. The emphasis on an industrial managerial elite was taken by some as an attempt to turn the Marxist socialist spotlight off the owners of capital and on to the more ubiquitous and less obvious groups of industrial managers. However, since the recent resurgence of Marxist and neo-Marxist analysis, the emergence and nature of the managerial class has not been given the prominence that its power and numbers justify. Yet perhaps the most significant development of the mid-twentieth century has been the growth of large scale organizations – both the instruments and the home of the managerial class. Those in control of large scale organizations are at the core of the managerial class. That a managerial class exists does not mean, however, that pre-existing classes of industrial property owners or landowners have been dispossessed and must be eliminated from current analysis; it does mean, however, that the latter's control and power has been reduced to such an extent that they can be seen as a part, or faction, of the broader managerial class.[5]

The objectives and ideologies of such a class are distinct and in particular cannot be associated with either the nineteenth-century small scale entrepreneur nor the large capital owner (so much the favourite of the more vulgar class analyses). While class objectives within labour control will be greater productivity and extraction, other goals may not be the ones of profit and accumulation as traditionally defined, for growth of organization (quantitatively and in power) perquisites and security may be equally important.[6]

There is a section of the managerial class that is in control of multinational organizations which are particularly concerned with world governance.[7] It constitutes a transnational elite or the international managerial class. While the main locale is the multinational corporation, members of the managerial class are also in public and quasi-public international organizations and internationally operating government agencies. This element is of particular importance to globally strategic systems of labour control. The study of the journals, technical and popular, aimed at this group provided considerable input for this paper and other such work.[8] In these journals the discussion of labour control is at its most overt, untrammelled by the niceties of liberal politics; the writing is sometimes frank about the myths deliberately promoted for uninitiate consumption (such as inter-firm competition, subsidiary autonomy and economic development).

Labour control and motivation is of universal concern to managerial groups and classes regardless of the nature of the society or the justice of the distribution of income and wealth. The universal need for labour control and motivation stems from the universal tendency for the pace and intensity of work to slow and decline when perceived, immediate, personal needs are satisfied. Managerial classes are particularly concerned to prevent such a slowdown when (i) part of a person's production is extracted in order to underwrite the higher standards of living or better conditions of work of other people, that is, when labour is exploited and (ii) when production is socialized in the sense that the division of labour is advanced and therefore consumption is indirect, either being effected through the medium of exchange, or composed of a high proportion of collective goods.

The universal concern of managerial classes with labour control and motivation does not invoke the 'convergence' theories of the 1960s simply because it includes groups within both socialist and capitalist countries. That a concern is universal means that similar attitudes, language and even cultures may be produced but it does not mean that the different settings or social formations in which this concern is situated converge. Thus the goal of low labour cost, universally shared by managers, does not mean that child labour is permitted universally; there are psychological, cultural and social barriers to the expression of the extremes of labour control methods.

In the first case of the special need for labour control mentioned above (when labour underwrites an extant higher standard of living for others), a mechanism is needed to maintain the intensity and pace of work after immediate needs are believed to have been satisfied; this is the phase of work the product of which accrues to the benefit of the more privileged and powerful. In the second case – in socialized production – a mechanism is needed to connect the work actually performed to collective, future or indirect consumption. Thus it is that even in a society in which distribution could be assumed to be perfectly just (i.e. with no exploitation), a system operating at the psychological level would be needed to connect immediate individual tasks with future collective consumption and to adjust return to individuals to achieve equality regardless of different productivities.

At the individual level there are three basic means available for the control and motivation of labour. These may be termed coercive, material and moral or normative.[9] Systems of labour control use a mixture of all these three, although some systems may be more associated with one particular means.

Coercion within systems of labour control may be physical or economic. Physical coercion is used when a worker is beaten, shot, imprisoned or arrested when work is not performed at the required intensity and pace at the offered return. Economic coercion refers to an economic sanction, usually, but not always, the threat of the removal of the source of income in conditions where it will cause a precipitous decline in living standards affecting the physical well-being of the worker and dependants. Material mechanisms are based upon positive rewards rather than negative sanctions. In return for an accepted pace and intensity of work the worker is promised material rewards; when the pace of work tends to decline further rewards are offered. Moral or normative incentives invoke psychological, inspirational and ideological elements – the incentive to work is not coercion nor material rewards but the acquisition of individual status or mental satisfaction derived from the belief that work is for some posited collective and higher objective.

The effectiveness of all these means decays over time and produces crises of stability. That different systems of labour control produce both different labour cost and different political instabilities and therefore investment risks are crucial to current discussions of international political economy.

Current Strategic Systems of Labour Control

Using the above definition it is apparent that the strategic concerns of the managerial classes are involved with four major systems of labour control. These cover either strategic proportions of total world output or strategic sections of the labour force. These may be termed agrarian coercion, employer domination, power bargaining and central planning. These will be briefly described before they are used to discuss the current policies within the international political economy and their impact on third world labour.

Agrarian Coercion

The agrarian coercion system of labour control is so named because extraction from producers is based on the ability of a class of landowners, money-lenders and merchants to be able to deliver physical sanctions against recalcitrant farmers, often through state organized police or army. This system exists in the rural areas of Latin America, Africa and Asia and through its operation peasant families surrender anything between 30–90% of their total production as 'rent'. This system, although not technologically efficient, is efficient in extraction, with the net result that its low labour cost produces cheap food for consumption in town and industry, or commercial crops, usually for export. Any change in the system of labour control would certainly mean increasing returns for producers without increasing productivity and hence higher prices for food which would have both national and international effects.

Social unrest in the agrarian coercion system is constant. The history of people suffering from agrarian coercion has been one of constant revolts, rebellions, resistance and revolutions. The successful peasant armies of the mid-twentieth century caused the system to be at the centre of international concern throughout the 1950s, accelerating after the Cuban revolution of 1959. Thus most major international agencies and dominant governments advocated land reform which was seen as the principle means of defusing political explosions and reducing investment risk. The clear failure of this policy by the late 1960s caused it to be replaced by one designed to increase productivity without challenging the agrarian coercion power structure – the so-called Green Revolution. The inability of this policy to alter patterns of political turbulence and the strategy of an international squeeze on peasants caused the abandonment of the policy in the mid-1970s.[10]

Employer Domination

The employer domination system of labour control uses economic coercion through employer's unmitigated power to dismiss, or refuse to hire, in conditions where such action means physical deterioration of the persons thus made, or left, unemployed and/or their dependants. The labour force has been prevented from organizing industrially or politically to reduce employers' power. The two essential features of this system of labour control are an unorganized labour force and the presence of a pool of unemployed whose living conditions are sufficiently bad to raise fear among the employed that they may become unemployed.

Employer domination as a system of labour control is found principally in third world countries but, as will be discussed later, is also increasing in scope in industrialized capitalist countries. It is most suited to production using low skilled or unskilled labour which can easily be replaced from the labour market. Employer domination produces the lowest labour costs in industrial production.

Like agrarian coercion the employer domination system of labour control produces constant crises. These arise from attempts to keep the labour force unorganized and employer power intact in the face of a social and political dynamic leading to the development of protective worker organizations within industrial production.

Employer domination was the system of labour control at the beginning of European industrialization; but it began to be eliminated by the growth of union power in the 1930s and was further reduced in Europe and North America with the growth of the welfare state in the 1940s and 1950s. It was on the way to being reduced to a residue during the late 1960s and early 1970s with the extension of unemployment benefits from their original transitory function to the longer-term role of dealing with structural unemployment. In third world countries, however, this system of labour control was increasing in use throughout the same period as the result of industrialization based upon private ownership of capital. Currently the system is to some extent being restored in capitalist industrialized countries and, by analogy, in some centrally planned socialist countries. In third world countries current policies are based upon attempting to secure the benefits of employer domination without running the risk of either organizational or social unrest risks to capital.

Power Bargaining

The power bargaining system of labour control abandons the economic coercion of employer domination and rests mainly on the motivational mechanism of material rewards, the level of which are determined by bargaining between different parties on the basis of their different power capabilities. Normative incentives, particularly in relation to nationalism and national security, are used to reduce labour protest. A positive attitude towards work and productivity is maintained through constant reassurance that it will be rewarded by ever-growing material benefits. Demands beyond certain limits at any point in time are protested against as being unnecessary, unpatriotic or socially unacceptable.

Unlike the constant crisis of the employer domination and agrarian coercion systems of labour control, the power bargaining system produces periodic crises of increasing severity. This is because both material and normative motivations decay over time. Material incentives must be constantly increased to prevent them losing their motivational power and this raises problems of both supply and demand: supply because there are limits to the ever-increasing supply of material benefits; and demand, because there are limits to the consumption of material goods. Normative incentives of the type used also have a limited life and renewal is difficult as they involve large questions of inter-state relations which cannot always be controlled.

There is a third world variant of power bargaining in which the legitimacy of trade unions is recognized but their power is institutionally and legally constrained by the state. In it the state also constrains employer power but never to such an extent as worker organizations. This system, often known as state corporatism is, however, in the management literature, generally subsumed under power bargaining inasmuch as worker organizations are legitimate and have to be dealt with, unlike within employer domination in which only the *potential* of worker organizations must be dealt with.

The basis for the power bargaining system was laid down in the 1930s in Europe when trade unions were legitimized as production partners. The essential condition was that unions abandon the broader goals of the labour movement in favour of income maximizing organisations, often based on the enterprise, and representing a diminishing and minority proportion of the total labour force. The process gained momentum during the late 1940s and early 1950s, assisted by interdictions on protest activities arising from the Cold War. Thus by the mid-1950s the system was in optimum operation. The crisis of a declining rate of productivity and increasing money wage demands which started in the late 1960s is crucial to the development of the current situation and will be discussed in a following section.

Central Planning

Central planning as a system of labour control uses most extensively moral incentives in the framework of conditions of work and return which are set by a central authority capable of wielding coercive power to enforce its decisions. Moral incentives take the form of awarded status at the place of work or the assignment of value to work as serving a higher purpose. The decay of these incentives in a relatively short space of time – sometimes known as the ten-year period of enthusiasm – means that, invariably, material incentives are added to the system.[11]

The crises of the system are periodic as moral incentives decay and are refurbished. The introduction of material incentives and the consequence of differences in income also unsettle a system which is based upon the acquisition of social rather than material prestige within a framework of material equality.

The basic lines of the central planning system were laid down in the Soviet Union in the 1920s and 1930s but the refurbishing of moral incentives took place after the 1939–45 war. The Chinese Revolution in 1949 and the inclusion of the Eastern European countries have substantially increased the proportion of the world's labour force covered by the system. Since the mid-1950s, however, all countries operating this system of labour control have begun to show continuing problems of labour productivity and unrest resulting from the decaying belief in the validity of future goals and the introduction of material incentives. The Soviet incentive factory reforms of 1957 and 1965, the 1971 resurrection of the symbol of socialist emulation (the miner Stakhanov), the redressment of wage differentials in the Chinese Cultural Revolution and inflation in Poland and Hungary are manifestations of these problems.

Of particular importance to the current situation were the 1970s attempts, especially in Poland, Hungary and Romania, to solve the crisis of declining productivity, not by refurbishing motivation or increasing material incentives but by the importing of foreign capital and technology. This has produced the unique structure of buy back deals (barters between capitalist and centrally planned socialist societies) which are part of the cause of the more overt manifestations of crisis such as those in Poland.

Systems of Labour Control and Third World Trade Unions

It is now possible to begin to apply the concept of a system of labour control and the specific systems identified above to the development of third world trade unions, the emergence of the current situation and the directions of trends. The emphasis will, however, largely be on the international aspects affecting third world trade unions and the perceptions and strategies of past and present internationally active managerial classes.

Labour Control in the Development of Third World Trade Unions

A system of labour control once established and once dominant in any particular society clearly affects the institutional exports of the society. When that society is in a dominant position in the world the 'model' which is exported is the formal, perceived model of the system of labour control. This dynamic affects all parties which are organized within any particular system. Thus trade unions as well as capital owners, government agencies, voluntary organizations and development groups will tend to attempt to export the model with which they are most familiar. However, as the objective is labour control in the target society, the model is invariably exported in a form modified to best facilitate that goal.

In terms of labour control it is possible to see the third world as going through three stages which were determined by dominant powers concerned with the labour cost surrounding the products which were to be extracted. The three periods could be called the early colonial period, the late colonial period and the neo-colonial period.

In the first period metropolitan powers were interested in extraction from traditional farming, plantations and commercial farming. Agrarian coercion prevailed in the non-commercial sector based upon the use of distortions of the indigenous power structure because metropolitan managers had little experience in such systems. The plantation system, a form of employer domination, is one of the unique products of the early colonial period.

Metropolitan managerial classes had little interest in establishing employer domination at this time as manufacturing was not a major form of international extraction. Labour costs were important in farming, in plantations and then in mines. As agrarian coercion ruled in the countryside, plantations were considered as enclaves and labour costs in mining were generally not significant (gold being an exception), it was easy for metropolitan powers to advocate the use of power bargaining with its comcomitant increase in labour costs.

The most noticeable attempt in this respect, and one which has had a profound effect on third world trade unionism, was the 1929 Passfield Memorandum issued by ex-trade union theorist Sidney Webb as British Secretary of State for the Colonies (disguised as Lord Passfield) in which colonial governors were instructed to legalize trade unions by a system of registration as

> without sympathetic guidance, organisations of labourers without experience of combination for any social and economic progress may fall under the domination of disaffected persons, by which their activities may be diverted to improper and mischievous ends.[12]

Webb's objective was to preserve imperial domination through the imposition of power bargaining. In short, the political advantages of absorbing social unrest was not at that time matched by an economic cost to the metropolitan power.

The result of this policy is well known. Trade unions in some ex-British colonies preceded political parties and were the base for struggles to achieve formal independence. But it also bequeathed two aspects of labour control and trade unionism which were sustained for nearly thirty years. First, power bargaining was established in almost enclave conditions and the new internal governments were left to deal with the management of the largely domestic issues of wages and distribution. Second, it laid the foundations for the state corporatist variety of power bargaining in which workers' organizations are legitimate but, in accordance with Passfield, are registered, controlled and regulated by the state.

The neo-colonial stage saw the consolidation of power bargaining in certain large organizations or enterprises (for example, railways, mines, public services and sometimes plantations), the establishment of the state corporatist variant and, of course, in some cases the attempt to develop a third world version of centrally planned socialism.

This situation prevailed until the early 1970s when international management became interested in labour costs within manufacturing as well as plantations and mines. At the same time the capital-intensive nature of modern production facilities meant that there was a growing concern to minimize investment risk. The interest in labour costs within manufacturing meant that the power bargaining system had to be curtailed, eliminated, or at least contained in favour of employer domination. It would not be possible to establish employer domination in the conditions of power bargaining (legal structures, political cultures) for there would be risks that it could not be sustained, that is, there was a risk of the organization of the workforce and wages being influenced not by the market but by power bargaining in the organized sectors. The symbolic response was the overt enclaves of employer domination in the Free Industrial Zones; but these were only institutional manifestations of political policies being pursued in order to dismantle the power of trade unions established at a time when power bargaining was the internationally oriented system of labour control. These strategies and policies will be discussed in the concluding section after considering the reasons for such changes towards third world labour and unions.

Development of the Current Situation

The two world dominant systems of labour control and motivation – power bargaining and central planning – which were established in the 1940s were functioning at the peak of their efficiency in the 1950s and began to decline in the 1960s. The periodicity is of crucial importance to world politics and the fact that the 1950s configurations of both systems were laid down in the late 1940s has meant that there has been a convergence of productivity decline and labour unrest which cannot only be explained by the inter-societal effects of the world political economy.

The productivity and political stability problems within the centrally planned system of labour control has had an impact on the third world only as a weakening of the potency of an established model for emulation. This decline in the interest of central planning as a viable model for third world countries and the search for more creative solutions may have a longer-run importance greater than that of the more immediate and material effects on the third world arising from crises in power bargaining. However, this latter point must be deferred in order to devote more space to the more manageable topic of the policies and strategies developed out of the crisis within power bargaining.

The power bargaining system was subjected to a conjunction of trends in the late 1960s which emerged into what has become known as the international 'economic crisis' or the international 'crisis of capitalism'. First, managers of the power bargaining system have in the past been able to deal with declines in productivity by increased applications of capital and technology as well as increased material incentives. Such applications, however, were expensive in their use of raw materials and also had some limits to the extent and depth of their possible application. The pressure this put on raw material prices at a time when limits to innovations were being reached weakened the technological means to restore the rates of productivity growth. Second, the power of unions began to move beyond bargaining over the level of material incentives and moved further in the direction of job security and substantially improved conditions of work. The first caused labour to move nearer becoming a fixed cost[13] and the second towards a massive expenditure on 'unproductive capital' in work-floor health and safety provisions and general environment and pollution controls.[14] Coupled and associated with this was the state system of social security which began to undermine the disciplining power of both the need for work and the threat of its removal.

Third, for a complex of reasons, the material base of the power bargaining system began to be undermined in that the material goad to work began to lose its power as more producers opted for non-work rather than material goods.[15] Fourth, the normative aspects of the power bargaining system in key economies such as that of the United States began to lose their potency. The dampening effect of the Cold War on labour militancy began to be lost both as part of an inevitable ageing process and the obvious impact of the Vietnam War. Fifthly, the growth of the tertiary sector in which productivity is notoriously hard to measure brought further inefficiencies in the productivity/reward structure of power bargaining. Finally, the late 1960s saw not only a staging point in the growth of the managerial class but also the beginnings of its reaction to the closing gap between incomes of the managerial and production workers – the beginnings of erosion between the salaried and the waged worker.

These are some suggested reasons for the decline in the rate of productivity growth in the 1960s. Providing reasons for this phenomenon has become a favourite game in management literature; for example, Samuelson, with nineteenth-century simplicity, attributes the decline to a loss of managerial power over labour which resulted from a decline in 'the hungriness motive' of workers.[16]

Reasons aside, the effects were clear; with productivity declining but worker organizations continuing to use their social power to bid up the wages, the wage demand had become redistributive, acting against the managerial classes particularly. The first reaction was to inflate. This restored the differentials and stopped the erosion of managerial privileges. Throughout the 1970s, while production workers were taking real cuts in income or advancing only slightly, real and money wages for the managerial classes leapt ahead, especially when the real value of non-monetary payments (company cars, stock options and other such benefits) were added.[17]

The other responses were basically a direct attack on union power, the creation of a section of the labour force outside of union power and state assistance and an attempt to dismantle the 'welfare' state.

The attack on the unions was in a direct and traditional fashion – through legal restrictions, disturbing established bargaining patterns, dismantling indexation systems, easing laws on dismissals and job security and creating a corps of experts for use in 'union busting'. The creation of an army of low wage workers, unorganized and usually in small to medium enterprises was intended to restore to the managerial class in so-called rich countries the real benefits of wealth–a personal service economy based upon a labour-surplus lifestyle. Hence in the United Kingdom there has been a re-emergence of the indigenous household domestic servant who had been in eclipse since the 1920s. To be successful, however, either the attack has to bring wages below social security benefits or social security benefits must be reduced or eliminated. This is a major reason for the now global attack on the welfare state with its associated social security benefits. The fundamental strategy is, then, to create an institutionalized dualism characterized by the high productivity, oligopoly employed and organized workers and the managerial class on one side of the divide and the unorganized low productivity, low wage, part-time and socially disadvantaged workers on the other.[18]

The difference from the more familiar dual labour market is that the duality now being created is pervading all aspects of society–education, housing, food, transport, and work and state derived benefits. It is a return to Disraeli's two nations with the fundamental difference that those in the privileged nation are not necessarily in the minority. The coming of the managerial class and the inclusion of the more privileged workers means that the privileged section may include as much as 40% of the population. It is, then, essentially the institutionalizing of two systems of labour control–power bargaining and employer domination–within one social formation.

The complications and contradictions that this reconstruction of a new duality engenders will form the base of all political and social movements in the industrialized capitalist countries of the world for some time to come. The focus in this paper is, however, the effects of this strategy on third world labour and trade unions.

Priorities of Extraction From Third World

The basic means of extraction from a third world country are via the internationally traded goods or services of raw materials, agricultural produce, industrial products and leisure facilities and from the returns on direct investment derived from internal production and sales and from interest on loans. Each of these has a different utility and is perceived differently by the global managers.

The place of these in the basic strategy of a structured duality of systems of labour control and industrialized countries can now be considered in turn. In the case of raw materials many of them, like oil, have been integrated into a price and labour market structure which is the basis of the high productivity sectors. The maintenance of supplies and the prevention of precipitous price increases become of primordial importance. To take one example, the replacement of copper for galvanized iron in the modern construction industry has revolutionized that industry in both cost and labour terms; the use of copper requires much less capital and a much lower skill level than iron. A similar situation prevails with the use of aluminium. Thus the maintenance of the supplies of bauxite and of copper and the restriction of prices will be pursued at all costs. This situation, of course, has effects on the policies directed at labour and unions within these industries.

In contrast, agricultural products are of less strategic interest having value only to those specific industries involved. As already mentioned it is for this reason that, once the fear of rural based revolutions evaporated, the third world farmers have been left mainly to the rigours of the domestically imposed and maintained labour control of agrarian coercion.

Exportable industrial products play a role in the strategy which has yet to be completely realized. In general, the literature has wildly exaggerated the importance of industrial exports from third world countries.[19] Penetration in the markets of industrialized countries is insignificant. The products themselves are of little interest to the managerial class as consumers and in the maintenance of their lifestyle. Furthermore, the returns from direct investment in third world manufactures are still in aggregate inferior to a similar investment in industrialized countries, especially when investment risk is taken into account, as the direct investment figures clearly show. However, there is an important role that cheaper industrial exports from the third world may play in the structured duality strategy and that is the reinforcement of the duality of markets, with the low wage army consuming the cheaper and poorer mass consumption goods from the third world. This cuts the cost of maintaining a low wage labour force, (especially those among it who are unemployed) by enabling wages and social benefits to be reduced. The 'adequate' consumption pattern, by analogy with 'basic needs', also dampens social protest. Thus via unequal exchange the structured duality can be reinforced.

Leisure activities centred on the third world, of which the various types of tourism are the most important examples, while not strategic are of extreme importance in maintaining the lifestyle of the managerial class and the perception of international power and command. This is particularly so with the international section of that class. The ability to travel anywhere, to open a subsidiary or branch office and use all the facilities for spouse accompanied and company financed trips looms large in the reward package of the managers; they will fight for it in much the same way that other groups will fight viciously simply to maintain a labour-surplus lifestyle. Access is the crucial objective in this case and the ideology of nationalism and other access restricting movements will be roundly condemned.

Direct investment via multinational companies is the mechanism which serves the managerial class most readily. The returns are received directly by that class and their associated workers and represents extraction from the third world to which other groups and organizations have little claim. The apparent need for each large company to acquire international operations in third world countries then has a lot to do with the possibility that such operations can accrue directly to the salaries and benefits of the ensemble of the organizations. The extraction via loans serves another section of the managerial class which is closer to the traditional image of a capitalist class. Part of the dynamic for third world loans was precisely the move to self-financing of multinational companies which squeezed out bankers and rentiers from profitable domestic investment. The contradiction is that the demands on the third world for debt servicing, for which the IMF is the spokesman of the principal investing and loaning countries, contrasts with the need for a high level of domestic demand by the foreign owned subsidiaries serving the domestic markets.

Third World Labour in Global Management

In this brief conclusion it is intended to combine the analysis of systems of labour control, managerial global strategy, the existing structure of third world trade unions and the various utilities of different forms of extraction from the third world.

The remnants of power bargaining left by the late colonial period, as described above, are under attack in two basic areas: the first where the system would create higher labour costs in exportable manufactures and second where the dynamic of 'free trade unionism' would be a possible foundation for a broader based labour movement likely to threaten investment and access. The attack, however, is not one of elimination but one of containment. The objective is twofold, first to contain the activities of trade unions in the sectors where labour cost is of little importance, usually raw materials or high capital ratio direct investment and then to corporatize these unions into what has been called the 'enterprise corporatist' variant of power bargaining.[20] The basic lines of this policy are the granting of relatively high rates of pay and privileges derived from the company. This tactic is even being pursued in social formations in which unions are official within state corporatism. It issues from an international managerial class most interested in the direct investment, raw materials and exporting manufactures. On the other hand, the third world creditors argue for the incorporatization of trade unions via the 'social democracy' slogan which, in effect, means wage restraints and incomes policies. Both are incompatible with the 'free trade union' slogan of global management in the neo-colonial period.[21] Clearly this tactic assists in the destruction of a broader based labour movement by making enclaves of the very workers whose high wages, productivity and strategic position surrounding either high capital industries of primary foreign exchange earners make them a financial and tactical power within any labour movement.

The firmer establishment or re-establishment of employer domination in sectors where labour cost is important to global managers is then made easier by the isolation of the potentially powerful unions. However, the growth of the Free Trade Zones is to some extent an expression of the fear of failure of such a policy. They are islands of employer domination which have had to be protected and shielded by the state and its agents of law and force from the possibility of the spread of unionism. If then there is any extension of the role of manufactured exports it is likely that there will have to be a move beyond the perimeters of the Free Industrial Zone and it is for this reason that there has been a promotion of small and medium enterprises under legal conditions and practices in which organization is impossible or difficult.

The emerging interest in labour cost in manufacturing has resulted in a deliberate lack of concern with agrarian coercion. Fear that land reform or disturbances in the countryside will put up labour costs has meant that landlords, money-lenders and merchants – the triumvirate of extractors within agrarian coercion – have been actively supported, if not left in peace (or rather violence), in delivering food to urban workers.

If this be the correct analysis of plans which emerge from the interests of an international managerial class and its international labour specialists within multinational companies, agencies of governments dealing with foreign affairs and international public organizations then, of course, a counter-strategy may be devised. Such counter-strategies and responses would have to fasten on the contradictions within such global policies, some of which have been identified here.

The objective of this paper has specifically not been, however, to devise strategies and tactics for the response of third world organized labour – these must always emerge from the social environment of the impact of the policies and not from the environments which are the source of such global policies. The objectives of this paper are then modest; first, to record how one person reads the current thinking, policies and strategies of managerial classes in dominant powers and second, to present such identified strategies and policies in a way which may help develop insights into current actions and assist in the anticipation of future initiatives or reactions.

Notes

1. This is to be published in the form of a study entitled *Power and Production* which comprises of four free-standing volumes, viz: R.W. Cox, *Production, Power and World Order: Social Forces in the Making of History* (forthcoming, Columbia University Press, New York, 1987); J. Harrod, *The Unprotected Worker: The Social Relations of Subordination* (forthcoming, Columbia University Press, New York, 1987); J. Harrod, *The Established Worker: Corporatist Social Relations* (forthcoming, Columbia University Press, New York, 1988); R.W. Cox, *Redistributive Social Relations* (provisional title – forthcoming Columbia University Press, New York, 1988).

2. This definition is in accordance with one of the four ways in which Marx used the concept but not, of course, with the traditional historical epoch definition of a mode of production.

3. Other authors who refer directly and indirectly to concepts similar to this definition are Richard Scase (ed.), *Industrial Society; Class, Cleavage and Control*

(Allen and Unwin, London, 1976); H.A. Spalding, 'Ideologies and Mechanisms of Labour Control in Latin America' (mimeo, 1977) and R.W. Cox, 'World Systems of Labour and Production' International Political Science Association (IPSA) (Conference Paper, 1974).

4. J. Harrod, 'Informal Sector and Urban Masses: A Social Relations of Production Approach' (unpublished paper, mimeo, available from author, 1980) and J. Harrod, *The Unprotected Worker: The Social Relations of Subordination* (forthcoming Columbia University Press, New York, 1987).

5. For a review of the literature on the theories of the development of a managerial class and the conclusion that managers do control large business corporations see Edward S. Herman, *Corporate Control, Corporate Power* (Cambridge University Press, Cambridge, 1981). On the reduction of capital owners to part of a managerial class see the concept of a 'unified business class' in John Scott, *The Upper Classes: Property and Privilege in Britain* (Macmillan, London, 1983) and for similar conclusion from an empirical study see Thomas R. Dye, 'Strategic Ownership Positions in US Industry and Banking', *The American Journal of Economics and Sociology,* vol. 44, no. 1, 1985, pp. 9–22.

6. See Herman, *Corporate Control.*

7. A discussion of the growth of a 'transnational elite' and its impact is found in J. Harrod, 'Transnational Power', in *The Year Book of World Affairs 1976* Vol. 30 (London: Stevens & Sons 1977), pp. 97–115. See also Alejandro Portes and John Walton, *Labour, Class and the International System* (Academic Press, New York, 1981).

8. For example, *International Management, Business International, Duns Business Month, Intersocial, Harvard Business Review, Columbia Journal of World Business, Euromoney, Economist Intelligence Reports, The Hudson Letter, L'Usine Nouvelle, Forbes, Fortune, L'Expansion, Multinational Business, International Management* and industry trade journals.

9. Although this is similar to Weber's three methods of legitimization in fact it was derived from A. Etzioni, *Modern Organisations,* (Prentice Hall, New York, 1963).

10. For a discussion of this point see Harry Cleaver, 'Internationalisation of Capital and Mode of Production in Agriculture', *Economic and Political Weekly Review of Agriculture,* March 1976, pp. A2–A16.

11. See, for example, 'Cuba increases productivity with incentive payments', *Latin American Report,* 5 January 1979, p. 7.

12. S. Webb, *Labour in the United Kingdom Dependencies* (HMSO, London, 1957). See also J. Harrod, *Trade Union Foreign Policy* (Doubleday, New York, 1972).

13. This is often an assumption made in company strategies, see also M. Bienefeld, Martin Godfrey and H. Schmitz, 'Trade Unions and the 'New' Internationalisation of Production', *Development and Change,* Vol. 8, 1977, pp. 417–39.

14. On the importance of increased worker power at the workplace see Giovanni Arrighi 'The Labour Movement in Twentieth Century Western Europe', in I. Wallerstein (ed.), *Labour in the World Social Structure* (Sage Publications, London, 1983) pp. 44–57.

15. For some different analyses of this development see Richard B. Freedman, *Labour Economies* (Prentice Hall, New York, 1972) pp. 22–4; Peter Chinloy, 'Sources of Quality Change in Labour Input', *The American Economic Review,* vol. 70, no. 1, 1980, pp. 108–115.

16. *Fortune,* 1979, December 3, p. 80. An overview of the 'productivity discussions' is found in 'Decline in Productivity Growth After 1973: A Further Look at Explanatory Factors', in *United Nations Economic Survey of Europe in 1982* (United Nations, New York, 1983), pp. 36–52.

17. This is evident from most official and private surveys and statistics; see Charterhouse Group, *Guide to Management Remuneration in the UK* (annual) and Hay Associates (US) annual survey of executive salaries. For the non-monetary elements in the managerial class 'reward packages' see, for example, Pierre Beaudeux, 'Au Paradis des Advantages en Nature: Comment Payer les Cadres quand on ne peut plus les augmenter', *L'Expansion,* 25 November 1982, pp. 133–40 and 'Top Management: The Company Pays-Everything', *ICEF Chemical Industries Bulletin* (Geneva), Autumn 1981, pp. 8–9.

18. One author refers to this as a 'split level' economy: see Mike Davis 'Late Imperial America', *New Left Review,* no. 143, 1984, pp. 6–38. The expansion of the 'underground economy' is part of this process. On the use of marginal workers, consider the following headlines: 'Convict Labour Has the Unions Worried', *Businessweek,* 1984, April 16; 'Labour Camps in Louisiana Provide "Warm Bodies" for Oil Companies', *The Asian Wall Street Journal,* 1983 June 29; 'Hopes for Factory Run by Jobless' (in fact, youths paid 60p per hour), *The Guardian,* 7 April 1983. For an academic economic argument to pay US sub-minimum wages see Daniel S. Hamermesh, 'Substitution and Labour Market Policy', *Challenge*, vol. 22, no. 6, 1980, pp. 44–7.

19. Another author who has noticed this exaggeration is Rhys Jenkins, 'Divisions Over the International Division of Labour', *Capital and Class,* no. 22, 1984, pp. 22–57. For the argument that third world industrial exports based on cheap labour will become even less important, see Moises Ikonicoff, 'Economie Souterraine, Accumulation et Tiers Monde', *Revue Tiers-Monde,* vol. 25, no. 98, 1984, pp. 318–37.

20. See R.W. Cox, 'Approaches to the Futurology of Industrial Relations *International Institute of Labour Studies Bulletin, no. 8,* 1971, pp. 139–164; R.W. Cox and J. Harrod *et al., Future Industrial Relations: An Interim Report* (Geneva, International Institute of Labour Studies (IILS), 1972) and J. Harrod, *The Established Worker: Corporatist Social Relations* (forthcoming, Columbia University Press, New York, 1987).

21. For a discussion of these policies see J. Harrod, 'Rethinking Development: From Change to Stabilisation', in R. Apthorpe and A. Krahl (eds), *Development Studies: Critique and Renewal,* (Brill, Leiden, 1985).

2 Types of Industrialization and the Capital–Labour Relation in The Third World

Maja Bjorkman, Laurids S. Lauridsen and
Henrik Secher Marcussen

It is extremely ambitious to propose a holistic approach to the study of types of industrialization accumulation structures and capital–labour relations in the third world, if only because any approach pitched at a high level of abstraction will inevitably attract criticism on empirical grounds. None the less, despite all the risks that such a task involves, this paper will attempt a theory generating analysis; only by so doing is it possible to provide the generalization needed for a better understanding of global dynamics and thereby provide a point of departure for political analysis and strategy. Of course, this does not mean that we deny the importance of detailed case studies of the conditions and constraints under which third world trade unions and labour operate; but such analyses have to be incorporated into a theory generating framework. In brief, our approach is largely deductive, serving thereby as a heuristic base for the formulation of hypotheses which may be applied to the study of capital–labour relations in specific situations.

Much of what follows is based on assumptions regarding the changing international division of labour and its dynamics. We shall briefly summarize our assumptions here, focusing on one particular aspect of the international division of labour: the relationship between the internationalization of capital and types of industrialization in the third world. This brief sketch will serve as background for the main topic under discussion: the relation between types of industrialization/structures of accumulation and labour market relations.

In our view of the changing international division of labour, the internationalization of capital is the process whereby capital's tendency to ever-broaden its sphere of operation, its inherent disposition to establish capitalist production and reproduction processes wherever possible, is exemplified. With the increased socialization of production and with capitalism penetrating and encompassing all sectors of the national centre economy, its sphere of operation is increasingly global. However, the built-in mechanisms to transcending national barriers are only potential and have to be realized historically. In this connection the peripheral state is one, perhaps *the* most important, element within peripheral social formations which may activate such built-in tendencies.

The internationalization of capital on the one hand and the peripheral state on the other are the most important, related determinants in shaping the changing international division of labour.[1] The actual outcome of the division of labour emerging – the historical origins, periodization and causes of which would take us too far off track – is an increasing differentiation among the countries of the third world. This differentiation is not only manifest when measured in national economic terms like GNP per capita but is also reflected in *structures of accumulation* (the way in which class forces or socio-economic factors facilitate or inhibit capitalist growth) and *types of industrialization* (that is the political-economic development strategies implemented by the state as they relate to the industrialization process).

This brief sketch of global dynamics and its elements neglects, of course, a number of problematic issues and makes a number of assumptions which we do not have space to discuss here. Rather than going in to these we shall try to outline the main elements in our model (presented graphically below) which are needed to understand the central issue, that is, how the internationalization of capital and the peripheral state – in symbiosis or in conflict – shape both the predominant type of industrialization and the capital–wage labour relation.

In the figure below the part of the centre accumulation process to which we devote our interest is that which causes the internationalization of productive capital. It is this internationalization, rather than that of other forms of capital, that has historically most affected the pattern of industrialization at the periphery. In quantitative as well as qualitative terms[2] it is still the most important.

The internationalization of productive capital takes various forms, of which foreign direct investment in the form of relocation or the establishment of complex, total plants – in contrast to the relocation also via direct investment of fragmented, parts production processes – must be singled out. Others requiring special mention are capital-intensive and technologically sophisticated production processes (often associated with the establishment of complex plants) – as opposed to more simple and relatively labour-intensive processes (often associated with the relocation of parts production processes).

It is assumed that the internationalization of productive capital, whatever form it takes, is directed towards specific types of industrialization[3]. This means that a working hypothesis could be formulated as follows: the establishment of complex production plants – most often via direct foreign investment but also via the import of capital goods from the centre – is most likely to be associated with an import-substituting type of industrialization.

The policy of import substitution, with its home market protection, often forces foreign companies to invest either to keep a market formerly held through trade or to exploit a growing internal demand. The plants established through investment are, however, most often of the complex

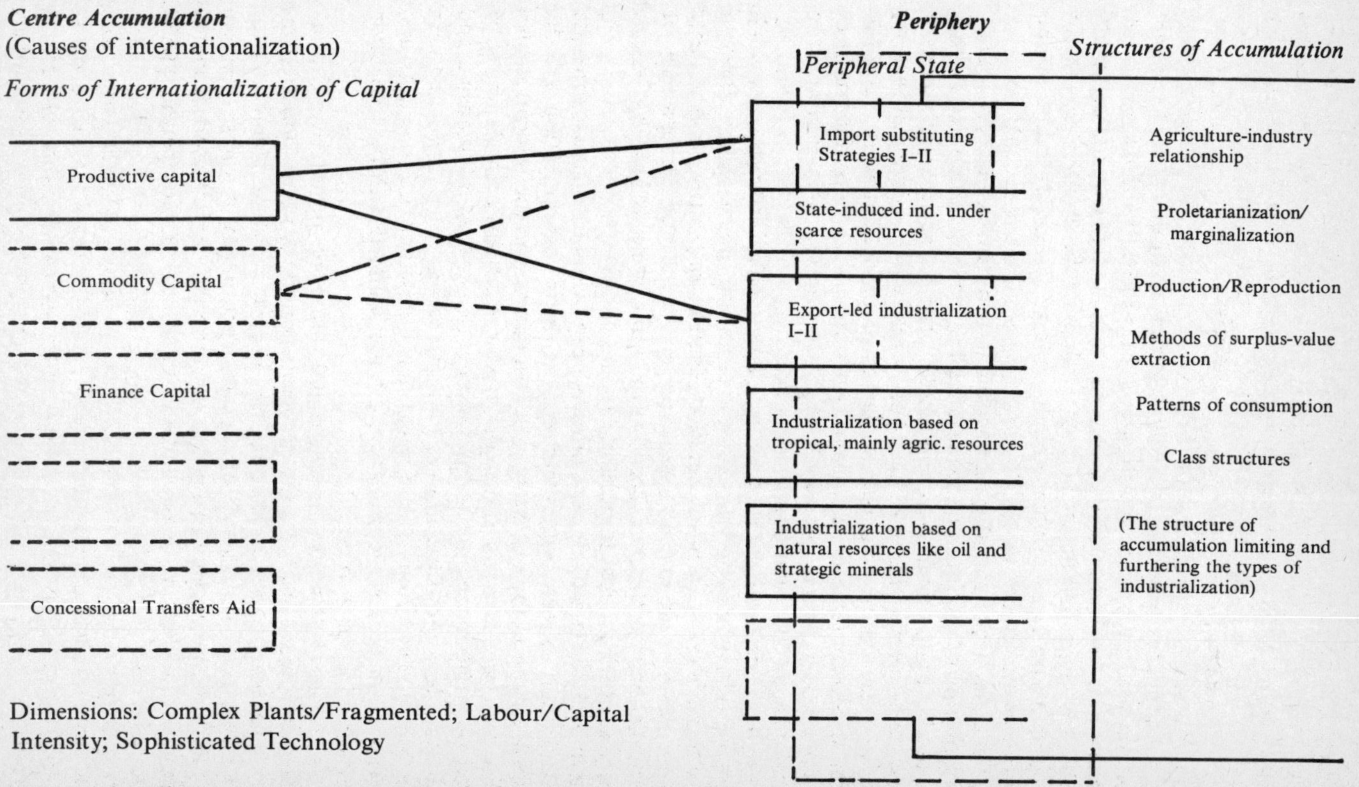

Figure 1 Dominant types of industrialization

and capital-intensive type, a factor confirmed by most of the present research in the field. This research has also demonstrated that only marginal technological adaptations, if any at all, are made by foreign companies when they invest in third world countries pursuing an import-substituting strategy.[5]

In contrast to this, it is assumed that the relocation of parts processes takes place in countries following an export-led industrialization strategy, where specific investment incentives (tax holidays, duty free import of raw materials, state subsidies and so on) and costs of local production factors favour and legitimize precisely this strategy of industrialization. Once more, the actual form in which fragmented parts processes are relocated may vary with respect to such factors as capital intensity, technological sophistication and in accordance with the actual phase of the specific explort-led industrialization strategy; although the investments generally are more labour- than capital-intensive and to a greater extent are technologically adapted to the local conditions and factors of production.[6]

In the figure we have sketched out only two major, characteristic phases within the import-substituting and export-led industrialization strategy respectively. Of course, no country pursues only one industrialization strategy; we are here defining the *dominant* type of industrialization.

It is not possible in a short space to cover all the complexities implicit in our model. We will simply discuss the relationship between the forms of internationalization and four major types of industrialization in order to explain how this affects the capital–wage relationship. These latter are, first, the rather simple, and secondly, the more complex and inter-related import substitution strategy; thirdly, the simple export-led strategy of industrialization based on the relocation from the centre of fragmented and relatively simple, labour-intensive production processes and, fourthly, the export-led strategy based on technology-intensive and rather sophisticated production processes where the end product is no different from what is produced in western countries or Japan.

'New' Perspectives on Division of Labour Studies

The discussion on changes within the international division of labour has shifted its focus in recent years from an almost exclusive concern with capital to a more recent emphasis on labour. On the one hand, the international division of labour has been analysed from the point of view of the internationalization of capital, but focusing on the labour market consequences of the penetration of foreign capital. Within this perspective employment, salary structures, qualification structures and working conditions are among the topics studied, somehow reducing labour to a subsumed and passive role. On the other hand, many studies have analysed labour in its socio–economic context and emphasis has been put on the developing working-class and labour market seen from a historical and structural perspective. Here labour has been regarded as the actively acting subject. A more holistic approach would combine the best of both these two worlds.

In the neo-classical paradigm the term labour market refers simply to the determination of wages and employment by the forces of supply and demand. In contrast, we view it as a somewhat broader concept comprising not only the capital-labour relation but also the economic, political and institutional bargaining mechanism behind it.

Capital accumulation requires a certain amount of capital and a sufficient, cheap, adequately disciplined work force. Labour as a commodity has, like all other commodities, an exchange value equivalent to the quantity of abstract labour needed for the reproduction of the workforce. It is, perhaps, a platitude to stress that labour is distinguishable from other commodities in two respects. First, labour has the peculiar quality (use value) of being able to create value. Secondly, labour is a conscious and acting production factor. Hence, labour has the possibility of adapting to, limiting or directly opposing and resisting capital subsumption.

The study of the industrial labour market is, then, the study of the relative strengths in the capital–labour relation. It is our basic assumption that the type of industrialization and the structuring of the industrial labour market are closely inter-related. More precisely, it is our thesis that the specific type of industrialization affects the capital labour relation in a specific way, leaving its mark on certain basic structures. Conversely, a specific type of industrialization presupposes a specific structuring of the capital–labour relation in order to function in an optimal sense. In each of the four types of industrialization, we would argue, the capital–labour relation is affected by certain basic structural features (leaving, of course, room for historically concrete variability).

It is, however, our view that the study of the industrial labour market in the third world cannot be separated from movements in the international division of labour and the internationalization of capital (or more particularly the internationalization of productive capital). Our second thesis is that the internationalization of productive capital affects the capital–labour relation qualitatively differently according to whether it takes the form of complex, integrated production plans or segmented production processes.

Our third major thesis is that the internationalization of productive capital, regardless of its specific form (whether complex or fragmented plants), affects the local industrial labour market disproportionately in relation to the amount of capital involved.

Delimitation

Bourgeois labour market theory has been under fire for many years, not least from Marxist sociology, wherein it is possible to distinguish two major orientations: on the one hand the so-called new international labour studies, and on the other studies focussing upon how employers' control of labour is exercised via either the labour process or the labour market itself.

The New International Labour Studies

These studies fundamentally characterize the worker as the central social agent. 'Workers as general social agents' rather than 'workers as employees' seems to be the focal analytical point of departure.[7] Two basic messages are offered by the new international labour studies: it is a myth that only a few workers exist in the third world and it is a myth that workers in the third world are passive and adapt easily without resisting the suppression and exploitation to which they are exposed.

Much conventional research tends to underestimate the importance and magnitude of the working class in the third world. It concentrates largely on the permanently employed labour force in middle sized and large industrial firms or in mines and plantations. But this group of workers forms only one element of the labouring poor in the third world (even if a rapidly increasing group). The primary focus on this one form of labour excludes from the analysis that often decisive fraction of the labouring poor which is directly or indirectly subsumed by capitalist production for shorter or longer periods. In the rural areas this includes the seasonal, often migrant workers and semi-proletarianized peasants and in the the urban areas contract workers, temporarily employed, casuals and unregistered labourers (e.g. children) together with persons indirectly or directly associated with industrial production through sub-contracting arrangements and so on.

The exclusion from analysis of these important and large groups of labourers introduce a serious bias in the studies, especially since capitalist development in the periphery 'rather than destroying petty production . . . simply increases the levels and the incorporation of petty- and small-capitalist enterprises'.[8] Furthermore, according to Cohen *et al.*[9] we ought to investigate 'the whole spectrum of underclasses drawn into relations of capitalist production, distribution, and exchange'. The focal interest is not 'the working class' but rather 'the working classes'. A number of hitherto invisible groups then appear: the urban poor, the women and peasants indirectly or directly involved in production and/or reproduction. In other words, the central issue for international labour studies ought to be the whole spectrum of labourers and others, not only the working class as such but also the marginalized masses in the cities and the women employed in the households and/or in simple commodity production, all of whom contribute to the reproduction albeit at a low level, of the workers employed in mainstream capitalist production.

With this broad approach to the study of the working class in the periphery, the emphasis has shifted away from the proletariat *per se* to the more inclusive process of proletarianization, with this in turn related to a movement in analysis from the study of unions to the study of labourers as general social agents.

> While we concur that the trade union cannot be ignored as a significant unit of analysis, the focus has shifted from union to worker, from organized labour to the working classes and its allied and related elements in the population – the peasantry, rural workers and the urban poor.[10]

The broader analytical approach at the theoretical level is then supplemented by a broad political strategy, formulated by Peter Waterman.

> The essential implication is the necessity for political alliance of the organized working class with the movements of women and of the massive and permanent petty-commodity producers/circulators, this evidently requiring action in both the domestic and community sphere. The problem is not the worker–peasant alliance but the worker–peasant–woman–'urban poor' alliance.[11]

This naturally leads to the other important issue for the new international labour studies: evaluation of the resistance potential of the labouring poor in the third world.

It must first be stressed that not all revolutions in the third world have been peasant revolts wherein the working class has played only a marginal role.

> On the contrary . . . we see the dominant form of successful political struggle as a constellation of class forces, as alliance and combination of peasants and workers (rural and urban) often cemented together by revolutionary intellectuals and appropriate revolutionary ideology and organization.[12]

Secondly, the new labour studies have emphasized the need to go beyond the assessment of workers' resistance by such manifest factors as the number, extent and duration of strikes, the number of lost working days, the labour rotation ratio, the degree of unionization, participation in social movements and demonstrations; for although important, such measures tend to overlook hidden and latent forms of resistance, thereby contributing to the myth about the passive and apolitical third world working class. Among the hidden forms of resistance, for example, Cohen[13] mentions enforced proletarianization: desertion, community withdrawal or revolt. He also stresses hidden resistance through task-, efficiency- and time-bargaining, sabotage and creation of a work culture. Finally, accidents and sickness, drug use and theft are mentioned as resistance forms connected to psychological adjustment. If such issues are addressed, workers' resistance naturally assumes more rounded and more extensive dimensions than conventional assessments of working-class revolt and protest would indicate.

In sum, by focusing on the workers as general social agents, the new international labour perspective has made a fundamental contribution to the understanding of the extreme differentiation among the dominated classes in the third world, and their different expressions of resistance and to the study of processes of proletarianization, class formation and the development of class consciousness.

Nonetheless, in our opinion such studies have as yet contributed only marginally to our overall understanding, and as far as our approach is concerned, the utility of the new international labour studies lies more in defining the conditions for and effects of the reproduction of the labour force than in delineating the conditions for industrial labour market creation in third world countries pursuing different strategies of industrialization. It is therefore important to stress that the immediate applicability of the new international labour studies, as related to our approach, lies in defining the conditions for and effects of the reproduction of the labour force.

Studies of Capital's Control of the Labour Process

The departure point for a focus on capital's control of the labour process is the criticism raised against neo-classical labour market studies for seeing the cost of labour as determined by supply and demand. In contrast, the new approach sees labour not as an ordinary commodity, but rather looks at production itself – or more precisely, the contradictions and the struggle between capital and labour in production.

Two major trends can be distinguished. On the one hand there is a focus on the possibilities for employers' control over the labour force through the organization of the labour process and technology, with class struggle, as waged and mediated by unions, often being a major concern. This is central to the work of, for instance, Coriat,[14] which studies workers and unions within the context of Taylorism, Fordism and neo-Fordism.[15] It is also the perspective contained in the works of Braverman.[16] On the other hand the radical segmentation theorists like Edwards, Gordon and Reich[17] are primarily looking at the employment situation. According to their theories, the segmentation developed in centre economies, when adapted to third world conditions, gives employers the opportunity of introducing strategies to control and fragment labour. Examples are:

—selecting a particularly adaptive workforce, like the young female workers recruited for the Free Enterprise Zones in South-East Asia;

—excluding unionized workers, or suppressing attempts at unionization by allowing only selected groups to unionize, thereby splitting the work force;

—using job rotation as a systematic means of preventing a large group of permanently employed workers organizing, or as a measure to prevent the employed workforce from gaining wage increases.

The studies of the production process and the place of work are valuable for understanding how the labour market is affected by struggles in production; they make an essential contribution to understanding the many forms and direction which workers' struggle can take. Their limitation would seem to be that the production process and the class struggle are studied, if not in isolation, then at least before the factors explaining the process which frames the condition and constraints for the struggle. Hence, these studies are not necessarily false or inaccurate descriptions but risk being partial because the struggle is not located in the context of the predominant structure of accumulation and type of industrialization.

A Holistic Approach

Once again, we would stress that our subject here is the industrial workforce, its permanence of changeability and its main determining factors. It is our further intention to look onto the conditions under which it is subsumed in the sphere between capital and state, but we will deal with the labour market only in so far as our interest extends to the recruitment and reproduction of labour.

The holistic approach is often abandoned at an early stage, in favour of detailed case studies which are easier to understand. Behind this predominance of country studies lies the consideration that apparently similar tendencies in industrial development can have different consequences for labour precisely because of the diverse and not easily comparable conditions present in different social formations. Hence, even if ambition may overleap itself, the *attempt* at a holistic approach is justified not least by the difficulties in summarizing and generalizing the multiplicity of historical specific country studies.

Historically concrete country studies are indeed a valuable, even perhaps, the only relevant approach when it comes to the study particularly of political, (but also labour market) developments in a given geographical space. But failure to develop a holistic approach leads to a number of shortcomings, two of which may be mentioned here. Extra-societal factors such as the internationalization of capital, and these factors' influence and importance, are often taken for granted, and not specified or analysed in any great detail. And the historically concrete case study has to form the basis for certain generalizations, which, due to the inherent limitations of restricted empirical material, often take the form of the unsupported extrapolation of trends drawn from one particular case study.

The Three Main Factors Outlined

The Internationalization of Capital and the Industrial Labour Market

The internationalization of capital does not affect the structures of the industrial labour market in the third world in a simple way. There is a difference between, on the one hand, the internationalization of integrated production processes and, on the other, the internationalization of segments of production, that is an international segmentation of the production process. However, it is argued here that the internationalization of complex production plants is by far the most important form of internationalization in the third world.

Integrated production plants: Extensive research demonstrates that there is minimal adaptation of technology when integrated (complex) production processes are transplanted to the third world.[18] Any adaptation which does take place is within marginal areas only, as for example when the transport of material from one production line to another in centre countries is automatized, while being done manually in the periphery. In either case the technology is essentially the same. This kind of internationalization will therefore not create more employment than it does in centre countries, even though integrated production plants may be more or less capital-intensive.

Because technology is not adapted, the rationale of production will rather be to adapt labour to technology. Consequently, the control of labour is a means to secure its optimal adaptation, to make the production process continuous and smooth and to maximise the utilization of the transferred machinery and equipment. The way in which labour is adapted will be specific, and may very well imply relatively high wages for some workers.

> With any given technology, in fact, there is not a single 'best way' to organize the division of labour and form and control labour. Indeed, management has to confront a series of contradictory aims when creating and controlling labour. The need to minimize wage costs contradicts the need for the best quality labour. Stability of labour may undermine control. Managerial and engineering control of work may stifle labour force initiative.
>
> In this situation, the variety of employment practices is likely to be enormous, particularly in countries where unions are not strong enough to equalize working conditions between firms and sectors. The pattern found in any one firm or industry will depend partly on technology, but also on labour supply, labour legislation, educational levels, family structures, union power and gender.[19]

In this connection it is important to stress that the lack of adaptation means that the technology struggle does not take place in the periphery. Rather, transferred technology reflects the technology struggle that has taken place in the centre, where the labour and trade union struggle has had its impact in shaping the technology which is subsequently exported.

Global segmentation of the production process: The internationalization of segments of production as part of the global division of production process does, on the other hand, require certain adaptations of technology. This is because the relocation from the centre to the periphery of parts of the production processes has been furthered not least by the abundant and cheap labour available in, for example, South-East Asian countries pursuing an export-led strategy of industrialization. It is likely that labour-intensive technology and machinery possibly old and superfluous in the centre context, will be transferred to countries pursuing this strategy.[20] In sum, the technology will to some extent be adapted to the prevailing labour force and its composition, which may be more or less qualified. In these cases the control of labour will be directed towards maximum exploitation, the effect of which will be rapid exhaustion and replacement of the employed labour force. In other words, attempts will be made to secure a surplus-value extraction in both absolute form i.e. an intensification of the labour process and via extended working hours. Low wages (or rather low unit labour costs) will of course be central, motivating factors for the relocation of labour-intensive parts of production.

It is proposed, therefore, that the way in which the two different forms of capital internationalization affect the local industrial labour market structures differ fundamentally. Yet, in conclusion, what we want to stress is that these two forms of internationalization still have a central feature in common: the internationalization of capital, regardless of its specific form, whether via complex or fragmented plants, makes a disproportionate impact upon the local labour market structure. The influence of foreign capital on the structures of the labour market goes further than might be expected from the mere quantitative importance of this capital in a given social formation.

This is particularly obvious in the countries where the industrialization strategy is export-oriented and where the labour market conditions *per se* are important for attracting international capital (that is, where any particular country is competing with others in order to offer the most attractive labour market conditions to international capital). Apart from offering low unit labour costs this competition also often means a shift in state policy, for example with regard to the implementation of the ILO's international labour standards.[21]

In countries pursuing an industrialization strategy which is predominantly home market orientated (via import substitution), it is more difficult to point to the impact which foreign capital will have. None the less, we argue that international capital will have a disproportionate influence on the formation of the labour market in the sense that it shapes the technological conditions of production in decisive and important branches, thus influencing the capital–labour relation which obtains in locally owned enterprises. This becomes evident particularly when this influence is mediated by the interventions of the state.

The Role of the State

The development of capitalism in the periphery – which is often more advanced than is normally thought, and definitely more advanced than dependency theorists would have us to believe – is implanted from the outside; it has generally not occurred from the inside because of internal contradictions. A peripheral state cannot be directly compared with a capitalist state in the centre where capitalism has penetrated all sectors of the economy. The penetration from the outside and the only partial subsumption to capital of the periphery mean that the capitalist class structure is weak, with a merely embryonic national bourgeoisie. In other words, the predominantly external reproduction of capitalism in peripheral social formations and the underdeveloped nature of the bourgeoisie (in contrast to countries in the centre wherein that class played the leading role in developing capitalism) imposes particular demands on the peripheral state, even when the latter cannot be viewed as the mechanical instrument of the local capitalist class. The class nature of the state, therefore, is rather complex, with diverse fractions of classes and other elements (for example the bureaucracy) often enjoying some access to state power. This obviously brings into question any crude assumption that because many peripheral formations are externally dominated, the peripheral state necessarily lacks any autonomy and hence ability to intervene or regulate national economic development.

A peripheral state must generally undertake functions similar to those performed by a centre state. This includes providing the necessary, general preconditions for capitalist production (physical and social infrastructure), although the extent of such provision will differ widely. The national bourgeoisie in the periphery being weak, the peripheral state must in many ways replace the bourgeoisie. This means that the state will take a more directly productive role than in the centre state and will often have to invest directly in the productive sector.

Mathias and Salama[22] stress that the state in developed centre formations intervenes much more in the field of the reproduction of labour and less in the productive sector, with the opposite generally being the case for the state in peripheral formations. Hence the active role of the state in various productive operations in the periphery is of crucial importance.

We are, however, rather more doubtful than Mathias and Salama as to whether the state is less interventionist in the reproduction of labour in the periphery. In certain Latin American countries, for example, the import-substitution strategy has – in the words of Lipietz[23] – ‘brought together an autonomous local capital, relatively abundant urban middle classes, and experienced nuclei of a working class’ during the seventies. A process of coupling intensive accumulation and expanding consumption patterns, which in the literature is often labelled peripheral Fordism,[24] has been initiated. The integrated production plants established through foreign investment demand state intervention in order to ensure that labour adapts to the complex technology involved. The control and disciplining of the workforce are vital not only for the internal process of accumulation but also to maintain investment by international capital and hence for the continuation of this type of industrialization. In those countries which have reached a more advanced stage of import substitution, broader consumption patterns have developed and certain room has been allowed (fostered, of course, by class struggle) for unionization and political activity at plant and regional levels. This 'relative' political freedom has, however, its limits; these are easily reached during the time of crises, when once again state intervention in the labour market is required, usually in dictatorial form.

Export-led industrialization similarly demands state control over the capital-labour relation, not only to provide a legal–political framework but also in a much more direct sense. In the global segmentation of the production process, decisions of relocation are highly dependent on labour market considerations, such as the level of labour's renumeration, employment conditions, and the qualifications of the workforce. Although it is management which exercises direct control over labour, the state in, for example, the Free Enterprise Zones often directly intervenes in order to control and suppress strikes, putting restrictions on unionization and even providing guards and security forces to ensure a smoothly run production process not disrupted by any political activity. Because of the intense competition for investments, export-led industrialization broadly speaking seems to require a firmly controlling, indeed politically repressive state (as in South Korea, Malaysia and the Philippines under Marcos). Hence it is that the control of unions, minimum wage regulations, prohibitions of strikes by law and other more direct measures related to unions and union activities are typical state activities intimately associated with this type of industrialization.

To conclude, it can be argued that the interventions of the peripheral state in the economic and political sphere (and consequently in the regulation of the labour market, which is of primary concern in the present context) are of utmost importance and have to be seen as a result of the relations between types of industrialization and the form of internationalization of capital, whether this relation is one of symbiosis or otherwise.

Types of Industrialization

As previously mentioned, our model rests on the relations between, on the one hand, the internationalization of capital, the interventions of the peripheral state and types of industrialization, and on the other, the basic structures of the industrial labour market. We now turn to the relation between the type of industrialization and the labour market.

By type of industrialization we mean a specific strategy of industrialization formulated and mediated by the state; we are talking about economic policies which are actually being implemented. The four types of industrialization have been selected according to two criteria: the first is whether production is intended for the home market (import-substitution) or for export (export-led). The second is the complexity of the technology utilized in production.

The last criterion is essential because the demand for labour is dependent on the form of production technology. The first, however, needs some specification. What is decisive is not the actual market or the sphere of circulation, but rather whether production for the home market or for export imposes very different demands on the capital–labour relation according to different competitive conditions. Hence a strategy of industrialization oriented towards the home market (import substitution) – substituting for actual or potential imports of industrial commodities – is basically characterized by state protection against competing imports. This is implemented through high customs and tariffs and a comprehensive use of import restrictions in the form of import licences and import quotas. However, this protection against competing imports does not mean that foreign competition as such is absent. As mentioned above, international capital, by its norm setting position in internal (oligopolistic) competition, is largely responsible for sharing the set of production and the technical conditions of production in the locally owned enterprises in the dynamic industries.[25]

The strategy of export-led industrialization, on the other hand, is directly dependent on world market competition, partly because the commodities produced must compete with corresponding commodities from other places, but also because exporting countries have to compete among themselves in order to attract vital foreign capital.

Apart from the different types of industrialization it is also of crucial importance for an historical concrete analysis to take into account the structure of accumulation in which the dominant type of industrialization is located. This is important as the structure of accumulation conditions and limits the actual development prospects inherent in the type of industrialization: the totality of production and reproduction of economy and classes in society. Hence, for us, an understanding of the conditions for successful capitalist development – or the lack of it – ought to take into consideration the following four elements in the structure of accumulation.

a) *The relation between agriculture and industry:* It is decisive whether a virtuous or vicious circle can be created between these sectors in society. By a virtuous circle we mean increased productivity in agriculture which both lowers the cost of food (thereby contributing to the lowering of reproduction costs for the working class) and avoids squeezing direct producers to the extent where the creation of a broader market for industrial goods is forfeited. A vicious circle, which is typical of many third world countries, is the neglect of food production in agriculture (often in favour of cash crops) and consequent deprivation.

b) *The relation between production and consumption.* Among the factors to be investigated are the extent to which commodity production has replaced subsistence production, and whether consumption patterns based on 'Fordism' are developing and, if so, which classes and strata are benefiting.[26]

c) *The reproduction of labour:* This is the next important element, where the extent to which the industrial labour force is reproduced partly outside the capitalist sector is vital. Other aspects are the relation of the industrial proletariat to other social classes, the existing qualification structures, the stability/instability of the industrial labour force, its composition and the size and nature of the reserve army.

d) *The role of the state:* It is important to investigate the extent to which the development of capitalism in a given social formation has taken place parallel to the development of a national capitalist class or whether the state has acted as an entrepreneur in the absence of such class. In other words, what is of interest is the class determination of the state and its potential for pursuing a long-term capitalist development strategy.

Noting that any historical concrete analysis of the relation between industrialization and the labour market must take into account these four elements of the structure of production we may now proceed to an examination of the four types of industrialization.

The simple type of import substitution: This is characterized by the production of non-durable consumer goods and light semi-manufactured goods intended for the local market. Production is protected from world market competition in different ways and is usually financed by the extraction of surplus from the agricultural sector together with external financing. However, the strategy contains two fundamental constraints, one external, the other internal. First, just as import requirements are determined by the dynamism of the industrial sector itself, so import capacity is determined by the export earnings stemming from the agricultural and raw materials sector. Hence, if the volume of exports and/or the terms of trade deteriorate, this type of industrialization will soon fall victim to external constraints. Secondly, the limited internal demand introduces another constraint, resulting in stagnation after a shorter or longer period.

The advanced type of industrialization based on the home market: This may be regarded as an attempt at solving the contradictions of simple import substitution. In this model the production of durable consumer goods and production in ancillary industries are destined to become dynamic elements in a process of continued accumulation which gradually broadens to include the capital goods sector and semi-manufactured basic goods.

However, technological knowhow is typically imported, often from transnational corporations. Meanwhile, an increased, although still restricted, demand is created, often via a policy of income concentration through inflation and the creation of a layer of functionaries and skilled workers with effective purchasing power and systems of consumer credits.

Simple export-oriented industrialization: This is the most likely strategy in countries with limited internal demand and limited natural resources. A continuous process of industrialization must necessarily take the form of export of manufactured industrial goods. The external constraint contained in simple import substitution, dependence upon fluctuating export earnings from agricultural commodities, is then partly solved, just as the problem of limited internal demand is eliminated (given that production will be geared towards external demand). Production may cover the same range of products as in simple import substitution, together with labour-intensive products relocated as part of the global segmentation of production processes.

Advanced export-oriented industrialization: This means the restructuring of production to new product areas with high local value added and technology- and knowhow-intensive (such as machine tools, industrial electronics and computers). The traditional labour-intensive export-directed industries (such as garments and textiles) are reduced and transformed through rationalization and automation.

Simple export-led industrialization is founded on certain preconditions, particularly an expansive world market for non-durable consumer goods and cheap labour power. However, towards the end of the 1970s these preconditions were eroded as a result of both falling international demand and protectionist measures. At the same time 'The Four Little Tigers' in the Far East – South Korea, Taiwan, Singapore and Hong Kong – were met by fierce competition from 'late-comers' such as Malaysia and the Philippines, while a gradually developing lack of manpower resulted in increase real wages among wage earners at home. Struck by import quotas and increased competition from automated plants in the western industrial world, the restructuring of production towards more technology-intensive products became a necessity.[27]

Types of Industrialization and the Capital–Labour Relation

Different types of industrialization affect the capital–labour relationship differently. The table below illustrates the elements in the relationship which have to be included in the analysis.[28]

Table 2.1 Capital–labour relations – a scheme of analysis

A. *Relations of production* (workplace conditions)	B. *Exchange relations*
1. Actual performance	1. Level of compensation – purchase of labour
a. Productivity – unit labour costs	a. Wages
b. Working hours and working intensity	b. Fringe benefits
c. Quality of work	c. Living conditions
	d. Indirect wages (incl. social expenditures)
2. Managerial control	2. Selection of the labour force – performance capacity
a. Control mechanisms —segmentation —labour turnover etc.	a. Skills
	b. Extra-production capabilities —industrial discipline —adaptability —patience etc.

The capital–labour relation includes, then, two fundamental dimensions – the production relation and the exchange relation. Among relations of production or workplace conditions we distinguish between the actual performance of labour in the production process and aspects related to the control of labour. Exchange relations or the labour market represent a link between the relations or production and the reproduction of labour and differentiate between the manner in which labour is purchased and the way in which it is selected. The relative strength of capital and labour may be assumed by examining these various dimensions together. But this is also affected by the institutional form for conflict resolution and labour control already in existence, such as the forms of union formation and struggle, mechanisms for the regulation of labour market issues, any labour code and ways and means for state intervention and institution building. For instance, the labour legislation system created by the populist Vargas regime in Brazil during the thirties was still influencing the balance of forces between labour and capital during the post-war period.)[29]

Simple Import Substitution Industrialization

This produces a high degree of variability in the character of the capital–labour relation because it has a weak effect on it. However, it should be stressed that simple import substitution as a result of an internationalization of integrated production processes has the characteristic mentioned earlier.

Advanced Import Substitution

At the level of production it is the norm for low unit labour costs to be primarily secured by high productivity resulting from mechanization/

automation, i.e. a high capital intensity. Thus relative surplus-value production is considered dominant, with capital's control over labour requiring a continuous and smooth running of the production process. However, it is not possible to specify the actual mechanisms introduced to adapt labour to the production line, for these rather reflect the actual stage of class struggle and its historical origin.[30] Meanwhile, in the sphere of exchange relations it is stressed that labour compensation does not necessarily imply maximal cutting of wages, for among the preconditions for this type of industrialization is the requirement that elements of the labour force are also able to demand durable consumer goods. At the level of production, moreover, relatively high wages also serve as means of adapting labour to the prevailing work system. As demonstrated by John Humphrey, a combination of relatively high wages and labour instability (high labour turnover) has been utilized in the Brazilian car industry in order to get acceptance of discipline and high work intensity. Moreover, labour control is secured by means of artificial internal labour market strategies resulting in a layer of so-called *qualificados*, i.e. a splitting of the labour force.[31]

When selecting labour it is in the interest of capital to secure an industrially trained work force which easily adapts to new functions. For the state, however, it is not only a matter of securing capital's control over production, but also enabling it to regulate wage income for parts of the working class and hence allowing the type of industrialization to continue without facing a restricted demand.

Simple Export-oriented Industrialization

At the level of production it is of crucial importance to secure very low unit labour costs in order to compete with third world exporting nations. Production is kept at a relatively labour-intensive level, and high productivity is provided not through the development of the productive forces, but by the method of double absolute surplus value extraction (that is via intensification of work and the extension of working hours). Control over labour in the production process is aimed at securing this end. The mechanisms of control may vary but high job rotation seems to be a preferred means, reflecting monotonous and depressed working conditions. The high labour turnover involves only segments of the labour force and thereby creates an internal segmentation of workers as another means of control.[32] Meanwhile, in the sphere of circulation, direct labour costs are depressed as far as possible and indirect wages are practically absent. In these cases, the reproduction of labour is taken care of by the extended family.

The selection of labour aims at getting a workforce which can rapidly be trained to undertake relatively simple jobs. The monotonous, repetitious and uniform labour process seems to imply that a young, female labour force in particular is demanded. In Taiwan, for example, women constituted 53% of manufacturing workers in 1980.[33] Meanwhile, the state policy is aimed at securing the total freedom of capital, which among other things may entail an abandoning of work rules and regulations introduced under simple import-substitution industrialization.

Advanced Export-oriented Industrialization
Increased productivity is secured through the development of productive forces by the introduction of automatized and other more capital-intensive production processes in very much the same fashion as in the western countries and Japan. This goes for countries such as South Korea, Taiwan and Singapore – and, if the "Look East" policy of Malaysia is believed to be of any substance, perhaps also for this country in the longer perspective.

Although still tightly controlled by the state – as external vulnerability is still a major problem – a scarcity of manpower and increase in demand for skills may allow for labour to increase its political muscle. Subsequent increases in real wages and more widespread internal consumption may then allow for a general labour market situation not basically different from the one which prevailed in Western countries at an early stage of their industrialization.

Concluding Comment

It has to be stressed that our framework for analysis is intended primarily to facilitate study of only one major aspect of the capital–labour relation, that is, strategies adopted by capital (and the state) towards the subordination of labour. This, it must be emphasized, cannot operate to the exclusion of the analysis of labour resistance to which it forms the complement. Likewise, we stress that the survival or collapse of a given type of industrialization is essentially dependent on labour strategies. The dissolution or breakdown of a dominant type of industrialization might very well result from a crisis of labour, i.e. the incapacity of capital (and state) strategies to control labour and the general strength of labour resistance.

Notes

1. To avoid misunderstanding: neither the internationalization of capital nor the activities of the peripheral state can be fully understood without due consideration of the class forces behind them.

2. The internationalization of productive capital may take the form of direct foreign investment or the export of capital goods (machinery and equipment). Both affect the type of industrialization and the capital – labour relation in much the same way.

3. It has to be stressed that the forms of internationalization of capital mentioned in the figure are not exclusive catagories but rather predominant ones. The internationalization of productive capital in the predominant form of direct

foreign investment will often be supplemented by other forms of internationalization such as commodity capital and finance capital.

4. The plants established—either through investment or export—vary a great deal in technological complexity, and in accordance with the actual historic phase of the specific import-substituting strategy in question. The export of complex plants from centre to periphery is often achieved via a transition stage of assembly (parts production) operations.

5. Ample evidence of this is presented in, for example, Lawrence Marsh, Richard Newfarmer and Lino Moreira, *Employment and technological choice of MNCs in developing countries: A literature review and a case study.* Working Papar no. 23 (ILO, Geneva, 1983); A.S. Bhalla (ed.), *Technology and Employment in Industry* (ILO, Geneva 1975) and Susumu Watanbe, 'Multinational enterprises, employment and technology adaptation', *International Labour Review*, vol. 120, no. 6, 1981.

6. The generally labour–intensive parts production processes, technologically adapted to the local costs of factors of production and exploiting investment incentives are most often relocated to countries in South-East Asia, and in particular, perhaps, to the so called free enterprise zones.

7. For a presentation of what is part of the new international labour studies, see Robin Cohen, *The 'New' International Labour Studies: A Definition*, Working Paper Series No. 27, Centre for Developing Area Studies, McGill University, Montreal, 1980.

8. Peter Waterman, 'Understanding Relations amongst Labouring People in Peripheral Capitalist Societies', *LABOUR, Capital and Society*, Vol. 14, no. 1, 1981, p. 91.

9. Cohen, Gutkind, Brazier (eds.), *Peasants and Proletarians: The Struggles of Third World Workers* (London, 1979), p. 12.

10. Cohen, *The New International Labour Studies,* p. 7).

11. Waterman, 'Understanding Relations amongst Labouring People', p. 10.

12. Cohen, Gutkind and Brazier, *Peasants and Proletarians*, p. 13.

13. R. Cohen, 'Resistance and Hidden Forms of Consciousness Amongst African Workers', *Review of African Political Economy*, no. 19, 1980.

14. See Bejamin Coriat, *Science, technique et capital* (Seuill, Paris, 1976) and *L'Atélier et le chronomètre* (Christian Bourgeois, Paris, 1979). See also his 'Ouvriers et Automates: Procès de Travail, Économie du Temps et Theorie de la Segmentation de la Force de Travail', in J.-P. Gaudemar (ed), *Usines et Ouvriers* (Maspero, Paris, 1980) and 'Transfer de Techniques, Division du Travail et Politique de Main d'Oeuvre: une Etude de Cas dans l'Industrie Brésilienne', *Critiques de l'Économie Politique*, vol. 14, 1981.

15. Definitions of Taylorism, Fordism and neo-Fordism are given in Michel Aglietta, *A Theory of Capitalist Regulation: The US Experience* (New Left Books, London, 1979), on pp. 114, 117 and 168 respectively. See also Christian Palloix; The labour process: from Fordism to neo-Fordism', Conference of Socialist Economists Pamphlet No. 1, (London Conference of Socialist Economists, 1976).

16. Harry Braverman, *Labor and Monopoly Capital: The Degradation of Work in the Twentieth Century* (Monthly Review Press, New York, 1974).

17. David Gordon, Richard Edwards and Michael Reich, *Labour Market Segmentation in American Capitalism* (Cambridge, Massachussetts, Harvard Graduate School of Education, 1973) and David M. Gordon, Richard

Edwards and Michael Reich, *Segmented Work, Divided Workers: The Historical Transformation of Labour in the United States* (Cambridge University Press, Cambridge 1982).

18. See the works mentioned in Note 5 and Benjamin Coriat's study on the transfer of technology of a French firm, which uses largely the same technology in France and in Brazil, but redefines jobs and work teams so as to adapt to the labour power available in Brazil (Benjamin Coriat, 'Transfer de Techniques'). Also Helena Hirata's study of French and Japanese multi-national companies operating in Brazil gives similar results (Helena Hirata, 'Internationalisation du capital, techniques de production et division sociale du travail: les firmes multinationales Françaises et Japonaises au Brésil', *Critiques de l'Économie Politique*, Vol. 14, 1981).

19. John Humphrey, *Theoretical Issues in the Study of Industrial Labour Markets in Latin America,* (June 1983) pp. 8–9. Originally published in Danish in *Den my Verden*, 2/3, 1983, pp. 18–27.

20. C. Cooper, R. Kaplinsky, R. Bell and W.Satyarakwit, 'Choice of Techniques for Can Making in Kenya, Tanzania and Thailand' and C. Cooper and R. Kaplinsky (with the collaboration of R. Turner), 'Second-hand Equipment in Developing Countries: Jute Processing Machinery in Kenya', both in A.S. Bhalla, *Technology and Employment in Industry*.

21. See Hans Günter, *ILO Research on Multinational Enterprises and Social Policy: An Overview,* ILO Working Paper No. 15 (1982) and *The Tripartite Declaration of Principles concerning Multinational Enterprises and Social Policy (History, Contents, Follow-up and Relationship with Relevant Instruments of Other Organisations*), ILO Working Paper no. 18 (1981); Gus Edgren, 'Spearheads of Industrialisation or Sweatshops in the Sun?', in Eddy Lee (ed.) *Export Processing Zones and Industrial Employment in Asia* (ILO/ARTEP, Bangkok, 1984) and Arne Wangel's contribution to this collection.

22. G. Mathias and P. Salama, *L'Etat surdéveloppé: Des Métropoles au tiers monde* (Maspero, Paris 1983).

23. Alain Lipietz, 'How Monetarism Choked Third World Industrialization', *New Left Review*, no. 145, 1984, p. 74. See also his 'Towards Global Fordism', *New Left Review*, no. 132, 1982.

24. Cf. Lipietz. 1982. See also Note 26.

25. In the case of Brazil, for example, it could actually be argued that this phenomenon has become progressively more important for local capital because transnational companies have diversified their investments over a wider spectrum of industrial sectors. See Helena Hirata, 'Internationalisation du capital'.

26. In the French 'regulation approach', the term 'Fordism' has been attributed to the accumulation system and the mode of regulation which combine strong productivity gains and rising wage earner purchasing power. 'Fordism' is thus the principle of an articulation between process of production and mode of consumption, which constitutes the basis for mass production. The characteristics of the mode of consumption of 'Fordism' can be found in Michel Aglietta *A Theory of Capitalist Regulation*, pp. 155–66.

27. The restructuring process going on in South Korea is probably the most outstanding example. Major South Korean conglomerates, such as Samsung, Hyundai and Daewoo, are investing huge sums in micro-computer manufacturing. In Taiwan, the machinery and information equipment industries have been selected to spearhead the industrial restructuring and in 1980 the government established an

advanced type of export-processing zone–Hsinchu Science Based Industrial Park–designed to attract foreign high technology firms. See *Far Eastern Economic Review*, 4 June 1982, 7 April 1983, 21 July 1983, 31 May 1984, 8 November 1984 and *South*, July 1984.

28. The figure is inspired by Michael Storper and Richard Walker, 'The Theory of Labour and the Theory of Location', *International Journal of Urban and Regional Research*, vol. 7, no. 1, 1983.

29. See Gilberto Mathias, 'Transfer de Techniques et Transfer de Théories: Du 'Dualisme' du Marché du Travail aux Nouvelles Formes de Résistance Ouvrière en Amérique Latine', *Critiques de l'économie politique*, no. 14, 1981.

30. Humphrey, *Theoretical Issues*, pp. 8–9.

31. John Humphrey, 'Labour Use and Labour Control in the Brazilian Automobile Industry, *Capital and Class*, no. 12, Winter 1980/81 and Michael Storper, 'Who Benefits from Industrial Decentralization? Social Power in the Labour Market, Income Distribution and Spatial Policy in Brazil', *Regional Studies*, vol. 18, no. 2, 1984.

32. Besides high labour turnover rate, companies often use changes in the wage package as a control mechanism. Instead of rising the base salary a set of non-base wage additions are introduced, such as performance bonuses which are easily forfeited in case of tardiness, sick leave, etc. See Linda Gail Arrigo, The Industrial Work Force of Young Women in Taiwan, *Journal of Concerned Asian Scholars*, Vol 12, no. 2, April-June, 1980, pp. 30–32.

33. Calculated from *Yearbook of Labour Statistics*, Republic of China (1982), DGBAS, Taipei, p. 82.

3 Third World Industrialization and Trade Union Struggles

James Petras and Dennis Engbarth

Third world industrialization has become an increasingly important theme in the development literature. The shift in emphasis from underdevelopment to industrialization has been dramatic. Only a short decade ago, many writers, especially those associated with the dependency school, looked upon the industrialization of the third world as an impossibility or at best a phenomenon only possible through a radical rupture in the global capitalist system. Today the intellectual trend is generally in the opposite direction. Rapid and dynamic industrialization of the third world is assumed to be part of the new economic realities. Within this perspective some writers have elaborated a theoretical framework arguing that a new international division of labour (NIDL) has evolved in which the third world, specializing in labour intensive industries, complements the high tech enterprises in the advanced capitalist countries.

While such analysts provided a corrective against the early and more dogmatic assertions of dependency theory, their version of third world industrialization suffers from some of the same flaws and misconceptions as their rivals': the same tendency to project limited country experiences on to a global pattern and to extrapolate from favourable conjunctures and formulate generalizations that cut across economic cycles. In order to understand the implications of third world industrialization for trade union struggles it is necessary to correct several misconceptions concerning the process.

The Realities of Third World Industrialization

More precisely, the immense diversity, dynamics, and limitations of the process of industrialization in the third world have generally been overlooked by NIDL theorists intent on tailoring the richness of this experience to fit their vision of global capital redeployment.[1] However, the dynamics of the development process – and its implications for trade union movements – can only be comprehended by close examination of the scope (i.e. the share of gross domestic product [GDP]) accounted for by the industrial, particularly manufacturing, sector), depth (degree of growth of

Table 3.1 Index numbers of industrial production (1975=100)

Branch of Activity	*Developed Market Economies*		*Developing Market Economies*	
	1970	*1980*	*1970*	*1980*
Manufacturing	90	122	69	134
Light manufacture	91	116	77	127
Heavy manufacture	90	125	65	140
Food & beverage	86	116	79	138
Textiles	96	109	80	111
Clothing	95	102	70	113
Wood products	92	102	70	113
Paper & publishing	97	126	66	132
Chemical, petroleum, & plastic products	85	128	68	134
Non-metallic mineral products	92	121	69	143
Basic metal industry	102	113	75	150
Metal products	88	142	55	141
Electrical machinery	85	142	52	134
Transport equipment	86	118	53	134
Mining	97	125	90	110

Source: *UN Yearbook of Industrial Statistics*, United Nations, New York, 1981, Volume 1.

capital goods or high technology sectors) and diversity of industrialization in third world countries and regions. We find intensifying differentiation between various types of third world development patterns (including some of the dynamic newly industrializing countries [NICs]) evolving from sharply divergent reactions to cyclical movements in the world economy and the problems arising from both the success and failure of individual developmental efforts.

The Scope of Third World Industrialization

The spread of industrialization throughout the third world is evidenced by the rapid increase in manufacturing production and employment. During the 1970s, third world growth rates rose over a wide range of manufactured products. Manufacturing production has climbed by 85.5% in developing economies (DEs) during the past decade compared with a rise of only 37.7% in the developed market economies (DMEs), (see Table 1). While industrial and manufacturing employment declined in the DMEs, the third world industrial workforce showed steady growth of 5% over the same period (see Table 2).

However, the scope of industrialization in most developing countries is still quite limited; most middle income economies (defined by the World Bank as having per capita GNP over $410 in 1982) have less than 25% of their productive activity in manufacturing (see Table 3). Despite impressive growth figures, third world economies have yet to overcome the critical

Table 3.2 Index numbers of industrial employment (1975=100)

Branch of Activity	*Developed Market Economies*		*Developing Market Economies*	
	1970	*1980*	*1970*	*1980*
Manufacturing	103	99	73	122
Light manufacture	104	96	74	123
Heavy manufacture	102	101	70	121
Food & beverage	101	100	74	125
Textiles	116	84	77	109
Clothing	103	94	63	146
Wood products	100	96	72	116
Paper & publishing	105	97	82	119
Chemical, petroleum, & plastic products	99	102	66	122
Non-metallic mineral products	103	97	76	124
Basic metal industry	105	92	57	118
Metal products	101	104	70	122
Electrical machinery	—	—	—	—
Transport equipment	—	—	—	—
Mining	109	103	88	102

Source: *UN Yearbook of Industrial Statistics,* United Nations, New York, 1981, Volume 1.

Table 3.3 Percentage of GDP in manufacturing

Type of Economy	*1960*	*1982*
Low income	13	14
Middle income	21	20
Oil-exporting	14	17
Oil-importing	22	23
Capital surplus oil-exporting	—	4
Industrial market	30	24

Source: World Bank, *World Development Report 1984,* Oxford University Press, New York, pp. 222–223.

Table 3.4 Index numbers of labour productivity in industry (1975=100)

Branch of Activity	*Developed Market Economies*		*Developing Market Economies*	
	1970	*1980*	*1970*	*1980*
Manufacturing	89	120	104	108
Light manufacture	89	116	108	105
Heavy manufacture	89	123	94	114
Food & beverage	85	112	105	105
Textiles	85	122	104	104
Clothing	92	109	100	96
Wood products	94	116	108	116
Paper & publishing	95	121	114	112
Chemical, petroleum, & plastic products	86	129	115	106
Non-metallic mineral products	91	123	90	104
Basic metals	96	127	126	120
Metal products	89	120	85	118
Mining	97	105	99	109

Source: *UN Statistical Yearbook*, United Nations, New York, 1981.

advantage enjoyed by DMEs in the high growth of labour productivity; until they do their capacity to compete in international markets will be limited (see Table 4). The small size of the developing countries' share of total world manufacturing exports – despite substantial growth from 6.3% in 1970 to 9.7% by 1980 – provides little support for theories based upon notions of an extensive *global* realignment of productive forces.[2] Although most third world countries have become increasingly integrated into the global economy, only a minority are rapidly improving their competitiveness *vis-a-vis* the advanced industrial countries; the majority still play a marginal role in the international division of industrial production.

Growth in manufacturing production and exports in the third world is highly concentrated. Seven economies (Taiwan, South Korea, Hong Kong, Singapore, Brazil, India and Mexico), with about 30% of the third world's population, accounted for 65% of third world manufacturing export value in 1980 (up from 55% in 1965). Although a few other countries have also recorded strong export performances in recent years, the limitation of rapid manufacturing growth to a relatively small and diverse assortment of countries suggests that the critical issue in successful third world industrialization may be the interaction of particular configurations of more or less internal factors – class structure, state composition and policy, domestic resource endowments – with transformations in the world economic and political environment.

For example, the continued predominance of agriculture among many low and lower middle income countries often reflects strong class linkages between primary producing classes and the state. The enduring power of traditional divisions of labour and a lack of strong public or private industrial entrepreneurial groups often inhibit domestic capital accumulation and the launching of sustained development efforts that can take advantage of shifts in the world political economy. The presence of powerful landowner–exporter classes and their influence on state development policies, particularly favouring the importing of finished manufactured goods and the promotion of primary exports, could weaken efforts at national industrial development and perpetuate traditional divisions of labour in the domestic economy. The inflow of overseas manufactures and the competitive disadvantage of local industry would encourage investors to place their capital in service, real estate, trading, consumer goods, overseas bank accounts or other speculative activity.

Not all constraints on industrialization are political or social. Limited resources, poor geographical locations, inadequate infrastructure or the lack of basic market or productive systems (e.g. subsistence agriculture) often impede domestic saving and private industrial investment, given better profit and interest earning opportunities elsewhere. Third world countries distant from the cutting edges of superpower confrontation are also far less likely to receive large grants or loans aimed at the creation of strong military allies and developmental showcases. (Such outlays were *initially* important for poor countries like Taiwan and South Korea; but effective utilization of the opportunities for development brought about by association with a superpower is also conditioned by the capabilities of local states and entrepreneurial strata).

Not only is the scope of third world industrialization fairly limited, but past assumptions about the smooth ascent of third world economies have surely been shattered by the blows delivered to many of even the most dynamic developing nations by two energy crises and a deep recession over the past decade. Average growth in industrial production among low income oil-importing countries slowed from 6.6% per year in 1960–70 to 4.2% from 1970–82. Industrial growth among middle income oil-importers fell from 7% per year to 5.5% per year, while oil-exporters recorded a slight improvement from 7.4% per year to 7.6% per year over the same periods.[3]

Overall, third world countries suffered more from the 1980–82 recession than from the 1973 energy crisis. Middle income oil-importers were especially hard hit, but even oil-exporters proved vulnerable after the recession and worldwide energy conservation efforts led to an oil glut and the collapse of the petroleum market in 1981-82 (Table 5). Contrary to most expectations, the export-led East Asian countries were the quickest to recover from the sharp shock administered by the 1980–82 recession. Although the immediate impact on semi-industrialized Latin American nations (such as Brazil and Mexico) was less severe, they have had negative rates of economic growth since 1981 and appear to have dim hopes for an early recovery given their massive debt burdens. Intensifying differentia-

Table 3.5 GDP growth rates, 1960–73 (averaged annual percentage change)

Country Group	*1960–73*	*1973–9*	*1980*	*1981*	*1982*	*1983 (est.)*
Developing countries	6.3	5.2	2.5	2.4	1.9	1.0
Low-income	5.6	4.8	5.9	4.8	5.2	4.7
Asia	5.9	5.2	6.3	5.2	5.6	5.1
China	8.5	5.7	6.1	5.2	5.6	5.1
India	3.6	4.3	6.9	5.7	2.9	5.4
Africa	3.5	2.1	1.3	1.2	0.5	–0.1
Middle income oil-importers	6.3	5.6	4.3	0.9	0.7	0.3
East Asia & Pacific	8.2	8.6	3.6	6.7	4.2	6.4
Middle East & N. Africa	5.2	3.0	4.2	–2.4	5.5	2.0
Sub-Saharan Africa	5.6	3.7	5.5	3.9	1.1	0.3
Southern Europe	6.7	5.0	1.5	2.3	0.7	–0.9
Latin America & Caribbean	5.6	5.0	5.8	–2.3	–0.4	–2.2
Middle income oil-exporters	6.9	4.9	–2.4	2.4	0.9	–0.7
High income oil-exporters	10.7	7.7	7.4	0.0	—	—
Industrial market economies	4.9	2.8	1.3	1.3	–0.5	2.3

Source: *World Bank, World Development Report 1984 p. 11*, Oxford University Press, New York

tion among third world countries and the continued uneven development of the scope of industrialization seem to be inevitable outcomes of these developments.

The Depth of Industrialization

We can see a similar pattern when we examine the depth of third world industrialization (here measured in terms of the growth of producer goods, chemicals and transportation equipment sectors).[4] Only 12 of 55 capitalist middle and low income countries surveyed by the World Bank have 25% or more of manufacturing value added derived from capital goods, transportation equipment or chemical sectors (see Table 6). Twenty countries, on the other hand, have less than 10% of their manufacturing value added in these lines (see Table 7). Industrialization for most third world nations has apparently taken place overwhelmingly in light consumer goods industries. Most third world countries must therefore import the bulk of their capital good requirements from advanced industrial economies. Only the NICs can fulfil most of their needs through domestic production, and, of these, only South Korea and Brazil have emerged as significant exporters of capital goods and technology related services.

Countries with strong capital goods and chemical sectors tend to be oil-importing, middle income economies in Latin America or Asia; only two (India and Kenya) fall into the low income bracket of World Bank statistics. The high concentration (9 of 12) of upper middle income economies (with per capita GNP over $1500 in 1982) suggest that the deepening of industrialization may be partly related to growing internal markets and associated with increasingly differentiated class structures.

The deepening and widening (of the scope) of industrialization by third world countries is thus clearly possible, if only for a select few. Yet analysis of relatively successful experiences also shows that the deepening process is multilinear and historically conditioned by the interaction of a complex matrix of internal and external factors. This state of affairs severely mitigates the utility of imposing any single strategy or explanatory theory on developing countries. Moreover, it is also evident that substantial industrialization can occur under a variety of socio-economic conditions and resource endowments, leading in turn to crucial variations in the types of class structures that emerge from these experiences.

Historically, the deepening of industrialization beyond the production of consumer goods in the third world has been associated with two broad (and not mutually exclusive) types of development strategy. Several older, larger countries in Lation America have been able to develop substantial capital goods and chemical industries (primarily because of their sizeable internal markets and rich natural resources) in successive stages of primary and secondary import substitution, along with some efforts at export promotion in recent years. Development efforts in such nations have usually featured powerful and extensive state leadership and direct

Table 3.6 Distribution of manufacturing value added (1981 Percentages, 1975 prices)

Country	*Light industries*	*Capital Goods/ Chemicals/Transportation Equipment*
Low Income:		
Chad (1980)	83	0
Bangladesh	68	20
Ethiopia	54	2
Burma	45	5
Malawi	64	0
Upper Volta	81	11
Uganda	79	0
India	31	34
Rwanda (1980)	58	2
Haiti (1980)	52	1
Central African Republic (1980)	87	2
Madagascar (1980)	66	12
Sri Lanka	56	0
Togo (1980)	78	0
Ghana (1980)	28	0
Pakistan	60	23
Kenya	34	39
Lower Middle Income:		
Liberia (1980)	22	0
Senegal (1980)	58	8
Indonesia	36	19
Zambia	38	24
Honduras (1980)	61	8
Egypt (1980)	42	24
Thailand (1980)	57	18
Philippines	51	21
Zimbabwe	38	21
Nigeria	51	23
Morocco	43	19
Cameroon (1980)	41	9
Nicaragua (1980)	67	0
Congo, People's Republic	42	7
Peru (1980)	41	21
Dominican Republic (1980)	86	6
Ecuador	41	17
Turkey	35	27
Tunisia	40	24
Columbia	47	23
Paraguay	48	14

Country	*Light industries*	*Capital Goods/ Chemicals/Transportation Equipment*
Upper Middle Income:		
Syria	59	8
Malaysia	39	24
South Korea	39	29
Panama	63	8
Chile	20	26
Brazil	25	37
Mexico	27	32
Algeria	40	13
Portugal	30	36
Argentina	23	36
Uruguay (1980)	49	19
South Africa	25	29
Venezuela	33	16
Greece	46	18
Israel	27	33
Singapore	8	59
Trinidad & Tobago (1980)	28	16

Source: *World Bank, World Development Report 1984,* Oxford University Press, New York *pp. 230–31.*

involvement in the industrialization process. Significant strata of domestic capitalists have also evolved, along with large volumes of direct TNC investment (generally aimed at local or regional markets) and extensive state and private sector ties with western financial capital.

More recently, several small, resource poor East Asian economies (e.g. South Korea, Taiwan, Singapore and Hong Kong) have capitalized on large pools of surplus labour to rapidly develop labour-intensive, assembly based industries producing inexpensive consumer goods largely aimed at external markets. Considerable amounts of export-oriented TNC investment and tight integration with the world market are well known features of this export-led industrialization path. Yet despite the free market rhetoric often espoused by their political leaders and overseas backers, these countries have also had energetic and powerful states with major direct economic involvement. The expansion of light export-oriented industries has been accompanied by state efforts to build intermediate and upstream heavy and chemical industries, often with sizeable foreign capital inputs; moreover, rapid economic growth and the expansion of

Table 3.7 Low and Middle Income Countries: Share of manufacturing value added in capital goods, chemicals and transportation equipment 1981

	(Number of Countries)	
Percentage	*Middle Income*	*Low Income*
over 30%	6	2
25–29%	4	0
20–24%	8	2
15–19%	9	0
10–14%	2	2
under 10%	9	11
Total	38	17

Source: World Bank, *World Development Report 1984,* Oxford University Press, New York, p. 11.

employment in labour-intensive industry and the rise of large middle class strata have enlarged domestic markets for manufactured goods.

Both routes have successfully promoted relatively deep industrial development in Latin America and East Asian NICs and have given rise to strong strata of domestic industrial capitalists. This latter process reflects several trends, including the conversion of local traditional elites to industrial activity, the growth of industrial capital in association with the state and the associated growth of many domestic capitalists with transnational corporations (TNCs) from the US, West Europe or Japan. Indeed, examples of large scale local industrialists rising *without* links with state or foreign capital are quite rare, especially in East Asia. Nevertheless, not a few local entrepreneurs have effectively exploited such linkages to gradually bolster their own competitive strength. Ultimately, regionally based TNCs have been organized, particularly from Brazil, South Korea and Taiwan, to compete quite effectively with foreign capital.

However, these economies now confront urgent problems of adjustment and upgrading to overcome the pressures generated by both the strengths and weaknesses of their developmental paths, the recent worldwide recession and the new challenges of the present development decade.

The 1980–1982 recession brutally exposed the mortal weakness of the externally financed developmental efforts of Latin American NICs. These countries, among many others in the third world, had turned to transnational banks (TNBs) and Eurodollar funds in the mid-1970s to cover rising oil bills and the costs of the massive capital good imports required for ambitious state led development projects. In several Latin American nations the state was either unable or unwilling to obtain sufficient amounts of capital from domestic sources, perhaps because of

Table 3.8 External public debt service as percentage of exports of goods and services

Country	*1970*	*1982*
Argentina	21.5	24.5
Brazil	12.5	42.1
India	20.9	7.1
Kenya	5.4	20.3
Mexico	23.6	29.5
Philippines	7.2	12.8
Singapore	0.6	0.8
South Korea	19.4	13.1

Source: *World Bank, World Development Report 1984,* Oxford University Press, New York, *pp. 248–9.*

either the economic weakness or political strength of local capitalist interests and inadequate levels of domestic savings from other social classes.

The sudden eruption of the second oil crisis in 1979, the subsequent recession and sluggish export growth and contractive western industrial policies deepened the crisis. Service ratios on external public debt alone soared to 42.1% for Brazil and 29.5% for Mexico by 1982, sparking a flurry of debt reschedulings and raising the spectre of defaults (see Table 8). This process has left many Latin American nations subordinate to the severe austerity programs of the International Monetary Fund (IMF), which may actually lead to a degree of de-industrialization, with deleterious effects on the local populations.

The proposed shift to growth oriented, export expanding adjustment may not provide a cure[6]. This prescription is based on the successes of East Asian NICs (see below); but the context of its proposed adoption in Latin America is strikingly different. Export substitution in East Asia has been a means to make maximum use of limited capital resources and technology to produce light industrial goods for overseas markets. Export earnings were then used to finance imports of raw materials, capital goods, and more advanced technology and to expand production and employment further. In contrast, the current export promotion effort in Latin America is accompanied by the IMF's stringent measures to severely *contract* employment, wages and imports, primarily at the expense of the working classes. While some degree of painful economic adjustment will be required to resolve the present crisis, the best prospects lie in policies that can catalyse intensive economic growth through expansion of both local employment and consumption of locally produced wage goods and export of manufactures that can be truly competitive on world markets without artificial compression of wage costs. Whatever the answer is to the debt crisis, it surely does not lie in slashing the already low levels of consumption of working people.

The East Asian NICs have been far less *substantially* reliant on foreign capital. Export earnings and high rates of domestic savings (thanks to the mushrooming of smaller export related firms and high levels of employment) have contributed to the greater availability of local capital resources as well as to the steady expansion and intensification of home markets. Direct foreign investment has been strategically less important for capital inputs than for the provision of production and management techniques and markets in the advanced industrial countries. While East Asian NICs have borrowed extensively on overseas capital markets to finance their own large scale state sponsored infrastructure or heavy industrial projects as well as private endeavours, huge export earnings have provided them with a far greater capability to support and pay back these funds. Based upon these strengths, the East Asian NICs were able to bounce back from the recent recession very quickly, after experiencing a brief period of deflation due to the sharp external shock. Not only were the local states less dependent on externally generated funds (given high rates of domestic savings), but foreign banks were still eager to lend funds to the East Asian NICs at favourable rates given their superior export performance and lower debt service ratios. Moreover, state promoted efforts to boost productivity, adjust the industrial structure (by, for instance, discouraging energy intensive lines) and develop high tech lines may have contributed to a faster recovery. The revival of key export markets in the US and the strong US dollar also helped the East Asian NICs to record strong export and economic growth rates in 1983 and 1984.

The critical issues for the East Asian industrial nations in the coming decade involve problems arising from their economic *success*. The export competitiveness of their light industrial products has declined as growth in real wages has far surpassed increases in labour productivity given the virtual elimination of surplus labour, rising standards of living and more effective labour activity at the point of production. Rising protectionism in the West and a new wave of entrants into labour-intensive export lines (mainland China and some South East Asian nations) are pressuring for the 'four little dragons' (South Korea, Taiwan, Singapore, and Hong Kong); a rough indication of their comparative advantage in labour costs can be obtained from Table 9. Moreover, the potential for trade reversal from the introduction of new computerized production technologies in advanced industrial countries (such as fully automated factories) may affect the long term viability of the export-led model.

The East Asian NICs have thus intensified efforts to upgrade their industrial structures through promotion of more technology- and capital-intensive export lines and through liberalization of remaining barriers to imports and foreign investment. Rich domestic capital sources and high levels of scientific and technical education augur well for these efforts, but the obstacles are still formidable. In addition to the external pressures mentioned above, the East Asian NICs must confront fierce internecine competition from each other as well as from firms in developed countries such as Japan that are threatened by their rise.

The domestic difficulties are also daunting. A new type of developmentalist role for the state, emphasizing industrial policy through less direct, parametric forms of involvement (like Japan's Ministry of International Trade and Industry) may be needed to build a more advanced economic structure in the context of tighter integration with the world economy. Yet bureaucratic and some capitalist strata with vested interests in the previous pattern of assembly based export growth and its associated form of direct state intervention can be expected to oppose such efforts to revamp the local industrial and state structure. Moreover, rising living standards and education levels have spurred movements for the democratization of authoritarian states and for greater attention to social welfare and environmental issues. Such pressures may be heightened by the potential threat posed by industrial upgrading to the prosperity of small and medium enterprises.

Labour movements in the East Asian NICs face a period of crisis and opportunity whether industrial upgrading suceeds or fails. The shift to skill and knowledge-intensive high technology industries should improve the structural bargaining positions of skilled and semi-skilled workers. This

Table 3.9 Average hourly wages in manufacturing in Asia

Country	*1983 (US$)*	*%increase 1978–83 (current prices)*
Australia	7.9	73.8
Japan	6.6	14.8
New Zealand	4.79	91.1
Singapore	2.05	—
Taiwan	1.51	60.2
South Korea	1.47	51.5
Hong Kong	1.39	18.7
Thailand	1.15	—
Malaysia	0.91	—
Indonesia	0.50	—
Philippines	0.46	121.4
Pakistan	0.41	—
India	0.38	40.1
Sri Lanka	0.19	45.9
China	0.17	—

Source: *Business Asia*, 14 December 1984, p. 399.

tendency is reflected in the recent shift of local East Asian states (especially Singapore) from repressive labour policies to attempts to stimulate the expansion of official labour federations and implement a high wage regime. While this shift offers more opportunity for union activity, its main thrust is still to pre-empt the potential emergence of a more radical labour movement and to secure the stabilization of the disciplined and productive labour force that is critical for the growth of skill-intensive lines. The campaign to develop high tech industries and boost productivity is likely to entail sizable unemployment and growing income inequality if compensating opportunities for displaced unskilled labourers are not created by faster economic growth. However, massive unemployment and sharp increases in inequality will surely result from the stagnation which would follow in the wake of the failure of industrial upgrading projects.

Industrialization prospects for third world nations which have not yet broken into the exalted ranks of the NICs by the mid-1980s are clouded by expectations of continued slow growth in the advanced industrial countries as the industrial restructuring of the OECD economies continues. This process and the diffusion of new technologies in automated and computerized production management may diminish opportunities for export-led industrialization given the possible reinforcement of protectionist barriers and the potential reversal of some kinds of TNC investment as the new technologies reduce labour costs for domestic production. Development efforts by less industrialized third world nations may focus more on the home market and establishment of tighter links between rural and industrial acitivity.

Expansive Industrializing Countries: Development versus Exploitation

Discussions of third world industrialization have focused almost exclusively on the issues of develpment or more specifically on the growth of the productive forces. This one-sided concern with emphasizing economic changes was perhaps a natural reaction to the obstinate tendency among dependency theorists to deny these developmental possibilities. In the process, however, this techno-productivist bias has blinded development students to both the dynamics of the new socio-political reality which successful industrialization has created in these more advanced regions and its human cost.

The benefits of substantial industrialization and economic growth have generally not been equitably distributed. Extremes of income inequality and swelling masses of sporadically employed poor characterize many of the urban centers of the newly industrializing countries, especially in Latin America, where industry is often quite capital-intensive. Early land reform and the rapid growth of labour-intensive light industries in the East Asian NICs have permitted relatively equitable income distribution through high levels of industrial employment; however, a huge proportion of these newly absorbed workers are young, unmarried women filling low skill jobs with low wages and labouring under strict, paternalistic work disciplines.

Unionization has been impeded not only by political repression, but also by the perceived temporary nature (only before marriage) of such employment. Social benefits have often been minimal, despite the stressful and often hazardous working conditions.

Moreover, the capacity of NIC states for forceful political economic involvement has also been fully manifested in vigorous repression of political opposition and extensive violation of human rights, particularly by military regimes (most infamously in Chile, Argentina, South Korea). The industrial working class has often been singled out for special treatment by such regimes. Latin American history has been punctuated by recurrent confrontations between highly politicized trade unions and worker movements with authoritarian or military regimes. Fierce repression as well as forcible incorporation into state controlled union structures have been common in efforts to tame labour militancy. Firm state or party control over unions has also characterized East Asian factories, especially since the maintenance of low wages to undergird export competitiveness was more important than in Latin America's often capital-intensive and protected industries. The right to strike is usually effectively prohibited and trade unionism outside of ruling party directed corporatist structures is virtually proscribed.

NIDL analysts have pointed to these conditions as the key to the redeployment of labour-intensive segments of the production processes to labour surplus export platforms in East Asia and other regions. However, their techno-productivist bias and narrow focus on TNC activity has led many researchers to overlook the social impact of this investment and the general expansion of third world industries. As noted above, the rise of various middle class strata and skilled workers (along with the economic crises) has led to heightening pressure for political democratization throughout Latin America and East Asia.

More relevant to our purposes here has been the emergence of a new generation of workers located within the new productive facilities and their deepening perception of the basic issue as one of exploitation and not development. The growth of industry – whether or not TNC-inspired – and the incorporation of labour into industrial employment has created a new point of departure for the second generation of workers. The problems raised by segments of the working class in the NICs no longer merely concern employment but increasingly the *conditions* of employment as well: the very development of the productive forces has brought the issue of the social relations of production to the fore, at least among some layers of the industrial labour force. While it would be a mistake to attribute the emergence of new layers of class conscious workers to merely techno-productive changes, there is evidence suggesting that in some of the more advanced industrial countries of the third world there is increasing discontent with the organization and type of work which was previously acceptable to the first wave of workers recruited to the factory system. This is particularly the case as the industrialization process becomes more advanced and complex, drawing in its wake strata of skilled workers with greater education whose qualifications cannot so easily be replaced. Simultaneously, social mobility *out* of the working class has become more difficult in the more developed and highly populated societies; as more and more workers, male or female, perceive factory employment as a long-term occupation, concern for the quality of the workplace environment and wage levels will become ever more intense. Under such circumstances, the push for greater worker autonomy should proceed apace.

Free Enterprise Ideology and Statist Practice

One of the most frequently misunderstood aspects of third world industrialization has been the relationship between free enterprise ideology and statist practice. The growth of industry in close association with the growth of statism is well illustrated by the experience in Latin America. The region's three leading industrial countries – Mexico, Brazil and Argentina – have very substantial public sectors involved in basic industry and resources. In Asia, the state has played a pivotal role in regulating and directing the growth of private capital in Taiwan, South Korea, and Singapore even as local private capital has increased its role over the past decade. Thus, despite the apparent official adoption of free enterprise ideology in name by some of these states (more precisely, their neo-classical economist boosters), statism plays a much bigger role in practice than is usually recognized.

Perhaps the major substantive differences among third world countries has not been over the role of the state but rather over the relative importance of the domestic market in stimulating growth. Latin American countries have generally fostered industrialization aimed at supplying local markets, whereas the labour surplus economies of East and South East Asia have placed more emphasis on manufacturing production for export. Thus Brazil exports only about 10% of its manufacturing product, compared to 30% for South Korea. Yet this latter figure (low compared to other East Asian NICs) does not adequately reflect the strategic importance of the export-oriented sector as a dynamic generator of large scale (albeit low paid) employment, foreign exchange and domestic investment capital. These functions have often been fulfilled in Latin America by state or TNC associated heavy or intermediate industrial projects for import substitution and by greater amounts of foreign direct and indirect (loans) capital investment. Still, one should also not neglect the major role of domestic markets in the East Asian NICs, whose high employment policies have stimulated the growth of (and ever more sophisticated) markets for both light and durable consumer goods.

Moreover, while industrial exports have been playing a larger role for most third world countries, the marketing patterns of these exports has varied with the level of industrialization. Rising shares of the exports of less industrialized nations are going to other third world countries, while the more advanced regions are expanding their trade with the industrialized west and Japan. Even this trend is not unilinear: South Korea has hiked its share of manufactured exports which go to developing countries from 17% to 28% from 1962 to 1981[7]. These trends, added to the emergence of *regional* economic networks (e.g. between Japan and East and South East Asian nations), contradict notions of core centred or TNC determined industrial redeployment patterns as suggested by the NIDL school. Growing protectionism in metropolitan nations and the rising number of proponents of heightened intra-third world exchange suggest that development of more complex trade patterns will continue.

Sources of Foreign Financing: Banking Capital and Multinational Corporations

Besides the NIDL school's insufficient appreciation of the importance of the state, local capital, and local markets in third world industrialization, this perspective often exaggerates the role of multinational capital and understates the centrality of finance capital. In the 1960s and 1970s, foreign capital financed at most 10–20% of the total investments in the third world. Despite the often strategic contribution of foreign invested projects or associated technology transfer, capital accumulation in third world nations has usually come overwhelmingly from domestic sources, including earnings by local entrepreneurs from exports.

Moreover, during the 1970s and 1980s, there was a dramatic shift from direct to indirect investments in the form of commercial or, less common, official loans[8]. The rapid expansion of the Eurocurrency market and the flood of petrodollars in the 1970s, combined with slow growth in the metropolitan countries, prompted transnational private banks (TNBs) to boost lending to developing countries. Floating interest rates and syndicated lending passed on market risks to the borrowers and spread default risks among a multitude of private and official lending agencies. Low risk high profits were seemingly assured by concentration of lending to the more developed third world nations. The added insurance of local state guarantees and immunity from expropriation due to nationalist or class struggles enhanced the attractiveness of such lending over the financing of direct TNC investment projects.

Third world governments often preferred foreign commercial loans over direct TNC investment or official credits as being less likely to perpetuate dependence and allowing them to invest or spend the funds as they wished without conditions or strings. International private financing thus stimulated growth through state sponsored investment projects in heavy industry or infrastructure during expansionary periods and provided local governments with funds for countercyclical pump-priming or subsidies during contractionary phases of the world economy.

Yet this process was not without its traps. External financing to local states and private capital may have led to greater local ownership and appeared to enhance state autonomy from international and local capital, but at the cost of a burgeoning debt burden propelled by soaring variable interest rates. The seductiveness of easy and almost unconditional credit married to nationalistic or militaristic ambitions encouraged some states (e.g. Argentina) to waste valuable loan funds on armaments or ill considered infrastructural projects (nuclear power plants in hydropower-rich Brazil). Moreover, the economically beneficial efforts to expand heavy industry and build up needed transport and power facilities were usually long gestating, and have begun only recently to pay off. Efforts by some states (notably Brazil and Taiwan) to sidestep the structural implications of the energy crisis of 1973-4 through subsidizing energy prices were also proven unwise and expensive by the onslaught of the second energy crisis in 1979–80 and the belated shock that accompanied domestic adaption to world energy price levels. Stagnation plagued not a few third world economies after the growing risk of default began to deter foreign bankers from further lending coincided with peak interest rates and a downturn in export earnings from both primary resource and manufactured commodities due to the 1980–82 recession.[9]

The cyclical nature of world capitalist development and the increasing dependence of locally owned state and private capital on finance capital created a new set of contradictions after the debt crisis exploded in the 1980s. The struggle between the third world and the TNCs postulated by the NIDL school has been dwarfed in the eighties by the struggles emerging over debt financing and interest payments – a far more serious drain on development resources.

Moving Beyond the New International Division of Labour

New theories on the formation of new international divisions of labour through transnational capital expansion constitute an advance over the static conceptions of the dependency school. NIDL theorists have recognized the rapid progress of industrialization in the third world and have drawn attention to the tendency of transnational capital to create new forms of worldwide intra- and inter-firm divisions of labour based on exploitation of cheap labour in export-oriented assembly and processing industries (notably, but not exclusively, in East Asia).

However, the process of third world industrialization is much more complex and contradictory than has been envisioned by the proponents of a new international division of labour. Both the size and scope of industrialization has to be specified to determine the balance of social forces in analysing trade union strategies. Nor has industrialization been as core centred or TNC determined as NIDL theorists claim: the continuing strong trade *among* industrializing third world nations is but one indication (see Table 10).

Through neglect of socio–historical analysis of developing countries, NIDL theorists have overlooked the ability of third world states to actively

Table 3.10 Destination of manufactured exports (percentage of total)

Origin	*Industrial market economies* 1962	1981	*Developing economies* 1962	1981
Low income economies	57	50	—	28
Middle income economies:	50	57	43	31
Oil-exporters	61	57	27	37
Oil-importers	48	57	46	31
Lower middle income	53	52	38	39
Upper middle income	50	58	44	31

Source: World Bank, *World Development Report*, Oxford University Press, New York, pp. 242–3.

intervene in the development process. In East Asian NICs, for example, the thrust of such intervention has been to seize the opportunities offered by association with emerging international and regional specializations to build strong foundations for sustained *interdependent* development. The real importance of statism and its paradoxical legitimation by free market ideology raises important issues regarding the relationship between state and civil society and, in particular, the need to deepen internal class analysis as the major research strategy in determining the significance of third world countries' insertion in the world market. This is particularly important in discussing the moves from state controlled to autonomous trade unions. The linkages between locally owned industries and foreign private banking capital has in many cases created a new set of global contradictions between the local labour force, the state and foreign bankers. The problem of debt payments involves a new set of alliances and conflicts in which the process of extraction of economic surplus for interest payments becomes a central concern for the trade union movement.

Finally, the almost exclusive focus placed on the formation of TNC centred subordinating divisions of labour has often led NIDL proponents to overlook the substantial degree of social transformation that has taken place in rapidly industrializing third world nations. Failure to comprehend the dynamism of economic development has spawned a blindness to the implications of the differential patterns of industrialization on the working-class and trade union movements in the third world. In the expansive third world countries, shifts in levels and types of industrialization have raised new strata, new issues that go beyond the perspectives of development and raise basic issues relating to the social relations of production. It is to this critical dimension that we now turn.

The Implications of Industrialization for Third World Trade Union Struggles

The specificity of third world industrialization raises concrete issues and particular points of departure for trade union struggles that are substantially different from those found in the industrialized West. Rather than bemoaning these differences (or castigating third world unions for deficiences), it is important to explore the ways and means by which the specificities of third world industrialization can be turned into advantages in the trade union struggle. On the basis of our previous discussion of industrialization, we shall proceed to analyse the implications for trade union struggles. At the outset, we should emphasize that the following remarks aim at stimulating new thinking in analysing existing and evolving conditions for the development of trade unionism; they are not meant to apply to all third world countries but are rather offered in the spirit of recognition of the great variety and rapidly changing nature of socio-political life in developing societies.

Limited Scope of Industrialization

In most third world countries, industrialization takes place amidst a sea of rural producers, petty commodity distributors and a multiplicity of small household manufacturing enterprises. In many cases industrial workers, recently arrived from the countryside, retain ties with their family and land in rural areas. The generally limited scope of industrialization and the concomitant small size of the industrial working class means that trade unions must develop ties with other strata and organizations to be politically effective. Workerist orientations, with their exclusive focus on factory issues and organizations, will thus tend to isolate the workers and perhaps make them more vulnerable to repressive forces. Three strategic groups – small farmers and peasants in the countryside and petty producers and distributors in the cities and urban underemployed – are central to any coalition building effort. Without underestimating the difficulties involved in a coalition building strategy (and without underestimating the dangers of trade union organizations becoming subsumed in populist forms of socio–political movements), there are specific sets of issues that can serve to bring the trade unions in a working relationship with these strata: workers share with unemployed petty commodity producers and distributors a whole set of common demands at the point of habitation (such as housing, infrastructure, potable water) that could be articulated through community organizations linked to the trade unions. Communication between workers and petty urban producers is facilitated by the frequent multiple employment practices of working class segments. The social and geographic proximity of workers and other urban strata facilitates the intervention of trade unions in community struggles *and* the mobilization of community support for trade union struggle. Trade union struggles divorced from wider community demands of the non-factory urban poor constitute open invitations to employers to recruit strike breakers from the mass of surplus labour.

The second strategic group, peasants and farmers, has been in some accounts counterposed to the industrial working class because of differences in income and standard of living. Yet an earlier study showed how highly organized miners were able to exercise a radicalizing influence on peasants in surrounding agrarian regions through mutual interaction and provision of legal and material support for the peasants' struggles[10]. Frequent visits between urban and rural areas provides a useful channel for the diffusion of ideas of organization and struggle. At a more formal institutional level the creation of issue specific overlapping institutions between rural producers and trade unions– such as producers and consumer cooperatives– could serve as a bridge toward broader sets of working relations.

At the ideological level then, the often narrow scope of industrialization and the relatively small size of the working class requires that trade unions elaborate an ideology of solidarity between industrial and other workers and the mass of petty producers and distributors. Without *dissolving* the basic trade union organization into a heterogeneous movement, it is incumbent on trade unions to transcend the factory setting and help establish institutions at the community level and at the intersection of rural and urban exchanges in order to be able to muster sufficient force to establish a national presence. Involvement in community issues is no less vital in societies where the working class is quite large, as in the East Asian NICs. Broad sections of the population are deeply affected by widespread environmental pollution, virtually non-existent consumer protection, nuclear power, rising crime rates and other social problems that have emerged as negative consequences of the type of rapid industrialization they have experienced. Opportunities abound for popular movements dealing with these issues, which are likely to be seen by state authorities as less of a direct threat than sharper but more narrowly defined workerist struggles.

Limited Depth of Industrialization

In most third world societies, manufacturing activity has been located primarily in consumer goods sectors such as textiles, clothing and electronics. The relative simplicity of the technology employed and the low level of capital investment per worker makes these industries particularly susceptible to greater capital mobility. Trade unions in such industries must pay special attention to the vulnerability of these lines, particularly when there is a substantial component of foreign capital involvement, and link up when necessary to nationalist sentiments to avert the possibility of capital flight without sacrificing their essential class perspective.

More central to trade union organization in this context is the female-intensive character of employment in such industries, especially in East and South East Asia and som export-oriented enclaves in other regions. Within the textiles, clothing and electronics industries there is a preponderance of women at the level of mass production, while technicians and maintenance workers (along with the union leadership) tend to be males. The fundamental problem facing trade unions in this context is their capacity to create the specific institutional and cultural support structures that would allow women to play a significant role in the mobilization and struggles of the union. Some of the basic difficulties of trade union work in textile and electronic sectors revolve around the domination of the female majority by household concerns, their manipulation and exploitation at the hands of alternately paternalistic and authoritarian employers and their subordination to male trade union leaders. They usually have virtually no time, space or energy left for the trade union struggle – unless a major crisis (sharp reduction in salary, factory closing or mass revolt) disrupts routines and allows women workers to change their agenda of priorities and take part temporarily in trade union struggles.

The vulnerability of light industry makes it incumbent for trade unions to develop ties with strategic trade unions, usually in the public sector, such as light and power workers, port and transport unions. While employers can usually sit out a strike in consumer goods sectors (or bring in strike breakers from among the surplus labour force), strikes among the usually highly organized utility and transport workers would have an immediate and highly damaging effect on the economy as a whole and on the state – thus providing greater leverage in bargaining for the weaker unions in consumer industries. The spread of workers across consumer goods sectors thus requires the formulation of nationalist and gender programmes that broaden alliances to protect industries and mobilize internal support. Alliances with strategic sector unions can enhance bargaining power and compensate for internal structural weaknesses. However, the forging of such alliances is apt to be arduous given the high degree of direct political control exercised by the state over public sector unions precisely because of their strategic importance. Official favouritism and cooptation through higher wages and better working conditions is likely to widen the gap between public sector workers and their counterparts in privately owned light industry. Nor should potential leverage of workers in light industries be neglected. The pressures of seasonal demand and tight delivery schedules in exported consumer goods, for instance, leave local and foreign capital in these lines vulnerable to slowdowns or other worker action at the point of production at critical times.

Statism and the Trade Unions

One of the most salient facts about third world industrial development is the permeation of society and economy by the state; whether it be in the elaboration of development agencies to promote investments, or in the expansion of patronage appointments for followers or to extend control over potentially oppositionist associations, the state is everywhere. The centrality of politics in both promoting the productive forces and determining how its product will be allocated clearly suggests that trade union struggles must be political. Whoever controls the state controls the character and direction of the heavy state involvement in society and economy that seems to be necessary in all third world development. The problem, however, is that to the degree in which trade unions enter into political struggle over the state they greatly increase the likelihood of provoking repression.

The centrality of the state and its important role as broker and partner between national capital and the multinationals also suggests that the struggles against multinational capital frequently involve conflicts with the domestic capitalist class and its political collaborators. The formidable array of forces and resources at the disposal of the state and TNCs may lead trade unions to adopt a two step approach of first building up strength within the realm of economic and trade union issues and then, after a period of accumulating forces, deepening and extending the struggle to the political terrain. The ubiquitous state institutions and their highly centralized structures penetrate and control trade unions at the apex–the leaders of federations and confederations frequently appear to be functionaries of government labour ministries. In this context the national or industry-wide union structure appear to be less representative and responsive to rank and file demands than local factory based unions. In the context of centralized state control of national trade unions, the spread and growth of locally controlled factory unions (union decentralization) could be a positive step toward autonomous class unionism. Strengthening of local unions may well in turn promote tendencies in industry-wide federations for democratization and more autonomy *vis-a-vis* the state. However, there is the danger that enterprise based unions, if counterposed to wider federations, could become little more than isolated company unions dominated or even organized by employers. In avoiding bureaucratic state control there is thus the risk of becoming captive to employer designs.

Perhaps the most salient issue facing trade union struggles is the extensive statification of economy and society. Nationalization, heralded by many as a progressive step toward socialism or national economic independence, frequently means bureaucratization and tighter state controls over the trade unions. Subsequently, the range of permissible labour protest and exercise of the right to strike is sharply curtailed as job action against the enterprise becomes redefined as a threat to the state and national security. The trade union movement thus must critically re-examine the whole issue of centralized statification as a progressive step in the transition to socialism. Nationalization has often been the first step toward the subordination of the trade unions to one party states with few compensatory trade-offs. For trade unionists the issue of autonomy of organization–independence from the state–has become a general demand throughout the third world. What has yet to be forcefully pursued, however, are the necessary concomitant programmatic changes, including self-administration by local producers of the social services heretofore administered by the state. For the state's subordination of the trade unions is linked to and legitimated by its broader role as general dispenser of social services. *The issue of decentralized and producer controlled productive and distributive units is crucial to creating legitimate space for autonomous trade union activity*. The autonomy so often violated by the state is in part legitimated by workers themselves who look to the state to intervene on their behalf in the economy and society to provide pay-offs. What these same claimants cannot subsequently do is contain and limit that same state to its positive role, but must also suffer its negative intervention in trade union life. Hence comes the painful and perhaps unnecessary dilemma of having to weigh the pros and cons of state intervention.

Finally, on the ideological plane, the trade unions must demystify the doctrine of national security, particularly as local bourgeoisies have increasingly used the doctrine to oppress indigenous ethnic minority groups and expand into neighbouring territories. The doctrine of national security serves to mobilize popular support for centralizing state power and repression of class demands as divisive–thus de-legitimizing trade union struggles. The permanent crises engendered by the constant evocation of national enemies requires that the trade unions unmask the class interests behind these chauvinist displays. To the extent that trade unions are mobilized to support nationalist expansion they increasingly sacrifice both the immediate interests and historic goals of labour: by strengthening the military components of the state and by providing the ruling class with the halo of national saviour they provide material and ideological support for their enemies once the national crisis subsides.

Externally and Internally Oriented Development

It is frequently noted that externally and internally oriented developments are not antithetical–that both are necessary to development. Having said that, however, there is a strong tendency, particularly by the World Bank and the IMF, to stress export promotion as a means of earning of hard currency to service and repay the massive debts of many third world countries. If exports of existing commodity lines are boosted and imports slashed merely to finance debt servicing and repayment, the benefits to these societies and to labour will be minimal. Both products and foreign exchange earnings would thus be exported, leaving labour to purchase fewer goods with possibly lower real wages. Promotion of manufacturing industries aimed at export markets can be beneficial only when it can spark development of new commodity lines and expansion of production, employment and investment. Rising protest among trade unionists, particularly in Latin America, against neoconservative efforts to simultaneously promote exports and compress real wages and domestic consumption is only to be expected and welcomed. Such a pattern of export promotion may well result in sacrificing the production or import of essential commodities for local consumption and deprive the economy of investment funds which could upgrade or expand productive forces.

The subsequent emphasis on developing manufacturing for the home over the export market may thus be a healthy tendency, as long as it does not lead to the growth of overly protected industries that, although locally owned, basically siphon off monopoly profits from selling high cost goods on the internal market. Trade unionists travel far by merely attacking the consequences of austerity programmes, but, perhaps in conjunction with other popular political forces, must work to formulate alternative development strategies that can subordinate export expansion to the building of solid foundations for long-term industrialization and rising social welfare. Simple defence of jobs in stagnant industries provides the most potent ammunition for the enemies of trade unionism: the trade union programme of industrial conversion to advanced production and the expansion of internal markets must recognize the need to be competitive in the world market, both to develop the capacity to exploit opportunities opened through considered linkages with the world economy and to promote utilization of more advanced and efficient production processes. What trade unions can and should do is to ensure that competitiveness does not become an excuse for increasing inequality between owners and workers.

The current world crisis has been used by many third world states, local capitalists, and international capital to lower labour costs. Yet the crisis offers an opportunity to challenge the current models of accumulation. The sluggishness of external markets, exploitative financial arrangements and exorbitant interest rates converge with trade union demands to expand production for the local market, through structural changes that increase income and purchasing power for the masses. There is among the local bourgeoisie a push in the same direction, mainly as a means of preserving their precarious enterprises from foreign competition and vegetating on state subsidies. Thus in taking advantage of the world crises and turning toward the revitalization of the internal market the basic question trade unionists may ask is: what classes in the internal market will benefit from the shift in development strategy?

Metropolitan Redeployment or National Capital

Contrary to the theories of NIDL, the impetus to industrialization has not been primarily a phenomenon designed and directed from the metropolitan countries. The expansion of multinational capital (as important as it has been) largely complements major inflows of capital from local, state and private sources. Most third world labour is employed in thousands of locally owned industries or in state enterprises. The predominance of national forces has forced trade unionists to critically re-examine the prevalent nationalist and anti-imperialist doctrines which have provided some of the offical animus to class conflict. Nationalism as the ideology of capitalist (private or state) industrialization has obscured the worst forms of exploitation in the third world: the mass of locally owned sweat shops that exploit child labour, recent women migrants and urban slum dwellers. Unlike the TNCs, with their concentrated work force and unionized wages, the small and medium national capitalists operate in highly competitive markets, frequently extracting a surplus through the systematic violation of labour laws, health controls and minimum wage restrictions. Contrary to the folklore of traditional leftists, at the shop-floor there is nothing progressive about this national bourgeoisie. The few and scattered attempts by trade unionists to organize labour in this sector have been violently resisted not only by right-wing regimes but by supposedly progressive populist governments, who fear that a significant sector of their poly-class coalition (small and medium size business) will be alienated and driven to the right by the extension of union militancy.

In general, trade unionists may choose between two strategies to cope with this complex situation: one approach involves an anti-monopoly strategy focusing on the organization of a small core of workers in larger enterprises and joining forces with sectors of business and the middle class to promote national development and ensure the legality of collective-bargaining; the alternative is a radical class strategy which seeks to mobilize workers and employees in a broad array of enterprises for deeper structural changes against a formidable alliance of small and large business. The former strategy maximizes allies across class boundaries but slows or limits socio-economic changes; the latter strategy deepens the process of change but broadens the base of opposition. While proponents of the anti-monopoly strategy argue that their approach does not preclude a second more radical stage, in fact the consequences of their approach has been to help consolidate a new configuration of capitalist power. The radical approach, on the other hand, offers greater social clarity among the organized workers' movement at the cost of heightened isolation from non-working-class political forces in the face of a more unified capitalist class. Where this line has been defeated more intensive repression of labour movements ensues.

Finance Capital, Third World Industrialization and the Debt

Trade unionists in many third world countries are increasingly aware of the macro-economic processes affecting their members. The 1970s and 1980s witnessed the increasing importance of finance capital and the relative decline of direct investment. Rental income which accrued to the petroleum exporting countries was recycled through western banks into loans to the third world. The rent and interest collecting oil rich third world countries became a new source of extraction of surplus from the rest of the third world. The loans in turn were directed toward third world state and local ruling classes to invest or spend as they saw fit. With the onslaught of the recent world economic crisis, rising interest rates, and sluggish export markets, the debt payments became an albatross on the development of many third world countries. Both industry and labour were put through the wringer to maintain interest payments: devaluations, cutbacks in public spending and investment, re-allocation of resources from domestic consumption to exports and restructuring in credit led to massive unemployment, inflation and widespread bankruptcy, especially in Latin Amerian oil-importing nations. The IMF played a crucial role in enforcing discipline on the borrowers and in intervening to control many crucial aspects of economic policy. Short-sighted and unselective pressure from IMF to liberalize trade controls and tariffs and the squeezing out of debt payments from exports led to a weakening of productive structures and to a return to neo-mercantile economic policies. The decisive historical role of state involvement in third world industrialization was neglected by the IMF, whose efforts to drastically reduce the economic role of local states may well be leading to a significant degree of de-industrialization in affected countries instead of the anticipated redeployment of industry from the metropolitan countries.[11]

Trade unionists clearly perceived the effort by the banks and the IMF to reconcentrate income, industry, employment and markets through their debt collection policies. In this context labour joined with sectors of the local bourgeoisie and technocrats to attack this generalized assault on labour standard of living and the overall productive structure. The mobilization of this *de facto* coalition against the IMF enforced austerity programmes reflects the new global contradictions that have emerged between the West and the third world.

Trade unionists in this conjuncture may choose to form alliances with the local bourgeoisies to preserve the foundations of their national productive structure against the de-industrializing implications of IMF and private foreign bank pressure – even as they resist becoming politically subordinate to capital in the operation of the productive system. In countries less affected by the debt crisis, trade unionists can work to secure protection of labour rights and welfare in cyclical downturns and particularly in the current effort to revamp the industrial structure toward more high tech lines.

In the face of cyclical shifts in the economy and shifting sources of exploitation, trade unionists need the flexibility to shift coalitions according to the priority needs of their members – both at the level of the international economy and at the level of shop-floor. No less crucial is active trade union involvement in wider political issues, including questions of national importance such as the presence of foreign military bases or resistance to IMF conditionality. There is little room for dogmatic deductive approaches which bind trade unionists to one set of coalitions, given the shifting contours and problems facing the industrialization process in the third world.

Technological Change and the Uneven Transformation of Labour

Among the more industrially advanced third world countries, the movement toward technologically sophisticated industries is deepening the uneven transformation of labour. In Latin America, an increasingly skilled, educated and highly organized workforce is rising along side of a growing mass of marginalized rural migrants dissociated from or unable to obtain permanent factory employment. In the labour–intensive industrial sectors of East Asia's NICs, efforts to shift to more skill and knowledge intensive lines may accelerate stratification and differentiation among the working class as a better educated and more skilled minority obtains higher wages and improved working conditions while most factory workers either stay mired in lower wage and less skilled employment or get pushed out into the service sector.

Yet the growth of skilled technical labour and the increasing demand for it has also opened new opportunities for unionization as some third world states manifest a greater willingness to tolerate economic bargaining by limited segments. The progressive bifurcation of labour increases the danger of isolation in a dual sense: skilled workers are being divorced from the mass constituency necessary to carry out deep structural changes, while the mass of unskilled labour is isolated from a potential leadership group. Economic and skill differentiation, however, is not an insurmountable obstacle to common action. In most advanced third world industrializing countries there are fundamental overarching issues that adversely affect both skilled and unskilled workers: authoritarian and repressive political structures, inflation, austerity policies, restrictions on autonomous organization, excess concessions to foreign enterprises and so on. As multi-polar conflicts emerge, the challenge facing trade unionists is to determine whether the skilled segments of labour will become incorporated into subordinate elements of the ruling power bloc or whether they can lead less advantaged or excluded masses in struggles against the power bloc.

State Socialism, Industrialization and Trade Unionism

Several third world countries have pursued industrial development under socialist auspicies, primarly through collectivization of the agrarian economy, the nationalization of industry and subsequent promotion of state owned heavy industry. These state socialist regimes have secured more egalitarian norms of distribution of goods and services, higher levels of employment and the fulfilment of many basic needs of the labouring masses. Nevertheless, the stark contrast between the democratic ideals of socialism and the reality of authoritarian bureaucratic control has given third world unionists much food for thought. The structure and style of these regimes, combined with their solid economic progress, has engendered new tensions. One of the most basic issues of concern to workers has been the failure to realize substantive social ownership of the means of production, a process stymied by the lack of autonomy of trade unions and other worker organizations *vis-a-vis* the ruling workers' parties. Hence, one of the most crucial working-class struggles is precisely the effort to democratize the union structure in state socialist societies, either through internal reform or by the creation of parallel unofficial unions or labour organizations that can articulate workers' demands. The very successes (however limited) of state socialist societies in addressing basic needs lay the foundations for the demands of workers for better working conditions, broader participation in management and a greater variety and better quality in consumer goods. Skilled workers in an increasingly complex economy demand different incentive systems that can modify rigid egalitarian norms in favour of rewards linked to merit. Reforms aimed at boosting worker participation and decentralized planning move to the foreground. The emergence of trade unions responsive to the new generation of workers and oriented toward new democratic forms of planning would provide new hope for revitalizing socialist ideas, within and without state socialist societies.

What are the prospects for the growth and strengthening of trade unionism in the third world? Although this question is a fundamental one that underlies much of the above discussion, the high – and rising – degree of differentiation among third world societies, in historical as well as economic and social development, precludes any simple answer. Indeed, identifying the strength of working-class or trade union movements is by no means a simple process. We can observe widespread trade union or labour militancy in many countries at various stages of industrial development. But *militancy* may as easily be an indication of weakness (e.g. an isolated working class in a sea of peasants or a desperate response to economic or political crises) as of strength. More pertinent may be concrete analysis of the political, social, and economic conditions that are apt to lead to strengthening union or labour movements.

While it is difficult to draw any direct connection between early or advanced stages of industrialization and the extent of trade union activity or militancy, a strong case can be made for the relative importance of the larger political setting in shaping the conditions for union development. The existence of an open political climate and broader social and national movements challenging the structure of state and society can be seen to stimulate trade union activism. On the other hand, the establishment of an authoritarian regime and the defeat of major popular social movements (including trade unions), followed by a period of rapid and intensive industrialization, leads to a prolonged period of trade union quiescence. Military regimes may attempt to suppress independent union activity entirely; more moderate regimes may allow limited forms of struggle controlled by official trade unions to appear. As noted above, virtually all the newly industrializing countries in Asia and Latin America display this pattern. Development imperatives have been given precedence over the rights of trade unions to autonomous existence. This has been true regardless of whether the regime in question promoted internally-oriented national development or export-led industrialization, or whether the regime was radical nationalist or pro-western conservative. Whenever development has been a transcendent goal to which trade unionism and workers' rights are seen as a subordinate element, states have generally endeavoured to integrate trade unionism into official administrative structures and thus control it.

Yet this trend should not be perceived in a static manner, nor should overly pessimistic conclusions be drawn. Recent changes in Latin American and East Asian NICs point to the importance of structural factors that may undergird prospects for a long-range strengthening of trade unions, especially in more advanced stages of industrialization. The severe crisis or fall of military regimes in Latin America signifies the failure of attempts by these regimes to solve the present economic crisis and the problems of ever more complex industrial societies by excluding labour and other popular forces from the political sphere and repressing their autonomy in the socio-economic spheres. In several East Asian societies the emergence of new middle-class strata and the rapid growth of the industrial working class has stimulated pressure for political democratization and liberalization of restrictions on trade union activity. In contrast to previous labour-repressive strategies, some East Asian states are moving to encourage the expansion of official unions in order both to establish more effective means of stabilizing and disciplining labour through integration (vital for development of more skill-intensive high-tech industries) and to pre-empt the possible rise of more radical labour movements (the likely result of a continued reliance on repression).

The success of more liberal corporatist labour policies in these regions depends on many factors, not the least of which is the re-establishment or continuance of solid economic expansion. While this seems somewhat problematic, especially for some Latin American nations, trade union activists should endeavour to respond creatively to these new trends. In some countries, the long historical development of relatively autonomous and militant trade unions with mass bases in key industries provides positive conditions for struggle to resist cooptation into government sponsored structures and against corporatist developmental projects. Activists in other countries, however, may well have few options besides working within official labour unions for greater autonomy from state or party control and for broader inner union democraticization.

Activists should be alert to corporatist attempts to keep one step ahead of labour; awareness of other experiences (e.g. Japanese rationalization of industrial management) and new techniques (e.g. new management and production methods) is necessary to identify both upcoming managerial strategies and possible points of danger or opportunity to labour. The communication of such knowledge to union members and other workers is central to the further development of trade unionism, expanded union democracy, and long-term prospects for democratic socialism. The experience of state socialist societies outlined above indicates the difficulties involved in achieving substantial labour participation in political and economic management in states with official pro-labour ideologies. The task of promoting active and effective labour involvement in political, economic and social decision-making in openly capitalist societies is surely no less arduous. Perhaps the best hope for achieving progress toward this ideal within the limits of trade unionism lies in the steady growth of (at least relatively) autonomous trade union organizations and their continuous efforts in expanding democratic participation and education and thus enhancing the capacity of the working class for self-management.

Notes

1. By industrialization, we refer here only to manufacturing and other secondary activity. However, the progressive mechanization of agriculture and the linkages between manufacturing, mining, agriculture and related service sectors need to be incorporated to obtain a fuller picture of the industrialization process.

2. *United Nations Yearbook of International Trade Statistics, 1981*, United Nations, New York, vol. 1, p. 114.

3. World Bank, *World Development Report 1984*, Oxford University Press, New York, pp. 220–21.

4. The concept of depth is by no means a static one, nor limited in principle to the growth of capital good sectors. It varies with the development of the world economy. High technology electronics, for example, could now be included. Moreover, the capacity for industrial upgrading should be estimated through evaluation of data on educational levels, availability of trained scientific and technical personnel, research and development expenditures and so forth. Indicators to show the quality of life (e.g., health, education, equity) should also be considered.

5. The third world countries with the strongest capital goods sectors include Brazil, Mexico, South Korea, India and Argentina. The People's Republic of China and Taiwan also have strong capital goods industries but were not included in available World Bank data.

6. See World Bank, *World Development Report 1984*, p. 29 for the case in support of this switch.

7. See World Bank, *World Development Report 1984*, p. 243 and Table 9 below.

8. The share of net direct foreign investment in net foreign capital inflow for Brazil plunged from 33.8% in 1967–71 to 22.9% in 1972–6 and from 36.6% to 16% for Mexico over the same period. South Korea, on the other hand, showed a slight increase from 3.7% to 7.9%. See Larry Westphal, *Korean Industrial Competence: Where It Came From*, World Bank Staff Working Paper No. 469, July 1981, p. 12.

9. For a recent succinct analysis of these trends see Stephany Griffith–Jones and Ennio Rodriguez, 'Private International Finance and Industrialization of LDCs' in *Journal of Development Studies*, Vol. 21, no. 1 1984.

10. See James Petras and Maurice Zeitlin, 'Miners and Agrarian Radicalism', *American Sociological Review*, Vol. 32, no. 4, 1967, pp. 578–86.

11. Our rejection of the IMF approach does not imply a denial of the validity of numerous critiques of the often ineffectual and inefficient character of many state sponsored industrial projects and other forms of state economic involvement. Extreme fiscal irresponsibility on the part of the Brazilian, Argentine, and other regimes in their investments and attempts to borrow through the two energy crises and evade necessary structural adjustments played a major role in bringing on their subsequent vulnerability to IMF conditionality.

Part 2 Industrial Restructuring, Repression and the Third World Union Response

Introduction

Roger Southall

The differential extent and impact of industrialisation throughout the third world – stressed by Petras and Engbarth in terms of its varying scope, depth and diversity – is strikingly illustrated by the contrasting trade union and working-class experiences featured in this section. Demonstrating the truism (even if now challenged by the changing international division of labour) that working classes are *nationally* formed, the first five papers are all studies of trade unionism (or its equivalent) in individual countries, yet they none the less all reflect wider continental or regional realities.

The survey of resistance to the process of capital restructuring by the military in Argentina which is offered by Ronaldo Munck exemplifies a related dilemma in other Latin American semi-industrialized countries whereby capital, national and international, is inhibited in its freedom of manoeuvre by the social weight of trade unions and the assertive consciousness of a sizable working class. Summoned up historically by the process of dependent, import-substituting industrialization, the Latin American working class provides a counter to capital which now urgently argues the imperative of fragmenting labour if continental competitiveness in the global economy is to be restored. But in Argentina, as elsewhere on the continent, the militance which makes of unions an effective *defensive* combination may produce a shift from millitary to civilian forms without indicating a concerted capacity for carrying through an offensive socialist project.

Similar situational muscle is displayed by Nigerian unions which, according to Nic Van Hear, have hitherto parried various impositions by the state, even in a time of retrenchment and repression, because of the organization of workers in strategically important sectors of the economy (notably oil distribution and production and the ports). Ironically, however, their relative strength reflects the overall weakness of labour in Africa which, as Howard also notes, remains largely locked into the old rather than the new international division of labour, transnational capital being drawn to the continent (South Africa partially excepted) principally by the prospect of raw materials' extraction. The achievements of Nigerian unions are therefore based, somewhat exceptionally in Africa, upon the fissiparous system of federal government which even the military cannot manage by coercion alone, as well as upon its populous, oil-fired economy providing a market whose potential international capital is reluctant to ignore even in times of recession. Even so, Van Hear surmises that Nigerian labour's relative strength will likely be eroded over the long term to the extent that country and continent are restructured by transformations in the global economy.

Laksiri Fernando and Peter Wad situate their analyses of trade unionism in Sri Lanka and Malaysia respectively within the context of export-oriented industrialization. In both papers, whilst there is assertion of the underlying imperative which causes labour to struggle and combine, there is admission also of the division and disorganization of the working class which is not atypical of conditions in newly industrializing countries in Asia and which are therefore attractive to international investors. If, in the case of Malaysia this is entailing the attempted subsuming of the labour market to Japanese forms, then this will require, as Wad insists, a sympathetic assessment of working-class resistance which takes place within what are generally considered to be the highly restricted confines of employer structured unionism. Meanwhile, the segmentation of Sri Lankan workers into what Fernando labels new and old elements implies an organic class disunity flowing from the disarticulated nature of export-orientated industrialization which may well have wider applicability.

Valentine Moghadam's fascinating account of workers' councils in revolutionary Iran draws attention to a country and region which have been very largely ignored in studies of both trade unionism and the changing international division of labour. Yet the Middle East cannot be excluded from such debates, for the pattern of economic development in Iran, and particularly oil-exporting countries, displays the salient features of new industrialization elsewhere in the third world. Notwithstanding that the predominance of oil production within an economy imposes the associated forms of a rentier state and an inward looking, non-competitive mode of (import-substitution) industrialization (not so very different from the Nigerian situation described by Van Hear), a re-organization of social productive relations is wrought which centres around the accelerated growth of an industrial working class and its assumption of a strategic role within the economy. The distinctive feature of such a class in the Middle East, however, would seem to be most certainly *not* its lack of political consciousness (and Moghadem depicts Iranian workers' attempted overturn of autocratic despotism on the shop-floor) but how this blends with Islam and – in the present era – the revolutionary yet repressive impetus towards theocracy.

The case study papers, taken as a whole, illustrate the challenges posed to trade unions in the third world by the changing international division of labour and thereby demonstrate the value of locating working class struggles within the context of the international redeployment of capital.

In both Argentina (where the organized strength of the working class had historically required its incorporation in the Peronist populist alliance) and in Nigeria (where the military had in 1976 enforced an amalgamation of four rival trade union centres to clamp down on industrial unrest and secure labour's control by the state), reduction of the active wage labour force and the expansion of the reserve army of labour brought about by the recession (as well as by the more direct result of government policy) provided the backdrop to the attempted restructuring of the economy and the re-composition of the working class (whereby its capacity for collective resistance would be undermined). Meanwhile, if the rapid rate of new industrialization in both Malaysia and Iran under the Shah was based upon the ability of capital to suck labour out of agriculture at will, then the availability of a very large surplus of particularly female labour – combined with an extremely uneven and generally low level of organization of the working class – enabled the Sri Lankan government to carry through the shift to an economy more open to international capital as an investment site.

Segmentation of the working class in third world countries is an inevitable accompaniment of uneven development, yet as Bjorkman *et al.* suggest, different strategies of industrialization shape the labour market in different ways. Two observations emerge from the case studies here.

First, in that import-substitution industrialization customarily involves entry into at least some relatively heavy industrial spheres (in manufacturing directly as well as the extensive infrastructural developments involved), there is a requirement for the summoning up of a sizable skilled and semi-skilled stratum alongside the mass of unskilled workers in both formal and informal employment, the latter often swelled in number by a bottom tier of foreign labour (as in Iran and Nigeria by Afghani and neighbourng country immigrants respectively). Almost inevitably, such differentiation lends itself to the development of something of a subordinate primary labour market for the minority of more skilled workers, and thereby lends itself to attempts by capital and/or the state to divide workers by forging a labour aristocracy: Munck reports a conscious policy in the generals' Argentina to sharpen wage differentials and thereby weaken the traditional solidarity of workers, whilst in Iran the Shah sought to stem working-class agitation and bolster productivity by introducing a profit-sharing scheme for a privileged layer of workers in certain sectors of large scale manufacturing. In Nigeria, at a somewhat different level, the Shagari regime sought to shore up its rapidly diminishing popular support amongst citizens by scapegoating and expelling many thousand aliens.

Second, as argued previously, the world market orientation of relocated labour-intensive industrial operations encourages the absolute minimization of labour's cost in order to ensure national competitiveness. The emphasis on light manufacturing implies a lack of requirement for skill, and in consequence segmentation of the workforce is more likely structured along age, sex and often ethnic lines in whatever combination is calculated by capital to maximize both production and passivity. Hence it is that the once militant trade unionism of Sri Lanka's old proletariat (which was located in the strategic sectors of the conventional post-colonial economy) have been substantially undermined by the expansion of the secondary casual labour market via recruitment of a mainly female new proletariat in the export processing zone which is effectively denied the right to unionize. In such a circumstance, communal divisions between Sinhalese and Tamil workers have been easily exacerbated.

Segmentation of the workforce along ethnic lines–via the state's intervention within the market to favour the employment of Malay at the expense of ethnic Chinese and Indian workers–has been used to divide organized labour in Malaysia. More significant, however, is the fact that the increase in real wages conceded to workers (and allowed for by the transition to rather more capital-intensive export-oriented industry) has encouraged the impetus towards Japanese-style enterprise unionism whose design is to block the evolution of class solidarity by containing worker organization within individual factories or companies and to entrench differentiation between privileged and disadvantaged workers by excluding non-permanent employees of corporations from unions. Doubtless, segmentation of any particular labour force is more or less likely according to the specific characteristics of the social formation concerned, yet in the Malaysian case at least, it has been amplified by the requirements of export-oriented industrialization.

That the change in the international division of labour entails a shift to authoritarian corporatist state forms in the third world and autocratic despotism on the shop floor is illustrated most schematically–as might be expected–in the Asian cases studied here. Hence although the deradicalization of the trade union movement in Sri Lanka must in part be explained by reference to the policy failure of the centre-left coalition which ruled during the period 1970-77, the subsequent drive towards export orientation has been accompanied by a crackdown on union activity, which has extended from defeat of a widespread general strike in 1980 by mass dismissal from government service to exclusion of unions from the Export Processing Zone and the imposition of highly authoritarian workplace practices. Meanwhile, in the more complex case of Malaysia, Wad writes of the extensive writ of anti-labour laws, the increasing repressive capacity of the state and a strengthening of the security police network alongside the promotion of enterprise unionism whereby the autonomy of labour is curtailed as much by direct management ordinance as by the rhythm and pace of work.

Despite continuous worker resistance, state intervention in both Sri Lanka and Malaysia has worked effectively to curtail and contain trade union activity in the present era. Not so in Argentina where open warfare by the military against organized labour–entailing the murder and imprisonment of many thousand trade unionists–was not able, in the ultimate analysis, to overcome the mobilizing power and defensive strength of the unionized workforce. If, as Munck opines, the trade unions are seen as brokers between capital and labour (even though they do not threaten to transform the social order), then it appears that elements of an hegemonic incorporation of the union movement will remain central to the survival strategy of any civilian regime–unless a shift of capital away from Argentina over the long term allows for the restructuring of the labour market which the military's overtly fascist methods failed to accomplish. If, in turn, Nigerian unions have been able to resist neutralization and incorporation by the state, this flows as much from the latter's incapacity and fragility as their own rather limited strength.

Of the countries studied here, it is only in Iran that new industrialization has brought forth a working class which has threatened to transform production relations in the process of establishing a new social and political order. Why this should have occurred in Iran–and not in any other NIC–must in all probability be explained by reference to the specific nature of the Pahlavi state and of Iranian society in general, even if such explanation must necessarily be situated in the context of how under the Shah the economy was drawn more closely into the modernizing orbit of international capital. Whatever the case, although the Workers' Councils mounted a concerted challenge to industrial hierarchy and relations of domination/subordination in the workplace, the revolutionary regime has been able to re-impose managerial and technicist control over the shop floor principally because the workers' movement failed to evolve a viable political alternative to Islamic autocracy.

As Moghadam notes, the defeat of the worker's movement in Iran poses major questions about the response of industrial workers in the third world to a concerted accumulation strategy and the prospects for autonomous working-class organization. Such, indeed, is the central problem addressed in this book. However, an important query is raised as to whether this should be so by Rhoda Howard, who in a bold, germane and critical paper flays Marxist analysis for ignoring the issue of human rights (just as liberal analysis has ignored the role of trade unions in buttressing human rights). Distinguishing between *substantive rights* and the *right to have rights*, Howard argues that abuse of both occurs as much under socialist corporatism as under peripheral capitalism. In so doing, she challenges a wide range of assumptions which she sees as having underlain the analysis of trade unions and labour in the third world, arguing strongly against what she perceives as the irresponsibly utopian strand in much Marxist analysis (i.e. that socialism will guarantee human rights to the extent that Marxism admits that these exist) when, in practice, the evidence suggests that it is capitalism (which has less requirement for a tightly centralized state) which is more likely to provide the conditions for the existence of civil and political rights. In the African context at least, where prospects for any significant economic development are limited precisely because the continent is *not* caught up in a new international division of labour, we should not have unreal expectations of unions, whose economism should not be lamented but celebrated as embodying the perpetual struggle for basic rights.

Whether or not Marxists will agree with the manner in which their analysis has been portrayed, perhaps the most important assertion contained in Howard's paper is that, for all their many deficiencies, trade unions in third world countries are basic organizations which are absolutely necessary to defend and promote the rights of workers both materially and as humane beings. The very existence of trade unions, in other words, is rooted in struggle, and in consequence, Hyman's qualified optimism must be allowed to prevail!

Taken together, the papers in this section all reaffirm the importance of focusing upon relations between workers, unions and politics. Whatever our concern, if it be with labour, then quite simply third world trade unions – despite their weaknesses – cannot be ignored precisely because the working class in newly industrializing countries plays a disproportionate role in both the politics of production and the politics of the state. This is not, of course, to deny the importance of other socio-political movements concerned with mobilizing the poor, women, peasants or the otherwise oppressed, nor – by any means – to proclaim the primacy of trade unions in any and every situation. What it does insist upon, however, is that further advance within the field of labour studies – old or new – must be informed by recognition of the increasing centrality of the working class, and analysis of its capacity for collective organization, within the contemporary third world.

4. Capital Restructuring and Labour Recomposition Under a Military Regime: Argentina (1976–83)

Ronaldo Munck

Argentina was integrated into the international division of labour between 1890 and 1930 as a primary goods exporter.[1] This expansive cycle came to a close with the international capitalist crisis in 1929 which ushered in a period of chronic economic and political instability. This crisis led to the emergence of a nationalist movement, based largely on the trade unions, which promoted a process of industrialization. Its leader, General Perón, held office from 1946 until 1955 when he was overthrown by the armed forces. During that decade Argentina became a semi-industrialized country and the trade unions emerged as a major element in the political process. Following the overthrow of Perón in 1955, the movement which took his name (Peronism) was led by the trade unions which thus became the political as well as the economic expression of the working class.

Between 1955 and 1973 there was a succession of military and civilian governments based on opposition to Peronism. In the early 1960s a vigorous process of industrialization based on an influx of foreign capital took place. This internationalized sector of the economy can be distinguished from the state led national capitalism promoted by Perón and it lay behind a new military takeover in 1966 which attempted a corporatist strategy whose intent was to firmly wed the trade unions to international monopoly capital. This venture collapsed in the wake of a series of urban uprisings in 1969 of which the *Cordabazo* (named after the interior city of Córdoba where it occurred) was the most famous. These events, protagonised fundamentally by the working class, exacerbated contradictions between the various factions of the bourgeoisie and culminated in the military withdrawing to barracks in 1973.

When free elections were held in 1973, the Peronists triumphed in a landslide victory, but their euphoria was shortlived as General Perón died in 1974. Deprived of its populist leader the country collapsed into a state of virtual civil war between, on the one hand, the government of Isobel Perón (the General's widow) supported by the trade union leaders, and on the other, the left-wing Peronist guerrillas, the Montoneros and much of the rank and file of the labour movement. This confrontation led, amongst other things, to a general strike in 1975 which unprecedently pitted the workers against a Peronist government. The economic crisis was deepening – largely as a result of the international economic recession of 1974-5 – and the political situation was becoming untenable. Eventually, the armed forces again took power in 1976 and launched a coherent economic and political strategy designed to permanently overcome the chronic instability of the country.

The bureaucratic-authoritarian regimes which came to power in Brazil in 1964, Chile in 1973 and Argentina in 1966 and again in 1976 all had a similar underlying dynamic. In a general sense these regimes can be seen as a reaction to the crisis of hegemony in Latin America since 1930 and, more precisely, as a result of the sharpening of the class struggle on the one hand and the internationalization of capital on the other. As O'Donnell notes, this new type of state corresponded to a deepening of the productive structures of dependent capitalism.[2] In all cases it led to a closer integration of the country concerned into the international circuit of capital accumulation. The economic and political weight of the trade unions in Argentine already stood in the way of such a strategy so that their weakening was to be a key element. Likewise Peronism, which had discredited itself in 1973-6, would be further weakened by breaking its connection with the trade unions. In 1976 the needs of international capital and the dominant economic interests in Argentina itself clearly coincided. It was a question of overcoming the economic and political stalemate in Argentina between the sector of monopoly capitalism in alliance with the landed and financial interests on the one hand, and the small and medium sized industrial interests allied to the working class on the other hand. To accomplish this a far-reaching process of capital restructuring and labour recomposition was required.

The concept of *restructuring* refers to that process whereby capital seeks to overcome a crisis by restoring the conditions for expansion through structural transformations of the capital accumulation process. It is a social as much as an economic process as capital strives to impose its mode of social organization on labour. This capitalist offensive alters the composition of the working class, but labour *recomposition* cannot be reduced simply to the effects of capitalist restructuring. The resistance of the working class to capital's initiatives and the adoption of political counter-strategies also plays a role in this recomposition of the working class. We must recognize that capitalism is a social relation, which pits the working class against capital and state. Thus the class struggle can be seen as a series of cycles in which capital and labour take initiatives and counter-initiatives. The state, for its part, plays a major role in integrating labour within the parameters of capital accumulation. The capitalist crisis is therefore not simply an economic event but must be seen rather in terms of the power relations between classes being aimed essentially at re-establishing capital's mechanisms of control over the working class.[3] This chapter is thus dedicated to the study of how capital restructuring and labour recomposition occured in Argentina between 1976 and 1983, effecting a radical re-making of the Argentine working class.

Restructuring

The repression of the working class and the trade union movement after 1976 took many forms. In the weeks following the coup armed police detachments stood at the doors of offices and factories to arrest shop stewards and union activists. Army detachments marched into factories to settle disputes at the point of a bayonet. The disappearance of militants was stepped up, and the less dramatic sacking of troublemakers became a routine practice. All this must be mentioned first; but terror in itself would not have been sufficient to inflict a historic defeat on the labour movement. To do that Argentina's capitalists and new military rulers needed to restructure the economy so as to reduce the social weight of the working class. Thus it was that the monetarist policies of the military junta aimed at returning Argentina to the pre-1930 golden era based on a thriving agro-export economy with only a subsidiary industrial sector.[4] The public sector was to be reduced and uncompetitive industrial sectors would simply be allowed to sink. The main beneficiaries were to be the argrarian oligarchy and a new financial oligarchy dedicated to profiting from the de-industrializing economic system. The strong national industrialist class, which had been an important element in the Peronist alliance, was destined to disappear or at best become a minor partner in the new arrangements. In the event, these economic policies did not come to fruition but they were none the less effective in reducing the homogeneity of labour and causing considerable disorganization in the ranks of the working class.

The drastic restructuring of the labour market since the coup is best indicated by the decline in the number of workers in manufacturing from 1,030,000 in 1976 to 790,000 in 1980. The effects on the labour movement are obvious: for instance, the car workers' union, SMATA, lost 36,000 members and the textile workers' union. AOT, calculates that only 40,000 of its 120,000 members in 1976 still had work in 1980. We see in Table 1 what monentarist economic policies led to in some key industrial plants.

Table 4.1 Employment in selected firms (1976–81)

	Personnel		*Reduction*
Firm	*1976*	*1981*	
Sevel (Fiat and Peugeot merger)	6,000	2,400	60%
Mercedes Benz	4,000	3,200	20%
Dodge-Volkswagen	4,000	2,200	45%
Deutz	2,000	240	88%
Renault	8,000	5,800	27%

Source: various SMATA press statements.

In the state sector, half a million employees lost their jobs over this same period.[5]

The remodelling of the labour market severely weakened the traditional solidarity of the working class which had been based on a homogeneous labour market and strong links between the factory and the community.[6] Thousands of workers were thrown out of work to become self-employed or move to another area. In turn, this process of atomization was sharpened by a conscious policy of increasing wage differentials. The wage structure in Argentina had been traditionally homogeneous, a factor making for increased solidarity and union power. Wages for skilled workers and those in bigger firms were allowed to rise disproportionally to create an internal hierarchy within the labour force based on wage differentials of up to 75% between industrial sectors in 1978.

The restructuring of the labour market did not lead immediately to an increase in unemployment.[7] In fact the military government was keenly aware of the effects a drastic rise in unemployment could have on labour militancy. Several factors served to mark the decline in the labour force from 8 million to 7.2 million between 1974 and 1978. The approximately 800,000 people withdrawn from the labour market were made up by some 300,000 who became self-employed in the service sector, 150,000 women and youths who left waged employment and some 300,000 immigrant workers from neighbouring countries who were expelled. Thus the official unemployment rate was kept around 3-4% until 1980. By 1981, however, the government was admitting that unemployment had doubled and one report suggested that fully 40% of the economically active population was underemployed.[8] The service sector could no longer act as a refuge for those thrown out of the industrial sector and the economic recession was deepening. By 1981 there were possibly 1.5 million people unemployed (although some studies put the figure as high as 4 million). Though full employment had always been a myth, this was the first time that the Argentine labour movement had had to cope with such a level of unemployment. The divisive effects of such a large reserve army of labour were bound to test the traditional solidarity of the workers' movement.

A key condition for increasing the rate of profit in industry was the reduction of the cost of labour. The stark result of the political defeat and military repression of March 1976 was a reduction of wages by 50% within a year. Another way of looking at it is that the workers' share in the national income fell from nearly 50% in 1975 to around 30% in 1980. The economic recession meant that there was less overtime, social benefits were cut and so on. Thus the decline of real wages cannot be fully expressed even in these figures. However, the continued resistance of the working class was able to halt this decline in living standards by 1979, as we see in Table 2. Whereas wages were generally falling (and the 1980 rates were still well below 1975), labour productivity was increasing dramatically as restrictive practices were eroded. Indeed, although manufacturing product per capita fell by 11% between 1975 and 1980, productivity rose by an incredible 37%,

Table 4.2 Real industrial wage 1976–1980 (1977=100)

Year	1975	1976	1977	1978	1979	1980
Wage	175	114	100	95	114	125

Source: *Boletin Semanal de Economía* no 408, 1981, p. 2169.

for there was an increased work effort due to repression and unemployment and an introduction of new technology in key areas designed to accelerate the process of de-skilling (and hence the interchangeability of workers). The effects of this super-exploitation of labour are borne out by one report which states that the biggest industrial plant at Córdoba required 172 man-hours to produce one vehicle in 1975 whereas in 1979 it only required 90 hours; in another plant 1,300 workers had been required to produce 2,000 engines per month, whereas in 1979 half the number of workers produce twice as many engines.[9]

Having examined the social and economic effects of the military government's policies on the working class we must now turn to the junta's offensive against the trade union movement. As had happened after previous military takeovers in 1955 and 1966 the Central General de Trabajadores (CGT) was subject to intervention by the government as were some 45 unions representing 75% of the unionized working class. Amongst these were all the major unions in terms of influence or numbers: the metalworkers' (UOM), the constructions workers' (UOCRA), the bank workers' (Associación Bancaria), the textile workers' (AOT) and the car workers' (SMATA) unions. These organizations had effectively structured the organized labour movement since the 1940s. In addition, the military government took further legislative measures to reduce the power of the trade union movement as a whole:

Law 21,356 (July 1976) suspended all trade union activity, banned assemblies, conferences, meetings and elections; the Ministry of Labour was now empowered to replace shop stewards and *comisiones internas*;

Law 21,400 (December 1976) concerning Industrial Security banned any concerted measure of direct action, go-slows (*Trabajo a desgano*, literally sad working), with striking workers being brought under military jurisdiction.

Law 21,297 (December 1976) anulled most of the measures favourable to workers existing in the previous labour contract law: the onus of proof was hereafter on the worker in any dispute. Workers could now be dismissed before guilt was proved by a tribunal.

Law 21,576 (December 1976) changed the collective bargaining conventions so that special pay structures, holidays, union participation on tribunal and other advances were cancelled; all previous declarations regarding unhealthy work conditions were declared subject to revision.

Law 22,269 (August 1980) withdraw from trade union jurisdiction all social services including clinics, rest homes and so on.

This battery of repressive legislation was unprecedented in Argentina's labour history and its effects were considerable.[10] It deprived the unions of all their basic functions; the social services law (22,269) broke the link between union and basic welfare rights and greatly weakened the economic power of unions; and many of the historical conquests of the working class were anulled at a stroke. For the conservative newspaper *La Nación* these measures were designed to put an end to 'the economic and political power with which the trade unions had overpowered the state and the political parties for more than two decades'. If ostensibly the aim of the government was to democratize and depoliticize the unions, in reality it aimed at fragmenting the basic organizations of the working class in order to further disperse the labour movement.

If the trade unions as institutions were severely attacked, so too were the grassroots of the labour movement in the factories. Where the trade union structures were concerned the military government was careful not to jeopardize the role of the leadership completely. Their role was merely suspended and taken over by military overseers who, it was intended, would hand back the unions in due course to a suitably chastened bureaucracy. But when tackling the real or grassroots labour movement in the workplace the military rulers were far less ambiguous in their mission. Hence the new Law of Professional Associations finally approved in 1979 after some hesitation decreed a number of measures in this respect:

i) the number of shop stewards was reduced to 1 per 100 workers instead of 1 per 50 as previously;

ii) to be eligible to serve as a shop steward, candidates had to have worked for four years in the plant and have no police record;

iii) the Ministry of Labour was empowered to intervene in union recognition, negotiations, and union finances at a local level;

iv) branch meetings were to be able to discuss items only on a pre-approved agenda, and there were now to be no speeches or debates, nor were they to engage in politics;

v) the closed shop system was abolished.

All these measures were directed at destroying the element of workers' power at the factory level established during the first Peronist period and revived during 1973-6. The main targets were the *comisiónes internas* and the democratically elected union representatives. Many of these were simply killed in the so-called dirty war waged against the people by the armed forces after 1976. (The civilian government which came to power in 1983 launched the Sabato Commission which found that the majority of the 10,000 victims had not been connected with subversive organizations). Others were sacked by the internal factory security services, and others simply resigned given the very real climate of terror. The result was that a major factory such as the General Motors plant in Buenos Aires only had one union representative (*delgado de empresa*) for every 2,000 workers in

1979. A visiting trade union delegation found that 'at Ford in Córdoba the number of shop stewards was lowered from 300 to six, depriving workers in the plant of any effective means of communication.'[11] In other plants, such as Mercedes Benz and the Deutz tractor works, a shop steward structure was the exception rather than the rule, and this lack of a generalized organic union structure at the factory level greatly impeded working-class resistance in the years following the coup. It is well to remember, when the military justified its repression in terms of a guerrilla campaign, that out of 15,000 prisoners in Argentina's jails in 1978, fully 5,000 were workers and trade union activists; and that of those killed during the dirty war between 1976 and 1978, nearly one-third were workers and union activists.[12]

Labour Resistance (1976–1978)

Though the labour movement did not mobilize to defend the government of Isabel Perón, there was a widely felt need to confront the offensive of the military dictatorship. At the Renault plant in Córdoba there was a strike on 24 March, the very day of the coup, and the metal workers of Buenos Aires launched strikes in various plants around the city. These first actions against the regime were of great importance because they laid the basis for the accumulation of forces and a concerted fightback campaign in the months that followed. Despite the repression unleashed by the government the working class was able to organize strikes, go-slows, lightning stoppages and various ingenious forms of sabotage. At the IKA–Renault plant in Córdoba production dropped off from 40 to 14 units a day in June 1976 and the government administrator declared that 'obviously this was caused by industrial sabotage'. One of the most persistent and effective forms of labour protest was the so-called 'sad working' (*trabajo a tristeza*) which was a widespread form of passive resistance. The Montoneros somewhat rashly called for a 'CGT in the Resistance' to replace the body suspended by the government and to help co-ordinate these struggles. This proposal, as they themselves later admitted 'was incorrect, because it proposed a totally clandestine structure, forcing legal non intervened structures to go underground, thus ceding, gratuitously, spaces of legality'.[13] Nor could this type of vanguardist movement mobilize the millions of Argentine workers and it rapidly became a propaganda front which did not really impinge on the life of the masses. After this attempt energy was focused on recovering the trade unions from their military overseers as in the 1956-8 period.

The early strike movements were largely defensive, designed to ward off government attacks on strategic sectors which had in the previous period been in the forefront of labour struggles. One of these was the car industry which in the course of 1976 was marked by partial stoppages in the Fiat, Renault and Ford plants which by September had been generalized across the industry. Repression against car workers was severe. Early in 1977 six workers were kidnapped from the Mercedes Benz works and only one re-appeared in spite of the protest by the workers. A strike at the Renault plant in Córdoba in October 1977 led to an intervention by the armed forces to restore order resulting in 75 arrests and 175 dismissals. In June 1978 a paramilitary group entered the Deutz factory and took away busts of Perón and Evita to intimidate the workers who were in dispute with management over wages; the *comisión interna* called a general meeting and a half-hour protest strike was called. Another form of repression was the dramatic increase in the level of exploitation in the plants. A report from Ford's notes how the already rapid pace of production on the line was accelerated, the working day was extended from eight to nine hours (ten for the late shift) and that those who did not accept the new working practices were summarily dismissed.[14] The true significance of the coup was becoming brutally clear: it has little to do with fighting corruption and a lot to do with implementing conditions which would favour a super-exploitation of workers and the virtual destruction of the organized labour movement.

With the most combative unions taken over by the military government, some previously less militant unions came to the fore. One of these was that of the electricity company workers (organized in Luz y Fuerza) which faced a general revision of working arrangements, including an increase in the shift from six to eight hours. In October 1976 they launched a go-slow and a series of partial stoppages in defence of their rights; they were to continue for six months. The workers engaged in widespread sabotage actions and when their general secretary, Oscar Smith, disappeared they mounted an unprecedented march on the Ministry of Labour.

Though the power workers' struggle was defeated, it none the less served as the starting point for a general process of re-activation within the union movement. This culminated in October 1977 with a rail strike in Buenos Aires which spread to the underground workers and saw the power workers out again. At the same time as the first power strikes, the port workers of Buenos Aires began a work to rule over wages and conditions which seriously hindered the grain export drives. In June 1978 another port workers strike began in Buenos Aires which rapidly spread to other ports throughout the country calling for extra pay for overtime. Unlike a defeat of the port workers in 1966 which led to widespread demoralization, this dispute transmitted a spirit of resistance to the whole labour movement. However, during the remaining months of 1978 there was a downturn in labour struggles, albeit marked by some highpoints such as the national rail workers' strike in November which not only achieved its economic demands but succeeded in securing the freedom of the union leaders detained by the Junta.

We must now attempt a systematic analysis of the causes of strikes, the sectors involved and the forms of struggle during this period. Based on the data in the Appendix (which understates by around one-third the number of disputes because of its reliance on the press but which is nevertheless reliable for trends) we can draw several conclusions. In 1976, 1977 and

1978, wage demands constituted 60%, 87% and 65% of all disputes. Clearly there were no anti-bureaucratic struggles as in 1969-76, and where working conditions were at issue (10% of disputes in 1978) these generally concerned the defence of previous gains rather than a demand for new concessions. In short, the struggles of labour in this period were purely defensive. In 1976 80% of all disputes occured in the manufacturing sector but this declined sharply to 44% and 48% in the two following years, whereas the services sector *increased* its share in disputes from 15% to 49% and 53% between 1976 and 1978. In terms of the number of workers involved we find that the transport sector alone accounted for three-quarters of all disputes in 1978. This reflects the serious state offensive against the transport sector after the industrial working class had been forced to retreat after the confrontations of 1976. As to the forms of struggle, nearly half of all disputes took the form of stoppages and a quarter were work to rules (*quite de colaboración*). On the other hand there was only one factory seizure in the whole three years and just nine public demonstrations. This again goes to show that the whole tenor of labour activity in this period was defensive.

Data on the result of strikes is very difficult to obtain. However, a survey of 174 major disputes between March 1976 and March 1981 found that in 61 workers' demands were fully met, 54 saw workers' demands partially met and in 59 they were completely rejected.[15] This means that over the whole five years an almost equal number of disputes were won and lost by workers, not counting a further third in which negotiations led to some advance. In the context this was a considerable achievement. However, when we consider that the vast majority of all disputes during this period were called at plant level, with very few regional, national or solidarity strikes, the dominant tone is of dispersed, isolated struggles. The labour movement had lost its cohesiveness and its mass mobilizing power based on its centralized structure. It had not, however, lost it totally and the junta was unsuccessful in its bid to use widening wage differentials as a source of disunity. The extent of strikes in the metallurgical and mechanical sectors, and the lead given by the highly skilled workers in many disputes, shows that no labour aristocracy was created by the new policies. A confirmation of this tendency is given by the fact (see Appendix) that between one-third and half of all disputes occurred in the largest and leading industrial establishments (where pay was usually higher than average). Our conclusion can only be that the drive by the junta to atomize the labour movement was at most partially successful. The trade unions maintained a residual element of mobilizing power and developed a vigorous – though defensive and dispersed – resistance to the government's austerity policies and naked repression.[16]

One of the most remarkable features of this period was the emergence of a new rank and file leadership in the factories. It is estimated that of the 100,000 shop stewards present in Argentine industry in 1976 fully 10,000 were killed or imprisoned by the regime. After the coup it was not surprising then that most struggles were not led by an organic plant leadership. Instead, previously unknown people were elected unofficially as provisional union delegates; they took turns in leading negotiations with management. Given the weakness of the *comisiones internas* this new semi-spontaneous leadership structure came to play an important role in more than half of all disputes after 1976. Sometimes this leadership was recognized by the firm and in some cases the unions concerned would declare a dispute official. In most cases however they remained a fluid, somewhat amorphous presence in the plants. One newspaper report in 1977 expressed a general concern with this phenomenon when it noted that though the industrial guerrilla had been rooted out in most plants since March 1976, 'in many firms it has been discovered that the true thinking and organising agents of trade unions activity did not appear on the list of union delegates.'[17] This concern even took the ludicrous form of military detachments entering factories in dispute and demanding that management allow union representatives to negotiate freely. Once again the reserves of combativity and the dense supportive social networks of the labour movement had allowed at least a partial recovery from what was after all the worst defeat in its history.[18]

As for the trade union bureaucracy, there was a split after 1976 reflecting previous divisions in the mid-1960s between openly collaborationist and supposedly hard sectors. The so-called Group of 25 followed the *verticalista* line of the last Peronist government based on a strict hierarchy within the Peronist movement– its main strength lay in the smaller unions not subject to intervention by the government. A second federation, the *Comisión Nacional de Trabajo* (National Labour Commission), based on many of the larger unions under military overseers such as the textile workers', metal workers', construction workers' and power workers' unions, concentrated on putting forward a more professional image along US business unionism lines. The Minister of Labour distinguished between one sector which defended the interest of workers through 'an appropriate dialogue with the different productive sectors . . . and belief that dialogue and participation is most appropriate' whereas others, less to his liking, 'believe that it is appropriate to carry out the defence [of workers' interests] through "days of protest" or direct action methods.'[19] It was this body, more attuned to the international labour federations, which usually represented Argentina at the tripartite (state, business, labour) meetings of the International Labour Organization (ILO). With much of the national field of action closed to the trade union leaders they took an unprecedented interest in the annual ILO delegation, which provided an international platform. At home they were constantly competing for the favours of the government, the hard line merely going about it in different ways. This division within the organized labour movement was undoubtedly a source of weakness and some unions, such as the metal workers' UOM, split over the claims of the rival federations. The rail workers' union *La Fraternidad* took a more principled line emphasizing 'its efforts to unify the labour movement without participating in any sector'.[20] It would take several more years before the pressure from the rank and file would lead to a process of re-unification of the CGT.

Labour Recovery (1979-1980)

After the downturn of labour struggles in 1978 a new phase of recovery in 1979 culminated with the first general strike against the military dictatorship on 27 April. In March 1979 a series of disputes in Córdoba brought that city to the brink of the kind of struggles it had known ten years previously. Workers at the State Mechanical Industries (IME) run by the Ministry of Defence began a series of stoppages in support of wage demands. The authorities decided to apply the redundancy law and dismissed 50 workers and the Labour Ministry applied the new Security Law. This dispute spread to the car parts manufacturer Thompson Ramco and to 6,000 workers in four Renault plants. At the Renault works the demand was for a 50% wage increase timed to coincide with a visit from the managing director of the French parent company. After a hundred workers were sacked negotiations began with the military overseers of SMATA, the motor mechanics' union, and the dispute was settled favourably for the workers. This example led to a series of strikes in Buenos Aires metal-working plants such as Santa Rosa, Centenera and Decker. A business review made the following worried comment after the events:

> The chieftains of the labour movement . . . are out of touch with popular demands and the prospects for continued labour peace are going to be complicated by a series of shop floor strikes. For all its defects, union bureaucracy acted in the past as a shock absorber, and this is not possible at the moment.[21]

Indeed there was a real prospect that union leaders would be brushed aside by shop-floor members because of their failure to secure wage increases, and militant action was seen to be the only way forward.

It was partly as a result of these pressures that the union leaders called for a National Day of Protest on 27 April 1979. The stoppage was called for by one of the union fronts, the Group of 25, in protest at the government's economic policies and for the release of imprisoned trade unionists. Given the fact that only one of the federations called the strike, the approximately 30% turnout was quite respectable, and in the circumstances the other federation, the CNT, lost ground because many of its member unions supported the strike. The unions had effectively re-established their role in national politics and at grassroots level the stoppage created an increased level of self-confidence.

In the months which followed some disputes (such as that of the Peugot plant) were successful; others were hard and long (over a month at the Santa Rosa metallurgical plant) and there was even a workplace occupation (ITT). The crucial links between unions and the community were being re-established and the unions' structures themselves were being rebuilt. This movement of recovery culminated in October 1979. The Ministry of Labour even began issuing a daily bulletin on the strike movement and was at pains to stress that it arose from a misinterpretation of the new wage guidelines and not subversion. Many disputes were solved by ministerial intervention, as a snowball effect could have led to a general strike. As it was, the last week of October saw 17 concurrent disputes involving nearly 10,000 workers. In these circumstances the Secretary of Finance, Juan Alemann declared openly that union power in Argentina was too strong and that the government's economic policy was designed explicitly to weaken it.[22] Considering that strikes were still illegal this upsurge of labour activity was most significant.

In several ways October 1979 represents a turning point in the pattern of strikes. Essentially, from now on struggles against the effects of the economic recession–factory closures, lay-offs and so on–were to achieve more prominence. In the 12 months before October 1979, nearly 80% of all conflicts were about wage demands and only 9% were related to the recession.[23] By contrast, in the 12 months after October 1979, the disputes over wages had fallen to 40% and those concerned with the effects of the recession had risen to 44%. Another way of describing this trend is to note that whereas in the earlier period the large and leading firms had accounted for nearly 45% of all disputes, this proportion had fallen to 30% in the second period; this appears to indicate that those firms squeezed by the capital concentration process implicit in the recession were becoming more strike prone. This change in the rhythm of strike activity was also reflected in the type of unions in the forefront of labour struggles. In the first years after the coup those unions which were previously in a strong economic position–such as the metal workers' UOM and the power workers Luz y Fuerza–were in the forefront of the struggle. Later it was unions such as the car mechanics' SMATA, operating in a sector which was hard hit by the recession, which came to the forefront, playing a key role in the 27 April general strike and the massive mobilizations of labour in subsequent months. New sectors also came to the forefront in 1980 such as the bank workers who carried out several combative stoppages at regional levels obtaining important economic concessions.

In the course of 1980 there were several important disputes. In June there was a national seamen's strike to protest against new laws allowing foreigners not resident in the country to serve on Argentine ships. The strike was organized by unofficial struggle committees (*comisiones de lucha*) bringing together the various trades involved. The Admiral in charge of the Secretariat of Maritime Interests pointed out that 'the legitimate union leaders had neither declared nor led the strike, and they had shown themselves to be impotent to control the activities they were supposed to be in charge of.'[24] The union leaders meekly responded that the strike was 'a spontaneous reaction by the workers'. The strike marked a new level of autonomous working-class organization. In July, a major rail strike was led by a coordinating committee of the various unions involved, train drivers, signallers, guards, and the 'intervened' union of unskilled rail workers. Demands centred around the closure of railway workshops as well as wage increases. The government remained intransigent but as one contemporary account noted: 'this is the fourth railway strike in four years of military government and [it is the fact that] the railway workers' union is intervened which makes the spontaneous activity the more surprising.'[25] It is also significant that the seamen's and railway workers' (also the taxi drivers' and cinema operators') disputes were not led officially by the union but by local rank and file committees. In a way the militant tactics of *clasismo* were being adopted, more because of official union inactivity than through choice.

Another area of disputes in 1980 was the fight against lay offs and sackings in many car, mechanical and textile factories. Though these produced worker protests there was little response from the union hierarchy and each group tended to act alone. The closure of General Motors and Citroen affected other related industries and it appeared that the crisis would spread to Villa Constitución, epicentre of the 1975 struggles. In Córdoba there were uninterrupted dismissals in Fiat controlled companies and one business magazine speculated on the possibility of a repeat of the *Cordobazo* 'which will shatter ideas about general tranquility that have been gaining ground lately'.[26] These disputes came to a head in November when the Deutz tractor company announced that it was to cease production. The 800 workers at the plant held a meeting and decided to occupy the factory as a reaction to the first 100 sackings. The car workers' union SMATA declared a state of alert in defence of its members' jobs and in solidarity with the Deutz workers. The company rapidly re-instated the 100 workers and pledged to negotiate over the proposed closure. At the same time the workers at the Inort chemical laboratories started a go-slow to force management to discuss poor working conditions. Four years of frozen collective bargaining had left a vast area of accumulated grievances over safety, hygiene, lighting and hours worked.

Using the data in the Appendix we can now draw some general conclusions about the strikes in 1979 and 1980. We find that stoppages in the manufacturing sector increase in importance once again, representing 71% and 66% of all disputes in 1979 and 1980, whereas the service sector share declines from over half to 27% in 1979 and 29% in 1980. Wages are still the main cause in three-quarters of all disputes in 1979, but as we have already mentioned this proportion declines to one-third in 1980, whereas recession related disputes rise from 11% to 50% over the same period. The stoppage is still the main form of struggle in over half of all disputes, but we see a dramatic increase in the number of assemblies and petitions and even a handful of workplace occupations. Sabotage on the other hand practically disappears. It would seem that strikes were becoming more structured and organic as a certain level of organization and confidence was recovered. This is confirmed by the level at which disputes originated: whereas previously there were few regional stoppages and virtually no sympathy strikes, in 1979-80 there were at least 44 strikes called by regional union bodies and 56 major sympathy strikes. Though the facts are hard to come by it seems that many strikes were being won in this period, though this masks the fact that many, if not most, struggles over the effects of the recession were unsuccessful. This should lead us to a qualified picture of a certain recovery by labour but with a growing number of struggles occuring on the unfavourable terrain set by economic recession and growing unemployment. The closure of the State Mechanical Industries (IME) in Córdoba in April 1980 without a major union response was a clear example of this.

During the course of this period the question of the trade union bureaucracy became an important issue again. Time and again the employers lamented the lack of a representative interlocutor (*interlocutor válido*) for labour. We have mentioned several strikes above in which observers lamented the lack of a regular union structure. By mid-1980 this pressure had become severe and one economic journal said that 'the government, by depriving union leaders of room for manoeuvre, are leaving a vacuum that may be filled by moderates today, but by someone quite different tomorrow.'[27] A visiting delegation of the AFL–CIO had earlier concluded that the 'junta's subversive paranoia is misplaced in the strongly anti-communist CGT'.[28] As the trade union federations began regrouping in 1979, one of their statements pointed out that if the government did not normalize union affairs rapidly, 'alien structures' would grow within the movement which would be much more difficult to control.[29] True enough, another source of pressure towards normalization came from the rank and file, for there were numerous incidents in these years where workers called on, and obtained the solidarity of local union leaders, even in cases where there had been bitter anti-bureaucratic struggles under the previous Peronist administration. There were, in short, pressures from all directions – if for different reasons – for a restoration of normal trade union structures. The government, however, had not yet decided to accept defeat of its bid to virtually decapitate the union structures and prohibit the operation of a central union confederation.

Meanwhile, the trade union hierarchy also made a degree of progress towards unification in this period. In September the CNT and Group of 25 mentioned above came together to form the *Conducción Unica de Trabajadores Argentinos* (United Leadership of the Argentine Workers) which, although illegal, began in a limited fashion to play the role of the old CGT, (although an independent sector, the Group of 20, remained on the sidelines composed of a heterogeneous group of unions such as *La Fraternidad* and the collaborationist *participacionista* current). However, this unity was short-lived, and after several permutations, a rump CGT was formed by the end of 1980 as the 'big battalions' (such as the metal workers' UOM) began playing a more prominent role, displacing the smaller and marginal unions which had played a disproportionate role until 1979 because of the anomalous legal situation.

Labour Offensive (1981–1983)

By 1981 the recovery of the labour movement had become consolidated to such an extent that we can realistically speak of a labour offensive from then on. Now it was the military regime which was on the defensive (as was the labour movement during the difficult period of 1976–8). In early 1981, strikes and go-slows spread with unheard of frequency in spite of the junta's anti-strike laws, as one firm after another laid off workers or simply closed down. In March the workers at the Borgward clutch factory in Buenos Aires occupied the plant for 12 days until a court order forced them to leave; the strike then continued until the police dispersed the picket lines. The bank and insurance company workers also launched a battle plan against the new regulations dropping job security, involving go-slows and lightning strikes. The union also accused the Economy Minister, Martínez de Hoz, of corrupt banking deals and fraudulent bank closures.[30] The economic struggle of workers was now being extended to a general offensive against the dictatorship and its economic policies in particular. In April the new Labour Minister, General Porcile, promised to seek social peace and an agreement between capital and labour. This all reflected a new climate in which indiscriminate repression was no longer viable and workers frequently resorted to wild-cat strikes and factory seizures. Around this same time internal union elections were allowed for the first time, in the first instance for five small unions; but in the next two years normalization of union affairs accelerated. By mid-1983 the government was forced to repeal law 21,400, thus restoring the right to strike, and ended military control over the key car workers' union SMATA and eventually reformed the Law of Professional Associations to allow the formation of third level union organizations, i.e. confederations such as the CGT.

In July 1981 the car workers' union SMATA called a 12-hour national strike to protest against the growing rundown of the industry and in support of Mercedes Benz workers' fight against redundancies. In the course of the strike the union leaders and more than 1,000 workers who were meeting at the union headquarters were arrested and a strong police contingent blocked the march of car workers coming from the industrial suburb of Avellaneda towards the capital. This street mobilization of a key sector of the working class had a deep impact on the whole labour movement. The pressure from this action and other strikes at Borgward again, the Celulosa Argentina plant and others led towards a general strike on 22 July 1981. One union federation denounced the strike call and demanded instead a social truce. In the circumstances many reports suggested the strike was a failure when important sectors such as the rail workers did not heed the strike call. However, participation in the strike was solid in the industrial belt around Buenos Aires with absenteeism in some sectors, such as engineering and the paper industry, surpassing 50%. In the provinces the response was more patchy but there was more support in Córdoba, Mendoza, Santa Fé and Tucumán than during the previous national stoppage on 27 April 1979.[31] The level of organization was stronger with labour activists mounting strike pickets, distributing leaflets and in parts using miguelitos (bent nails) to stop traffic. In spite of the division in the trade union leadership over two million workers demonstrated their rejection of an economic policy which was leading to daily factory closures and lay-offs.

1982 was of course the year of the Malvinas war which represents a watershed in Argentina's recent political history.[32] Even as the military adventure was starting the labour movement was challenging the dictatorship with a major demonstration of 30 March 1982. It seemed at first that the protest would be called off because of the impending confrontation but the labour leader declared that 'the role of the people cannot be subordinated on the sole grounds of defending national sovereignty.'[33] In the circumstances the union demonstrators met with police repression in the course of which 400 arrests were made and in Córdoba four people were seriously wounded when the police opened fire. During the war the unions supported the recovery of the Malvinas Islands and repudiated the attack by British imperialism, even though they did not go as far as the political parties did in actually supporting the junta. In tours abroad the union leaders were at pains to distance themselves from the dictatorship and its military adventure which was designed to distract attention from the growing labour unrest in the country. In fact, after the war, there was a concerted drive to obtain higher wages to meet the rising cost of living. In August when the railway workers', transport workers' and seamen's unions all threatened industrial action the new Labour Minister, Héctor Villaveiran, took the side of the unions arguing their case in cabinet meetings. The defeat of Argentina's armed forces in the South Atlantic had given a boost to the labour movement and seriously weakened the cohesion of the regime.

In the course of 1982 'normalizing committees' were established for many unions to manage the transition back to normal democratic procedures. This of course was a concession to the labour bureaucracy, which was again necessary as a stabilizing element, as it had been during the 'decompression' of 1972. But, as a General Nicolaides declared, the military government 'could reconsider recognising the CGT and study the question of the [CGT's] social services, but there can be no movement on the rule of one union delegate per 100 workers'.[34] Even so, there were a series of shop floor elections during this period which helped re-establish the *comisiones internas*. Union delegates were elected in the railways, for Buenos Aires municipal workers, in the banks and above all in the metallurgical plants. Normalization was in many cases overflowing official channels and regulations, as the rank and file made a leap forward in factory-floor organization. This pressure from below led inexorably towards a new general strike which a united union leadership called for 6 December 1982, partly to defuse the groundswell of protest. The one-day strike was highly successful being joined this time by the independent unions such as the rail workers', bus drivers' and railway workers' which had remained aloof in the July 1981 general strike. On 16 December 1982 the opposition parties organized another protest march in which the workers' movement was clearly the main force involved. As Alberto Piccinini, a leader of the 1975 Villa Constitución strike recently released from jail proclaimed: 'the climate has changed dramatically. There is a real resurgence of a determination to join in activity, to act.'[35]

This resurgence went wider than the ranks of organized labour. There were mobilizations of small farmers in many areas, not to mention the agricultural workers; there were popular movements against the increase in municipal rates; the Mothers of Plaza de Mayo received increased popular support for their denunciation of disappearances; even the police force kept to barracks in Buenos Aires in a protest over wages. An important strike early in 1983 which showed a new pattern was the three week stoppage at the Volkswagen plant near Buenos Aires. Led by young left-wing activists the strikers obtained massive support from the neighbourhood and showed total determination. The upsurge of activity came to a head with a new general strike on 28 March 1983 which was successful in spite of being declared illegal by the government: even the Ministry of the Interior spoke later of an 85% effectiveness. Two days later a mass rally was called and several newspaper reports commented on the presence of a far left contingent which came close to matching the organized columns of the official trade union movement.[36] This turn to the left was also reflected in the trade unions. The MAS (*Movimento al Socialismo*) had become active in the car workers' union SMATA and with building and transport workers. The Trotskyist-oriented Partido Obrero re-established a presence in the metal workers' union UOM, with journalists and teachers, and also played a prominent role in the 1983 Volkswagen dispute. However, the Communist Party was by far the most successful in breaking out of the intellectual world, establishing a significant role in the UOM, the port, railway, bank and state employees' unions, not to mention its control over approximately one-fifth of the union delegates in the staunchly Peronist power workers' union *Luz y Fuerza*.[37] The time now appeared to be ripe, as some labour activists suggested, for the left to strive not only for union democratization but to build class struggle tendencies which could actually assume the leadership of unions and change their policies and form of operating.[38] This was particularly the case because there had been a serious split between the top level and middle level union leadership (especially in the provinces) since 1976 which could be to the advantage of a new combative union movement.

The trade union leadership went through further splits and re-alignments during this period. By the beginning of 1983, one sector known as CGT–RA (*República Argentina*) had brought together the ostensibly hard-line Peronist CGT–Brasil led by Saul Ubaldini and most of the non-aligned unions. A smaller sector, CGT–Azopardo followed a more conciliatory line, although it too was forced to take militant action in this phase to protect its credibility. The military government had favoured the Azopardo group but towards the end of 1982 turned more towards the CGT–RA and particularly Lorenzo Miguel, leader of the 62 Organizations and effectively the 'king-maker' in the Peronist movement. There was even considerable speculation in 1983 that sectors of the armed forces were proposing a new military–labour alliance to Miguel. However, the terms of the military withdrawal to barracks were increasingly set by the mass movement after the defeat of the regime in the Malvinas adventure. The union leaders, although they emerged as a credible political force once again during this period, had their terms of reference also set by the mobilization of the masses. The freezing of most anti-bureaucratic struggles for around seven years did not mean that the issue of union democracy was resolved. In the new democratic political period which opens up the vitality of the rank and file, organizations will mentally seek a democratic renewal of their trade unions. The recent establishment of 'co-ordinating commissions' outside official union structures points to a resurgence of the type of bodies which emerged after the 1975 general strike. The union bureaucracy has not yet realized to what extent a new generation of trade unionists has emerged who have had to defend wages and conditions with no help from a national organization. As one report states,

> The real trade union power at present is in the hands of factory delegates, and local coordinating committees. No one speaks for them, or can claim to represent them, at national level. Yet they may well determine the future shape of Argentine trade unionism, and of the Peronist movement itself.[39]

The general elections of October 1983 saw the unexpected victory of the middle class Radicals over the Peronists. Wide sections of the working class voted for the Radicals in protest at the undemocratic practices of the Peronists within the trade unions and in favour of a clean break with the military regime. The labour movement remained on the offensive until the very eve of the traditional Christmas bonus (*aguinaldo*). After the Radical victory there was an eruption of the demands which had accumulated under the dictatorship. In the first place, there were a series of struggles to regain lost purchasing power with claims for 50% and even 100% wage rises. Many strikes also reflected concern over working conditions; we must remember the sharp rationalization bid carried out under the military regime which had flouted health and safety laws and regulations on working hours. Finally, there were many disputes over job losses and fights against further redundancies and for the re-employment of those dismissed under the old regime. As Delich predicted,

> After the deluge there will be neither a new working class or new trade unions. There will be a new contract and new forms of action. But the fresh and bitter memory of these years will persist, years which no one who lived through them will be able to forget.[40]

A major election promise of the Radicals was the democratization of the trade unions, which helped gather support from wide sections of the left and the more radical currents within the unions. These illusions were soon dispelled, however, once President Alfonsín assumed office. In fact, his real motive emerged in a speech made shortly after the election: 'the worker has a right to his political beliefs; what he has not a right to is to put his union at the service of a political party' (i.e. Peronism). The related aim of trade union pluralism was designed to break the established link between the unions and the Peronist movement. In fact, the CGT was re-unified in January 1984 and mounted a strong campaign against the proposed law of trade union reorganization. Eventually, the project was dropped, seemingly after the trade union leadership came to an understanding over the International Monetary Fund imposed austerity plan. Within the factories (notably at Ford and Volkswagen), the radical currents had won internal union elections. When these were disallowed by the government, the real aims of the Radicals were becoming clearer: simply to win a space for their supporters in the union, and not to encourage a class struggle tendency. The new government did not keep its promise to re-activate the party commissions (*comisiones paritarias*) which regulate wages, on the basis of free collective bargaining, making it clear instead that productivity bargaining would apply. Having survived nearly seven years of fierce military dictatorship, in spite of grievous losses the labour movement took the offensive in the new democratic interlude.

It should not be concluded from the above account that the working class in Argentina simply advanced inexorably against the military regime. What is being questioned however is an interpretation of the 1976-83 period which ascribes the decline of the regime to its own internal contradictions. The workers hardly constituted a threat to the new regime until at least 1979; but the fundamental point is that they were not defeated. An historic defeat of the working class would have almost certainly allowed the military to consolidate its power. As it was, the military steadily lost allies and became isolated, whereas the trade union movement gradually recovered its legality and helped structure a broad opposition movement. The political parties emerged again after 1980 precisely because political space had been won for them by the struggles of the working class. This is not meant to minimize the political defeat inflicted on the working class in 1976, a defeat from which the political side of the Peronist movement seems unlikely to recover. Nor does it alter the severe impact which the government's economic policies had on the working class, which was dispersed socially and geographically, and lost much of its economic bargaining power.

The trade union question was indeed a central one for the post-1976 military governments. Like monetarists elsewhere, they believed that trade unions exercised an undue monopoly over the labour market. The deregulation of the factors of production entailed a systematic dismantling of the trade union structures. In economic terms this was largely successful, with the withdrawal of the social works from trade union control representing a severe blow to their corporative weight. Yet ever since 1955 the trade unions in Argentina had also been the key vehicle of working-class political expression. This could be less easily quelled by military power. Effectively, the political identity of the working class remained strong and was reconstituted in the factories and working class neighbourhoods progressively after 1976. The trade unions are generally seen as brokers between labour and capital, expressing class divisions but not threatening them. This is true in Argentina, as elsewhere; but they also represent one political pole in the country's political alignments (the other being the armed forces). Between 1976 and 1983 the military, the monetarists and their international backers, could not withstand the alliance mounted by the trade unions which articulated the political aspirations of the vast majority of the population. The international economic recession of 1980-82 led to a depression in Argentina and thus created the conditions for the success of this broad alliance which led to the return of civilian rule in 1983.

Notes

1. For an introduction to Argentina's economic history see A. Ferrer, *The Argentine Economy* (University of California Press, Berkeley, 1967).
2. G. O'Donnell, 'Reflections on the Pattern of Change in the Bureaucratic Authoritarian State', *Latin American Research Review,* vol. XIII, no. 1, 1979, p.6.
3. This approach is developed by H. Cleaver, *Reading Capital Politically* (Harvester Press, Brighton, 1979).
4. On the economic policy of the military government see A. Ferrer, *Nacionalismo y Orden Constitucional* (Fondo de Cultura Económica México, 1981) and G. Hillcoat, *Notas sobre la evolución reciente del capitalismo. El programa económico del regimen militar, 1976–1980* (CIAL, Université de Paris VIII, Paris, 1981).
5. On changes in the labour market after 1976 see L. Beccaría, 'El mercado de trabajo urbano en Argentina 1975–1978' *Desarrollo Económico*, vol. 20, no. 78, 1980.
6. This interpretation is developed in G. Almeyra, 'La clase obrera en la Argentina actual', *Coyoacán*, no. 9, 1980, pp. 87–113.
7. On unemployment see Sanchez, C. Ferrero, F. and Schultness, W. (1979) Empleo, desempleo y tamañio de la fuerza laboral en el mercado de trabajo urbano de la Argentina. *Desarrollo Económico* Vol. 19, no. 73.
8. Report cited in *Buenos Aires Herald*, 2 July 1981.
9. Report cited in *Somos*, 9 May 1979.
10. For a discussion on the effects of the new labour legislation see B. Galitelli and A. Thompson, 'La Situación Laboral en la Argentina del 'Proceso', 1976-1981', in B. Galitelli and A. Thompson (eds), *Sindicalismo y Regimenes Militares* (1982) p.182 and F. Delich, (Después del Diluvio, la Clase Obrera, in A. Rouquié (ed.), *Argentina, Hoy* Siglo XXI, Mexico, 1982), pp. 129–50.
11. M. Boggs and A. McLellan, 'Argentine Trade Unions', *AFL–CIO Free*

Trade Union News, no. 33, 1978, p.16.

12. Vance Report, cited in B. Galitelli and A. Thompson 'La Situación Laboral en la Argentina' (1982) p.153.
13. G. Chavez, 'Movimiento obrero-consecuencias del plan económico', *Vencer*, no. 6, 1981, p.9.
14. Política Obrera leaflet, cited in Latin American Bureau, *Unity is Strength: Trade Unions in Latin America: The Case for Solidarity*, London, (Latin American Bureau, London, 1980) p.44.
15. R. Falcón, 'Conflicto Social y Regimen Militar. La Resistencia Obrera en Argentina (Marzo 1976–Marzo 1981)', in B. Galitelli and A. Thompson (eds), *Sindicalismo y Regimenes Militares en Argentina y Chile.* (CEDLA, Amsterdam, 1982) p.132.
16. N. Liffschitz, (Luttes Ouvriers et Repression), *Tricontinental*, New Series No. 2, 1981, pp. 90–100.
17. *Somos,* 27 May 1977.
18. For a development of this theme see J. Petras, 'Terror and the Hydra: The Resurgence of the Argentine Working Class', in J. Petras (ed.), *Class, State and Power in the Third World*, Zed Press, London 1981, pp. 255–64.
19. *La Prensa*, 7 July 1981, p.4.
20. *The Review of the River Plate,* 11 April 1979, p.492.
21. Ibid., 11 April 1979, p.492.
22. *La Prensa,* 23 October 1979, p.3.
23. From data in *Vencer*, no. 6 1981, p.7.
24. *The Review of the River Plate*, 18 June 1980, p.887.
25. Ibid., 18 July 1980, p.96.
26. Ibid., 8 August 1980, p.206.
27. Ibid., 11 June 1980, p.835.
28. Boggs and McLellan, 'Argentine Trade Unions', p.5.
29. *Latin America Economic Report,* 11 October 1979, p.329.
30. *Latin America Weekly Report*, 20 March 1981, p.11.
31. See report in *Vencer*, no.9 1981.
32. For an overview see A. Dabat, and C. Lorenzano, *The Malvinas and the Crisis of Military Rule* (New Left Books, London, 1984).
33. *Latin America Weekly Report*, 2 April 1982, p.6.
34. *Política Obrera,* 12 October 1981, p.5.
35. *International Viewpoint*, 18 May 1983, p.9.
36. *Solidaridad Socialista*, 7 April 1983, pp.4–5.
37. *Latin America Weekly Report*, 6 May 1983, p.10.
38. See J. Gaibur and F. Gutierrez, Documento presentado para la discusión del IV Encuento del TYSAP, *En Lucha*, p.2, 1980.
39. *Latin America Weekly Report*, 21 November 1980, p.6.
40. Delich, F. (1982). Después del Diluvio, la Clase Obrera, p.150.

Appendix: Table 4.3
Strikes by sector, cause, measures taken and result (1976–1980)

	Strikes					*Workers involved*				
Year	*1976*	*1977*	*1978*	*1979*	*1980*	*1976*	*1977*	*1978*	*1979*	*1980*
Total	89	100	40	188	261	191,660	514,710	212,140	318,020	362,447
Sector:										
Extractive industry	2	6	0	2	10	500	38,732	0	5,020	2,280
Manufacturing (large or leading firms)	71	44	19	133	171	118,610	69,600	49,080	164,757	136,844
Total Service sector	13	49	21	51	75	70,650	406,286	163,060	148,060	222,893
(Transport)	8	29	16	30	26	4,650	288,246	162,160	134,040	154,727
Cause:										
Wage demand	53	82	26	141	88	79,520	386,948	194,400	278,332	165,039
Recession	6	2	7	21	130	7,540	6,300	6,280	15,430	88,869
Working conditions	6	3	4	2	18	34,000	62,000	6,660	2,100	34,900
Union organisation	8	2	0	1	6	26,800	20,100	0	100	13,747
State sector restructuring	1	0	0	2	3	20,000	0	0	5,100	5,100
Others	1	0	2	2	13	100	0	1,100	0	52,170

Measures taken:										
Stoppage	43	54	19	113	132	180,120	356,022	145,480	244,744	194,218
Withdrawal of cooperation	24	23	11	28	21	64,020	113,150	52,200	30,410	21,841
Public demonstration	6	0	3	10	26	25,950	0	1,300	15,800	22,620
Factor seizure	0	0	1	5	5	0	0	2,000	8,200	2,660
Factor assembly	2	0	0	13	58	250	0	0	24,500	85,287
Petition	0	0	3	11	38	0	0	660	23,970	74,164
Sabotage	7	19	4	0	0	13,250	37,646	11,380	0	0
Strike call:										
Factory	51	46	19	69	155	101,790	97,470	46,600	138,140	133,271
Regional	3	7	9	15	29	6,100	118,232	47,200	16,300	81,190
National	3	8	2	7	3	60,000	182,200	115,200	105,100	114,100
Sympathy	0	0	1	17	38	0	0	115,200	45,330	155,092

Source: Vencer, no. 8, May–June 1981, pp. 6–7.

Notes: The data for 1976 begins with April. The data for 1979 does not include the general strike of 27 April.

5. Recession, Retrenchment and Military Rule: Nigerian Labour in the 1980s*

Nicholas Van Hear

The Nigerian economy is an integral and important part of the world economic order. Nigeria supplies a substantial portion of US oil imports, is one of the UK's largest markets outside the EEC, is the West's most important African market and has attracted major foreign investment. The country's mixed economy underwent substantial growth in the 1970s.

But Nigeria is not in the forefront of the current worldwide restructuring of capitalism. It does not accommodate the new kinds of industrial sites that have emerged since the mid-1970s. In such areas–typically in south-east Asia—capital is making use of leaps forward in transport and communications and of technological developments allowing the de-skilling of complex production tasks, to take advantage of pools of unlimited cheap, unskilled labour.[1] Nigeria's industries have in fact suffered seriously from the penetration of exports from these newly industrializing countries.

One reason why the regimen characteristic of the new third world zones of capitalist expansion has not been established in Nigeria may be the persistence of a relatively independent and effective labour movement in the country. Against that, it is also argued that the favourable position of Nigerian workers, relative to others in industrializing countries, may nevertheless be changing, for in common with many other countries whose economies crumbled under the strain of the world recession, Nigeria was forced in 1982–4 to take structural adjustment measures while negotiating with the IMF a way out of the economic crisis: as elsewhere it was labour which bore the brunt of the new austerity. Indeed, the military government which took power at the end of 1983 has squeezed labour harder than the civilian order it replaced and is fulfilling expectations that the new world capitalist order will generate repressive regimes to discipline the labour force.[2]

This paper is concerned with the impact of the recession and structural adjustment on Nigerian workers, the response to the crisis of the

*Thanks to Tom Forrest and participants at the Ottawa Conference for their constructive criticism of this chapter.

organizations claiming to represent them and the effect recent developments may have on the position of Nigerian workers in the international division of labour. It proceeds by first outlining the expansion of the economy and the labour force in the 1970s before going on to trace the establishment, overseen by the state, of the Nigeria Labour Congress and how this body conducted the general strike in 1981 and the agitation for a national minimum wage. The paper then charts the labour unrest that continued despite austerity measures imposed by Shehu Shagari's government in the wake of the world oil glut and recession before examining the assault on labour by the military government under Buhari as talks with the IMF proceeded. The labour movement's activity in 1979–84 is then reviewed and the paper concludes with some consideration of the prospects for Nigerian workers in the later 1980s.

Nigeria's Economy in the 1970s

The 1970s saw the transformation of Nigeria's economy from one based on the appropriation of agricultural surplus from peasant farmers to one based on capital-intensive petroleum extraction, the revenue from which financed investment in large scale agriculture and manufacturing industry. Oil exporting began in 1957, but it was not until the late 1960s that it began to have a profound effect on the economy. Oil production increased fourfold between 1969 and 1974 to a level of around 2.25m barrels per day. With the rise in world oil prices, particularly the hike of 1973–4, Nigeria accumulated vast foreign exchange reserves; resources for development came to be seen as virtually limitless and the third national plan of 1975 grew into the most ambitious ever launched by an African country. Notes of caution were sounded in 1975 and especially in 1978 when prices slumped and production fell, but the doubling of world oil prices in 1978–80 sustained the expansionary impetus.[3]

Economic expansion in the 1970s was most visible in the construction industry, as major infrastructural investments were made in transport, power generation, housing, water supply and telecommunications. Funds were allocated to develop large scale irrigation and other capital–intensive agricultural schemes. Manufacturing remained largely dominated by the production of consumer goods, but there was a significant shift towards heavier industry, seen in the development of oil refining, vehicle assembly, and the manufacture of petro-chemicals, cement, steel and liquefied natural gas.

The structure and development of the economy has much in common with other developing countries. As with other third world industrialization, much of the new manufacturing was limited to the conversion or assembly of imported materials with little integration of industrial production. Successive indigenization decrees have ensured majority Nigerian participation in many of the enterprises; but foreign capital retains an important hold and often commands managerial and technical control. Financial and administrative mismanagement and endemic corruption meant that the expansion of the 1970s was accompanied by all kinds of abuse: both Nigerian and foreign capital were involved in the plunder.

One result of the wild growth was a rapid expansion of the labour market. In 1975, Nigeria's wage and salary earners in recognized employment were said to number 1.5 million, while in 1980 it was estimated that there were 3 million in wage employment.[4] There may have been more wage earners unrecorded, and the labour force must have expanded subsequently, although an estimate by the Nigeria Labour Congress for 1983 that wage earners numbered 6 million is probably exaggerated. Nevertheless there were shortages of skilled labour and also of unskilled workers willing to take low paid manual work. Many of these gaps were filled by immigrants, attracted by Nigerian prosperity and impelled by circumstances at home to seek employment abroad; such workers may have numbered around one million in the early 1980s.

The Formation of the Nigeria Labour Congress

The history of central labour organizations in Nigeria since the formation of the Trade Union Congress in 1943 has been marked by the proliferation of rival bodies which have lined up with the various international federations.[5] In 1976, against a background of four years of industrial unrest, Nigeria's military government[6] stepped in to restructure the labour movement so as to further its incorporation into the state. The four existing rival trade union centres were currently attempting to amalgamate into a single central body; but this initiative to form a Nigeria Labour Congress (NLC) independently was stifled by the military government. The four centres were dissolved, probed and their assets seized; at the same time all international organizations except the ILO and OATUU were banned from the country.

In February 1978 a reconstituted NLC was launched by government decree with a large subvention of public funds. The country's several hundred unions and staff associations were rationalized into 42 industry based unions affiliated to the NLC; the unions were to be recognized by employers, with dues checked off automatically from wages. Strikes were forbidden in certain industries and procedures were laid down for settling disputes and for collective bargaining.[7]

That the government was looking for a tame labour movement to bequeath to its civilian successors was confirmed by interference in the elections for posts in the 42 unions and the NLC. Nevertheless, the results were not to the government's liking, since Alhaji Hassan Sunmonu, a left-wing and former member of the WFTU affiliated union central, was elected president of the Congress. Neither the NLC nor the restructured unions proved in subsequent events to be the compliant instruments envisaged by the outgoing military government.

The General Strike of 1981[8]

As well as inheriting a restructured labour movement when it took office in October 1979, the new civilian government headed by Alhaji Shehu Shagari faced growing unrest over wages. As elections took place and the constitution was finalized for civilian rule, pressure had been building up for pay rises to make good erosion of living standards wrought by inflation, particularly of food prices in 1970s. A fall in Nigeria's oil sales and earnings in the late 1970s led to the imposition of austerity measures including a wage freeze and import curbs which aggravated the increases in the cost of living.

Although the military were concerned to avoid confrontation with labour during the handover, General Obasanjo's last budget maintained the wage freeze and cuts in rent, transport and other allowances. The NLC responded by demanding a review of the allowances and the fixing of a national minimum wage; but negotiations got nowhere and at the beginning of 1980 the NLC issued an ultimatum threatening the new civilian administration with a general strike if a settlement was not reached shortly.

The government's handling of the wages issue was confused, for while favouring collective bargaining it agreed after bilateral talks to a monthly minimum wage of 100 naira – the current base level of pay for public employees was 70 naira per month – and improved fringe benefits.[9] Workers generally welcomed these improvements, but, unsurprisingly, found employers reluctant to implement them, and there were strikes to force payment of the new minimum wage, which employers opposed on principle.

The run up to the NLC delegates' conference and elections at Kano in February 1981 temporarily took some of the heat out of these developments, as a press campaign was launched to secure the moderate candidate, democrat David Ojeli (head of the Civil Service Union) as Congress president in the hope of tempering the NLC demands. But communist Hassan Sunmonu retained the presidency and his faction's slate took command of all NLC posts. A unanimous resolution to call a general strike in May was passed, with a demand for a N300 monthly minimum wage.

Ojeli's response in defeat was to form a caucus within the NLC which had some backing in the National Assembly and among business interests hoping to weaken the NLC. Ojeli and the eight unions supporting him condemned the general strike, but it went ahead at the appointed time. Transport was brought to a halt, power was cut, banking disrupted, water supply and health services were affected and schools were closed. As more workers, including some civil servants, joined the strike next day, negotiations began and something of a compromise was agreed: the NLC rejected an offer of a monthly rate of N120, but the National Assembly was to debate and fix a national minimum within 30 days; pensions were to be increased from N33 to N50 and allowances were to be increased or reviewed. The NLC called off the stoppage, but many workers were incensed by employer's assertions that they would not be paid for the days they were on strike, in defiance of one of the stipulations of the agreement ending it; this led to further stoppages.

After further prevarication by the National Assembly, a N125 minimum monthly wage was finally accepted by the NLC. The Congress meanwhile successfully beat off an attempt to undermine it by repealing the 1978 Acts which had made the NLC the labour movement's sole central body (a move which would have allowed recognition of Ojeli's caucus) and resisted other elements of the employer's counter-offensive – anti-strike measures and an attempt to abolish automatic check-off.

Nevertheless, disputes over payment of the minimum wage continued, and added to them was wrangling over pay scales precipitated by the imminent publication of the Onosode Report. The Onosode Commission had been set up in 1981, shortly before the general strike, to review the operations of the parastatals, including their salaries and conditions of employment, and the possibility of separating out the unified grading and salary system for civil servants and employees in parastatals established by the Udoji Commission of 1974. Some unions appeared to welcome the Commission's findings since removal of the workers they represented from the unified salary scale opened up the chance of independent negotiations to determine improved pay. Other unions were unhappy at the Commission's criticisms of inefficiency in the parastatals and recommendations for privatization or dissolution.[10] A wave of strikes and protests over the Onosode recommendations followed in 1982. There was a six-day stoppage by power workers, then strikes by Nigeria Airways air traffic controllers, by workers at the Central Bank and later other federal financial institutions, by Post and Telecommunications workers, by the Civil Service Technical Workers' Union, and by senior and non-academic staff at University Teaching Hospitals.[11]

The Recession

The campaign over the national minimum wage, allowances and pensions, and the disputes over grading, pay scales and privatization took place against a background of economic expansion following the recovery of world oil prices in 1979–81. After tumbling in 1978, world oil prices were sent shooting up again in the wake of the upheavals in Iran: the export price of Nigerian oil correspondingly rose from $14 per barrel in 1978 to a peak of $40 at the beginning of 1981. Borrowing abroad continued and the combined result of this and increased oil earnings was that foreign exchange reserves reached more than $10 billion by the end of 1980. Federal expenditure was doubled and public expenditure projected for 1981–5 almost trebled between the preparation and the publication of the Fourth Plan.[12] The large scale immigration of foreign workers – many from Ghana – to meet the demand for labour continued throughout the period.

But the high world oil prices on which this renewed expansion was predicated were short-lived, as a world oil glut developed in 1981. Nigerian production fell from an average of just over 2 million barrels per day to 707,000 in August 1981.[13] The export price was reduced and sales picked up, but the country's substantial foreign exchange reserves were rapidly evaporating, as the spending bonanza of the 1970s worked through.

Chronic financial mismanagement and endemic corruption had accelerated the foreign exchange haemorrhage, so that by the end of 1981 federal and state governments were in grave financial trouble. By then 7 of the 19 states could not pay teachers and government employees; by mid-1982 several months arrears were outstanding in Bendel, Benue, Cross Rivers, Imo, Oyo and Rivers states. Only by striking and threatening strikes did workers force payment of some of the arrears, marking the beginning of a long struggle by public sector workers to be properly paid.[14]

By April 1982 Nigerian oil production had fallen again and export prices had dropped further.[15] In response to the growing economic and fiscal crisis, the Shagari government rushed through a stabilization package. Import curbs were re-introduced on a more drastic scale by means of licensing and import duties; stringent financial restrictions were imposed and public expenditure cuts made: a new phase of austerity, more rigorous than the last, had begun.

In addition to continuing pressure to implement the gains won after the general strike and unrest over the Onosode Report, two other issues stemming from the recession now came to dominate industrial relations: securing actual payment of wages in the public sector, particularly by workers employed by state governments, and the general retrenchment that followed the austerity measures of April 1982.

Workers responded to government intimations that there were no funds to pay improved wages with another wave of stoppages. There were strikes by government workers over the non-payment of wages and allowances in Benue, Oyo, Ondo, Ogun, Rivers, Anambra, Gongola and Borno states in the second half of 1982: workers often struck repeatedly when state governments reneged on agreements to pay the arrears. Similarly, teachers' strikes in Kwara, Bendel, Benue and Rivers states were replicated in most of the country's 19 states by the end of the year. Not only were salaries irregular, or never paid at all, but pay was reduced and fringe benefits eroded, as states introduced their own austerity measures.

There were also strikes by steel workers protesting at non-payment and redundancies, by petroleum and gas workers of the Nigerian National Petroleum Corporation, by water workers and by agricultural workers demanding implementation of the new minimum wage. In addition to disruption in the ports over pay and the Onosode report, dock workers struck over the introduction of new cargo handling machinery – which would have halved the dock labour force – and secured its suspension.[16] According to Ministry of Labour figures, the successive waves of industrial action accounted for the loss of more than eight million working days in 1982, involving nearly 560,000 workers. But continuing retrenchment in both the public and private sectors was to dampen this militancy.

Added to the slump in markets brought about by the recession were difficulties for manufacturing in securing imported raw materials and spare parts, as a result of the import controls. The consequences were shutdowns and widespread lay-offs. Construction was one of the first industries to be hit. Private firms contracted by federal and state governments to build roads laid off many workers, maintenance workers on federal highways were sacked and much building work was abandoned. Steel, textiles, vehicle assembly, the ports and light manufacturing were also seriously affected, and some state governments began to lay off workers later in 1982.

The economic situation continued to deteriorate amid fears for the collapse of world oil prices. Nigeria's external payments fell more heavily into arrears and foreign banks were refusing to confirm letters of credit for importers. Further downward revision of the country's economic forecasts were made in the 1983 budget proposals.

The beginning of 1983 seemed to mark a new resolve by the Shagari government to try belatedly to get a grip on the economic situation and to quell the upsurge of labour unrest of the previous two years. In January the government introduced a further Economic Stabilization Order in an attempt to reduce imports from the prevailing level of N900 million a month to N600 million. Import of some items was banned altogether, the number of goods requiring import licences was increased and higher tariffs were set. The inclusion of some raw materials in the list of items subject to higher tariffs hit local manufacturing further.

Shortly afterwards the government announced that it was expelling from the country aliens living and working without proper permits. Around 2.2 million people, of whom perhaps half were Ghanaian migrant workers, were forced to leave the country in a mass exodus in January and February. It was a classic scapegoat ploy and gave the government temporary respite from growing public criticism.[17]

Although the expulsion no doubt went some way to sublimate Nigerian workers' discontent (the labour movement's reactions to the expulsion are discussed below), labour unrest nevertheless resumed. The disputes over arrears of pay spilled over into the new year. Teachers, civil servants, nurses, doctors and midwives struck over non-payment of salaries and there were strikes by brewery workers, oil tanker drivers and oil production workers. Despite authorization by President Shagari in February of a loan of N200 million (on top of the statutory monthly allocations) to help state governments meet their salary commitments, workers in many states were still waiting for many months' pay. There were further strikes, sometimes repeated, over non-payment of salaries by civil servants in Benue, Bendel, Imo, Cross River and Borno states and by teachers in Kaduna, Kano and Borno between January and July 1983.[18]

In an attempt to force the government's hand, the NLC threatened to transform this wave of stoppages into a nationwide public service strike if all arrears were not settled by the end of July. To add weight to this demand, the nationwide strike was strategically timed to coincide with the federal, state and presidential elections starting in August; the NLC argued that state governments should not go in for re-election with such huge arrears outstanding. The movement of federal funds to state governments was accelerated just before the elections and the NLC called off the strike. A meeting between Sunmonu and the Minister of Labour resulted in an increase in the federal loan to N519 million and some state governments began to draw their entitlements in September. But dilatory disbursement of the funds made available for salaries ensured that the grievance was not resolved in many states. There were also suspicions that the funds were being diverted, despite monitoring by the NLC and federal and state governments. In addition, unrest at lay-offs in both the public and private sectors was growing.

As the domestic economic situation worsened, so too did Nigeria's external payments situation. The government had made approaches earlier in the year to borrow $2 billion abroad from a consortium of foreign banks to pay off short-term debts and to allow importers to secure letters of credit again. When the banks came up with just $1 billion the government had to reconcile itself to approaching the IMF; but it was reluctant to finalize a deal before the August elections, for the IMF standard stabilization package would have involved devaluation of the naira, credit and wage freezes and further spending cuts, all unpopular with voters. Negotiations with the bank consortium and the IMF continued throughout the year – indeed agreement with one was dependent on agreement with the other – but the sticking point was devaluation.

As the government attempted to secure loans abroad to finance the balance of payments' deficit, the economy showed little sign of recovery. According to figures from the Central Bank of Nigeria, GDP fell in 1983 by 4.4%, oil earnings dropped by 15%, and inflation, at 23.2%, was running at three times the 1982 rate.[19] The Manufacturers' Association of Nigeria described the year as 'the worst for Nigerian manufacturing industry in two decades'; manufacturing output fell 20% in the year overall, while some manufacturers were forced to cut production by 60%.[20] The consequence for workers was more shutdowns and lay-offs, while at the same time acute shortages of imported and locally produced commodities were intensifying the prices spiral and lowering workers' living standards.

Faced with this deteriorating situation, the government took further stabilization measures, anticipating the conditions likely to be laid down by the IMF in the ongoing negotiations. Late in the year a committee was set up to review all projects costing more than N30 million to implement: the most important schemes were to be identified and others postponed or abandoned. More austerity measures were contained in Shagari's budget announced late in December, but the New Year's Eve coup intervened before the civilian regime could implement them.

The Military Coup, Retrenchment and the IMF Talks[21]

Like many other sections of Nigerian society, the organized labour movement welcomed the coup on 31 December which ousted Shagari and the civilian politicians and installed Major-General Buhari and the Supreme Military Council in power. But the honeymoon did not last long. Three issues dominated industrial relations, just as they did under Shagari. Non-payment of wages to public sector workers was a continuing grievance; lay-offs in both the public and private sectors gained momentum with the new regime's purge of civil servants; and there were fresh assaults on wages and fringe benefits, with wage restraint being a likely ingredient of the package under continuing negotiation with the IMF.

In his New Year broadcast made on the morning after the coup, Buhari pledged to clear the backlog of salary arrears – some of which still stretched back as far as 1980 – and directed the new state military governors to settle the arrears within four months. Compliance with this order was patchy, but some of the outstanding salaries were paid.

The government's purge of civil servants – ostensibly to rid the state administrations of officials implicated in corruption under the Shagari regime – began to develop into another area of serious contention. Sacking of civil servants became widespread and appeals of redundant workers to be redeployed were largely ignored. To those civil servants still in work, attendance registers, punishments for poor time-keeping and other disciplinary measures were meted out by the military.

Lay-offs from the manufacturing sector led to more confrontation. In January, a long-running dispute over arrears of pay at Kaduna Textiles (KTL) came to a head with the summary dismissal of 3,000 workers. When they marched on the military governor's office in Kaduna – he had ordered payment of the arrears – the workers were baton-charged by police, and 22 of them were arrested. The predicament of KTL – which is part-owned by the state government – was typical of the condition of much of Nigeria's manufacturing industry. A slump in the textile market, obsolete equipment, cash flow problems and lack of raw materials and spare parts led to retrenchment at the company and the austerity measures worsened KTL's position. But the textile workers' union claimed that the company had deliberately provoked confrontation to effect redundancies it intended anyway. Eventually, re-instatement was won, but management cut the pay owed by half – as elsewhere, workers were made to pay for the recession. In another state owned manufacturing industry–Bendel Brewery–1,300 workers were made redundant following a directive by Bendel state's military governor that all such companies should be made viable within six months. Although the dismissals violated labour legislation about notice of redundancies the union was unable to secure re-instatement.

The implications for workers of the IMF negotiations was another contentious issue between the labour movement and the new military government. Shortly after the coup the NLC declared itself completely opposed to devaluation, but a showdown on this and the other issues was postponed during the elections late in February for the NLC leadership, when the union bureaucracies' energies were directed into jostling for positions in the NLC hierarchy. A measure of continuity was assured when Alhaji Ali Chiroma was elected successor to Hassan Sunmonu; Chiroma was in the Sunmonu camp, but was less forceful and outspoken than the former NLC president.

Some indication of the climate to come was given by Buhari in his speech to the NLC delegates' conference. First he spoke of a 'real wage policy', suggesting that workers' purchasing power would be increased by controlling prices through a 'fundamental restructuring of the distribution system' in which the NLC would participate 'as an active collaborator'. But Buhari continued by warning that the government would not tolerate 'frivolous industrial actions', spoke of 'a number of unreasonable industrial disputes', and asserted that the 'principle of no work, no pay' would be 'strictly enforced', a statement that must have seemed ironic to many public sector workers who had not been paid for several months. The NLC responded by demanding another rise in the national minimum wage, increases in pensions, reforms of the social security system and measures to lessen the impact of redundancies.

While the government and NLC were firing their initial exchanges, protests at lay-offs and pay cuts were gathering pace. As well as the KTL and Bendel Brewery disputes, there were protests in federally based parastatals. The Nigerian Union of Railwaymen threatened a strike after the Railway Corporation announced it was suspending leave allowances as an austerity measure–allowances that had been won over several years, and were included in the settlement after the 1981 general strike. In late March, Nigeria Airways pilots, flight engineers and cabin crews struck in protest at curtailment of their night allowances. Summary dismissal of all strikers broke the strike; around three-quarters of them were re-instated after signing undertakings of good behaviour and accepting new conditions of employment. Although there was little public sympathy for the pilots, this and other defeats further reduced workers' confidence in their capacity to resist redundancies and wage cuts.

The purges in the public sector meanwhile accelerated. NLC branches in Kwara and Bendel states threatened strikes over large scale lay-offs. The NLC national executive soft pedalled and ruled out immediate industrial action against the sackings; but when other states announced even more drastic measures later in the month the NLC was forced to make a stand. As an indication of the new scale on which retrenchment was being implemented, Plateau state's military administration announced that all workers taken on since December 1981 were to be sacked, all workers over 50 were to be retired compulsorily, all salaries were to be reduced by 20% and all allowances cancelled. Other state governments were said to be contemplating similar measures and in several states health charges and education fees (abolished for primary schooling in the 1950s) were introduced.

The NLC leadership's response was to threaten another nationwide protest strike–this time from a position of weakness–but it soon backtracked and sought dialogue instead with the government over the purges, health and education charges and the unrealistic level of the minimum wage. Chiroma argued that retrenchment and redundancies were at the IMF's insistence, but at the same time he pledged the NLC's cooperation with the government. Not surprisingly, this gingerly voiced protest made little impact. Nevertheless, the government did announce that state governments were to receive N600 million in federal loans by the end of April to help them pay salary arrears–some of which still stretched back two years. Only 6 of the 19 states had met the government's April deadline to clear the pay backlog.

The NLC was not far off the mark in its argument that the economic stringency imposed by the military regime was largely determined by the negotiations with the IMF. After initial fears that the new government might not honour the debt accumulated under its civilian predecessors, talks resumed with the banking consortium to refinance the $2billion arrears on letters of credit into a medium term loan. Talks with the IMF were not disrupted and negotiations continued over rescheduling overdue trade credits underwritten by Britain's Export Credit Guarantee Department (ECGD). In January 1984 Nigeria's short-term arrears were estimated at $6billion.[22] To gain credibility with its creditors, the new regime imposed an import ceiling of £4billion for 1984, allowing imports only of food, raw materials and spare parts, and excluding most previously imported manufactured goods.

As negotiations to reschedule the external debt proceeded, lay-offs in Nigeria continued unabated. The NLC was unable to mount much opposition and further protests that the government was being overzealous in anticipating the conditions for an IMF loan were ignored. The construction workers' union claimed to have lost 80% of its membership through retrenchment since 1981, and motor workers were also losing jobs, closures at Volkswagen and Peugeot resulting in many lay-offs.

Frustration within the labour movement at accelerating redundancies led to criticism of what some saw as weak resistance by the NLC's national executive. When the recently elected leaders of the NLC met officials of the Nigeria Ports Authority Workers' Union they were castigated for not putting enough pressure on the government to stop indiscriminate sackings. NLC state branches joined in criticism of the Congress's national executive. The Lagos state NLC branch accused the national leaders of inaction and said jobs could have been saved if they had opposed the government more forcefully.

The military government's first budget, announced in May, tightened the screw still further. Like previous measures, the budget - a more stringent version of the one presented by Shagari just before his downfall – was designed to impress Nigeria's creditors. Agreement had been reached with uninsured creditors to reschedule arrears; but negotiations to refinance the British trade debt underwritten by the ECGD remained deadlocked. More important, no agreement was finalized with the IMF; devaluation - which would of course have meant dearer imports – still proved the stumbling block. The budget's proposed 40% cut in capital expenditure and 17% cut in current spending were meant as a prologue to the IMF talks scheduled to resume in June on a $3.2 billion extended credit. No new projects were to be undertaken, but the steel, petro-chemical and LNG programmes were to go ahead. Thus, although much associated with an IMF-style package – including a wage freeze – was proposed in the budget, the government stopped short of devaluation; nor were subsidies on petroleum products removed. Refusal to devalue led to the suspension of the IMF talks again at the end of June. Since then the official position appears to have shifted to the view that through good housekeeping Nigeria could survive without recourse to the IMF. This has inevitably meant further austerity. The 1985 budget maintained the wage freeze, and cuts in pay and allowances have proceeded briskly since. Subsequently the NLC has come in for further criticism from member unions for failing to resist retrenchment fiercely enough. More significant, though, is rank and file disenchantment with the official labour movement; at the 1985 May Day rallies, for example, both government officials and NLC leaders were jeered by irate workers, and the celebrations were brought to an abrupt end.[23]

Sackings have continued relentlessly in both the public and private sectors. The NLC estimated that around one million workers were laid off between 1981 and 1983. Estimates of redundancies since the military took power vary, but one report maintained that nearly 55,000 federal and state government employees were sacked or retired in the first six months of 1984, and this total included figures from only 10 of the 19 states. According to the Manufacturers Association of Nigeria around 50 factories were shut down in 1984 and 50,000 workers laid off from the manufacturing sector.[24]

Nevertheless, Nigerian labour has not been cowed by the threat of sackings and government warnings against indiscipline. Forty-seven trade disputes were recorded between January and March 1984, resulting in 24 strikes, involving 32,120 workers and the loss of 261,395 working days. Another 97 trade disputes were reported between May 1984 and March 1985, reportedly involving nearly 300,000 workers and more than 6.5 million working days lost.[25] Although these figures represent a decline

Table 5.1 Industrial unrest in Nigeria 1981–85

	Working Days Lost	*Workers Involved*	*Disputes*
Jane. 1981–Feb. 1982	2 million	366,323	278 (leading to 188 strikes)
1982	8 million	559,552	340
1983	—	—	—
Jan.–March 1984	261,395	32,120	47 (leading to 24 strikes)
May 1984–March 1985	6,564,347	298,440	97

Source: Nigerian Ministry of Labour

Table 5.2 Oil industry production: '000 barrels a day

	1975	*1976*	*1977*	*1978*	*1979*	*1980*	*1981*	*1982*	*1983*	*1984*
January	1,985	1,989	2,197	1,638	2,441	2,157	2,092	1,754	833	1,351
February	1,796	2,070	2,196	1,566	2,428	2,148	1,943	1,400	673	1,546
March	1,713	1,998	2,255	1,521	2,436	2,156	1,868	938	910	1,566
April	1,621	2,064	2,258	1,693	2,416	2,189	1,623	900	1,168	1,359
May	1,545	2,069	2,210	1,720	2,398	2,141	1,293	1,308	1,622	1,190
June	1,608	2,095	2,236	1,893	2,405	2,195	1,352	1,649	1,526	1,279
July	1,636	2,048	2,065	1,913	2,381	2,100	771	1,259	1,711	1,127
August	1,755	1,937	2,020	2,000	2,185	2,049	707	1,106	1,291	1,142
September	1,917	2,047	2,027	2,109	2,116	1,577	1,061	1,165	1,214	1,420
October	1,909	2,113	1,950	2,114	2,135	1,901	1,250	1,489	1,290	1,445
November	1,954	2,185	1,918	2,276	2,151	2,062	1,582	1,365	1,300	1,533
December	1,980	2,190	1,852	2,384	2,151	2,018	1,786	1,203	1,300	1,737
Year	*1,785*	*2,067*	*2,098*	*1,909*	*2,303*	*2,058*	*1,440*	*1,294*	*1,237*	*1,391*

Source: *Financial Times,* 26 February 1985.

from the level of militancy in the later years of the Shagari administration (see Table 1), they show that Nigerian workers have not acquiesced to their grim situation.

Labour Activity and the Recession, 1979-1985

Three periods may be identified from this account of Nigeria's recent labour history. During the first, 1979-81, the economy was recovering from the downturn of 1978, buoyed up by the doubling of world oil prices. The labour movement, orchestrated by the NLC under the capable leadership of Hassan Sunmonu, was able to win improvements in wages and allowances. The base level pay of public employees of N70 per month was increased to N100 in 1980, and then, after the general strike of 1981, N125 was established as a national monthly minimum wage. Improvements in 'fringe' benefits were also won, including transport and housing allowances for most workers and pensions were raised. Although gains were no doubt eroded by inflation during this period these were significant advances for organized labour as instanced by the opposition of the business community to the principle of a national minimum wage. The pay increases greatly enlarged employers' wage bills and must have contributed substantially to the subsequent crisis of capital in Nigeria, as well as to the fiscal crises of both state and federal governments.

The second period 1982 was the turning point, when the recession bit and labour struggles moved to the defensive. Nevertheless labour was still relatively confident. There was unrest over the Onosode Report which recommended that certain parastatals should be removed from the unified salary scale established by the Udoji Commission. This presumably meant that wage bargaining could now be conducted as in the private sector, which was welcomed by some unions, while others resisted the Report's recommendations for privatization of parastatals.[26] More widespread were strikes by public sector workers to secure from bankrupt state governments or federal institutions payment of wages and allowances just won. These disputes and struggles against lay-offs made 1982 the high point of labour militancy in recent years.

The third period, 1983-4, coincides with negotiations between the government, IMF and Nigeria's creditors to bail the country out. Further measures of economic stringency were imposed by the Shagari government early in 1983 as a prologue to talks with the IMF, which led to more shutdowns and lay-offs. The expulsion of foreign workers in January and February 1983 can be seen partly as a move to deflect Nigerian workers' unrest over mounting redundancies. Indeed some unions, including reportedly, the Dockworkers' and Hotel workers' union (whose members worked in industries using much immigrant labour) had appealed to the federal government shortly before the expulsion to restrict the immigration of alien labour. While some unions – notably the construction workers – did take steps to help immigrants regularize their papers, the labour movement's response to the expulsion was at best low key.

The muted reaction of the NLC did little to allay a surge of anti-alien chauvinism which was sadly somewhat justified. Allegations that aliens acted as blacklegs in strikes came from several quarters of the labour movement. The employment of foreign workers without proper work permits gave Nigerian employers the advantages typically associated with utilization of migrant labour that is technically illegal. Their insecurity forced such workers to tolerate poor wages and conditions, and, with the threat of betrayal to the authorities hanging over them, they were readily disciplined by employers. Further, the presence of large numbers of unemployed immigrants depressed wage rates and increased insecurity among indigenous workers. After the expulsions there were immediate shortages of labour in some industries and wage rates improved: daily rated casual workers in construction, for example, demanded and won increases of up to 50%. But the labour market rapidly re-adjusted and such short term gains at the expense of immigrant workers were hollow.

Despite this spectacular diversion, labour unrest at non-payment of wages and at redundancies resumed. The threat of a nationwide public service strike, made astutely by the NLC leadership just before the August elections, forced the federal government to increase by 150% its loans to state administrations and won some improvement in the pay backlog. But aside from securing its actual payment, real wages were eroded drastically by inflation in 1983-4.

After the military takeover, which was closely followed by the election of a new NLC leadership, the labour movement found itself in a greatly weakened position as the new regime imposed swingeing cuts in public sector jobs as part of a series of measures to woo the IMF and Nigeria's creditors. Lay-offs accelerated throughout the economy as stringent import controls added to the general effects of the recession. The NLC, whether through weak leadership or through an untenable bargaining position, was unable to mount much opposition and came under criticism from its member unions; it probably also lost the confidence of Nigerian workers at large. Demands for another increase in the minimum wage were merely ritualistic, made from a position of weakness. Labour protest pursued by individual unions nevertheless continued, although in several well publicized cases strikes were severely repressed. However, some groups of workers in strategically important sectors– such as oil production and distribution and the ports– were able to put up some resistance to the onslaught. Nigerian labour had not succumbed wholly to the new climate of austerity, retrenchment and repression accompanying prospective IMF intervention.

That the NLC has survived and remained relatively independent in such parlous circumstances is no mean achievement, especially in view of the fissile history of previous Nigerian central labour bodies. The NLC overcame attempted secession by a conservative oriented, business backed union caucus and successfully campaigned against legislation that would have hamstrung its effectiveness. The labour movement has also continued to function, although in a muted way, under the military. As well as pressing more narrowly economic demands for wages and job security, it has opposed–though with little success–cuts in the social wage, in particular health and education, and has spoken out against the gagging of the press.

The Nigerian labour movement is very much in the traditional mould. Its leaders, particularly Sunmonu, have shown the capacity to manage labour unrest so as to wrest limited gains from the government or private employers. The general strike of 1981 was so orchestrated, as were later manoeuvres. This hierarchically structured, bureaucratically managed labour movement contrasts with labour activity in the early 1970s which was carried on by more autonomous, accountable and local level unions and strike committees geared to local needs. These organizations, often acting outside official union hierarchies, successfully struggled to secure from private employers increases in pay recommended for the publication by the Adebo Commission in 1971. Similar activity surrounded the Udoji Commission increases in 1975.[27]

State intervention in the labour movement from the mid-1970s was designed to channel this activity into a more orderly and manageable system of industrial relations. As part of this process there was a departure from the pattern, dating from the colonial era, of periodic general wage reviews by government appointed commissions–which precipated labour unrest - to collective bargaining within an incomes policy. But, as was seen above, far from promoting industrial harmony, this strategy culminated in the minimum wage battle of the early 1980s.

The centralization and bureaucratization of the labour movement has not meant that Nigerian workers no longer take militant action on their own initiative. The years under review in this paper saw numerous actions by individual unions as well as wild-cat activity without union approval.[28] Nevertheless, control of their struggles was often out of the hands of the rank and file. The circumstances of recession and retrenchment also limited the scope for worker managed struggles. Workers have often defied the web of legislation restricting strikes and union activity (many of the stoppages described above were illegal); but the formidable repressive forces the state has at hand, and the new determination the military goverment has shown in using them, means that Nigerian workers have to ponder seriously the forms their activity can take.

Prospects for Nigerian Labour in the Later 1980s

Nigeria exhibits some of the features of 'new' industrialization, with many foreign manufacturing firms having established branches in the 1970s on the now familiar pattern of locating only part of their production process there. The vehicle assembly plants of Volkswagen, Peugeot, Mercedes, Fiat, Leyland and others are examples where Nigerian workers assemble imported knocked down kits. But this has been import-substitution rather than export-oriented industrialization for these and other companies have located themselves in Nigeria more to take advantage of the country's large potential market than to reap the benefits of a pool of cheap unskilled labour.

There are few indications that use of labour economizing technology is on the way. In the ports new machinery is to be introduced for cargo handling that may reduce the dock labour force from 35,000 to 7,000,[29] but further than this there is little evidence that capital in Nigeria is restructuring under cover of the recession by changing production processes fundamentally. There is little suggestion of utilization of forms of non-standard labour such as sub-contracting or outworking as seen in other parts of the world. No free trade or production zones have been established, nor is there large scale utilization of young female labour.[30] Such restructuring as is going on is rather a holding operation, as branches of foreign capital and their local counterparts try to maintain a level of operation adequate for survival until the hoped for upturn.

Nigeria does not seem to have been particularly attractive to the purveyors of the new world capitalist order. It has been suggested that one reason for this is the relative strength of the labour movement, whose struggles in the 1970s and early 1980s have ensured that the low wage regime characteristic of the new zones of capitalist expansion has not been established in Nigeria. But later sections of this paper showed that this may be changing under the impact of the recession. The expulsion of aliens, subsequently repented by the military regime, was a convenient way of shedding surplus labour before the assault on indigenous workers began. Under pressure from the IMF and its creditors, the Nigerian state has been buttressing capital through the imposition of public spending cuts, reduction of wage levels and allowances, and disciplining of the labour force. Until recently the military government presented itself as a benevolent dictatorship, harsh but fair, but since mid-1984 its actions have become less restrained and more repressive.

One prospect is the outright suppression of the labour movement and the setting up of a regime matching the gloomy prognosis of Frobel, Heinrichs and Kreye. Another possibility – probably more likely – is incorporation of the unions further into the state, a strategy attempted in the 1970s; it may now be that the conditions are ripe for fuller incorporation.

The rationalization of the labour movement in the later 1970s laid the foundations for a more orderly extraction of surplus value. Exploitation could be carried on more smoothly, with less disruption by unruly workers using their own impermanent, unstable organizations, as in the early 1970s. In the event the NLC and the restructured unions turned out not to be the pliant institutions planned by the Obasanjo regime. Acting like a powerful pressure goup, the offical labour movement won significant gains from capital and provided some resistance against the offensives of capital and the state in the initial stages of the recession.

The NLC and unions are no longer able to play this role. Apart from its much weakened bargaining position and the threat of suppression by the military government, the labour movement is in financial difficulties. Memberships have been falling because of lay-offs and employers have been refusing to forward check-off dues: most union contributions to the NLC were in arrears by 1983.[31] Recourse to the state for further funds may be the only way out with all the consequences for incorporation that this implies.

With the labour movement weakened by incorporation or suppression, Nigeria might become more attractive to transnational capital. It may be preposterous to suggest that the position of Nigerian labour will be reduced to South East Asian levels, but as social and political unrest mounts in some of these areas and they become less attractive, transnational capital may be tempted to seek out countries like Nigeria where labour costs are declining, workers are disciplined by a repressive regime, and where there is a large domestic market and a reasonably developed infrastructure – countries which combine the features of labour abundant South East Asia and market rich Latin America.[32]

What might be the response of Nigerian workers to such a scenario? Seeing the official labour movement suppressed, compromised or incorporated, workers might begin re-organizing themselves on the lines of the early 1970s; there might be a resurgence of more independent and accountable organizations in which workers are more in control of their activity. It may be that such organizations already exist, and have been conducting struggles over the past few years; but the over-riding impression is that Nigerian workers ceded the management of their protest activity to the official labour movement headed by the NLC, which performed reasonably effectively in the late 1970s and 1980s.

One model for such a resurgence of grassroots labour organizations might be provided by the Workers' Defence Committees in Ghana. Never fully endorsed and later suppressed by the Rawlings regime, they have since been eclipsed by the resurgence of the orthodox labour movement in Ghana. But for all their shortcomings, the WDCs did for a short time in the early 1980s embody the aspirations of sections of the Ghanaian working class; they waged struggles agains multinationals and state enterprises over lay-offs and other issues with some success. They did so in circumstances far more difficult than those facing Nigerian workers, who might usefully draw some lessons from them for the coming struggles with transnational and Nigerian capital.

Notes

1. F. Frobel, J. Heinrichs and O. Kreye, 'The World Market for Labour and the World Market for Industrial Sites', *Journal of Economic Issues,* vol. 12, no. 4, 1978, pp. 843–58 and A. Sivanandan, 'Imperialism in the silicon age', *Race and Class*, vol. 21, no. 2, 1979, pp. 111–26.

2. Frobel, Heinrichs and Kreye, 'The World Market for Labour and the World Market for Industrial Sites'.

3. On the Nigerian economy in the 1970s, see A. Kirk-Greene and D. Rimmer, *Nigeria since 1970: a Political and Economic Outline* (Hodder and Stoughton, London 1981); D. Rimmer, *The Economies of West Africa* (Weidenfeld and Nicholson, London, 1984); and B. Freund, 'Oil Boom and Crisis in Contemporary Nigeria', *Review of African Political Economy,* 13, 1978, pp. 91–100.

4. *Third National Development Plan, 1975–80* (Central Planning Office, Lagos, 1975) and *Fourth National Development Plan, 1981–85* (National Planning Office, Lagos, 1981).

5. For the post-war history of Nigeria's labour movements, see R. Cohen, *Labour and Politics in Nigeria, 1945–71* (Heinemann, London, 1974) and W. Ananaba, *The Trade Union Movement in Nigeria* (Hurst, London, 1969).

6. In July 1975 General Gowon was overthrown by Brigadier Murtala Mohammed, who was assassinated in February 1976 in a failed coup attempt; Murtala was succeeded by General Obasanjo.

7. D. Otobo, 'The Nigerian General Strike of 1981', *Review of African Political Economy*, 22, 1981, pp. 65–8 and Rimmer, *Nigeria since 1970*, pp. 105–06.

8. The following account draws on Otobo, 'The Nigerian General Strike of 1981', pp. 65–81.

9. One naira = approximately one US dollar.

10. The NLC's case against privatization was set out in its document *Nigeria: not for sale*, which argued that the real cause of inefficiency was the corruption resulting from political appointments to public boards: 'crude and primitive accumulation of capital at the expense of the health of the industry and the nation' (Nigeria Labour Congress, Information Department, *Nigeria: not for sale* (Lagos, n.d.).

11. *West Africa*, 8 March 1982; *New Nigerian*, 19 February 1982, 1–3 March 1982, 14–15 July 1982, 9–24 September 1982: *African Economic Digest*, 26 November 1982.

12. Rimmer, *The Economies of West Africa*, p. 129–31.

13. *Financial Times*, 23 January 1984 (see Table 2).

14. D. Otobo, 'The Political Clash in the Aftermath of the 1981 Nigerian General Strike', *Review of African Political Economy*, 25, 1982, pp. 109–112 and *African Business*, March & April 1983.

15. *FT*, 23 January 1984.

16. *African Business*, January 1983.

17. *Ibid.*, March and April 1983.

18. *Ibid.*, November 1983.

19. *Africa Economic Digest*, 6 July 1984.

20. *Ibid.*, 28 October 1983 and 6 July 1984.

21. The following section is based on Nigerian newspapers, *West Africa* and other periodicals.

22. *FT*, 1 January 1984.

23. BBC Summary of World Broadcasts, 3 May 1985.

24. *West Africa*, 9 July 1984 and *FT*, 25 February 1985.

25. Nigeria, Ministry of Labour; Maj. Gen. Buhari's May Day speech, 1985 and BBC Summary of World Broadcasts, 3 May 1985.

26. It is unclear how many of the Onosode Commission proposals have been implemented.

27. See A. Peace, *Choice, Class and Conflict: A Study of Southern Nigerian Factory Workers* (London: Harvester, 1979) pp. 150–67; P. Lubeck, 'Unions, Workers and Consciousness in Kano, Nigeria: A View from Below' in Sanbrook and Cohen (eds), *The Development of an African Working Class*, (London: Longman 1975) and 'Labour in Kano since the Petroleum Boom', *Review of African Political Economy*, 13, 1978, pp. 41–45.

28. Further investigation is needed to uncover the range of rank and file activity in this period, no doubt often in opposition to union leaderships.

29. *West Africa*, 6 August 1984. The Nigeria Ports Authority tried to introduce the machinery in 1982 but was thwarted by a dockers' strike. (see p. 150).

30. On female labour in Nigerian manufacturing, see C. Dennis, 'Capitalist Development and Women's Work: A Nigerian Case Study', *Review of African Political Economy*, 27/28, 1984, pp. 109–18.

31. *African Business*, April 1983.

32. Conditions conducive to industrialization in non-core locales are suggested by G. Arrighi in 'Stagflation and Labour Market Regulation in Historical Perspective', a paper represented at the *RoAPE* conference on 'The World Recession and the Crisis in Africa', University of Keele, 1984; see pp. 15–16 on labour rich and market rich locales.

6. The Challenge of the Open Economy: Trade Unionism in Sri Lanka

Laksiri Fernando

> The work force is highly productive. The average monthly wage in manufacturing industries in Sri Lanka is about US $35. Compare your wage bill with this! . . . The state machinery established for the regulation of industrial relations provides for the maintenance of industrial peace. When a dispute exists it is apprehended, so that the overall effect would not lead to work stoppage. A brochure – *The FTZ in Sri Lanka.*

The old international division of labour still defines Sri Lanka's overall position with the outside/metropolitan world in the sphere of trade. After thirty-five years of independence, Sri Lanka still continues to be an underdeveloped/dependent economy exporting mainly primary products and importing a major share of its industrial finished goods. Recently, however, there has been a noticable trend away from this pattern, partly conscious and partly forced by the circumstances within which the Sri Lankan economy operates. This emphasis on export-oriented industrial development is of course not of immediate origin, for it dates back to the mid-sixties. However, this trend has assumed a fundamental practical importance to the trade union movement in the country with the shift to an open economy policy since 1977 and the establishment of an Export Processing Zone (EPZ) as a part of this shift.

Since 1977 the economy has been opened up by the removal of import and exchange controls and other regulatory mechanisms as well as the creation of a legal and organizational infrastructure to encourage a liberal flow of foreign investment and aid. The consequent conditions – the expansion of export-oriented industries within and outside the EPZ, the process of social differentiation within the working class, state intervention in industrial relations and growing ethnic consciousness – have posed unprecedented challenges and problems to the whole spectrum of trade unionism in the country.

*Thanks all due to Mr Bala Tampoe (Ceylon Mercantile Union) and Mr Batty Weerakoon (Ceylon Federation of Labour) for their help in obtaining information and data; and to Dr L.C.D. Kulatungam for his help in the writing of this chapter.

The trade union movement, moulded on the British trade union model, reached its zenith under welfarism and parliamentary democracy. However, it has now been shaken to its foundations under the open economy and presidential rule. The purpose of the present paper is to examine how the trade union movement has responded to these new challenges in the context of the changing socio-economic conditions of labour under the open economy.

Sri Lanka and the International Division of Labour

At political independence in 1948 Sri Lanka was a typical underdeveloped/dependent economy. Primary products–tea, rubber, and coconut–provided 97% of foreign exchange earnings, 40% of the country's GNP and supplied employment for about 30% of the total work-force.[1] On the other hand, the great bulk of the foreign exchange earnings of the country was utilized to import manufactured goods for day to day consumption. The country's economic prospects thus heavily depended upon the world market forces controlled by the metropolitan countries. The policy-makers during the period, however, made no attempt to restructure the export–import economy inherited from the colonial past.[2] Sri Lanka was fortunate to be able to capitalize upon two export booms–the Korean War boom, 1950-2 and tea export boom, 1954-5–and was hence able to maintain a favourable foreign exchange situation. One consequence was that policy-makers became complacent and were more than satisfied with Sri Lanka's subsidiary location within the existing international division of labour.

After 1955, however, winds changed. Tea and rubber prices in the world market steadily declined, and as a consequence foreign reserves were rapidly depleted and the foreign exchange problems became continuous. In response, the populist-oriented regime which was elected in 1956 now sought to restructure the economy by turning to a determined strategy of import-substituting industrialization.

The import-substitution initiative first found policy expression in the Ten Year Plan, 1958-68.[3] The perspective of the plan was to develop industries to meet the local demand within a protected market. Beginning with the budget of 1957/8 Sri Lanka gradually implemented a system of protective tariffs to encourage import-substitution industries. In 1961 a system of direct import controls was implemented as the foreign exchange situation became increasingly critical, and Sri Lanka turned slowly into a closed economy.

The closed economy policy inherited certain weaknesses. There was a natural bias against exports. The highly protected domestic market 'implied relatively low profitability of production for the export market'.[4] The import controls implemented since 1961 had created an overvalued exchange rate thus lowering the rupee earnings of exports; one of the explicit objectives of the import-substitution strategy was to reduce foreign exchange spending on imports. However, the import-substitution industries themselves had to depend largely on imported raw materials and machinery thus frustrating the desired objectives of the policy. It was during this period that the importance of export-oriented industrialization was seriously discussed within policy-making circles. However, it was believed that the local entrepreneur class was incapable of initiating export industries independently and therefore that foreign investments should be invited and/or the state sector should take the initiative.

However, the nationalist democratic regime which came into power in 1970 was more oriented towards the policy of state initiated export-oriented industrialization schemes than encouraging foreign investment in this sphere. The foreign investment approval scheme, in fact, became restrictive. Only 20 economic ventures were approved with foreign capital participation during 1970-77 while the number of ventures approved during the 1960–65 regime was 40. There was a marked decline in direct foreign investment during this period. While new industrialization was taking shape through foreign investment in export industries in some developing countries[5] the environment in Sri Lanka was not conducive to this development, not least because of widespread fear of nationalization under the Business Acquisition Act (1971) and the discouraging strict criteria adopted in approving foreign investment projects. In contrast, the Five Year Plan of 1970-77 envisaged the development of a new industrial export sector initiated by the public corporations.[6] It was mainly in the sphere of the export of petroleum products that this objective was to be achieved.

Since 1977, when the present United National Party (UNP) regime assumed office, an overall change has been made in the field of industrial

Table 6.1 Export value of primary products vs manufactured goods 1965-1982 (percentage shares)

	1960–65	*1970–77*	*1978*	*1979*	*1980*	*1981*	*1982*
Primary products:	99.54	91.55	85.44	75.69	68.09	66.63	65.88
Traditional	89.40	77.87	72.25	62.29	55.21	51.22	46.2
Non-Traditional	10.14	13.68	13.19	13.40	12.88	15.41	19.68
Manufactured goods:	0.46	8.45	14.56	24.31	31.91	33.37	36.12
Garments	1.8	0.85	3.65	7.32	10.56	14.87	16.50
Petroleum Products	—	7.36	7.15	12.61	14.17	14.17	13.86
Other Items	.28	.24	3.76	4.38	7.18	4.33	5.76

Source: Athukorala & Jayatilake, February 1984.

strategy and in the general economic policy. The strategy has been an export-led development within a broader framework of an open economy.[7] By strengthening the market mechanism and linking the economy closely with the world system the increasingly moribund capitalist system in the country has been given a new lease of life. The open economy policy implemented under the guidelines given by the World Bank and the IMF has placed a greater emphasis on direct foreign investment in achieving the objective of export led-growth, with numerous 'more than normally attractive'[8] concessions having been offered to foreign investors.

The open economy policy has now been operating since 1977 and it is therefore not too early to assess its contribution towards the country's liberation from the old international division of labour. A look at the commodity composition of exports (see Table 1) certainly reveals a shift towards manufactured goods. Thus the percentage share of primary exports came down from 91.55% in the 1970–77 period to 65.88% in 1982, while the percentage share of manufactured exports went up from 8.45% in the 1970-77 period to 36.12% in 1982. However, it should be noted that among the manufactured exports, petroleum products accounted for about 40%, the export promotion dating back to the pre-1977 period, and being handled by a state run corporation. In that it is somewhat questionable whether petroleum products (mainly refined oil) can be considered as an industrial finished good, the main achievement of the open economy, so far, in the sphere of export-oriented industrialization, is the rapid expansion of the garment industry, whose percentage share of exports is in the range of 16 to 18%. Overall, however, while it is correct to say that there has been some effort to diversify exports with an emphasis on manufactured items, Sri Lanka still continues to operate largely within the framework of the old international division of labour.

The New Proletariat

The expansion of the working class is one significant development that has taken place under the open economy. It is estimated that around 1.5 million new jobs have been created since 1977.[9] The expansion of the working class has been both industrial and non-industrial. The expansion in trade, tourism, banking, private transport, construction and commerce has been more apparent under the open economy than expansion in industry. As a consequence, the number of the industrial proletariat has increased only marginally while the number of employees in tertiary sectors has increased greatly. The nature of the above expansion has necessarily had a profound impact on Sri Lankan trade unionism in that, first, the new employees in non-industrial jobs are scattered among numerous small business establishments (rendering collective organization problematic); and second, the new proletariat in industry is located in an Export Processing Zone from which unions are effectively excluded.

Trade Unions and the Expansion of the Service Sector.

The increased level of trade, both wholesale and retail, has absorbed a large amount of labour as sales workers, clerical employees, sales representatives, porters, drivers and many other diverse categories. However, because such labour is mainly employed on a casual basis and subject to high turnover, it has hitherto remained very largely unorganized.

Within the tourist industry, for instance, rapid growth has offered a wide variety of opportunities directly in hotels and indirectly in several servicing sectors. The total number of persons directly employed in the tourist industry was 26,776 in 1983. The majority were hotel employees such as waiters, cooks, receptionists, room boys, janitors and guards. The total amount of indirect employment generated by tourism as at the end of 1983 has been estimated at 37,486 jobs.[10] Employment in the tourist sector is partly seasonal, with many employees being out of work during the off seasons. Similarly it has been estimated that a drastic drop of tourist arrivals in 1983 after the July communal violence threw about 25,000 persons out of work.

A further sphere which has seen the development of new proletarian elements has been transport. In 1977, for the first time since the nationalization of bus services in 1959, passenger transport was opened up to private sector participation. This was further encouraged by the easing of restrictions upon the import of vehicles, so that by 1983 there were some 12,000 passenger vans and buses operated by the private sector.[11] These accounted for the direct employment of over 35,000 workers, mainly as drivers and conductors.

In building and construction, meanwhile, there were 57,881 employees registered under the Employees Provident Fund in 1980 (compared with only 23,774 in 1976). However, these were easily outnumbered by casual workers, so that the actual number of labourers employed by the construction industries may exceed 150,000, most of them employed on a short-term, unregistered basis. Such a situation, whereby employers can summon up a workforce from a pool of surplus labour, is hardly conducive to trade unionism. As a result, the only evidence of union activity appears amongst workers engaged on long term projects such as the Victoria Hydro Electrical Project.

The new employees in trade, tourism, construction and private transport represent an important segment of the new proletariat with some significant common characteristics. In brief, they are mainly casual workers with a high rate of turnover. They are scattered and fragmented among a large number of small business units with limited opportunities to see their problems and interests in common. But critical is the fact that, because they are employed in a highly competitive sector in which many concerns are marginal, they are made constantly aware that any increase in the return to labour may push their employers out of business. In such precarious circumstances, the prospects for organization of labour are inhibited by workers' perceived shared interest with employers.[12]

The EPZ and the Problems of Unionization

The Export Processing Zone (EPZ) is one area where the industrial proletariat has expanded. The concept of setting up an EPZ was first contemplated in Sri Lanka in 1974. However, this idea was soon abandoned for political reasons. After the change of government, in 1977, the Greater Colombo Economic Commission (GCEC) was set up in 1978, with the task of attracting and promoting export-oriented foreign investment.[13] The GCEC established an EPZ besides the Colombo International Airport at Katunayake. While the growth of the enterprises under the GCEC since 1978 may fall short of the projected progress, it is nevertheless noteworthy. Statistics put up by the GCEC record that, by the end of May 1984, the GCEC had approved 187 projects of which 75 enterprises were in commercial or trial production. The total number of employees in the GCEC enterprises amounted to 32,629 at the end of May 1984.[14]

Outside the investment areas covered by the GCEC the Foreign Investment Advisory Committee (FIAC) has been assigned to promote foreign investment in various spheres. Between 1977 and May 1984 FIAC had approved 686 enterprises with a heavy foreign investment component. The potential employment in these units was estimated at 88,500.[15] Most of these enterprises are in the tourist trade, construction, garments and similar light manufacturing ventures.

One consequence of the expansion of the foreign investment enterprises is the emergence of a new type of industrial working class. The social profile of workers in the EPZ is symbolic of this new industrial proletariat.[16] The predominance of women workers is one significant feature of these export-oriented industries. More than 85% of the workforce in the EPZ are women, primarily concentrated in the garment industries. There are two significant characteristics of these workers – age and civil status. It is estimated that close upon 75% of the workers in the EPZ are below 25 years of age. It is also observed that most of them are unmarried. These characteristics are not unique to Sri Lanka, for the new industrial proletariat which fills up the EPZs of other third world countries shows the same characteristics.[17] The economic logic seems to be that 'women are the cheapest of cheap third world labour'. The culturally conditioned Asian women are considered docile and capable of engaging in repetitive, dull and monotonous work without much protest. It is assumed that if men were subject to the same working conditions, they would protest and agitate through labour organizations.

Although the official GCEC brochure states that the workers are free to form trade unions, there are apparently strong pressures against so doing.

Some of the pressures come through the recruitment process itself. A special unit in the GCEC which functions as a job bank has been established to handle recruitment to the zone. Before recruitment a political screening is conducted. There are, in fact, no trade unions in the EPZ area proper. Indeed, it has been suggested that 'since the majority of workers are young women on arbitrarily extendable periods of apprenticeship and with no previous experience in industrial employment, they are incapable of being organised in unions'.[18] Furthermore, the workers are subjected to strict surveillance on grounds of security, with the EPZ having been labelled by its critics as a 'concentration camp'. It is virtually impossible for union organizers not only to enter the area but also carry out any kind of union activity near it. Furthermore the police use extra-legal means to prevent workers becoming organized: they prevent workers from assembling in private premises; they have prohibited picketing; they have banned the distribution of leaflets: and they even tear down union posters. A leading women trade unionist complained that

> when, recently, a member of my union was distributing leaflets against the attempt of the Government to repeal the law prohibiting night work for women, on the public highway leading to the airport, a police officer arrived in a jeep belonging to one of the companies in the EPZ and arbitrarily confiscated the leaflets apart from threatening to have our members arrested.[19]

The absence of trade unions in the PEZ has enabled the employers to practise the absolute exploitation of the workforce. It is claimed that at Esquire Industries Ltd which produces the well known 'Gloria Vanderbilt' jeans, the starting wage is Rs 350 (about US$ 17) per month rising up to Rs 450 (= US$ 22). These girls produce 20 pairs of jeans a day which sell in the US market at $40 per pair. Thus the daily output of each girl is worth $800 on the US market, for which she is paid less than one dollar.[20] Certain studies have revealed that the majority of EPZ workers come from families with monthly incomes of less than Rs 500. Even when these workers' incomes are added, the household incomes of most of the families still fall below the poverty line.

At the moment the reactions of the workers in the EPZ to their acute deprivation and exploitation have not been articulated. However, the very fact that they are paid at less than the rate of reproduction and further are victims of insecurity of employment, long working hours (including compulsory overtime), and rest and toilet facilities which can in no way be described as adequate, argues that there is considerable potential for organization and trade union activity. This may be demonstrated by reference to the experience of workers at Polytex Garments, an operation which runs outside the EPZ yet within the jurisdiction of the GCEC.

Polytex is the largest garment factory in the GCEC area of authority. Polytex employs 1,400 workers at its factory and 98% of the workers are women. At first there was no trade union at the factory. In March 1983, however, although without any formal organization, the workers went on strike demanding better working conditions. The strike lasted for one month and the workers managed to achieve their major demands including the recognition of their newly formed union by the management.[21] Since then, there have been three further strikes at the factory, each of which has ended satisfactorily. The last of these occurred in February 1984 and lasted for two-and-a-half months after the workers, led by the Industrial, Transport and General Workers' Union, downed tools when six colleagues were sacked for not meeting production targets. The union asked for eight demands including the re-instatement of the six sacked workers. The strike was supported by the radical women's organizations both within and outside the country,[22] and the upshot was that workers managed to win a two months bonus and a salary increase of Rs 75 per month.

The success of the Polytex workers has been a source of great encouragement to workers in other factories. As a result, there have been a number of attempts by workers within the GCEC area (albeit outside the EPZ) to form unions and to struggle for basic rights. Most of these have yet to make any obvious progress. At Monta Garments, for example, some 400 workers sought to form a union affiliated to the Ceylon Mercantile Union. However, their strike to demand the re-instatement of their leaders who had been dismissed once management learned of their activities ended unsuccessfully. None the less, it would appear that workers are becoming increasingly prepared to flex their muscles and to engage in struggle with employers.

Table 6.2 Strikes since 1948 (annual averages for selected periods)

		Private sector			Plantation sector		
Period	*Regime in power*	*Number of strikes*	*Number of workers involved*	*Number of days lost*	*Number of strikes*	*Number of workers involved*	*Number of days lost*
1948–51	UNP	28	4,034	14,294	248	829,411	1,338,150
1952–55	UNP	49	11,831	47,641	188	466,932	901,113
1956–59	SLFP	102	46,957	301,438	576	440,659	1,511,705
1960–64	SLFP	72	29,950	435,424	726	244,840	1,742,571
1965–69	UNP	48	11,796	183,188	818	408,926	3,142,999
1970–76	SLFP	54	11,984	160,386	1,025	414,471	2,323,336
1977–81	UNP	27	5,342	41,296	874	347,772	1,421,340

Source: Department of Labour.

Labour Market Segmentation and the Decline in Union Activity.

The period since 1977 has been characterized by relative industrial peace with a low level of class struggle and trade union activity. Table 2 indicates annual average strike figures in the private and the plantation sectors roughly during the different regimes in power since 1948. These figures show that the incidence of strikes was lowest in the private sector during 1977 and 1978 under the open economy. The number of workers involved in the private sector strikes was only slightly above the figure for 1948–51, when the size of the industrial working class was extremely small. The number of man days lost also was minimal compared to the previous periods. Figures relating to the plantation sector also show a relative lull in the strike movements during 1977-81 compared to previous periods.

While the size of the working class has expanded under the open economy, the trade union movement and its activities have stagnated. Table 3 reveals the stagnation and/or the decline trend of registered trade union membership since 1977. It is true that registration of trade unions has become more restrictive since 1977. However the declining trend in union membership mostly reveals a trend of demoralization within the working class.

The de-radicalization of the working class is due, in no small measure, to the increasing differentiation and segmentation of the labour market. This has occurred because the opening up of the economy has been accompanied since 1977 by impressive growth in terms of GNP and per capita real income. However, the nature of this growth has been such that the gap between the rich and the poor has been increased and the process of internal social differentiation within the working class accelerated; for although the open economy has brought important wage gains compared to the situation prior to 1977, these increases have not been substantial enough in many categories to offset the effects of inflation. Amongst lower middle class groups, for instance, government clerks and school teachers

Table 6.3 Trade unions, 1977-1982

	1977	*1978*	*1979*	*1980*	*1981*	*1982*
Registered	175	102	105	95	75	74
Cancelled	117	288	246	191	108	13
Functioning	1636	1450	1309	1213	1180	1241
Total membership	*1,399,902*	*967,795*	*1,440,720*	*1,337,664*	*1,010,112*	*1,220,110*

Source: Department of Labour.

have been most badly affected, with real wage indices revealing long-term stagnation in their earnings.

Before 1977, the socio-economic conditions of the working class were characterized by low wages and a high rate of unemployment. Internal differentiation within the working class was fairly minimal and workers experienced an equality of poverty. Although there were no substantial differences in wage levels between public sector and private sector employees, public sector employment was much preferred on account of its offering job security, pension schemes and other fringe benefits. Subsequently, however, the opening up of the economy has drastically changed the internal structure of the working class in that market forces have now become the major criteria of wage determination, and a result, wage levels in the private service sector (although not, of course, in the Export Processing Zone) are now substantially higher than in the public sector. In consequence, there are now substantial differences in wages from one sector to another and from trade to trade; for instance, bank clerks now earn three times the salary of government clerks, whilst the wages of skilled workers have similarly begun to overhaul those of clerical workers. Finally, the introduction of incentive systems even into state run industries has had the effect of widening the wage gap between skilled and other workers.

In sum, the segmentation of the labour market which has accompanied the opening up of the economy – between different elements of the new proletariat, between workers in the public and private spheres, and between skilled and unskilled – has broken down the homogeneity of the working class, and has made it much more difficult for the unions to unite and/or mobilize workers under a common cause.

State Intervention in Union Struggles

The working class in Sri Lanka has traditionally been in the forefront of militant trade union agitation and left-wing party politics. Militant trade unionism has a history of about a hundred years, the early period of which is well documented.[23] However the trade union movement has never been confronted with such challenges, problems and difficulties as they face at present, for if working-class unity has been rendered more problematic by its increasing social differentiation, then the working-class capacity for action has been additionally compromised by an increased level of state repression.

The present UNP government came into power in 1977 preceded by a strike wave in late 1976 and early 1977 against the previous regime. This wave was a backlash against the policies of the national democratic and centre left government of the Sri Lanka Freedom Party (SLFP), the Lanka Sama Samaja Party (LSSP), and the Communist Party (CP) which had led among other things, to food shortages and huge unemployment. There were clear indications by 1977 that broad sections of the working class had moved away from left-wing political parties toward the UNP, a party which was well known for its conservative and right-wing policies. The total strength of the left at the 1977 elections was a mere 500,000. The workers, of course, did not switch their trade union membership overnight. First many of them became politically aligned with the UNP at the elections, and thereafter, most of them joined the UNP unions. However, in the process, a large number of previously unionized workers became uninterested in trade union activities and as a result dropped out. At present the largest trade union outside the plantation sector is the Jathika Sevaka Sangamaya (JSS) controlled by the governing party – the UNP. The objective of the UNP unions was to deny an important element of backing and militancy to the left. Its method of action was not to win workers' demands through trade union action but to gain benefits to their members through the use of political patronage.

After the first budget under the open economy in November 1977, the left-wing trade unions mobilized against the rupee devaluation, price increases and subsidy cuts. The Joint Trade Union Action Committee (JTUAC) was formed with ten federations and six large unions representing important trade union centres of the oppositional political parties. The victory of the UNP at the election, however, has itself led to a demoralization of the left-wing forces and therefore the worker response to the left-wing call to protest against the budget was not very impressive. In January 1978 the government tabled a White Paper on employment with the hope that it would go unchallenged. This White Paper proposed to outlaw strikes in essential services and to prohibit strikes anywhere without 21 days notice, as well as introducing other stringent measures against militant trade unionism.[24] Surprisingly enough the JTUAC managed to organize a forceful protest against the White Paper and this protest showed that the old guard of militant trade unionism was still ready to fight back if their basic rights were at stake. One positive result of this agitation was that the government had to postpone the implementation of the White Paper for at least a year.

During 1978 there had been minor strikes and sporadic work stoppages at various places both in the private and in the state corporations. The one-day token strike by the Ceylon Bank Employees Union in July was the most successful among these. Encouraged by the success of the bank strike the JTUAC prematurely decided to stage a major confrontation with the government by calling a one-day national work stoppage on 28 September to protest against the escalation of the cost of living and the repressive measures of the government against the trade unions. This decision proved, however, to be a total miscalculation. The government immediately declared that the proposed strike was politically motivated and announced that every employee who did not report for work would be deemed to have vacated his or her post under the emergency regulations.[25] In the context of this forceful government offensive, the JTUAC felt no alternative but to call off the strike. The calling off of the strike, on the other hand, led to a recession in trade union activity.[26] The workers became demoralized about their strength and sceptical about the trade unions' capacity to safeguard their rights.

It was only in 1979 that the trade unions showed signs of revival against the implementation of some aspects of the White Paper in the form of a Parliamentary Bill – the Essential Public Services Bill (EPS).[27] Although the JTUAC organized forceful picketing campaigns throughout the country, they were not in a position, this time, to stop or postpone the passage of the EPS bill. However the trade union movement was successful in the early months of 1980 in its campaign against the proposal to curtail the holidays and to change the working hours of state employees. The reason for the success was obvious. The issue appealed to many workers and therefore broad support could be mobilized for the campaign. The government tactfully took a step back by withdrawing the proposal to curtail holidays in April.

There was another important reason for the revival of militancy among the working class in the early months of 1980. That was the sharp escalation of the cost of living. It was estimated that there had been a 75% rise in the cost of bare subsistence between May 1979 and May 1980.[28] The growing frustration of the workers was reflected when the JTUAC sponsored a trade union delegates convention in early March. Over 3,500 delegates from sixty odd trade unions affiliated to major oppositional parties were present. The convention put forward 23 demands to the government and decided to organize a day of mass protest.

The day chosen to protest against the government in a support of the 23 demands was 5 June. The protest turned into a confrontation with the government when the government sponsored trade unions organized a day of solidarity against the protest. The violent incidents of the protest day resulted in one dead and 40 wounded. However, despite the counter-attacks by the government supporters, the day of protest did register something of an advance. In particular, as a consequence of the death of a leading opposition trade union leader at the hands of government supporters on the protest day, there was growing resentment among the working class over the government's actions and policies.[29] The government provocatively used this situation as an excuse to victimize trade union activists who organized the protest day and the funeral of Somapala. It was these victimizations and the issue of cost of living which led first to the Rathmalana railway strike in early July which flared up into a general strike within a few days.

It is estimated that 70–75,000 public sector employees and 10–15,000 private sector employees participated in the general strike of July 1980. Participation in the strike was, however, unbalanced, as the plantation sector, employing over 600,000 workers, was totally unaffected; further, Colombo and other ports were not disrupted. Thus although there was long-term disruption of work in government departments, regional offices of central departments (Kachcheries) and local government offices, essential services where the strike could have been most effective were hardly disrupted during the strike. The supply of power, water, transport and food distribution continued undisturbed. The strike was effective mainly in the government clerical service. In this context, the government was able to lock out all those workers who participated through the use of emergency regulations. They also gave an ultimatum of dismissal to those who did not return to work by a given date. Overall, this strike, which led to the dismissal of about 40,000 workers, has to be characterized as a failure.[30] The failure of the July 1980 general strike marked a long term recession in trade union activity and class struggle in the country. Only at the beginning of 1984 did trade unions show new life with the formation of a new front of 21 trade unions.

Ethnicity and Class Consciousness

The demise of effective trade union activity since 1977 has been matched by incessant ethnic rioting.[31] The transition to the open economy, it would seem, has worked to divide the working class and to exacerbate tensions between the major ethnic communities.

The aftermath of the 1977 elections witnessed widespread anti-Tamil riots. Further, riots again broke out in 1979 with the Tamil plantation workers now being the main target of attack. Subsequently, numerous instances of localized violence both against the Tamil and Muslim minorities finally culminated in the anti-Tamil holocaust of July 1983. There is no clear evidence to determine the direct involvement of workers in these riots although a major government affiliated trade union has been prominent in propagating communal politics among the working class for some time. Such as there is, however, reveals that elements peripheral to the working class, such as intinerant workers, the urban unemployed and sections of the urban poor were in the forefront of these riots. It seems that the working class has not only lost its hegemony within the urban population but also has itself become vulnerable to ethnic and other non-working-class pressures. The low level of class consciousness which is revealed in the low level of trade union activity and the heightened ethnic consciousness within the working class are indicative of this.

During the period of the hundred years of its history the working class has gone through various phases of development and change. The first phase was the period between 1883 and 1915. It was during this period that certain sections of the workers (printers, railwaymen, harbour workers, carters and laundrymen) began to realize themselves as a class and to perceive that their interests were different from those of their employers. This is the period when trade unions were formed for the first time in this country and scattered and spontaneous strikes occurred. Religious leaders, social workers and philanthropists were the people who inspired the workers and helped them in organizing strikes and trade unions. However no particular ideology sustained the working class and the workers' consciousness was in a form of what can be called 'an awareness of common misery and problems'.[32] This period ended ironically with the first major communal conflict between the Sinhalese and the Muslims involving numbers of the urban working class.

The second phase of development (1915–35) was marked by the organization of trade unions on a national scale, the formation of trade union federations, and the corresponding emergence of a layer of professional trade unionists. The workers became more aware of their economic interests and expressed more courage and willingness to fight for their rights. Thus the period was marked by militant trade union struggles, at a time when a radical nationalist trend was also emerging. It was from this radical nationalist element that the leadership of the trade union movement came, a product of which was that the orientation and ideology of the workers' movement also became nationalist. During the period, also, there were a considerable number of immigrant South Indian workers within the urban labour force; yet initially workers belonging to different ethnic communities were organized under the same banner. However, the nationalist orientation of the workers' movement had its own logic. During the period of economic depression of the 1930s, in the context of severe unemployment, ethnic feelings against immigrant South Indian workers acquired a degree of prominence among the urban working Sinhalese workers.

A new phase opened up with the formation of the first left-wing party in 1935. Slowly but steadily the left-wing infiltrated the trade union movement.[33] More militancy and class awareness were injected into the working class. Strikes and general strikes were organized not only to champion economic demands but also political causes. The zenith of this phase was 1953 when a *hartal* (general stoppage of work) was organized and there was an open confrontation between the government and the workers' movement. During this phase a form of socialist consciousness was achieved. This consciousness, though not revolutionary, was nevertheless militant. It was during this phase that a genuine attempt was made to unite the urban Sinhalese workers and the Tamil plantation workers. The concept of nationalization, economic planning and welfarism were the basic notions of this socialist consciousness. However there was no concept of worker political power.

From 1956 onwards the workers' movement entered into a decisive and crucial period. It was a period of state capitalism where nationalization and policies of economic planning were implemented. This was also a period of Sinhala chauvinism and populism. Under state capitalism the incumbent regimes seemed to be implementing policies for which the left-wing parties had been agitating for decades. The workers' movement succumbed to this new trend stage by stage. Bourgeois parties which promised welfare measures organized their own working-class following. It was during this period that a deep gulf between the two major ethnic communities, the

Sinhalese and the Tamils, was steadily created, based mainly on language. A minor communal clash occurred in 1956 and a major riot in 1958. The left movement first tried to resist the discriminatory communal policy but soon succumbed to the Sinhalese nationalism which found echoes within the working class itself. The major working-class parties participated in a coalition government in 1970 to implement a programme of socialist measures with the bourgeois nationalist SLFP. The majority of the workers enthusiastically supported this regime in the hope that it would create a socialist society. This was the peak of their workers' false consciousness. They were left at the end with severe unemployment, galloping inflation and food shortages.

The maturity of class consciousness lies in the workers' capacity to recognize their own class interests. This, however, presupposes a certain understanding of the processes of the economic system. It is our view that the working-class movement in this country failed to grasp or erroneously grasped the operations of state capitalism since 1956. It was a failure that the workers identified their interests with state capitalism. However they became disillusioned during the period 1970–76. Without sufficient time to recover from their disillusionment, they have been confronted with a new economic reality since 1977. The new economic reality, which is money motivated, consumerist and with priority given to personal achievement, has at the moment taken broad sections of the working class and especially the new proletariat under its ideological hegemony. Class consciousness has ebbed and ethnic consciousness has become predominant.

The working class in Sri Lanka has experienced significant shifts and changes in its economic conditions, internal class structure, cultural orientations and political behaviour as a consequence of the shift to an open economy policy since 1977. The substantially greater emphasis on the export of low cost industrial goods has had ramifications which extend well beyond the exploitation of labour within the EPZ to entail, in addition, the increased repression and division of the trade union movement.

The expansion of the working class and the widening gap between the rich and the poor are two significant developments in the sphere of industrial relations since 1977. While money incomes of working-class families have increased as a result of wage increases and/or additional family members being employed, the high rate of inflation has meant that real incomes have increased only among certain sections. The growing consumerism, which can clearly be seen even among the lower income groups, has expanded the expectations of the working class. In such circumstances, the expected and natural reaction from the working class is the launching of strikes and other trade union agitation for higher wages and more fringe benefits. However, ironically, the period since 1977 has been characterized by relative industrial peace. There have been very few strikes of significance. The number of strikes and the number of workers involved has declined annually while the number of days lost has been minimal. Not only has militant trade unionism declined but the membership of the trade unions has dwindled. The main problematic of the present paper has been, therefore, to investigate the possible reasons for the apparent apathy and de-radicalization of the trade union movement in the recent period of Sri Lanka's history.

The open economy with its accompanying policies of encouragement to foreign investment and cuts in social welfare has necessitated the creation of political mechanisms which could keep opposition, dissent and strikes at bay. Such mechanisms have included a more authoritarian type of constitution as well as direct legislation against strikes and militant trade unionism. The open economy has, in fact, been accompanied by a closed polity. However, authoritarian policies cannot be the sole reason for the apparent low profile of the trade union movement. Socio-economic changes and changes in the level and form of class consciousness within the working class appear to account, among other factors, for the present low level of class struggle and militant trade unionism.

This paper has identified the expansion of the industrial proletariat as marginal mainly confined to young women workers in the EPZ and other garment industries. Although the mainly female new industrial proletariat demonstrates a high potential for organization and trade union activity, the process of unionization of these workers has not yet got off the ground. It is the author's view that women workers should be seen not only as workers but also as women if they are to be unionized successfully.

The demobilization of the older generations of the working class is basically political and largely the result of their experiences of disillusionment under the previous centre left regime during 1970 and 1977. The class solidarity of these traditional fractions of the working class has further been severely disturbed under the open economy as a result of new differential wage structures, internal social differentiation and the upward social mobility of certain sections. The trade union movement has to devise ways and means of reorganizing these workers without clinging to traditional styles, demands and slogans.

Finally, the Sinhala-Tamil conflict has clearly made the situation within the working class more complex. Given the obstacle that ethnic definitions represent to the development of class consciousness at this moment of particularly fraught communal tensions in Sri Lanka, attainment of a democratic and equitable solution to the ethnic problem is necessarily of paramount importance to the future of the trade union movement.

Notes

1. R. Amarasinghe, and P.V.J. Jayasekera, 'The Economy, Society and Polity from Independence to 1977', (ISS & SSA) Seminar Paper, Colombo, December 1983.

2. D.R. Snodgrass, *Ceylon: An Export Economy in Transition* (Richard D. Irwin, Illinois, 1966).

3. *The Ten Year Plan, 1958-68* (National Planning Council, Colombo, 1959), p.167.

4. P. Athukorala, and S.B. Jayatilaka, 'Export Development in Sri Lanka: Policies and Progress', (Mimeo, February 1984).

5. F. Frobel, J. Heinrichs and O. Kreye, *The New International Division of Labour* (Cambridge University Press, Cambridge, 1981).

6. *The Five Year Plan, 1972–76* (Ministry of Planning and Employment, Colombo, 1971), pp.65-72.

7 D. Ramanayake, *The Katunayake Investment Promotion Zone: A Case Study* (ARTEP, Bangkok, 1982), p.3.

8. 'Sri Lanka 81', *Far Eastern Economic Review*, 1981.

9. *Economic Review*, May 1983.

10. *Ceylon Report of the Central Bank 1983*, (Ceylon), pp.79-82.

11. Ibid., p.46.

12. L. Fernando, 'The Urban Poor in Sri Lanka: The Contemporary Scene', ISS & SSA Seminar Paper, December 1983.

13. The Greater Colombo Economic Commission Law No.4 of 1978.

14. *Central Bank of Ceylon Bulletin* (Ceylon), June 1984.

15. Ibid.

16. *Economic Review*, June 1983.

17. G. Edgren, *Spearheads of Industrialisation or Sweatshops in the Sun* (ARTEP, Bangkok, 1982), pp.8–12.

18. May Wickramasooriya, 'Problems of the Organisation of Women Workers in theFTZ' (mimeo).

19. Author's interview with Ms May Wickramasooriya, the Joint Secretary of the Ceylon Mercantile Union.

20. *Free Labour World*, 4 July 1981.

21. *Prathiravaya* (Sinhala bulletin of the Independent, Transport and General Workers' Union), March 1983, p.3.

22. *Island*, 29 April 1984, p.1.

23. See V.K. Jayawardena, *The Rise of the Labour Movement in Ceylon* (Duke University Press, Durham, 1972); R.N. Kearney, *Trade Unions and Politics in Ceylon* (Thomson Press Limited, New Delhi, 1971); V. Sarvaloganayagam, *Trade Unions in Sri Lanka* (Academy of Administrative Studies, Colombo, 1973).

24. Centre for Society and Religion, 'Memorandum on the White Paper on Employment Relations', 15 March 1978.

25. Public Administration Circular, 15 September 1978.

26. *Lanka Guardian*, 1 October 1978, p.3.

27. See Colvin R. de Silva, 'EPS Law and the Constitution', *Lanka Guardian*, 1 November 1979, pp.10–11.

28. *Satyodaya*, July 1980.

29. *Christian Worker*, August 1980, p.4.

30. L. Fernando, 'The State and Class Struggle in Sri Lanka: The General

Strike of July 1980', *Labour, Capital and Society*, November 1983.

31. N. Gunasinghe, 'The Open Economic Policy and Its Impact on Ethnic Relations in Sri Lanka', ISS & SSA Seminar Paper, Colombo, December 1983.

32. N. Gunasinghe, 'On the Class Consciousness of the Agrarian Proletariat in Sri Lanka', in S. Epstein (ed.), *The Paradox of Poverty* (Kapoor Art Press, Delhi, 1975), p.100.

33. V.K. Jayawardena, 'The Origins of the Left Movement in Sri Lanka.

7 Industrialization Strategy and Labour's Response: The Case of the Workers' Councils in Iran

Valentine M. Moghadam

Situating the Middle East in the Changing International Division of Labour

In the mid-1970s, the parallel developments of economic crisis in the advanced capitalist countries (ACCs) and the emergence of a special category of third world societies called the newly industrialized countries (NICs) led to new theoretical formulations on the structure of the world system. It also prompted research into the possible linkages between the two and their relations. Rationalization, automation and high technology industries in the West went hand in hand with redeployment to the third world and the growth of the NICs. Intensive accumulation in the latter was based on the extraction of surplus value, increases in productivity, improvements in technology – and repression. The internal market was growing, and a large proportion of production – now of manufactures – was for export. The changing international division of labour was expressed in developments in the labour process in manufacturing, the worldwide reserve of cheap labour, and the massive growth in technology, transport and communications. The trend towards global Fordism and the intensive accumulation occurring in the NICs based on 'bloody Taylorism' seemed to reflect a restructuring of the global capitalist system. Theorists such as Frobel, Heinrich and Kreye, Warren, Palloix, Aglietta and Lipietz examined these processes and offered new formulations on the relations between the NICs and the ACCs and the linkages between production, accumulation, and class struggle.

The issues raised by the theorists of the changing international division of labour include the depth, scope, linkages and replicability of third world industrialization; the origins of the world crisis and its relation to third world industrialization; the role of banks and the linkages between finance and industry; divisions within the third world itself; the authoritarian state in the third world and the implications for workers' solidarity, particularly in the wake of protectionist tendencies in the ACCs.

The literature on the internationalization of capital and the changing international division of labour has tended to focus on Latin America, South Asia and South-East Asia, with some discussion of Africa. However, the Middle East has been largely absent from the debate. There is, of course, the problem of conceptualizing the Middle East. What are its constituent elements and its boundaries? There are important differences between oil-producing Middle East states and the others. There is also the possibility that Turkey (if indeed it is considered Near/Middle East) and Tunisia, with their more developed economies, political structures, and trade unions, comprise a category of their own. It could be argued (and indeed, has been) that oil-producing Middle East countries are exempt from typical patterns of capitalist development because the predominant role of oil revenues has imposed a unique character on the state (rentier rather than capitalist) and, consequently, on domestic accumulation (restricted, non-competitive, and based on the export of oil rather than of manufactures). Economic development based on excess profits accrued from the monopoly price of a strategic commodity has been a mixed blessing, and one that has been more illusory than real.

However, if we agree that capitalist development globally has not followed a uniform path, and that the third world is not an undifferentiated, homogeneous bloc, then we can proceed with an examination of the ways in which developing societies in the Middle East are integrated into the global system of production and exchange, and of the inevitable peculiarities that have arisen in the process. Hence it should be noted that much of the oil revenue at the disposal of Middle Eastern states – representing a significant capital flow from the West, especially during the 1970s – has been channelled into productive capacities. Transnational capital's assistance in this broad strategy has taken the form of initial facilitating projects, assembly operations, engineering consultancy, managerial and technical services, direct investment, and training programmes – all of which have contributed to accumulation domestically and externally. It is also important to note that the oil revenue that has gone into non-productive activity – such as enormous military expenditures and huge deposits in western banks – represents a recycling of petrodollars that has been crucial to the international accumulation process.

Agrarian transformations, industrialization, technology transfer, direct productive investment and so on have occurred in many countries of the Middle East; these developments have been particularly striking in the oil-producing states, where change has come rapidly. Capital flows, labour migration and the circulation of oil revenue have been important features of capitalist development in the Middle East that ought to be situated in a global, as well as regional and domestic, context.

The pattern of economic development followed by Iran in the 1960s and 1970s had many of the salient features of development elsewhere in the third world: agrarian reform, import-substitution industrialization, foreign investment, growth of the manufacturing sector (private and state), growth of the industrial labour force. Indeed, the growth of the manufacturing sector was so impressive (by 1976 it has absorbed 19% of the economically active population) that in the 1970s development literature Iran was sometimes included in the varying lists of the NICs. However, there were important differences between the pattern of industrialization in Iran and that to be found elsewhere. For example, foreign investment in Iran was directed toward production for the local market; Iran's manufacturing was not export-oriented (as it was in other NICs). This remained the case for the 15 years of the accumulation strategy of the Pahlavi state (1962–77). Moreover, Iran's main commodity export was a *primary* product (oil), not manufactures. Oil was its major–and almost exclusive–source of foreign exchange earnings. No other commodity could compete on world markets with other capitalist producers.

Of course, 15 years may not be enough time to develop a firm foundation of industrial growth, or to develop productive resources in a competitive manner. And certainly Iran's idiosyncratic political features (such as the direct–and self-serving–role of the Shah in planning, as well as corruption, favouritism, and so on) hindered the processes of industrialization, accumulation and proletarianization.

In many third world countries, socio-economic processes that took centuries to unfold in Europe (and at least a full century in the US) have been telescoped into a few decades. The so-called primitive accumulation and capital accumulation proper in some places happen simultaneously and quickly. This was the case with Iran, where industrialization and changing land ownership patterns began–very slowly–in the 1930s. But it was not until the early 1960s that an accumulation strategy was launched, facilitated by rising oil revenues, that greatly accelerated the process of urban industrialization and rural transformation. Fundamental change came about so dramatically and rapidly that it left its own indelible imprint upon the structure of the economy, on social and political relations, on culture and ideological formations. Such a pace and rhythm of change could only create unique contradictions in both agrarian and urban sectors, including problems in agricultural production and a growing pool of urban marginalized masses. The rapid transformations and displacements being brought about by this sort of modernization also engendered serious resistance and contradictions, which came to the fore with tremendous force in 1977 and culminated in the Iranian Revolution of 1978–9.

In the course of just 15 years, then, a fundamental re-organization of social–productive relations occurred in Iran, expressed in changes in the structure of the economy, the social class structure and the labour process. The growth of the industrial sector and of modern manufacturing afforded industrial workers a strategic role in the economy and in the society. This allowed them to play a pivotal role in the Revolution, to articulate new demands and to create new forms of organization.

Industrial Workers in the Revolution

Between 1978 and 1981 the Iranian working class experienced a new form of organization and activity that was unprecedented in its history and significant in its implications. During the autumn of 1978, the urban centres in Iran were engulfed by street demonstrations and workplace strikes against the Pahlavi regime. While the massive street demonstrations –at times numbering some three million people in Teheran–did much to demoralize the Pahlavi state, the collapse of the regime may be attributed to the industrial and financial crises impounded by two critical strategic strikes: those of the oil workers and of the employees of the Central Bank.[1] In the industrial sector, other key strikes were waged by railroad workers and electrical workers, resulting in bottlenecks and blackouts that added to the regime's incapacity.

As the general strike gained momentum and numerous factories and bureaucratic organizations ceased operation, workers formed strike committees which co-ordinated the strikes and drew up demands that increasingly came to have a political orientation. The demands graduated from higher wages to independent working-class organizations to release of political prisoners and the trial of corrupt and repressive officials. As the once mighty Pahlavi regime crumbled, more and more power over its institutions came to be vested in the strike committees. These strike committees gradually evolved into workers' councils (called *shora* in Persian, the principal language of Iran) which spread throughout the urban centres during and immediately after the Revolution. The breakup of the highly centralized Pahlavi state resulted in a decentralized network of local, grassroots and workplace committees and councils that had far-reaching economic and political implications: the Revolution seemed to contain socialist and democratic elements in spite of the pervasive Islamic discourse and preponderant role of clerics. These new forms of organization and control, widespread in all modern bureaucratic organizations, were the seeds of a new social order, one that could be fundamentally different–economically, politically and ideologically–from the Pahlavi state.

The point of this paper is to move away from the focus on the revolution in the streets and draw attention to the revolution in the factories. It is an attempt to separate out of the mass movement a certain class movement that was not only crucial to the collapse of the Pahlavi state, but in the initial period of the Islamic Republic, also had a major impact on the Iranian economy and especially the industrial sector. The disruption in the capitalist organization of labour in the modern sector of the manufacturing industry threatened to transform production relations. The formation of workers' councils as the independent political and economic organization of the workers during and immediately after the Revolution, through which the workers proceeded to control the management of factories, signified a major interruption in the established labour process and production relations in the majority of industrial units. The new councils in the industrial sector also formed the nuclei of an alternative political authority which came into existence with the revolutionary disintegration of the old political order. Clearly, what was happening was not merely an economic struggle on the part of industrial workers but one objectively aimed at the restructuring of socio–economic relations. As their mechanism to effect this change, industrial workers chose councils.

The councils were, however, short-lived. The possibility of transforming a temporary movement into a permanent organization was eliminated by the regime's tactics. The process of maturation of the councils' movement was ruptured by the combination of force and concession, repression and incorporation on the part of the new state. The emergence of the post-revolutionary government and the increasing centralization of the new political rule meant that workers' councils as a parallel power centre with control over important aspects of economic activity could not continue and had to be emasculated. Workers' resistance was broken partly through coercion and partly through the Islamicization of the councils. Islamic councils tied to the Ministry of Labour came to replace the autonomous workers' councils in the factories, and even these were eventually eclipsed by Islamic associations, tied to the Islamic Republican Party (IRP), whose domain is ostensibly ideological. The economic functions that councils had delegated to themselves have now been completely taken over by the Islamic state.

The Iranian Revolution, then, is notable for the emergence of a distinctly class phenomenon: workers' councils, workers' control and the important role of urban industrial labour in the breakdown of the Pahlavi regime and the implementation of new practices and policies in the Islamic Republic. Industrial workers had a political impact, both during and after the Revolution, quite disproportionate to their relatively small numbers. The workers' councils and the idea of workers' control were products of the revolutionary situation and of the workers' heightened sense of consciousness derived from their critical role in the anti-Shah movement and the mass strikes. These developments are important not only in the evolution of the Iranian working class and socio-political processes in Iran, but in the broader historical evolution of working class initiatives around the world. While trade unions are the typical and universal organization of workers, it is important to recognize alternative and highly radical forms of working class self-activity and self-organization.[2]

The lessons of the Iranian Revolution are legion; but several stand out as relevant to industrial workers. The role of urban industrial labour in the anti-Shah movement and in the post-revolutionary struggle for power calls into question assumptions and simplistic notions about what is and is not possible for workers in an apparently backward context. It also undermines the conventional wisdom on labour aristocracies and the presumed conservatism of the skilled industrial labour force.[3] Because the historical incidence of workers' councils is so limited, and because of the significance of councils as a political–organizational project, it is important to recognize within the Iranian revolutionary process the emergence of new forms of organization and new demands. It is particularly important to take on board the activity of the industrial labour force in Iran.

But the limitations of the council's movement cannot be underestimated. They include structural factors such as the internal differentiation of the urban industrial labour force and small size of the concentrated proletariat; the youth of the industrial labour force and lack of working-class culture; the inexperience of industrial workers in political activity and self-organization (including independent trade unions); the absence of working-class parties, democratic traditions and institutions; and the nature of the new Islamic regime, whose populist discourse and practices, combined with coercion, compounded the difficulties and contradictions faced by the councils. The role of industrial workers in revolutionary Iran and the rise and decline of the councils underscore both the *possibilities* for advanced forms of working-class activity in a third world context and the serious *contradictions*, including the structural obstacles enumerated above, that surround industrial workers in developing societies. It is in this sense that an examination of the factory councils in Iran offers lessons of a wider relevance.

The Development of the Industrial Labour Force

Several features which encapsulate the peculiarities and contradictions of Iranian labour history may be briefly stated. The industrial labour force, like Iranian industry itself, is relatively new. While its roots lie in the partial and half-hearted modernization efforts of the Qajar rulers in the previous century, and in some expansion of the industrial working class during the 1930s, industrial workers remained a tiny proportion of an overwhelmingly agrarian social formation until the industrialization strategy initiated in the early 1960s. Notwithstanding their small numbers, however, Iranian workers have several times engaged in militant activity and organization. These activities have coincided with key stages in the development of capitalist relations in Iran, and came also at times of changes in international relations (such as socialist agitation and the October Revolution in neighbouring Russia, and during World War II). The first socialist movement in the Middle East emerged in Iran; so did the first communist party in Asia. The first trade unions in Iran organized the embryonic working class in 1906, and by 1922 over 20,000 workers were unionized under socialist leadership (see Table 1). Yet Iranian labour history is rife with discontinuities and fractures, and two crushing defeats stand out. The first came with the rise to power of Reza Shah. After abolishing the existing trade unions, he banned collectivist discourse and organizing altogether. The labour law instituted by his government had no provisions for strikes or trade unions and limited itself to questions of working conditions in industrial establishments. This period, then, saw a very repressed working class, but one that was growing as a result of the shah's industrialization strategy. By 1941 there were 200 industrial establishments with an estimated workforce of 50,000 (not including oil workers). In the period between the two dictatorships (1941–53) a

Table 7.1 Trade unions established, date and political organisation

Trade Union	*Year*	*Political Organization*
Printers' and telegraphers, union, Teheran, Tabriz	circa 1906	Democrat Party (later Communist Party)
Iranian labourers in Baku oilfields	circa 1910	Adalat (Justice) Party
Tenants' association; union of employees in Ministry of Post & Telegraph; Patriotic Women's Society	circa 1920	Socialist Party
Central Council of Federated Trade Unions in Iran (CCFTU): by 1925, 8,000 members throughout Iran: 32 unions, of which 6 represented workers in modern industry. Banned in 1933	circa 1920	Communist Party
Central Council of the Trade Unions in Iran	1942	Tudeh Party
United Central Council of the Unified Trade Unions of Iranian Workers (CCUTU). By 1946, it had 400,000 members with 186 unions. Affiliated to World Federation of Trade Unions. Newspaper – *Zafar*. Leader – Reza Rusta. Abolished in 1953.	1944	Tudeh Party

communist movement emerged in Iran which actively organized workers into what became the largest trade union in Asia. Capitalist development in Iran had produced a new social class, industrial workers, with the capacity to paralyse production and precipitate political crises through militant strikes. But the labour movement suffered its second historic defeat in 1953, when the *coup d'etat* against the Mossadegh government suppressed the Tudeh Party and the National Front (communist and nationalist organizations, respectively) and dismantled Iran's large and militant labour confederation. These breaks in the socialist movement and labour history – the cumulative effects of defeats and setbacks to socialists and to workers – are important factors in assessing the later capacity for working-class organization and struggle.

The royal restoration was a serious blow to trade union activity and put an end to independent labour action – in both its organized and spontaneous expressions. The incidence of strikes plummeted dramatically in the post-coup period, as first the military and later the secret police, SAVAK, moved into factories and all workplaces to instil and ensure discipline and subordination. Article 29 of the 1959 Labour Law banned trade unions and their confederacies from engaging in any political affairs.

In the early 1960s, in line with changes in the structure of the world economy and in international relations, the White Revolution was launched. It constituted a series of economic, political and administrative reforms which were part of a profound re-organization of Iran: land reform, nationalization of forests, electoral reforms, franchise for women, denationalization of state industries, literacy corps, and profit-sharing for workers in large industrial establishments. Like land reform, the profit-sharing measure was motivated by both political and economic considerations. As a political concession to industrial workers, it sought to win their support for the regime. It was, in addition, an economic measure to tie workers to one place and encourage productivity. Ultimately, its effectiveness was undermined by the fact that profit-sharing became little more than a form of annual bonuses, and as such lost its appeal as a strategy for increasing workers' identity with management.

Iran's development strategy was based on a programme of land reform and import-substitution industrialization that was facilitated by the massive oil revenues that accrued to the state. There was some assistance from foreign capital (primarily US, West European and Japanese transnational firms), though its share of gross domestic fixed capital formation and of Gross National Product was insignificant relative to state and private Iranian investment.[4] In the decade 1965–75, especially through the Third and Fourth National Development Plans, much progress was made in the development of infrastructure. Road construction and government investment in steel, heavy metal plants, aluminium smelters, and petro-chemicals followed state industrialization policy. Government policy was specifically designed to underpin the industrialization policy through the creation of a base level of heavy industry and large scale, capital-intensive plants held predominantly by state controlled organizations.[5] There was also a conscious policy of regionalization of industry during the Fourth Plan period. The main industrial centres became Teheran and environs, Tabriz, Isfahan, Shiraz, Abadan and Ahvaz, where petrodollars bought highly sophisticated means of production. They also brought in thousands of foreign managers, administrators, supervisors, advisors, technicians, and even skilled and semi-skilled workers to run the operations. The pattern of Iranian economic development and industrialization during the 1960s and 1970s included the following features: a rise in manufacturing employment, rapid industrialization largely financed out of oil revenues, the growth of a petro-chemicals industry, sophisticated consumer durables assembly plants (e.g. automobiles), steel complexes and designs for additional large industrial complexes. The massive oil revenues accruing to the state after the 1973 oil crisis prompted the Shah to revise the Fifth Plan and accelerate the pattern of investment in industrial activities.

Modernization resulted in a significant alteration in the structure of the economy, the pace of economic change and the living standards of many Iranians. Among other things, the rapid industrialization strategy created a layer of highly skilled workers whose incomes rose in order to develop the home market. Unemployment was almost non-existent.[6] Iran appeared well along the road toward realizing its leaders' ambitions of catching up with Japan by the end of the decade.

The importance of land reform in the expansion of the urban industrial labour force cannot be overestimated. The motivations for land reform were both development and political. There was, in the first instance, the need for the creation of a broad national market, which requires the destruction of pre-capitalist rural agrarian production. There was also a need to provide a popular base and mass support for the Shah's regime and weaken the political opposition. The land reform not only achieved both these aims, it also accelerated the process of proletarianization. In the 1960s rural–urban migration transferred about 400,000 job seekers to the towns from rural areas.[7] Between 1963 and 1972 the labour force increased fivefold. Urban industry expanded and drew hundreds of thousands of rural migrants while the agricultural labour force declined. Unskilled rural migrants invariably went into the construction industry, although manufacturing absorbed many as well. Both push and pull factors drew increasing numbers of rural residents to the cities, resulting in an expanded – and ethnically diverse – labour force, particularly in Tehran.[8]

By 1976, the industrial labour force had expanded to over one-third of the economically active population. The structure of the working population reflected the country's level of development, and the proportion of the working population in manufacturing was a key indicator. In Iran, 19% of the working population was engaged in manufacturing. This is high for a third world country (see Table 2).

The nature of the manufacturing sector in Iran requires some explanation. Neither the manufacturing sector nor the manufacturing work force was homogeneous. Both, in fact, reflected the uneven and differentiated nature of the development of the productive forces and relations in Iran. First, there was a high concentration of all manufacturing in light industry; the highest concentration was in the textiles and clothing industries. Tens of thousands of workers were involved in spinning and weaving, much of this in the rural areas. Second, whereas food, beverages, and tobacco had traditionally been the second largest manufacturing sector, by 1976 second place had been taken by metal products, machinery and equipment industries. This represented an important shift in the distribution of the labour force and in the composition of manufactures. Third, manufacturing was overwhelmingly small scale. Out of approximately 250,000 manufacturing units, only about 6,000 employed more than ten workers each. The vast majority of manufacturing firms were extremely small, each employing fewer than ten workers and on average about three workers. Fourth, a sizeable proportion of the manufacturing labour force was classified own-account worker and unpaid family worker. According

Table 7.2 Comparative distribution of workers in manufacturing in the third world

Country	*Percentage*	*Year*
Algeria	7.8	1977
Argentina	20.0	1970
Brazil	16.0	1976
Chile	17.0	1970
Egypt	14.0	1975
India	26.0	1976
Mexico	18.0	1976
Philippines	10.0	1977
South Africa	13.0	1970
South Korea	22.0	1979
Tunisia	15.0	1975
Turkey	8.0	1975
Uruguay	19.0	1975
Venezuela	16.0	1977
Iran	19.0	1976

Sources: *The Economist, The World in Figures* (1981); ILO, *Yearbook of Labour Statistics,* 1981.

to the 1976 Census, these categories together constituted some 46% of the total manufacturing labour force.[9] A very large percentage of those in the productive industries were therefore either self-employed artisans/home-workers or employed in very small shops using traditional methods. The Iranian industrial sector had a proliferation of workshops and medium-sized establishments (the latter employing between 10 and 50 workers). A much smaller proportion of all production workers was employed in large modern enterprises with a relatively advanced division of labour and a concentrated workforce (of, for example, over 100 workers).

A basic differentiation had emerged within the working class between a modern, highly socialized sector and a backward, traditional sector.This was particularly so on the national scale, where vast regional inequalities obtained. But it existed also in the cities. As a result, the urban working class was quite heterogeneous. Not only was there a considerable gap between those in the modern, highly socialized sector and those in the traditional sector, there were also considerable differences between those who were more or less fully socially integrated into urban working-class life (generally those whose parents had been workers or those who had been born in the cities) and the recent rural immigrants. Even in the modern sector of manufacturing there were substantial divisions within the labour

Table 7.3 Structure of employment in Iran 1976 (percentage)

Self-Employed managers and administrators		0.2
Employed managers, administrators and professionals		6.0
Self-employed professionals		0.5
Clerical and sales employees		6.4
Self-employed sales & service & unpaid family		6.1
Employed service workers		4.2
Employed agricultural workers		7.6
Self-employed agricultural and unpaid family workers		26.3
Employed production workers		25.0
Self-employed production workers & unpaid family		12.6
Other and unaccounted for		5.1
Self-employed	34.6	
Employed	54.1	
Unpaid family	11.3	
Total Workers		*9,732,500*

Sources: Compiled from ILO *Yearbook of Statistics, 1979.* (International Labour Organization, Geneva), Table 2B, p. 102; and *National Census of Population and Housing, 1976* (Plan and Budget Organization, Statistical Center of Iran), Table 21, p. 67.

force. These were based on gender, national/ethnic background, skill grade and education, and income level.

Manufacturing was thus both modern and traditional (in terms of both the labour process and the products), heavy and light, urban and rural. The industrial labour force was highly differentiated. The polarization of the urban industrial labour force of manufacturing corresponds to what is known in the Marxist literature as the division between production characterized by the *formal* subsumption of labour to capital, and that characterized by the *real* subsumption of labour to capital. The fundamental difference in the organization of the labour process is what distinguishes the two sectors. In the former, production is unmechanized, personal and patriarchal relations dominate, hours are long and remuneration low; but workers have some control over their tools and their products. The concentrated proletariat in advanced production units, working with sophisticated machinery and under modern managerial control, organized into syndicates and the beneficiaries of higher wages, health insurance, housing allowance, pensions plans and profit-sharing comprised only a very small percentage of the manufacturing workers: out of 24% engaged in units employing over 10 workers, about 17% percent were in units employing between 10 and 50 workers, and 7% in units of over 50 workers. The rest of the manufacturing labour force was dispersed over myriad workshops and small units (those in the cities were organized in and around the Bazaar), experiencing economic conditions and social relationships quite different from those of the concentrated industrial labour force.

The peculiarities of Iranian manufacturing were first noted by the ILO mission team that visited Iran in 1971/2. Among other things, they noted the supply of skilled labour in both sectors (traditional and modern). In the small sector, craft work and artisanal skilled labour was abundant. In addition, there had been a steady growth of workshops making not only numerous consumer goods but a wide range of engineering products.[10] A further point is that there was some movement back and forth between the two sectors. Workers who moved from the small sector into large firms could be employed either in a modern way (on the assembly line, for example), or by using their traditional skills in more labour-intensive subsidiary operations (for example, removing dents and warps in the factory products).[11] Likewise, workers in large factories who had acquired sufficient savings sometimes left to open up their own workshops, especially to service and repair electrical goods and automobiles.[12]

Labour Control and Resistance

Throughout the Shah's rule, the government exerted tight control over the industrial labour force in the large sector, especially by forming numerous and dispersed syndicates, to divide the workers, counter the effects of socialized production upon workers' consciousness and practice, and prevent the formation of a national labour organization. In the oil sector alone, there were 26 state controlled unions.[13] The automotive sector had seven. Syndicates operated on a factory by factory basis, not industry wide or regionally. By 1976 there were about 600 trade unions and 20 confederacies, but their existence was largely nominal. During the Pahlavi era many workers' representatives at the shop-floor level were officially employed by SAVAK.[14] The government also controlled workplace organization by means of the militarization of many factories, particularly the large ones employing over 500 workers. Here, retired army officers were often placed in security positions. Small wonder, then, that most workers were hostile toward the syndicates. Far from identifying with the unions, workers with grievances would often turn to the Ministry of Labour for recourse.[15]

The early 1970s was a period when working class protests began to break out once again. There were strikes, demonstrations, slowdowns and absenteeism, over wages, profit-sharing and job classifications. Less often there were protest actions over dismissals, the presence of semi-military personnel in the units, and mandatory attendance at official celebrations. These actions in the early 1970s were for the most part illegal and unreported. They were also sporadic and dispersed, which made it easier for the authorities to suppress them. One of the most dramatic incidents during this period was the strike by textile workers of the Chit-e-Jahan factory in Karaj (north of Teheran) for higher wages. The owner of the textile factory called in the police rather than negotiate with the workers and several workers were killed in the ensuing skirmish. The early 1970s had also witnessed the rise of an urban guerrilla movement with a strong orientation to the working class. One of these guerrilla forces, the Organization of the Iranian People's Fedaii Guerrillas, responded to this assault on the textile workers by assassinating the owner. (This organization was later quite active among the workers and within the councils.)

From the mid-1970s, there was a noticeable pattern in Iranian industrial labour disputes: textile workers, oil workers, transport workers, machinists, printers, miners and others were demanding higher wages and more fringe benefits, refusing to work as long, as meticulously, and for as little pay as before. In many instances, the authorities quickly gave in to workers' demands for wage increases. But more and more, the protests also focused on profit-sharing and job classifications – protests that indicated a questioning and challenging of managerial control and authority in the workplace and its capacity to re-organize production at will. In a sense, these worker protests were couching political demands in economic terms.

In 1975, in an attempt to stem working-class agitation and bolster productivity, the regime announced a divestiture scheme, which applied to enterprises of ten workers and over (excluding the oil, railway and tobacco industries). Under this workers' shares measure, workers were to receive up to 20% of the firm's profits (an additional 29% to be later divested to public ownership). This was to be distributed according to senitory and wages. Here the Shah's regime was attempting to replicate in the cities what it had accomplished in the rural areas with the land redistribution programme of the 1960s: creating a privileged layer of the labour force which could be counted on for support. The 1975 divestiture law was more effective than the 1963 profit-sharing law, but not so far-reaching as it sounded. The decree explicitly stated that workers were not entitled to participation in management; moreover, by 1977, just over one-third of the original target of eligible firms had complied, and the law completely bypassed the masses of workers in smaller manufacturing firms, that is, over 70% of the industrial workforce.

But the regime miscalculated in its attempt to divide the urban industrial labour force by creating an affluent, conservative stratum, as the events of 1977–9 demonstrate. In 1977 the latent contradictions in Iran's oil based development strategy and dictatorial political structure came to the fore, shattering the facade of economic miracle and social stability. The housing crisis erupted with considerable force, as both middle class victims of the enormous income gap and shanty town dwellers on the outskirts of Teheran began to protest at living conditions. Clashes between police and lower income people violating zoning parallelled open criticisms by the intelligentsia against political repression and censorship. *Bazaaris* and shopkeepers, targets of an official anti-profiteering campaign, turned to their traditional allies, Shiite clergymen, for support. A populist alliance was in the making.[16]

Between October 1977 and June 1978 several major strikes took place, and a number of factories were damaged by fires. The first indication that the labour force was turning overtly against the regime was in July 1978, when construction workers (many of whom had lost jobs when a recession was induced in 1976) joined the anti-Shah street demonstrations, swelling the ranks of the protestors into the hundreds of thousands. Strikes gained momentum in mid-September, when oil refinery workers in Teheran, Isfahan, Shiraz, Abadan and Tabriz struck to protest martial law. This was followed by cement workers, bank employees, and machinists, all of whom made explicit political demands.Industrial workers whose role in the general strike was indispensable include Ahvaz oil workers (37,000); Tabriz Machine and Lift Truck Co. workers (2,000); Tabriz Machine Tool Factory (1,000); Arak Tractor Assembly plant (3,000); Aryamehr Steel Complex in Isfahan (60,000 workers); textile workers of Gilan, Tehran and Isfahan; Sarcheshmeh (Kerman) copper miners; tobacco workers; thousands in the paper industries; railroad workers and electrical workers; and workers in the 40 companies related to the Behshahr Industrial Group (Teheran). In a joint statement issued on 4 November 1978, the workers of the Machine Tool and Tractor Assembly plants in Tabriz articulated their political and economic positions, demanding that the existing workers' organizations and yellow unions be dismantled, that genuine workers' councils and other working-class organizations be formed to 'defend the rights and social prestige of the workers', and that there be no intervention by the authorities in the factories' internal affairs.[17] All the striking industrial workers, but most notably the oil workers, displayed considerable imagination, courage and militancy in their tactics against the regime.[18] Their strike committees, even when underground, were by all accounts extremely well organized and effective organs. The strikes, strike committees, and combination of political and economic demands by the advanced industrial workers evidenced a new stage in the evolution of the industrial labour force.[19]

It is worth pointing out that the skilled workers and technicians in the military sector were also affected by the contradictions of the labour process and the general social conflict that engulfed Iran after 1977. In the Air Force – which had been the Shah's favourite, most privileged and pampered force, and the recipient of some of the most sophisticated military gadgetry anywhere – revolutionary committees emerged from the *homafar*, a special category of technical personnel whose social background was rural or urban working class or lower middle class. These revolutionary committees first mutinied at the main Air Force base in Tehran, and then, in conjunction with guerrillas from the communist Fedaii and the left-Islamic Mojahedin, fought and defeated the Shah's elite Imperial Guard (the so-called Immortals) during the armed insurrection of 9–11 February 1979.[20]

It is important to see the Iranian Revolution – notwithstanding its populist, Islamic and anti-imperialist veneer – as one in which diverse classes and social forces participated for their own reasons and advanced their own demands. The demands put forward by industrial workers during the general strike is evidence of this. A principal demand of such advanced industrial workers as oil workers, machinery workers, railroad workers and hundreds of thousands of workers in other production units was for the dissolution of yellow syndicates and the formation of independent working-class organizations. The strike committees were the seeds of the organizations to come. The experience of organizing and co-ordinating strikes in strategic sectors of the economy and key production units provided industrial workers with a greater awareness of their role and a sense of possession of their workplaces.

The Councils

The emergence of workplace councils, of the idea of workers' control, and in particular of the factory councils, was the product of a revolutionary situation. This was both the strength and weakness of the councils. As the Pahlavi order was being challenged in the most fundamental way, new structures emerged to fill the vacuum. Strike committees, organized to co-ordinate the strikes that engulfed the urban areas throughout 1978, were the seeds of many of the factory councils, creating a parallel power centre while the Pahlavi state was still formally intact. These strike committees gradually prepared the ground for council elections. The councils, then, came about in two ways. In factories where the owners and managers had fled – particularly those connected to transnational firms – workers took over in order to carry on production and preserve their jobs. In other cases, councils that had grown out of organized and militant strike committees insisted on control over or participation in the affairs of the factory. Although precise figures are not available, it is not an exaggeration to say that workers' councils were established in nearly every large and modern industrial plant in the period immediately following the February 1979 victory. By all accounts workers were overwhelmingly enthusiastic about the councils. Here was a situation that was fundamentally different from that before the Revolution, when there was no criticism, no open airing of grievances, enormous wage differentials between workers and managers, no participation in finances or production goals, and a rigid and authoritarian division of labour within the factory.

To understand the rise and decline of the councils movement it is useful to distinguish four phases. The first stage begins with the downfall of the Shah, when strike committees evolved into councils and these new working-class organs sprang up in nearly all factories. This first phase, characterized by the expansion of the councils movement despite official discouragement, covers most of the 1979 until the occupation of the US Embassy in November. During this period, not only were there factory councils, but students' councils were formed in high schools and universities throughout Iran, and peasants' councils were established in Kurdestan and Tukaman Sahra. The second phase begins after the Embassy takeover and Prime Minister Bazargan's resignation. This period is characterized by a more concerted effort on the part of the authorities to undermine the independent councils. Both the new president, Abolhassan Bani-Sadr, and his partners/rivals within the Islamic Republican Party (IRP) were involved in this effort. During this period, the Turkaman councils were violently smashed, the students' councils in the universities were suppressed, and the regime attempted to transform the councils by appointing managers and by creating Islamic associations. This period continued until the Iran–Iraq war, which ushered in a new stage. This third period saw the gradual decline of Bani-Sadr and his liberal/technocratic associates, and the ascendancy of the IRP. It also witnessed the increasing power of the Islamic associations as rivals to the workers' councils, and growing pressure on industrial workers to increase production and otherwise participate in the war effort. It continued until June 1981. The fourth and present stage begins with Bani-Sadr's ousting and includes the internal war against the left, the full takeover of the autonomous functions of the councils, and an attempt to codify labour relations.

A trend connecting the first three stages is the almost constant effort on the part of the new Islamic authorities to undermine the independent councils and gain control over them. This effort was undertaken by the managers, engineer-bureaucrats, and influential clerics, despite their own differences and rivalries, and involved both force and concession, repression and cooptation. A brief description of the immediate economic situation illustrates the power of the councils and the consequent need on the part of the new authorities to confront them. In 1979 the government began a programme of nationalization which eventually covered about 85% of all firms. This simply legalized the *de facto* expropriations by the workers' councils, and the workers welcomed and demanded further nationalization. (Insurance companies and banks were also nationalized). The government was forced to channel considerable capital into wages, although investment was cut back. In 1979/80 there was, for the first time, a negative growth rate. This was the inevitable result of the revolutionary disruptions, unavailability of raw materials and spare parts, as well as the capital flight of 1977–9. But a Central Bank report cited worker discipline as a major problem as well.[21] (At this time, the Central Bank and the other institutions inherited from the *ancien regime* were in the hands of the liberals, while the IRP was securing its hold over the grassroots structures that had emerged in the revolutionary process.) The liberal managers sent in by the Provisional Government were encountering serious difficulties with the workers' councils, and were not receiving much cooperation from their clerical allies. They were expected to fire all personnel connected with the Shah's regime, share power with the workers' councils (or the Islamic councils), and keep the unit operating without reviving old contracts with foreign corporations. In 1980/81 the government declared a $2.28 billion loss in state owned industrial units. But the decline in industrial output was not accompanied by a corresponding breakdown in industrial employment or a decline in wages. Employment in large establishments increased by nearly 2%, while output declined by 18.7% between the third quarters of 1979/80 and 1980/81. Despite the sharp fall in labour productivity, real wages increased substantially, shooting up in 1979 and 1980.[22] This was because the councils had doubled wages in many factories for blue collar workers, while reducing salaries of white collar personnel by one-third or even one-half. The political power of the councils during this period prevented redundancies and factory closures. The nationalization of banks and almost all large industrial establishments by the Provisional Government (the result of worker's pressures) was instrumental in maintaining the high level of manufacturing employment and of wages.[23]

The First Phase

In early 1979 the two main concerns were to discover and remove agents of the previous regime, and to resume production. The first was usually accomplished by either raiding the former office of the factory's SAVAK agent and examining files, or by setting up investigative committees. The need to resume production was felt by all in the early months; but the question of how it was to proceed was often critical. In some factories, the councils were able to reach an agreement with the qualified (and cooperative) technical management on the shop-floor. In such cases, production not only proceeded smoothly, but increases of 50% were not uncommon. Other councils encountered production problems almost immediately. This came about in cases where the council had fired engineers or other personnel associated with the Shah's regime, whose expertise was necessary. In those factories where production ground to a halt, the workers had to turn to the government, which gladly sent in its own representative to take control. In some factories workers resumed production but were not always paid. In addition, the new authorities interfered with orders and sales when they could.

In addition to ferreting out SAVAK agents and resuming production, the councils implemented various benefits for the workers. The minimum wage was doubled, and the top salaries reduced by one-third or a half. The councils set up libraries, where left-wing literature as well as radical Islamic writings were often on display. Various councils moved to provide workers with such benefits as a litre of milk per day, free lunches and transportation, and reduced rates for the products of the factory. They also introduced regular health examinations, free work clothes, increased housing allowances, and improved food services.

The forms of workers' control practiced by the councils in the first period were diverse. In Chit-e-Jahan textile factory, where the Mojahedin (a left-Islamic group) was influential, the council clearly ran the factory. General assemblies were held once a month. One account of that council notes that the original election of the councils seem to have been by acclamation, and that power was really not invested in the general assembly. The autarchic character of the factory was also mentioned.[24]

At the Iran National assembly plant, where 12,000 workers produced cars for the home market from kits imported from England, the head of the workers' council was a member of the factory administration during the Shah's time. According to one account, here talk was not of workers' control but of participation with the regime's appointed directors. The council was clearly pro-Khomeini. At the General Motors plant (which made parts for construction and agricultural machinery) there was an Islamic council of workers. The council had 21 elected members, composed of 15 manual workers and 6 office staff, one of whom worked full-time for the council. It met in full every two weeks, but had sub-committees to deal with production control, finance, buying and selling, education, discipline, arbitration, and sports. It also had a technical/research committee looking into ways of developing the factory's self-sufficiency (as a result of the cessation of supplies from the parent company). The full council countersigned all documents and inspected the books. What had emerged at the GM plant was a system of co-management, a situation of dual power between the council and top management, including the three directors sent in by the regime when the factory was nationalized. Such an even balance of forces characterized the situation within other factories.

The situation at the Caterpillar plant illustrates both the strengths and weaknesses of the councils. Here the council consisted of ten manual workers and two office staff, evenly divided between secular (pro-left) and religious (pro-IRP) elements. The new government had not yet sent in its new director, and in his absence, the operation of the factory was under the full control of the council, from signing cheques and controlling accounts, to determining wage levels. According to one account, the council held weekly meetings and was in the process of drawing up a constitution and preparing for new elections. Meetings took place in the office of the remaining director from the previous administration, who was ejected for the purpose when necessary. Even in this early period, however, the workers' council co-existed with an Islamic association, which had been set up for purposes of education. According to the observer, this association was clearly having an influence on some of the Islamic members of the council.[25]

During this period there were essentially three positions on and approaches toward the councils emanating from outside the factory itself. Prime Minister Bazargan was totally opposed to councils, openly said so, and threatened to resign if this revolutionary situation continued for much longer. A bill was drafted to prevent strike committees and councils from interfering in the administration of the production unit. This did nothing to endear him to workers. Some of his technocrats favoured a move toward corporatism, wherein the councils would replicate the Shah's labour councils. The latter had been bodies dealing with settlement of disputes that consisted equally of representatives of the workforce, of management, and of the Ministry of Labour. The IRP had a vague policy of co-management, and generally supported councils in public speeches and writings, although it always warned of counter-revolutionary and un-Islamic elements within them. Finally, the left-wing forces, particularly the Mojahedin and the Fedaii, were very interested in the councils, tried to have a presence in them, and warned workers in their literature of various attacks on the part of the authorities to undermine the councils. The Fedaii, for example, distributed pamphlets explaining the nature of nationalization and its differences with socialization. At this time, all the left-wing groups supported the councils. In their writings they urged that councils form the government, rather than the other way around. However they had neither a coherent programme for councils' and workers' control, nor the power to carry one out. While the left was consistently supportive of the councils and echoed their principal demands (minimum wage, a 40-hour work week, the right to strike, control of hiring and firing), their presence within the industrial labour force and the councils was limited. Moreover, the left was weakened by internal dissension, and by official harassment.[26]

At this time, the new authorities used a combination of force and concession to undermine the councils and infiltrate them with their own people. An example of a concession was the decision on the part of the IRP to make May Day a national holiday and commemorate it extravagantly—*after* the left had announced plans to celebrate the occasion. But force was applied too, and from time to time the so-called Imam's committees went into factories to ensure discipline in an authoritarian manner. But this was not yet the rule, and workers still on the whole supported the new regime, especially the anti-capitalist, anti-imperialist clerics. They were less impressed with the Bazargan forces, whom they identified with western economic interests. A good example of this is the attitude of the oil-workers toward the liberals/technocrats. By March 1979 the oil-fields were firmly in control of the new authorities, pictures of Khomeini were everywhere, and left-wingers were purged from the oil-workers' committees and councils. But the new chief of the National Iranian Oil Company, Hassan Nazih, was a technocrat and associate of Bazargan. His chief adviser characterized the NIOC's biggest problem in this period as management–labour relations. He complained that an enormous amount of management time had been expended on protracted discussions with the workers' committees. While precise information is unavailable, it appears that these discussions centred on government oil policy, production totals and export targets. The dismissal of Hassan Nazih in September 1979 did not reduce incidents of labour militance. Workers at Abadan gave the new oil minister, Ali Akbar Moinfar, an almost riotous reception on his first visit there, and he was apparently unable to venture into his Tehran headquarters for several weeks because of the danger of adverse worker reaction. While the drop in Iranian oil production to about one million barrels a day was due primarily to labour–management problems, there was also friction between oil workers—Islamic, radical left-wing and reformist—which may have contributed to the drop in exports.

Some attempts during this period were made to organize workers' councils above the factory level. The Mojahedin convened small conferences of councils at factories that were dominated by their own militants. The Fedaii, who had supporters among workers in Tabriz, Mazanderan and Teheran, were active in co-ordinating activities between councils and calling rallies and demonstrations. Because of the proliferation of councils during this period, the new regime was forced to accept and recognize them—albeit formally. The Constitution of the Islamic Republic, ratified in August 1979, recognized councils but reserved for the law the right to determine which were acceptable. Meanwhile, the authorities sought to divide workers by exploiting religious sentiments.

Phase Two

The second period begins with the US embassy takeover and the resignation of Bazargan. With this act, the Islamic forces were able to greatly improve their position within the country. Whether or not the clerics actually planned the act, the students who carried it out did so in their name and the clerics quickly defended and supported them. The act was very popular in Iran. In January 1980 there was a large demonstration by the Workers' Islamic Council, representing 128 factories, to show support for the seizure of the embassy and the hostages. The councils were still active during this time. In the mineral rich province of Kermanshah, the quarry workers' council of Marivan fought for wage increases and demanded that the mines be renationalized. Their demands were met, and the council proceeded to run the Marivan quarries. In Urumieh, Azarbaijan, among the first actions taken by the beet sugar workers' council was the expulsion of an engineer for obstructing the council and the demotion of the manager for opposing nationalization. There was even a Council of the Seasonal Workers of Gachsaran (near Abadan) formed during this period.[27]

Many councils drew up constitutions stipulating the duty of the councils to intervene in all aspects of the factory's operations: purchase of raw materials and machinery, hiring, wages, production goals and output targets, pricing, distribution. As such, the councils challenged both the technical and social divisions of labour. However, the effectiveness of these principles differed from factory to factory, depending on the balance of political forces within the factory and the preoccupations of the regime at particular moments.

An example of the efficacy of Islamic populist and revolutionary rhetoric is illustrated by the outcome of the Ahvaz steel workers' 56-day strike in early 1980. The workers of the Foster–Wheeler Teheran Jonub Company, part of the Ahvaz Steel Industry Contractors' Company and numbering 4,000, had demanded that the firm be nationalized and that employment be guaranteed. The first workers' council, an independent one, had been abolished and an Islamic council instituted. The strike ended when a leading cleric and the governor of Khuzestan (an engineer) promised them job security, back pay and new year bonuses. In a meeting with the council, the cleric and the engineer governor discussed problems of the Revolution, the general economic problems of the country and poverty in Khuzestan, the need for creative and productive work by industrial workers, and the role of Islamic ideology in strengthening the oppressed and fighting imperialism. According to a news account, the meeting ended with workers' prayers and wishes for Khomeini's good health and with slogans hailing his leadership.

Some of the factory councils, particularly those that attempted to co-ordinate their activities or those in which left-wingers were active, had running battles with the authorities. In Mazanderan (a northern province), the authorities withdrew recognition of the council at the Chooka Woodworking Complex on grounds that it did not conform to the standards and criteria set forth by the government and the Constitution. The plant was ordered closed for a month, ostensibly to search for SAVAK agents and counter-revolutionaries.[28] The councils of the oil workers and of railroad workers encountered difficulties with the authorities, and were eventually closed down. In Gilan province the most radical factory councils were those at Poushesh (textiles), Toshiba (electrical appliances), Iran Porcelain, Iran Fiber, Gilan Carpet and Iran Barak (one of the largest and most modernized textile plants in the country). In January 1980 they jointly drew up a nine-point resolution calling for official recognition of their councils and their right to control production and distribution, approval of their own job classification and profit-sharing plan, a new budget to expand production and hire additional workers, 'radical change in production to eliminate dependence upon imperialist countries', and a new labour law 'drawn up by the genuine representatives of the workers'. In March of that year, these six councils joined others, incorporating nearly 30,000 workers, to form the Union of Workers' Councils of Gilan.[29] The Union of Councils tried to affiliate itself to the Fedaii organization, but the latter was in the throes of an internal crisis centered on its approach toward the new regime. The Gilani councils were later closed down by the authorities. Eight factory councils in and around Tabriz (including those of the Machine Tool and Tractor Assembly plants) formed a co-ordinating council—only to be dissolved by the authorities in May.[30]

During 1980 and into 1981, the councils were pawns in the competition for state power between President Bani-Sadr and his associates and the IRP. The liberals and the IRP each attempted to dominate the councils, while both tended to oppose without reservation the left-leaning or independent-minded councils. Bani-Sadr was particularly interested in restoring order to the factories and this was effected mainly through his appointment of new managers, supervisors and administrators. In August 1980 new regulations issued by the Ministry of Labour granted only a consultative role to the councils, although because the state had not yet extended its authority throughout society not all the councils adhered to the new laws. During this period, there was an uneasy co-existence in the factories between the workers' councils and the Islamic associations. The latter were IRP organs formed in every factory, university, school and government office to implement IRP policies and expand IRP influence. There was initially a tenuous division of labour between the two structures whereby the councils were in charge of production matters and the Islamic association ostensibly limited to ideological considerations. The IRP sought to change relations within factories by expanding its network of Islamic associations. During this period, many councils were transformed into consultative bodies under the control of the state.

Phase Three

In September 1980, the Iran–Iraq war added another dimension to the fate of the councils, which brings us to the third phase. The Iraqi attacks on Iranian soil and southern inhabitants stimulated nationalistic emotions and provided both wings of the regime with the opportunity to undermine the councils by setting forth a new duty for industrial workers: increased production at all costs. Moreover, the state controlled councils, hand in hand with the Islamic associations, undertook to mobilize workers, provide basic military training and dispatch them to the war front. No one knows how many industrial workers died at the front; but the effect was certainly felt.[31] Moreover, the regime's exhortations to workers that higher productivity was a patriotic and religious duty impelled changes at the level of production to overcome technical failures quickly. Thus in many factories, the shop-floor had to turn to re-invent a managerial grade to ensure efficiency and continuity of production. Under these conditions, workers' economic and political struggles, not to speak of their autonomy, were forced to subside. There were, however, some notable protests in the factories, even where the councils had become ineffective, state controlled organs. Protests over profit-sharing, job classification, child care centres, and wages were staged at the Arj Factory (producer of electrical consumer goods in Teheran), Bafkar Factory (textile plant in Teheran), Bayer factory (in Teheran) and the Neishapoor Sugar refinery.

During this period there was an intensification of the struggle inside the factories between those in favour of independent councils and those in favour of a more corporatist arrangement. There were also struggles between pro-left and pro-government workers, between religious workers and non-religious ones, and between Bani-Sadr supporters and IRP supporters. While the move to tie councils to the Ministry of Labour was gaining ground, the Islamicization of the factories continued apace and was becoming more and more successful. The role of direct repression in the dissolution of certain councils must not be underestimated. This was the case with the most radical councils, where workers were purged, arrested and even executed. In other factories, the councils lost their strength and power because the concept of workers' control and the function of councils could not be fully developed and implemented in the new regime.

The Fourth and Present Phase

With the fall of Bani-Sadr, the IRP consolidated its control over both the institutions inherited from the Pahlavi state (banks, ministries, and the Army, which had been dominated by liberals/technocrats) and the new institutions that had been created in the revolutionary process (the neighbourhood committees, the Rural Reconstruction Crusade, the Pasdaran,[32] religious courts, and the workers' councils). In some cases, the regime reacted as brutally to factory workers' protests as it did to its left-wing and liberal opponents within the middle class. In many factories Pasdaran were installed. But the regime also exercised some caution in dealing with industrial workers. For some time following Bani-Sadr's ousting, workers' councils continued to co-exist with Islamic associations in some factories, although their role had changed drastically. The councils were no longer independent and had lost much of their control over internal decision-making. Their struggles mainly centred on wages, benefits and bonuses.

It should be noted that workers continued to have some influence and that the regime was still forced to make some concessions. The situation at the General Electric and the Arj plants in Tehran, described to me in 1982, exemplifies this. At GE, some 300 refrigerators were produced daily. The manager of operations was an Armenian. The workers had free transport to and from work, and subsidized lunches. White and blue collar employees had meals in the same cafeteria. There was both an Islamic association and a workers' council. As a result of demands by the latter, workers were given one refrigerator each at no cost. The Arj plant manufactured six lines of items: refrigerators, freezers, gas heaters, oil heaters, washing machines and dryers and air conditioning units. The plant had 3,000 employees: 2,500 blue collar workers and 500 white collar employees. A regularized work process had been restored, and foremen, supervisors and managers oversaw efficient production at 80% capacity (sometimes 90%) with storage space running out at times. Production was assisted by a 5,000-ton press from the GDR. The plant had suffered damage in May 1982 from a fire in the storage which may have been deliberately set, and was assessed at some 100 million rials (about 1.5 million dollars). Nevertheless, the damage was dealt with relatively efficiently and production resumed.[33]

At this time, most industrial workers in the large plants that were operating were receiving a wage of at least 30,000 rials per month (about $430). Transportation was free, and lunches either nominal or provided at no cost. In addition, workers received fruit, cigarettes and other items at discounted prices.

In 1983 the Minister of Labour, Ahmad Tavakoli, who had earlier issued a ban on the formation of new councils (even pro-government ones) caused an outcry with the labour law he had drafted. The law stipulated strict ideological preconditions for the membership in the councils, placed the Islamic councils under strict supervision of the Ministry of Labour and imposed severe restrictions on the individual and collective rights of the workers. It was so biased in favour of management that he had to be dismissed. A new labour law has yet to be passed by the Parliament and approved by the Council of Guardians. In the meantime, the Shah's Labour Law of 1959 is technically in effect.[34]

Balance-Sheet and Prospects

The councils were revolutionary organs, and may properly be called the socialist element of the Iranian Revolution. However, our assessment of the councils and recognition of their limitations must consider the fact that while workers had been unequivocal in the opposition to the Pahlavi regime (including Bakhtiar's government), their attitude and approach toward the new regime was ambiguous. Moreover, none of the councils explicitly called for a socialist republic or the abolition of *capitalism*; they directed their attacks against *dependent* capital and the domination of monopoly (*enhesari*) capital, foreign and domestic. The councils saw themselves as helping to lay the foundation for the construction of the new social order, but they were not clear as to what that new social order would be. The most radical, left-inspired workers in the councils called for a people's republic, or a popular democratic republic (calls made by the revolutionary left as well); but this demand was put forward by only a minority of the industrial workers (many of whom were fired, jailed or killed). Factory councils did not challenge or oppose the call for an Islamic Republic. According to various reports on and interviews with workers in the factory councils, they did not feel that an Islamic Republic (a theocracy) and the preponderant presence of clerics was contrary to or incompatible with workers' control and the management of factories by councils of workers. Moreover, contrary to the worker's beliefs, nationalization actually worked against them, inasmuch as the government could control the workplaces and undermine the councils by manipulating the supply of goods, inputs and so on. The councils did objectively (and often explicitly) challenge industrial hierarchy and relations of domination/subordination in the workplace, and were unalterably opposed to a return to a Pahlavi-style politico-economic system. But they did not posit the fully conscious task of transforming state and civil society, and were unable to carry through a programme for democratization and modernization. Nor were they very clear about the meaning of workers' control. For these reasons, the Iranian workers' councils must be seen as very different from the earlier Russian soviets.

While the Revolution brought about many changes, it did not qualitatively alter the basic social and production relations. Anti-capitalist and anti-imperialist discourse notwithstanding, the Islamic rulers were antipathetic to a socialist strategy and averse to sharing power with any other social force. Dual power in the factories, created by the councils, was therefore unacceptable. An aversion to democracy led them to establish an extremely authoritarian form of rule.

To conclude, the Iranian councils' experience must not be seen as an isolated phenomenon under exceptional circumstances, but rather as part of the ongoing proletarianization and politicization of Iranian workers—and part of on-going socio-political processes in Iran. All kinds of labour protest illustrate the rise of a working-class consciousness, and thus the councils' movement should not be seen simply as one manifestation of the populism of the revolutionary movement as a whole. Industrial workers who joined street demonstrations were not just protesting the person of the Shah but also the conditions of life and work and of the place of producers *vis-a-vis* managers and owners. On the other hand, there were definite limitations to the councils' movement, and constraints imposed upon them by their historical experiences, culture, the uneven and differentiated nature of Iranian industrialization, the size, youth and social composition of the urban industrial labour force, the absence of working-class parties, and the nature of the revolutionary 'Islamic state'. In the absence of a consistent and correct understanding of the character of the new regime, with whom even co-management or participation was impossible, the councils could not fully develop, further and implement workers' control. Instead, they had to settle for Islamic populism.

The period after the consolidation of the rule of the IRP saw a disorganized and bewildered working class, responding to the new state of affairs with a noticeable lack of enthusiasm and heightened sense of responsibility for production that workers had had in their factories during the first period of the Revolution and the councils movement. The new regime has gradually taken over all the economic functions that the councils had delegated to themselves, and has fully restored the old divison of labour. This poses potential problems for the state and the new Islamic managers. Even the Islamic associations, though IRP-controlled, are working-class phenomena. There have been reports of slowdowns and periodic strikes by factory workers. The ideology of the Islamic regime will become less opaque and its role and function more apparent when it comes out of its present transitional period, and becomes a coherent, cohesive state with a clear development plan that will no doubt replicate many of the features of the *ancien regime*'s accumulation strategy, including a re-linking with international capital. The story of the councils may be over for now; but the response of industrial workers to a concerted accumulation strategy and the prospects for autonomous working class organization is perhaps *the* intriguing question.

Notes

1. Like the oilworkers, the Central Bank employees occupied a sensitive position in the economic system and seemed to be fully conscious of this. They also devised creative ways of sabotaging financial activities, such as withholding deposit and withdrawal slips. In autumn 1978, rejecting the inviolate tenet of secrecy in banking, they released the names of those wealthy individuals who had withdrawn large sums of money or transferred their accounts to foreign banks.

2. Most of the writings on the councils are in Persian. Articles in English are the following: Shahrzad Azad, "Workers' and Peasants' Councils in Iran", *Monthly Review*, Vol. 30, no. 5, Oct. 1980; Assef Bayat, "Workers' Control After the Revolution", *MERIP Reports,* no. 113, March/April 1983; Chris Goodey, "Workers' Councils in Iranian Factories", *MERIP Reports*, no. 88, June 1980.

3. Both these sentiments are expressed by Fred Halliday in *Iran: Dictatorship and Development* (Penguin, Harmondsworth, 1979).

4. Farhad Daftary and Maryam Borghey, *Multinational Enterprises and Employment in Iran.* Geneva, ILO: 1976.

5. A good discussion of the Shah's industrialization policy is Keith McLachlan, 'The Iranian Economy 1960–76', in H. Amirsadeghi and R. Ferrier (eds.), *Twentieth Century Iran* (Heinemann, London: 1977), pp. 129–169.

6. According to a former official of the Plan and Budget Organization, nearly one million unskilled Afghani workers were working in Iran after 1973. Iranian skilled labour was in short supply and much demand.

7. International Labor Office, *Employment and Income Policies for Iran.* ILO, Geneva, 1973.

8. It should be noted that Iran is a nation of nationalities and ethnic groups. While Farsi is the dominant language, the inhabitants of Azarbaijan province speak a Turkish dialect (as do the Turkomans in the northeast), and the Kurds have a language and culture of their own. The ethnic differentiation of the Tehran industrial labour force – particularly the strong presence of Azarbaijani and Mazanderani workers – is documented by Assef Bayat in his unpublished Ph.D. dissertation on the councils and workers' control (University of Kent, 1984).

9. Islamic Republic of Iran, Plan and Budget Organization, Statistical Center of Iran, *National Census on Population and Housing, 1976* (Teheran, 1981). Table 26, p. 82. The figure for urban areas is 31.5% (p. 85).

10. In the small manufacturing sector the following could be found: tools, local foundries, castings, auto repair, masonry and carpentry, casting of small pieces such as fasteners, tea kettles, etc., sheet metal works such as assorted containers, buckets, gardening and small farming implements, and decorative handicrafts from brass, copper, silver, etc.

11. One writer describes a visit to a car assembly plant which, he had been told, was the last word in automation. There he saw workers sitting on the floor removing imperfections in the body of the autos, using hand tools identical to ones he had seen in handicrafts workshops (Walter Elkan, 'Employment, Education, Training and Skilled Labor in Iran', *Middle East Journal,* Spring 1977, p. 186.

12. Daftary and Borghey, *Multinational Enterprises*, p. 92.

13. ILO, 'Labour Legislation, Practice and Policy', Mission Working Paper IX (Geneva, 1973), p. 21.

14. The role of SAVAK in factories is stressed in the US Department of Labour

Report, *Labour Law and Practice in Iran*, BLS Report no. 276 (1964), p. 28.

15. In the factories, machinery was more modern than was management and supervision. In the early 1970s there was much discussion on the need to improve and modernize managerial and supervisory methods. A management institute affiliated to Harvard was planned. But by 1978 the division of labour in factories and other organizations was based less on scientific management than on the presence of SAVAK and retired or active military personnel, and high level manpower was determined primarily by family ties, connections, and educational achievement. According to one study, traditional social values formed the basic outlook of Iranian owners-managers. These values were reinforced by the political system of the Shah. (Gail Cook Johnson, *High-Level Manpower in Iran,* Praeger, NY 1980, p. 43).

16. The populist alliance was based on the convergence of all urban classes and social strata in the anti-Shah struggle: the urban poor, traditional petty bourgeoisie, new petty bourgeoisie, working class, clergy, students, and *Bazaaris.* The main slogan of the populist alliance was 'Independence, freedom, Islamic Republic.' After the Shah's downfall, the alliance began to break up into its constitutive elements.

17. 'Resolution of the Workers of the Machine Tool and Tractor Assembly Plants of Tabriz', 13 Aban 1357 (4 November 1978). Reprinted in Organization of Iranian People's Fedaii Guerillas, 'The OIPFG Salute the Advanced Workers of the Soil, Machine Tool and Tractor Assembly Industries' (leaflet), Teheran, 15 Aban 1357 (6 November 1978) (tr. by Iranian Students Association in the US).

18. A fascinating, first-hand account of the oil workers' strike is a document entitled 'How We Went on Strike and Paralysed the Shah's Regime'. It was carried in *MERIP Reports*, March/April 1979 and Peter Nore and Terisa Turner (eds.), *Oil and Class Struggle* (Zed Press, London, 1980).

19. The tremendous power displayed by Iranian workers during the anti-Shah struggle was acknowledged by the new authorities in various ways (recognition of councils, concession to demands that work on nuclear power plants cease and that shipments of oil to Israel and South Africa stop). Announcing the unilateral abrogation of the agreement under which the Iranian Oil Participants (the former Consortium) acted as purchasers of the bulk of Iranian oil, the new chairman and managing director of the National Iranian Oil Company said in a speech to NIOC employees on 28 February 1979: "We tell those companies that were imposed on us in the past that it is better for them to withdraw, because if they refuse, the workers will kick them out." (*Middle East Economic Survey* (Nicosia), vol. 22, 5 March, 1979, p. 8).

20. For a detailed description of these events, see Ervand Abrahamian's concluding chapters in *Iran Between Two Revolutions* (Princeton Univ. Press, Princeton, NJ, 1982).

21. Javad Salehi, "Economic Consequences of the Iranian Revolution". Paper presented at the 15th annual meeting of the Middle East Studies Association of North America, Philadelphia, PA, November 1982.

22. Massoud Karshenas and Hashem Pesaran, 'Islamic Government and the Iranian Economy', paper presented at the 18th annual meeting of the Middle East Studies Association of North America, Chicago, 1 November 1983. See also Plan and Budget Organization, Statistical Center of Iran, *Statistical Abstracts 1363* [1984], p. 71, demonstrating the dramatic reduction in the wage differentials between white-collar and blue-collar workers in large industrial establishments.

23. Karshenas and Pesaran (ibid.). See also *Statistical Yearbook 1363* [1984] (Plan and Budget Organization, Statistical Center of Iran), p. 400, showing wages, employment and output in the large industrial sector. During the period 1978–83, wages rose steadily and employment remained fairly constant despite the vicissitudes of output. Nonetheless, as Karshenas and Pesaran (ibid.) demonstrate, the gap between productivity and wages has closing up since 1981.

24. Goodey, op. cit., p. 6.

25. Ibid., p. 8.

26. Of the Left-wing forces, only the Tudeh Party was less than enthusiastic about the councils, preferring the formation of a nation-wide labour confederation such as had existed in the 1940s.

27. Organization of Iranian People's Fedaii Guerrillas, *Kar*, no. 49, 16 March 1980; no. 53, 13 April 1980.

28. Rah-e-Kargar Organization, *Rah-e-Kargar*, no. 9, February 1980.

29. Peykar Organization, *Peykar*, no. 49, April 1980.

30. Organization of Iranian People's Fedaii Guerrillas, *Kar*, no. 91, 21 May 1980.

31. Organization of Iranian People's Fedaii Guerrillas, *Kar*, no. 91, January 1 1980. This tragic development recalls the fate of Bolshevik workers during the civil war in Soviet Russia.

32. Pasdaran were the paramilitary "revolutionary guard".

33. Personal communication from an employee of the Bimeh Iran [Insurance] Company.

34. *Middle East Economic Digest* (London), Special Report on Iran, November 1984, p. 41, quoting the Minister of Labor and Social Affairs, Abolghassem Sarhadizadeh. (The report was written in Iran by Vahe Petrossian.)

8. The Japanization of the Malaysian Trade Union Movement

Peter Wad

The spectacular post-World War II economic growth in Japan and the continued Japanese expansion during the global economic recession since 1974 has attracted international attention, including attempts to emulate the Japanese model of development. One such attempt has been made in Malaysia, where since 1981/2, a Look East policy has been adopted which takes Japan and South Korea (mini-Japan) as its ideals.

Several explanations have been offered to account for the Japanese 'miracle'. Apart from massive transfers of US technology and favourable treatment of Japanese exports to the USA, emphasis has been placed on Japanese culture, the 'plan-rational' economic and industrial policy formulated and implemented by MITI (the Ministry of International Trade and Industry), and the three (or four) 'treasures' of the Japanese labour market: life-long employment, seniority wage systems, enterprise unionism and 'the social norms of the enterprise'.

In Malaysia, politicians have been aware of all these peculiarly Japanese factors and have tried to transplant a number of them to their own society. The latest step has been the formulation of the policy of enterprise unionism as an alternative to the dominant industrial unions in the private sector.[1] As might be expected, the Malaysian trade union movement has taken this threat seriously and has responded negatively.

The object here is to analyse the contemporary struggle surrounding enterprise unionism with particular reference to assessing, first, the strategy adopted by trade unions for their survival under the Look East policy and second, the appropriateness of conventional Marxist approaches to enterprise unionism. However, before proceeding to this task it is necessary to outline the historical development of trade unionism in Malaysia, the government's New Economic Policy (NEP) for 1971–90 and the background and content of its decision to Look East.

The Development of Trade Unions in Malaysia

The two main stages in Malaysian trade union history will here be called by the dominant union structure: *general unionism* from the 1920s to the defeat of the Communist trade union movement in 1947-8 and *industrial unionism* from 1948 until the present – when it now faces the prospect of being replaced by *enterprise unionism.*

General Unionism[2]

Having previously established trade and military centres in Penang (1786), Singapore (1819) and Malacca (1824), the British conquered mainland Malaya in the 1870s, whereupon they instituted an administrative system based on indirect rule through the various indigenous sultanates. However, with migrant Chinese workers strictly controlled by the Chinese entrepreneurs who were active in trade and tin mining, the British were faced by an acute shortage of labour until they resorted to the introduction of labour-saving technology on the mines and the systematic importation of Tamil (Indian) labourers to work on the rubber estates. Regulated by Indian and Malayan colonial government agreement, the estates' recruiting system used Tamil foremen as recruiters and work chiefs, with the employment and housing of Tamil workers being closely controlled by estate managers. Even so, the British still needed Chinese contract labour on a large scale, in skilled jobs generally, in mining and for particular tasks in the cultivation of rubber. But they never secured direct control over the migration of Chinese labour, for this remained very largely in the hands of Chinese *towkays* (rich men).

It was Chinese labour which was very largely responsible for the initial development of collective organization amongst workers in colonial Malaya, in particular under the aegis of the Chinese Communist Party (CCP). In 1926, the CCP and the international communist confederation of trade unions (Profintern) organized the Nanyang Federation of Labour (NFL) in Singapore to cover the whole of South-East Asia. However, the suppression by the Nationalists of the CCP in China was matched by the prohibition of the Singapore based NFL, after which a local Communist Party took care of union tasks. New waves of repression followed, but the Communists succeeded in re-organizing their labour movement into the Malayan General Labour Union (MGLU) in the early 1930s. They opted for organization along general lines not only because Chinese migrant labour was distributed through diverse sectors of the economy, but also to maximize prospects for political unity and recruitment across ethnic lines.

The subsequent expansion and development of the MGLU was severely hindered by four factors. First, the 1930s depression resulted in the massive repatriation of Chinese migrant labour; second, the MGLU constituents were suppressed by the British authorities; third, a craft-oriented movement of mutual aid societies expanded in size and scope, developing into union-like organizations; and fourth, Chinese dominance of the unions inhibited unionization amongst culturally different Indian workers. Although British pressure upon the MGLU was replaced by cooperation when war broke out between Germany and the USSR, the Japanese occupation again resulted in a fierce campaign against the Communists.

Despite initial Indian and Malay collaboration with the Japanese against British imperialism and Chinese economic influence, the Malayan Communist Party (MCP) became the leading liberation force against the Japanese. With the British re-occupation in 1945, therefore, the MCP was able to mobilize the Chinese and Indian masses together for an independent, democratic Malayan Republic with equal rights between the ethnic communities.

The MCP mass campaign effected the re-establishment of an alliance between the Malay aristocracy (which was able to mobilize the Malay peasantry in its support) and the British (in a bid to undermine the revolutionary communist potential). This was formalized in a new political structure under which Malays became privileged in regard to citizenship, whilst the Malayan aristocracy became constitutionally predominant within the new Federation of Malaya which replaced the Malayan Union in 1948. This new arrangement came under heavy attack from the MCP, which launched unsuccessful general strikes in 1947 and 1948 against the plan.

The MGLU, re-organized in February 1946 as the Pan-Malayan General Labour Unions (PMGLU), and again in August as Pan-Malayan Federation of Trade Unions (PMFTU), reached its peak in 1947, when it had 250,000 members, about 40% of wage workers and 80% of all unions. It had a centralized structure incorporating unions based on diverse trades, occupations, industries and regions. Co-ordinated from the top by officials, its unionization drive merged with spontaneous worker activity which sprang up in the conjuncture of renewed economic growth, a tighter labour market, colonial exploitation and the demystification wrought by the Japanese. The British responded with an abortive attempt to organize an alternative trade union centre as well as an implementation of the Trade Union Act of 1940 which forbade unions' political activity and which demanded registration. Militant unions were denied registration, and in addition, strikes were suppressed, union meetings dissolved and union organizers barred from the estates. Finally, a new labour law in 1948 banned general unions but allowed trade, occupational and industrial organization up to national level.

The new labour law was followed by the criminalization of MCP unions, mass arrests, retrenchment of union militants, violent suppression of strikes and so on. The MCP was finally banned after armed confrontations and the declaration of an Emergency. The Communist labour movement then went underground and into the jungle and merged itself with the ultimately unsuccessful guerrilla insurgency. The Emergency regulations were upheld beyond independence in 1957 and were only withdrawn in 1960 when they were replaced by a sweeping Internal Security Act.

In sum, the British counter-revolutionary policy succeeded in eliminating the MCP movement; but only at the price of conceding a political independence which recognized the anti-communist support received primarily from the Malay aristocracy but also the Chinese bourgeoisie. The result was a triple hegemony in the post-colonial era: Malay hegemony in the small holding agricultural sector and in the public sector, Chinese hegemony in the urban small and medium market economy, and British control over the capitalist export sector (principally the rubber estates and tin mines).

The precondition for the working of this neo-colonial solution was a supply of abundant and disciplined labour. Yet the inter-colonial migrant labour system did not now exist, for it was resisted by the (independent) Indian Government as well as by the Malays, and while the Communist labour movement had been crushed, it had left behind a vacuum in the labour market which might again be filled by MCP unionists. This dilemma was solved in two ways. First, agreement was reached with plantation owners whereby they would employ Malays on the estates, whilst simultaneously a reserve army of labour was created by forced resettlement and urbanization of Chinese peasants (squatters who had escaped into the rural areas under the Japanese repression).

Second, the British sponsored a new reformist labour movement. A subservient trade union movement was constructed on the basis of a few anti-Communist Indian estate workers' unions and public sector unions of principally Indian employees. Without competition from militant Communist unionists and within the scope of the more populist oriented Indian community, the new industrial unions made headway in terms of unionization and collective agreements. The Korean war boom for Malayan export products offered the opportunity to improve wages and working conditions, and the organizational framework was set up with the support of the British TUC and the newly formed anti-communist International Confederation of Free Trade Unions. The new national unions were finally combined into the MTUC (Malayan – later Malaysian – Trade Unions Congress), alongside which a British promoted Labour Party developed considerable support among the Indian population.

Industrial Unionism

By the time of independence, several national industrial unions had been created in key economic sectors, notably in the plantations, banking, commerce, mining and manufacturing. In 1957, too, a federation of unions in federal and state government services was formed, the Congress of Unions of Employees in Public and Civil Services (CUEPACS). While trade union legislation did not allow the formation of a national centre, the MTUC had operated since 1950 as a coordinating society, including most of the existing unions and advocating a programme for the restructuring of the union movement into 14 industrial federations.[3]

Since independence, the trade union movement has made little progress beyond this point in terms of further unionization and centralization (amalgamation); if anything the contrary, for although union membership has risen from 220,000 in 1957 to 500,000 in 1980, the level of unionization has remained at around 20% of the workforce. In addition, a number of leading industrial unions have been de-registered – including the Factory and General Workers' Union in 1958, the Mining Employees' Union in 1959, the United Malayan Estate Workers' Union between 1963–7, and the Airlines Employees' Union in 1979 – thereby leaving the scene to weaker unions (as in mining), in the control of a conservative union bureaucracy (in the estate sector), atomized in smaller industry unions (in manufacturing) and in airlines divided into separate organizations for foreign and domestic corporations' employees. Furthermore, the formation of Malaysia in 1963 by the confederation of Malaya, Sarawak and Sabah and Singapore did not enlarge the scope for unionization at the confederal level, for this was disallowed (although the MTUC – as a society and not a union – was allowed to encompass the entire territory). Meanwhile the number of trade unions has increased from 249 in 1958 to 276 in 1980, just over a third of these being located in the private sector which, accounting for in excess of half of total union membership, encompasses unions which are generally larger than in the public sector.[4]

The failure of the MTUC policy to reduce the number of unions to fourteen industrial conglomerates is often seen as a major factor in the trade union movement's stagnation, for as a result, there now exists a jumble of union types (regional/national; craft; occupation; industrial; enterprises; and department). Defining departments in the public sector as an enterprise, enterprise unions constituted 47% of all unions in Malaysia in 1981, equivalent to 25–30% of total membership, with some three-quarters of such unions located in the public sector. In manufacturing, enterprise unions account for only one-fifth of the number of unions and only 8% of membership (1979), for as in mining and agriculture, industrial unions still predominate – although, as will be related below, these are now subject to attack. Meanwhile, trade union unity was dealt a further blow with the disaffiliation from the MTUC (then representative of some two-thirds of total union membership) of CUEPAC unions in 1980 after further tightening of anti-labour laws and the MTUC's severe criticism of the government.[5]

The structure of Malaysian trade unionism in the 1980s is therefore very much a product of both colonial and post-colonial government policy. But whereas the British sponsored industrial unions were counterbalanced by national employers' associations, and industrial relations thus geared to centralized wage bargaining and collective agreements, the Malaysian government has sought to destroy the momentum towards working-class unity which such industrial unionism might bring in its train by promoting the disaggregation of the union movement in its stead.

In addition, the post-colonial government has made extensive use of security legislation and has implemented a succession of anti-labour laws. Further, it has intervened to curtail the right to strike in the public sector, upon which it has also imposed a controlled system of conciliation and arbitration. Meanwhile, industrial unions in manufacturing have been corralled within narrowly but arbitrarily defined occupational sectors.

The outcome of all this has been divergent union organization and policies. In the private sector, the older unions have developed into union bureaucracies without genuine union democracy and with persistent indications of corruption, while the newer unions in manufacturing have developed closer ties to members and a more critical attitude to the government and employers. In the public sector, unit unions have shown a very militant line from time to time even though CUEPACS has moved steadily closer to the government.

The rationale for the government's anti-labour line is three-fold. First, unions are seen as obstacles to the pursuit of a low wage strategy of national capital accumulation; second, unions have consistently supported opposition parties; and third, unions have organized across ethnic lines in contradiction to the ethno-political compartmentalization of the Malaysian polity. However, notwithstanding such a commitment to the mobilization of workers as a class, the trade union movement has drawn its support disproportionately from (mainly) Indian and Chinese labour.

The New Economic Policy

Within the context of changes in the world market in the 1960s, the class based labour market and the ethnic base polity worked to increase socio-economic inequalities and ethnic tensions.[6] Whilst the organized working class was able to secure improvements in real terms, rising unemployment among (Malay) estate workers and the urban poor rendered the unorganized majority worse off. These tensions erupted in 1967 with a general strike by workers and shopowners in Penang, culminated in serious reverses for the government in the election of 1969, and set off ethnic riots in the capital, Kuala Lumpur, in which several hundreds, mostly Chinese were killed.[7] The declaration of a new Emergency symbolized the breakdown of the neo-colonial triple hegemony which had come about through the decline of British control over the export sector (notably via the devaluation of the pound in 1967), the reduction of Chinese domination over the urban economy and the consolidation of control over the state by the Malay bureaucracy.

The Malay bureaucracy now formulated a New Economic Policy (NEP) for the next two decades; its objective was to restabilize the power bloc under the hegemony of the Malay aristocracy and itself by launching an assault upon the poverty of ethnic Malay (mostly peasants and unskilled workers) and upon Malay exclusion from the capitalist sector.[8] The plan target was to reduce the proportion of the population in poverty from about 50% to below to below 20% in 1990, combined with a redistribution of capital and jobs in the non-agricultural sectors so that Malays would control 30% of corporate assets and a little above half of the number of jobs.[9]

This massive restructuring of the economy along ethnic lines was to be realized by rapid industrialization, state intervention into the economy, land development schemes and decentralized regional development, Malay-oriented educational reforms and an overall tightening of civil, democratic and trade union rights. Positive discrimination in favour of the Malay population was to be practised for 20 years.

The NEP was designed to transform the Malaysian class structure by entrenching the hegemony of the Malay aristocracy and bureaucracy via the formation of a new Malay bourgeoisie and a new Malay proletariat, the Malayanization of the corporate sector and the displacement of the Chinese working class from employment in the modern sector. However, this restructuring was to be achieved, not through the expropriation of either capital or jobs, but rather via economic growth and employment generation, with the financial means coming from domestic savings and an inflow of foreign capital as direct investment, loans and aid.

Evaluated on the basis of its own criteria, the NEP may be judged a success as it worked out in the 1970s. In broad terms (i) the proportion of the population living in poverty was reduced from an official figure of 49% in 1970 to 29% in 1980;[10] (ii) employment has been substantially increased, unemployment reduced and jobs redistributed to the benefit of Malays;[11] and (iii) ownership of private industry by Malays has increased from 4.5% in 1970 to around 12.5% in 1980 (at the expense of foreign residents rather than of non-Malay citizens, who have registered their own increase in ownership from 34.0% to 40%).[12] Notwithstanding some exaggeration by a reduction of the official poverty line and shadow ownership of foreign capital by citizens, substantial steps were taken towards the realization of NEP objectives. This was facilitated by an average annual growth rate in GDP of 7.8% (or 5.0% per capita) and, in particular, a growth rate in manufacturing in excess of 12.5% with production for export increasing by some 26%.

Despite such success, the NEP ran into considerable trouble towards the end of the decade and in the early 1980s. First, the contraction of the world market effected a marked reverse in the Malaysian terms of trade from 95 in 1980 (1970=100) to 70 in 1982.[13] In consequence, steady public sector activity and deficit financing of the development programme led to a leap in the public sector debt and the external debt (whose servicing ratio rose from 1.8% in 1980 to 6.0% in 1983). The resultant clamp down by the state on development expenditures inevitably endangered the further realization of NEP goals.

Second, there was a growing resistance to the takeover (in particular) of British capital, Malaysian state and private interests having successfully bought into foreign assets in rubber, palm oil, tin mining, banking and trade. The UK government reacted extremely negatively when the Malaysian state bought the Guthrie Corporation in a dawn raid on the London Stock Exchange, and the resulting strained relations led to the Malaysian government adopting a 'Buy British last' policy and undertaking a re-assessment of its international orientation.[14]

Finally, a third obstacle to the continuing success of the NEP was an adverse reaction by Malaysian workers, who despite the general tightening of controls upon labour were able in the 1970s to secure a substantial increase in wages, particularly in manufacturing. Significantly, however, such gains were not made by militant strike activity so much as through shop-floor resistance and collective and industrial bargaining, taking advantage of the use of the industrial courts, falling unemployment, shortages of skilled labour and increasingly, rising capital investment per work place and a growing concentration of capital.[15]

Despite these developments, the British heritage remained strong within the trade union movement, not least in the middle sized industrial unions in the private sector; yet the working class had meanwhile been transformed by the proletarianization of Malays, who were now the predominant ethnic component of those in wage employment (from 35% at independence to 47% in 1980 compared with declines in the proportion of Chinese from 42% in 1957 to 38% in 1980 and of Indians from 23% to 15%). This was matched by a change whereby in 1950 Malays accounted for 16%, Chinese 26% and Indians 58% of total union membership to a situation in 1980 where the proportions were 51%, 22% and 27% respectively.[16] Despite their new numerical preponderance, however, the industrially inexperienced Malay workers were still largely led by Western-oriented Indian trade unionists. Further, although schooled in the virtues of positive discrimination, they were heavily concentrated in poorly paid unskilled or semi-skilled jobs. They therefore constituted a social mass which could be mobilized in pursuit of economic and social demands which might lower the rate of accumulation in industry. Not only might this negate the NEP imperative of rapid industrialization and capital restructuring, but it might also threaten the ethno-political restabilization of the Malaysian polity.

In order to counter the potential muscle of the unionized the state clamped down hard on any manifestation of militant activity; for instance, demands for higher wages by employees of the Malaysian Airline System were met by mass retrenchment, detention of officials and deregistration of the union concerned.[17] Indeed, the capacity of the state for repression has increased significantly as a result of a marked build up of military forces in the late 1970s and the strengthening of the security police network. Even so, wholesale suppression of the workers' movement could have disastrous consequences for the Malayan rulers' political project, precisely because intervention would fall hard upon not only Chinese and Indian but also upon Malayan workers as well.

Hence it is that the Malaysian government, faced by these various contradictions, had to wrestle with the dilemma of how to maintain rapid capital accumulation and preserve public order when at home the implementation of the NEP was likely to produce reaction to repression and abroad was causing a disruption in its traditional relations with the West. It found its answer in a new strategy of looking east towards Japan.

The Japanese Alternative

Malaysia's policy re-orientation towards the east took place in a context where Japanese economic expansion was already making an impact upon its trading relations, foreign investment patterns and foreign aid. Hence over the last two years, whereas exports to Japan had increased from 17% between 1961-4 to 22% between 1975-80, imports had increased from 9% to 22%, the exchange centreing on Malaysia's export of raw materials and import of industrial commodities (increasingly capital goods).[18] Similarly, foreign direct investment in Malaysia was increasingly originating from Japan, having increased from 12% of the total in 1971 to 24% in 1977 (compared to 19% from the USA, 18% from western Europe and 34% from the Association of South-East Asian Nations (ASEAN) in the latter year). Such investment was principally in manufacturing (notably chemical production and textiles), whereby 1979 Japanese foreign direct investment–at 19% of the total–exceeded that of the UK (18%) and the USA (8%) and compared with holdings by western European countries (including UK) of 28% and ASEAN countries of 27%.[19] Meanwhile, by 1982 Japan was providing 50% of the total amount of foreign aid received by the ASEAN countries, and 55% in the case of Malaysia.[20]

The relationship between Japan and Malaysia was clearly asymmetrical with the Japanese capital coming to assume a steadily more dominant position, especially in heavy industries. Despite this, the increasing Japanese influence was given a warm welcome, for not only were Japanese TNCs willing to co-operate with Malaysian capital (public and private) in joint ventures and (in theory at least) in the transfer of technology, but without ownership control of raw materials production like the British, Japanese capital did not antagonize the NEP. Further, Japanese investment was considerably assisted by the links which had been established with the Malay aristocracy during the Japanese occupation during the war.

Influential though it was, the growing Japanese impact upon the economy could not in itself account for the espousal by the Malaysian state of its strategy of Japanization. Rather, the Look East policy that was adopted had much deeper roots in the domestic soil of Malay–Chinese antagonisms (which ensured that Malays would not Look South to Singapore, a Chinese dominated city state). In addition, wartime collaboration apart, the Meiji and MITI models of industrialization made a strong appeal to Malaysian policy-makers in contrast to what was perceived as the stagnation, decay and crisis of the West. As the Prime Minister, Mahathir Mohamed, explained in 1982:

> Japan is the biggest investor in Malaysia. Our Look East policy is directed not so much at investment from Japan but at acquiring the kind of policies, systems and work ethics that the Japanese have. We see the Japanese have made headway while the West . . . appears to be regressing. So in order for Malaysia to

> progress, we have to learn from the better example. This is why we now want to Look East where before we were looking West.[21]

But from an initial, somewhat diffuse focus on Japanese (and South Korean) work ethics, management style and technology as the primary factors behind the Rising East, the Malaysian government has elaborated and enlarged upon its policy of Look East as its own wider strategy has matured. In 1983, therefore, the Look East policy was more closely related to other official approaches of 'Malaysian Incorporated', 'Privatization' and 'Leadership by Example' as well as, and critically, 'enterprise unionism'.

Under the Look East policy, enterprise unionism is regarded as perhaps the key factor lying behind the Japanese miracle. Hence it was that after propagating the ethic of 'Workaholism' without any great success, the government announced its intention to promote enterprise unionism in the cause of national development. Such a strategy, declared the Prime Minister, would not be carried out at the expense of the westernized industrial unions in Malaysia, which would continue to co-exist with Japanized unions for

> it was not the government's intention to negate the work of trade unions as it was well aware of the need for trade unions to protect the legitimate rights of workers in the country.

But what was equally important, he continued, was the

> national interest and the need for a successful system suited for Malaysia in its development efforts. . . There is therefore a need for Malaysia . . . to look into a new concept like in-house unions that have been used successfully by the Japanese 'who have easily beaten the West' which practises the old system of trade unionism.[22]

The government interest in enterprise unionism, he further explained, followed from its accommodation to the maintenance of wage differentials between enterprises with different productivity and profitability, and to its raising productivity and promoting smooth labour–management relations within a context of company solidarity instead of class solidarity. Such a system of industrial harmony at the plant level would clearly benefit capital, labour and the state:

> Some of our companies . . . have just been set up and are coming up but if forced to pay the same benefits as the more successful ones will definitely not succeed. Hence . . . it would be more meaningful for these firms, especially the new ones, to have in-house unions which have proved to be a big success in Japan . . . by having a union within a firm, the union could negotiate with the management concerned, while taking into consideration the various circumstances. And with workers totally involved in the company, which would result in increased productivity and higher profits, all sectors would benefit, including the Government through revenue. It would therefore be more meaningful . . . for the

> thousands of workers in firms and not represented by unions to have in-house unions.[23]

Clearly, this vision represented a significant shift by the Prime Minister away from a wholly negative stance he had adopted towards the very notion of trade unionism during a previous spell in politics when in 1970 he had declared:

> In a scheme to force Malay labour into the competitive field of skilled and semi-skilled work, trade unionism can find no place. Absolute security and good working conditions are not the aims . . . Trade unions are therefore superfluous.[24]

In brief, it would seem that the very success of the NEP in creating a larger and more powerful working class, and one which had given some indication of its determination to struggle for an extension of its material benefits and industrial rights, had made both state and capital increasingly aware of the considerable threat that the organization of workers into effective unions would represent to their respective interests. Accordingly, enterprise unionism was now seen as a method not merely of pre-empting the existing industrial unions (for, in truth, official regulation had already hampered these enough), but of shifting the very basis of trade unionism away from the collective representation of workers to a new model which should ensure their collective emasculation in such a manner, not simply to contain their discontents but rather to direct them towards pliability and positive commitment to the achievement of capital's objectives.

This, it would seem, was the general aim. However, lest it generate too hostile a response, enterprise unionism has not been imposed by law (although this may follow later as it has been in South Korea in 1981)[25]. Rather, the state has sought to avoid confrontation with the industrial unions by simply bypassing them and making the 80% unorganized wage workforce the principal target of the new model, with particular attention being devoted to the incorporation of labour into enterprise unions in medium and small enterprises and within newly established large scale factories which have been set up in Malaysia in recent years. Among the most immediate beneficiaries of enterprise unionism, in other words, are the emergent Malay bourgeoisie and TNCs—most notably from Japan—whose interests are compatible with the achievement of objectives laid down by the NEP.

Enterprise Unionism: Containment and Contradiction.

Company unionism in Malaysia has a history which long predates the Look East policy, having been previously activated by employers' opposition to craft and industrial unionism and facilitated by the low level of industrialization, the relatively small size and the dispersal of the working class and the state's policy of enforcing a rule of one union per department. Further, employers' resistance to trans-enterprise unions has greatly benefited from the assistance of the Registrar of Trade Unions, who in 1974 for instance, prohibited a regional textile union from entering a locally owned plant despite the fact that 50% of employees clearly supported it. Similarly, in-house unions became established at quite a number of TNCs including the British Perak Hydro, the US owned Union Carbide battery factory and the Japanese (now state owned) Malaywata Steel Mill, whilst in some cases (as at Dunlop, where the National Union of Employees in Companies Manufacturing Rubber Products split and an MTUC official was suborned into withdrawing the plant collective from the national union) divisions within pre-existent unions have been manipulated by management in their favour.[26]

Attempts by management to secure company unionism have not always gone smoothly, for in a number of cases workers have struggled hard and long to establish their own autonomous organizations. At the locally owned United Motorworks (UMW), located near Kuala Lumpur, for example, the Transport Equipment and Allied Industries' Employees Union (TEAIEU) attempted to organize, but the 16 members of its initial committee were dismissed the moment management discovered the plan. Subsequently, attempts by the union to picket the company with supporters from other plants were smashed when management resorted to strong arm tactics and called in the police. A yellow (stooge) plant union was then established by the company in a bid to demobilize the workforce, only for workers to transform the new union into their own instrument of struggle. After failing to buy the union leadership, the company then opted for mass retrenchment of unionists; and when this, too, failed, management sub-contracted work in all sections where key unionists were employed. Although this went far in eliminating the autonomy which the plant union had acquired, UMW has none the less had to adopt a rather more co-operative labour strategy as its expansion and diversification into a high tech, capital goods producer has required its dealing with a more skilled labour force.[27] In sum, while enterprise unionism had made significant inroads into the larger industries within the private sector even before the announcement of the Look East policy, even the limited structures of company unions had been utilized by workers to resist managerial domination.

Following the adoption of Look East, however, the entrenchment of company unions by individual employers has been transformed into a coherent strategy by enterprise unionism, albeit by administrative means and not yet enforced by law. Within this context, enterprise unionism is usefully analysed in relation to (i) the industrial unions: (ii) the Japanese TNCs: (iii) the response of the established unions towards the policy of Looking East.

Enterprise Unionism and the Assault on Industrial Unions.

Although the official line under Look East is that the promotion of enterprise unions will not adversely impinge upon the activities of industrial unions, it has become apparent that the objective is as far as possible to cut the ground from below existing unions' feet: and in particular, the intention is to contain the emergence of autonomous organization amongst workers in the new industries which are expanding rapidly under the NEP. What this has meant in practice is that registration has been denied to industrial unions except in such cases as it is apparent that a level of support obtains which guarantees that substitution of an enterprise union would entail a major confrontation.

Consideration of a number of cases may serve to illustrate the general trend. In October 1983, for example, a claim by the National Union for Petroleum and Chemical Workers (NUPCW) for recognition on the grounds that it had obtained greater support amongst the 4,000 workers at the Petronas plant than the already registered in-house union was rejected out of hand. The NUPCW subsequently accepted this decision without any further struggle and decided to transfer its organizing efforts elsewhere.[28] Similarly, at Tanaka Sdn Bhd (a subsidiary of the Dragon and the Phoenix garment factory in Penang)–previously organized by the Penang Textile Workers' Union (PTWU) which had been deregistered after its members took part in an illegal strike in 1979–a bid by the same union to represent the mainly female work-force was turned down. Although the PTWU then took this up with the MTUC, the Textile Workers' Asian Regional Organization and the International Textile Garment and Leather Workers' Federation, such action was inadequate to secure a reversal of the decision, and subsequently plans to amalgamate the four regional textile unions in Peninsular Malaysia into a national union were abandoned for a more defensive strategy of maintaining the status quo.[29] Meanwhile TEAIEU, which has successfully organized all six pre-existing car plants, will probably be blocked from recruiting workers at the new PROTON car project which is financed by the Malaysian state in partnership with Japanese capital.[30] Given a tiny Malaysian car market of 100,000 cars and an already overcrowded industry with surplus capacity, extensive state support for PROTON is widely expected to drive a number of its competitors out of the market–in which case, TEAIEU will lose its strongholds and be forced to fall back upon the more difficult task of organizing the small sub-contracting companies which make components.

In contrast, there have been a few instances where industrial unions have successfully resisted attempts to displace them. At the Dragon and Phoenix garment factory, for example, the Registrar refused to register an in-house union in 1983 which had been formed after the PTWU had already organized a majority of workers and applied to the company for recognition.[31] Similarly, the Registrar ultimately rejected an application in June 1983 to register an in-house union at ITT Transelectronics–a 1,000 workers factory in the Penang Free Trade Zone–as a result of a determined struggle waged by the Electrical Industry Workers' Union (EIWU) to organize the largely female workforce which had seen the government sorely embarrassed by the case receiving wide publicity and being taken up in the international arena as illustrating a gross violation of the right to organize.[32]

In sum, whilst both capital and state are determined to contain resistance amongst the new industrial workforce by establishing enterprise unions and to disorganize the already unionized, they have as yet pulled back from incurring the cost which might ensue from outright suppression of autonomous organizations, choosing rather a less confrontational strategy of encircling the latter by restricting laws and rulings and preventing their further expansion.

Enterprise Unionism and Japanese TNCs.

The labour practices of Japanese TNCs in Malaysia are clearly crucial to the entire project of Look East, for if these were to indicate a failure to implement enterprise unionism, then success could hardly be expected elsewhere. Accordingly, it is notable that an early survey demonstrated that the personnel policies of Japanese TNCs were generally more centralized – allowing local subsidiaries' management less room for manoeuvre – than those of their US and UK counterparts.[33] Further, Japanese management has made determined efforts to transplant such integral components of the Japanese industrial relations system to Malaysian subsidiaries as the notion of the company family, productivity drives via quality control circles and suggestion boxes, cost reduction campaigns, morning exercises, company songs and recitation of company principles, all of which are designed to promote vertical solidarity and eliminate conflict between the company and workers.[34]

Despite such initiatives, the indications are that wholesale Japanization is neither possible not intended. In the first place, the sharp differentiation of workers into permanent and temporary staff which is a principal feature of the industrial relations system in Japan does not accord to Malaysian law, whereby after six months on the job a probationary employee acquires normal rights and duties which extend not to life-long guarantees of employment (as in Japan) but to an indefinite period which may be terminated subject to benefits. In essence, what would seem to be the case here is that because the Malaysian labour market is much more mobile than the Japanese, life-long employment guarantees are regarded as inappropriate (not least by the employers of female, highly replaceable, labour). Further, although employed rather little in manufacturing (where Japanese capital is concentrated), contract labour is still used extensively in plantations and construction. Likewise, the wage system in the private sector is not based on seniority as much as on job ratings and qualifications.

Secondly, the company world is divided into two halves: one culture for Japanese management and another for the (often multi-ethnic) employees.

Necessarily, such a divide severely inhibits the development of Japanese-style company norms, thereby impeding the evolution of enterprise community consciousness, the primacy of vertical relationships and reciprocal obligations, and a consensual system of decision-making. In addition, the achievement of Japanese welfare corporatism is rendered extremely difficult by a relatively high rate of labour turnover, the very different lifestyles of management and workers and a number of legal restrictions on foreign companies (such as the prohibition on their right to buy land, which makes the provision of company housing for employees more problematic than it might otherwise be).

In brief, the relationship between management and the shop-floor, besides being structured very largely through industrial unions, is filtered through a very different context in Malaysia than obtains in Japan. Hence it is that the much vaunted family spirit of which Japanese capital boasts at home is but rarely found in the Malaysian subsidiaries of Japanese TNCs where extensive passive–and not so passive–resistance by workers has imposed limits upon cultural transplantation. Meanwhile, Japanese TNCs have themselves proved to be by no means automatic conveyors of their own domestic model in that they have followed the western example of retrenching Malaysian workers during slumps and have generally ignored such practices as housing their employees which are often carried out at home. The Japanization of the Malaysian industrial relations system, as far as Japanese TNCs are concerned, is clearly only a partial, not wholesale, process whose implementation is subject to considerations of local cost and practicality.

Enterprise Unions and Industrial Unions' Response

When the government first attempted to promulgate the Japanese work ethics and their model of management–labour cooperation, they were generally quite well received by the MTUC and the older, larger and rather more conservative unions, which welcomed the prospect of the benefits of Japanization might bring, including the life-long employment system. On the other hand, the smaller unions in the expanding manufacturing sector tended to be highly critical from the start, TEAIEU arguing for instance

> that Japan lags behind many other industrial nations in the West especially on human rights and social welfare. It has to be realized that the vast majority of Japanese workers do not enjoy the security of tenure, housing facilities and other welfare benefits. Discrimination against female workers is also rife.[35]

Yet whatever the attitude, there was widespread scepticism that the Japanese model could be easily adapted to the very different Malaysian labour market.

Subsequently, as the threat to industrial unionism has mounted with the concerted effort to promote enterprise unionism in its place, the Japanization initiative has met with increasing resistance among private sector unions (even though within CUEPACS the policy has enjoyed a degree of goodwill). Thus it is that the MTUC has now adopted a strongly hostile attitude towards the whole concept of enterprise unionism.

> It is simply another weapon which can be used to weaken and dismember an already sickly union movement. The collective strength of workers in one industry will be broken into separate house unions in each factory, where union leaders will be dependent on the goodwill of their bosses, and unable to champion the workers' interests.[36]

Notwithstanding this belated adoption of a principled stand, the MTUC–together, of course, with CUEPACS–is strongly criticized by grassroots oriented unions like TEAIEU as having wholly failed to provide the leadership necessary to counter the long term consequences of policy and legislation adversely affecting the working class. But if, as TEAIEU alleges, the MTUC has proved inadequate to what should have been its historic task, how will enterprise unionism affect the workers' struggle in the years ahead, and what is labour's most appropriate strategy for survival?

Enterprise Unionism and Working-Class Strategy in Malaysia

In that trade unions are class organizations which, historically, have embodied workers' aspirations under capitalism, conventional Marxist (and, indeed, non-Marxist) theorization has inevitably viewed company or enterprise unionization as primarily a managerial strategy for imposing control upon and diverting more radical action by a workforce; and certainly, there can be little quarrel with such perception when company unions operate in a straightforward manner to ensure the subordination of labour to capital and develop no independent life of their own. However, it is suggested here that rather than dismissing company unionism as beyond the pale, there is an increasing need for its analysis as an important labour phenomenon. In the first place, enterprise unionism has been put forward as a major factor behind the Japanese miracle, and as such, it becomes important to understand the forms of coercion and hegemony over workers that it entails, and whether or not it is a principle of managerial domination which is particularly rooted within a peculiarly Japanese-style of capitalism. Secondly, and of rather more importance here, is the fact that, like it or not, enterprise unionism is quite widespread throughout the third world and for one reason or another establishes the boundaries within which myriad disadvantaged workers must struggle. What is required, in other words, is a more subtle and dialectical discussion of labour's resistance to capital within the confines of enterprise unionism than has generally been allowed.

It must be recognized initially that enterprise unionism in Japan is not quite the docile creature that it is commonly alleged to be. Hence although the exclusion of non-permanent employees from the benefits of unionization, company influence on union policy and union integration into company personnel strategies are all legitimate foci of concern, these are not the exclusive attributes of Japanese unions, whose performance compares not unfavourably to trade unions in a number of OECD countries in terms of the proportion of the labour force organized, the wage gains they have made and the militancy they exhibit and express. In addition, although such properties as Japanese unions possess must necessarily be related to Japan's rapid economic growth, the long-term rise in life-long employment may be regarded as something of an important achievement. In sum, whatever the final judgement, the Japanese situation is much more complex than western Marxist and non-Marxist mythology generally admits.

Within the third world, meanwhile, enterprise unions have often been contemptuously pushed aside by workers upon which they have been foisted; but even where the state has intervened to support them, they have not always been able to contain militant activity on the shop floor. In Chile, for example, where the Labour Law of 1924 was instrumental in impeding the development of genuine national unions until the late 1960s, the working class was none the less able to forge a united and radical trade union movement in close cooperation with the left-wing labour parties, this being a key factor in the later arrival of the Allende government in office in 1970.[38] Indeed, even in Japan radical and militant tendencies struggled with reactionary influences within the dominant enterprise unions from an early period, as evidenced by the rise of the Communist Sanbetsu grouping between 1945 and 1950; the militant economistic phase 1955-62 (involving the strike waves of the Spring Offensive every year); and the subsequent rivalry of the Sohyo and Domei federations (representing battle between economic militancy and economic corporatism) before the final triumph of the latter with the formation of the united private sector federation (Zenmin Rokyo) in 1982 and the simultaneous erosion of Sohyo strength in the public sector.[39]

What, then, are the prospects for enterprise unionism in Malaysia, and how is it likely to impinge upon the working-class struggle? Clearly, in that the imposition of Japanese industrial relations forms on the Malaysian labour market is intended to neutralize shop floor struggle and to pre-empt independent organization by the emergent working class in the rapidly expanding industries fostered by the NEP, it represents a major threat to the trade union movement, whose historical development in Malaysia – through general unions, industrial unions and now enterprise unions – has been continuously funnelled by the state towards unmilitant and controllable forms. Yet that said, it may be argued that the current strategy may have contradictory results.

First, it appears unlikely that the labour market will be easily Japanized, even to the extent that is desired by the state. Even without reference to the unfamiliarity of non-Japanese TNCs with Japanese management styles, the latter are unlikely to prove wholly compatible with the ethnic and cultural heterogenity of the Malaysian workforce. Similarly, whereas in Japan the cooperation of enterprise unions with management is generally secured by the allegiance to the latter of white collar and supervisory grades, and the exclusion of a significant fraction of blue collar workers, the colonial past and extensive foreign ownership of capital in Malaysia has served to bind largely unskilled blue collar labour together. Whilst this, in turn, has somewhere developed into large established industrial unions with unwieldy bureaucracies that have been highly susceptible to corruption and impervious to union democracy, the other side of the coin is that the enforced fragmentation of the union movement in Malaysia may by that token actually assist in the widespread establishment of plant based, grassroots control over union policy. Ironically, therefore, enterprise unionism may democratize the decision-making process within worker organizations by removing it from trade union bureaucracies and encouraging shop-floor activity. Finally, voluntary enterprise unionism may only be resisted by union democratization, preventing local grievances against union bureaucracy from evolving into local unions.

If enterprise unionism is the path that workers of necessity must pursue, then the possibilities for struggle that emerge even within the confining structures of enterprise unionism will require the evolution of a framework for coordination across plants. Were enterprise unions then to develop their muscle despite the best efforts of government and employers, then it is likely that they will take up issues at the industrial level; indeed, although the Japanese Spring Offensives (Shunto) are a unique phenomenon, similar assaults by labour upon employers might well be possible with the emergence of strong shop-floor based enterprise unionism in Malaysia.

A further dilemma for the government is that a fragmented union movement is an unwieldy if not inappropriate instrument for the pursuit of any form of administratively directed incomes policy. The existence of trade union centrals and large union bureaucracies opens the way for co-opting labour into the framework of overall development policy. Indeed, with ethnic Malays now in a majority in terms of union membership, this option might appear increasingly realistic and attractive and has already been realized in the public sector through CUEPACS and is potentially embodied in MTUC leanings towards a corporate relationship with the state. However, in so far as the government resolves to enable or allow enterprise unions to develop links and form a central body, so might it set in train a return to industrial unionism and the entry of a re-invigorated labour movement into the political sphere.

Thus it is that although the attempted Japanization of the Malaysian trade union movement represents a concerted threat to workers' collective organization, it simultaneously opens the door to new avenues of struggle. Although seeking to ensure that the trade union movement is restricted to merely defensive concerns, the government may find that the enterprise unions fostered under the policy of Look East may yet provide for the emergence of an industrially based workers' movement to confront the rise of Malaysian capitalism and Japanese neo-imperial power.

Notes

1. First announced by Information Minister Encik Abib Adam, *New Straits Times* (NST), 24 January 1983. An enterprise union is defined here as a trade union constituted at the plant or company level, and is synonymous with 'in-house', 'house' or 'company union'.

2. Mohamed Amin and M. Caldwell (eds), *Malaya: The Making of a Neo-colony* (Spokesman Books, Nottingham, 1977); M. Stenson, *Industrial Conflict in Malaya* (Oxford University Press, London, 1970); Tai Yun, *Labour Unrest in Malaya 1934-41* (University of Hong Kong, Hong Kong, Diss. 1973).

3. International Labour Office, *The Trade Union Situation in the Federation of Malaya* (Geneva, 1962), p.34.

4. Ibid., pp.43-5, R. Sielaff, *Malaysia: Gewerkschaften. Wandlungen im Selbverstandnis einer Gesellschaftlichen Gruppe* (Friedrich Ebert Stiftung, Bonn, 1976), p.17; Ministry of Labour and Manpower, *Labour and Manpower Report, 1980* (Kuala Lumpur, 1981); Registrar of Trade Unions (RTU), *Annual Report 1979* (Kuala Lumpur, 1982); Malaysian Trade Union Congress (MTUC), *Report of the General Council, 1979–80* (Petaling, Jaya, 1980).

5. Ministry of Labour (1981); RTU, *Annual Report 1979*; G. Dunkley, 'Industrial Relations in Malaysia', *The Journal of Industrial Relations*, vol. 24, no. 3, 1982, pp.424-42; MTUC, *Report of the General Council.*

6. D.R. Snodgrass, *Inequality and Economic Development in Malaysia* (Oxford University Press, London, 1980).

7. N.L. Snider, 'What happened in Penang?', *Asian Survey*, vol. 8, no. 12, 1968, pp.960-76.

8. R.S. Milne, and D.K. Mauzy, *Politics and Government in Malaysia* (Times Books International, Singapore, 1980), Chapter 10.

9. *Fourth Malaysia Plan 1981-85*, Tables 3-1 and 9-4.

10. Ibid.

11. Ibid., Tables 3-10 and 9-5.

12. Ibid., Tables 3–14 and 9–7.

13. Ministry of Finance, *Economic Report 1982-83* and *1983-84.*

14. J. Saravanamuttu, 'The "Look East" Policy and Japanese economic penetration in Malaysia', in K.S. Jomo, (ed.) *The Sun Also Sets: Lessons in Looking East* (Institut Analisa Sosial, Kuala Lumpur, 1983), p.283.

15. P. Wad, 'Malaysian Industrialization and the Dilemmas of the Trade Union Movement', in I. Nørlund, P. Wad, and V. Brun, (eds), *Industrialization and the Labour Process in Southeast Asia* (Institute of Cultural Sociology, Copenhagen, Repro serie 6, 1984) pp.117-47 and International Bank for Reconstruction and Development, *Malaysia's Manufacturing Sector*, Vol. II (Washington, 1981).

16. C. Gamba, *The Origins of Trade Unionism in Malaysia. A Study in Colonial Labour Unrest*, Singapore (1962) p.361, and Ministry of Labour (1981).

17. MTUC *Report of the General Council*; Transport Workers' Union, *8th*

Triannual Report (Petaling, Jaya, 1982), pp.15-20; 4 May 1979.

18. Chee Peng Lim, *Changes in the Malaysian Economy and Trade Trends and Prospects* (mimeo, Faculty of Economics & Administration, University of Malaya, 1984).

19. C. Vaitsos, 'Transnational Corporations in the Asia-Pacific Region: Development or Maldevelopment?', in *Economic and Social Commission for Asia and the Pacific (ESCAP), United Nations Committee on Transnational Corporations (UNCTC)*; Publication Series B, No. 2 (ESCAP/UNCT, Bangkok, 1982): F. von Kirchbach, 'Transnational Corporations in the ASEAN Region: A Survey of Major Issues', ESCAP *Economic Bulletin for Asia and the Pacific*, vol. 33, no. 1, 1982.

20. *Asiaweek*, 2 September 1983.

21. *FEER*, 11 June 1982.

22. *NST*, 6 March 1983.

23. Ibid.

24. Mahatir Mohamed, *The Malay Dilemma*, (Federal Publications, Kuala Lumpur, 1982) p.108.

25. Michael A. Lanius, 'The State and Industrial labour in South Korea', *Bulletin of Concerned Asian Scholars*, vol. 16, no. 4, 1984, p.5.

26. Sielaff, *Malaysia*, pp.21-2.

27. Interviews with former UMW unionist and current UMW leaders, 1984.

28. *NST*, 12 March 1984.

29. Personal communication from the General Secretary of the PTWU. Now an offensive to amalgamate into a national (West Malaysian) union has been reopened (*Asian Workers Solidarity Link,* Malaysia, vol. 2, no. 1, 1985).

30. For the Malaysian car project see Chee Peng Lim, 'Malaysian Car Dream: Need for Reconsideration', in Jomo, *The Sun Also Sets*, pp.329-31.

31. *NST*, 12 March 1984 and *Suara Buruh*, December 1982.

32. See the article by Arne Wangel in this collection.

33. A.B. Sim, *Comparative Practices and Performance of American, British and Japanese MNCs in Malaysia*, Malaysian Economic Association Seminar, Kuala Lumpur, 1978.

34. Experiences from a study trip to Malaysia 1984.

35. Syed Sharir bin Mohamed, Transport Equipment and Allied Industries Employees Union (TEAIEU) and Mohn, V.C., Sahabat Alam Malaysia (SAM) *Country Report on Malaysian Workers Reality*, Penang: Asian Workers Solidarity Link (AWSL) Document 8 (undated) p.2.

36. *NST*, 12 March 1984 and *Suara Buruh*, April 1983, May 1984.

37. Therbon G, "The Prospects of Labour and the Transformation of Advanced Capitalism", *New Left Review*, 145, 1984, pp.5-38.

38. A. Angell, *Politics and the Labour Movement in Chile* (Oxford University Press, London, 1972).

39. Iwao F. Ayusawa, *A History of Labor in Modern Japan*, (East-West Center Press, Honolulu, 1966); Okochi Kazuo, B. Karsh and S. Levine (eds), *Workers and Employers in Japan* (University of Tokyo Press, Tokyo, 1973); Muto Ichiyo, 'Class Struggle on the Shopfloor–The Japanese Case 1945-1984', *Ampo*, vol. 16, no. 3, 1984, pp. 38-49.

9. Third World Trade Unions as Agencies of Human Rights: The Case of Commonwealth Africa*

Rhoda Howard

The new international division of labour is a political and social as well as an economic phenomenon. New roles in the world market (e.g. the provision of world market enclaves)[1] often presuppose new political regimes. As preventive counter-revolutions[2] against possible labour unrest occur in countries such as Chile, the issue of social justice is brought once more to our attention. Even in countries whose role in the international division of labour is still primarily within the old rather than new framework (as suppliers of primary agricultural and mineral goods) trade unions are a very important political force – one of the few, if not the only, defenders of the working class against new corporatist states. Trade union rights and human rights are under attack.

This paper considers the relationship between trade unions and human rights in several countries in Commonwealth Africa, from the point of view of a specialist in human rights.[3] I contend that trade unions are extremely important agents in the pursuit and protection of human rights, but that they are far from the only necessary agent. The field of study of trade unions in Africa, dominated as it is by neo-Marxist perspectives, makes some rather crude assumptions about the nature of human rights and how they are realized. These contribute to a general disregard of human rights among Marxist intellectuals. In my view, Marxists need to be more critical of their assumptions that a real, non-perverted socialism can solve all human rights problems.

My criticism of the Marxist perspective on human rights starts from a philosophical acceptance of human rights as individual rights. In its genesis, this philosophical position is classically liberal. However, its western liberal origins do not limit its relevance to non-western, non-liberal regimes, either logically or empirically. I base my interpretation of the substance of human rights upon internationally agreed standards, specifically as outlined in the two 1966 United Nations Covenants on Civil and Political, and on Economic, Social and Cultural Rights.[4] These two

*I am grateful for comments to Jack Donnelly, Linda Freeman, Nigel Haworth, Jon Kraus, Michael Piva, Richard Sandbrook, Roger Southall and Peter Waterman. Thanks also to the Social Sciences and Humanities Research Council of Canada for funds enabling me to conduct the research for this chapter.

Covenants contain many 'red' rights, such as rights to subsistence, rights to work and trade union rights. They exclude property rights, substituting instead the right of national sovereignty over productive resources. Indeed much liberal thinking also now excludes property rights: for example Shue says property rights must always be susidiary to the vital interests, specifically subsistence rights, of all human beings.[5]

Some Implicit Assumptions

To discuss the potential for trade unions to contribute to the realization of human rights in Commonwealth Africa, it is first necessary to analyse some implicit assumptions about the relationships between human rights, trade unions and revolution which are generally not articulated, but which dominate the thinking of the Marxist school on this question.

Assumptions about the Meaning of Human Rights.
The philosopher Elaine Pagels suggests that Marxists have no concept of human rights. Marxists, she argues, take the position that 'only as one contributes to the community can one expect to derive benefits from it.'[6] Marxism contains, as liberalism does, a concept of human justice; but it is not grounded in a concept of rights as inalienable claims by the individual on or against the state. Rather, Marxism grounds its concept of justice in claims by groups (social classes) against other groups (classes); and it assumes that once the correct group, that is the proletariat, controls the state, the right to make claims on or against the state will no longer be necessary.

In the liberal tradition, human rights are rights which people enjoy merely because they are human; no other qualification is necessary. But Marxists tend to exclude entire social classes from the enjoyment and protection of rights, on the grounds that they take from, rather than contribute to, the wider community. The bourgeoisie, in Marxist theory, ought not to have a right to the private ownership of the means of production; in practice, under socialist rule, real or alleged members of the bourgeoisie are deprived of all other rights as well. Thus people accused of economic crimes in Tanzania are frequently imprisoned under the Preventive Detention Act, without basic civil rights such as the right to trial.[7]

The liberal interpretation of rights as inherent in everyone solely because of their human status is, in fact, more radical than the Marxist interpretation. It forces consideration of whether and how the whole range of human rights can be guaranteed to all people, regardless, for example, of sex, ethnic origin, or class position. It demands that rights be revoked only under carefully adjudicated and circumscribed conditions, and it does not permit A's violation of B's rights (e.g. a property owner's violation of someone else's right to eat) to be used by C (the state) to deprive A of all rights (e.g. the right not to be executed or tortured) in retaliation.

The entire range of human rights elaborated in the two 1966 United Nations Covenants is adopted, with some modifications, in the recent African Charter on Human and Peoples' Rights.[8] But the African Charter also includes a communitarian interpretation of the relationship between rights and duties which resembles the Marxist view of class based justice. Part II of the African Charter states *inter alia* that 'Every individual shall have duties towards his family and society, the State and other legally recognized communities' (Article 27, 1), and further that 'The individual shall also have the duty . . . to serve his national community by placing his physical and intellectual abilities at its service' (Article 29, 2).

The effect of this tying of rights to duties, or to contributions to the wider community, is to ease the subordination of trade unions to the state in Commonwealth Africa. The community as such does not exist: it is represented by the state. But the state is not a neutral entity: it is composed of a body of people promoting their own class interests. Thus Marxism's implicit concept of human rights, meant to protect the wider (proletarian) community against abuses by the (capitalist) few, is turned on its head to protect the emerging African ruling class against one of the few institutions capable of effectively representing parts of the wider community, trade unions.

In the broad general outlines of its thought, then, Marxist theory does not have a concept of human rights. There is the further difficulty that Marxist theory has been used, and corrupted, by allegedly socialist governments in Africa to justify denial of human rights and repressions of organizations seeking to attain human rights, especially trade unions, in the name of so-called 'development dictatorship'.[9] Many scholars acknowledge these dilemmas and attempt to integrate undeveloped notions of human rights into their research agenda. Thus Southall suggests that equity and democratization are two key variables for consideration.[10] But he leaves these concepts undefined. Does equity mean equality (including equality of poverty), or does it mean fairness, including the possibility that large numbers of people accept inequality of distribution of resources as fair? Is equity, whatever its meaning, to apply to everyone, or only to workers and peasants? Does democracy mean socialist democracy/dictatorship of the proletariat, or does it mean allegedly bourgeois democracy, the right to effective participation in government by all adult citizens, regardless of class origin or position? These questions cannot be answered in this paper, but are raised to point out the undefined concepts of human rights in the Marxist social science literature.

Assumptions about the connection between Human Rights and Revolution. There is a generalized unarticulated assumption among many Marxist scholars that the attainment of socialist revolution will remedy all human rights abuses of capitalist society. There will be no injustice once private property, and with it the expropriation of surplus value from the proletariat, is abolished. Socialist revolution is, therefore, the *sine qua non* of human rights. Thus John Saul writes that

> The 'structures of domination' in contemporary Africa are such that only *revolutionary* solutions to the development problem seem promising and viable ones. Therefore the main point of interest concerning the role of the working class (and concerning the trade unions . . .) must be the extent to which the role so played either facilitates or cuts against a radical challenge to the *status quo* of underdevelopment and neo-colonial domination.[11]

Human rights are not discussed directly by Saul, but undoubtedly if they were, underdevelopment and neo-colonialism, remediable by revolution, would be taken as the chief cause of their abuse.

I believe that it is naive and dangerous to continue in the assumption that if only a true, rather than a perverted, socialism could be attained somewhere on this earth, all social injustice or abuse of human rights could be remedied. Capitalism in practice ought to be compared with socialism in practice. Even in their limited aim of preventing the expropriation of surplus value from the proletariat, socialist regimes in practice have manifestly failed. Socialist governments continue to extract surplus from proletariat and peasantry alike. Trade unions are unfree, incorporated into the state structure, and incapable of defending either their substantive rights to a fair share of the country's material wealth, or their political rights to associate, assemble and strike. Lenin's views on the party as the political vanguard of the revolution, and on the limited appropriateness of internal party debate, both reasonable strategies for revolution against the Tsar, are now incorporated into much practical Marxism as appropriate ways of running post-revolutionary governments. Thus trade unions are denied both a mass and a critical role, while new socialist ruling classes consolidate themselves through control of the party, government and bureaucracy.

In a review of research questions, Cohen notes that

> [W]ithin established socialist societies, there are particular questions relating to the relative autonomy (and reactionary character) of the party, the state organs and managerial cadres; the suppression of independent workers' movements and the particular forms of alienation present in states where the means of production are legally owned, but in practice not controlled, by the workers themselves.[12]

The questions Cohen raises cannot be answered unless the general propensity of socialist regimes to deny all civil and political rights is seriously confronted. The right to material security valued by all socialists cannot be guaranteed unless civil and political rights, including particularly the right to form trade unions genuinely independent of the state, are also guaranteed.

To confront directly the denial of civil and political rights by socialist regimes requires also a willingness to entertain the possibility that genuine reform of capitalist societies is possible and may be a better path to human rights in some instances than revolution. There is a real difference between the highly exploitative nineteenth-century capitalism exposed by Marx, and the welfare capitalism practised in many western societies today. This difference has been caused, to a significant extent, by the active role of trade unions in acquiring and defending workers' rights in the past hundred years. Civil and political rights to organize were the key, in early European capitalism, to the acquisition of economic (welfare) rights by the masses.[13]

It is facile to reject the reality of the achievements of trade union organization in capitalist societies by arguing that reforms merely reflect the relative autonomy of the state, which can be interpreted as taking all its actions for the long-run benefit of the capitalist class until the mythical collapse of the capitalist system. It is more important to direct inquiry to the structural conditions which permit such successful trade union activity in capitalist society, but prohibit it in socialist. Without in any way arguing that only civil and political rights are real rights, I maintain that it is precisely the civil and political rights permitted in theory, and attainable in struggle, in capitalist society which provide the conditions for successful trade union organization. Thus it is not incidental that relatively successful trade union activity, including a general strike, was possible in Nigeria in 1964, 1971 and 1981, and is possible in Zambia, two countries where trade unions are not completely controlled by the state, but is not possible in Tanzania, where trade unions are incorporated into the state structure.

Assumptions about the Relationship between Trade Unions and Revolution. The two assumptions discussed above are that human rights can best be realized by socialist governments, and that therefore non-socialist governments must be overthrown by revolution. A corollary of these two assumptions is that the proletariat, led by its trade unions, is to be the chief agent of that revolution. Thus the question 'Can trade unions promote human rights in Africa?' is rephrased to be 'Can trade unions promote revolution in Africa?' The result, among Marxist scholars studying trade unions in Africa in the last two decades, has been an obsession with the labour aristocracy thesis. Study after study has sought to determine if the organized proletariat in Africa is in fact a privileged labour aristocracy, or whether it has revolutionary potential. Richard Sandbrook has concluded, after extensively reviewing this literature, that the gap in living standards and lifestyle between the so-called labour aristocracy and other urban and rural inhabitants is too modest to generate political conservatism.[14]

It would be useful as a further corrective to the predominance of the labour aristocracy debate to take seriously Claude Ake's warning that

> The state of the development of productive forces in Africa threatens to turn socialism into caricature, even with the best of intentions: for instance, it tends to encourage political authoritarianism and reduce socialism to the management and redistribution of poverty.[15]

Given that socialism in Commonwealth Africa today in fact consists of various forms of economically disastrous left populism (as in Rawlings' Ghana), of state centred bureaucratism (Tanzania), or of rhetorical cover up for the continued accumulation of wealth by a state capitalist ruling class (Kenya), surely the most urgent political question even for those who accept that socialist revolution is the best road to human rights is how trade unions can contribute to the development of the productive forces necessary for a real transition to take place. Although a full answer to such a question cannot be proposed in this paper, an empirical argument can certainly be made that a better fed, healthier, wealthier and more politically active labour force is an inducement to greater productivity, hence to the entrenchment of a more advanced capitalism and possibly, in the long run, to genuine socialism. That is to say, human rights for workers facilitate the development of the productive forces, as well as being valuable in their own right.

Given this perspective, attention should be paid to the real capacity of trade unions in Africa to use, generate and/or preserve two kinds of rights, namely i) the substance of rights; the material benefits and improved working conditions presumably consequent upon trade union action and ii) the right to have rights; the general civil and political rights to association, assembly, and freedom of speech and the particular rights of free trade unions to closed shop, check-off and the strike which make the attainment of substantive rights possible. In Commonwealth Africa, corporatist governments such as that of Tanzania are willing to protect (at least in principle) the substance of rights, without guaranteeing the rights themselves.[16]

A long-term, and far from discouraging, perspective on the relationship between trade unions and human rights in Africa, therefore, would investigate the on-going struggle by trade unions against the state and capitalist class (where it exists), for the attainment and protection of both substantive and civil/political rights. Economistic trade unions, so lamented by scholars who long for a dramatic leap from capitalist injustice to socialist justice, in fact engage in precisely such a struggle for rights. They are not, nor should they be expected to be, the only agency struggling for human rights. Nor are they immune from charges of internal injustice and disregard for the rights of others, for example women workers. But they are, as Waterman states, 'the typical and universal organization of the worker, the one that he cannot do without and through which he both discovers himself and imposes himself on society'.[17]

We ought to consider African trade unions as effective and worthwhile participants in the struggle for human rights if they slowly organize the permanent wage labour force, if they improve their organizational capacity, and if they are able and willing to take large scale political action. To achieve this much in the context of the present economic crisis in Commonwealth Africa and the corporatist response it has generated among many governments, is to achieve a great deal. Unrealistic and ahistorical expectations should not be laid at the feet of trade unionists, either as agents for revolution or as actors for the gradual achievement of human rights.

The Economic/Political Setting of Trade Unions in Commonwealth Africa

The general economic, organizational and political factors affecting trade unions in Commonwealth Africa are well known and will be elaborated upon here only briefly. Conditions for trade unions are generally extremely unfavourable. In such a situation, it is wiser to look for incremental improvements in their capacity to organize and achieve their goals than it is to look to them for any significant, large scale political activity in the near future.

Historically, trade unionism has presupposed fairly advanced capitalism and the creation of a large, urbanized proletariat. But there is very little true capitalist production in Commonwealth Africa. Commonwealth African workers have not yet been necessary to the world economy as producers of industrial goods, although some heavy industry, mainly of the conversion/assembly type, developed in Nigeria in the latter stages of the oil boom to fulfil local demand.[18] At the moment, the labour power which Commonwealth Africa has to sell in the new international division of labour is not as 'cheap to buy, abundant and well-disciplined'[19] as labour in other underdeveloped areas such as South-East Asia or Brazil. The population of Commonwealth Africa is still by and large a surplus population[20] from the point of view of developed industrial production. Because Africans are not yet necessary to the world economy as industrial workers, there has been very little international investment in them as human capital.

Capitalist production in Africa consists mainly of extractive activities. The major type of extraction is mineral, and it is not coincidental that the most developed working class, (with, as well, the most classically Marxist working-class consciousness) in Commonwealth Africa are the copper miners in Zambia. Mineral extraction which employs African workers elsewhere is limited. Nigerian oil extraction is conducted almost entirely by transnational corporations using highly sophisticated technology which entails the employment of relatively few, relatively highly paid Nigerian workers.[21] Many Malawian males migrate routinely to work in the mines of South Africa; but their transformation into a classical proletariat is blocked by the fact that they do not maintain their permanent homes in the same place as they work.

Aside from such mineral extraction, industrial production in Commonwealth Africa is confined to low level value-added operations, for example automobile assembly in Nigeria, often uneconomically protected by the state as infant industries. As Shaw points out through analogy with infant industry development in Latin America, trade unionism may be permitted by the state in the early phase when it seems that infant industries will be profitable, but the state becomes increasingly authoritarian and anti-union when the sector declines, as it apparently is doing now in Kenya.[22]

In such an underdeveloped industrial economy, and moreover in an environment in which trade unions were either prohibited outright or strictly controlled until very late in the colonial period, it is not surprising that those unions which exist are organizationally very weak. In the early independence period, before co-optive organizational measures had been taken by the state, trade unions tended to be small and fragmented, and their leaders easily corrupted. Leadership was, for many, 'an entrepreneurial enterprise'[23]: a means of obtaining marginally higher incomes, material wealth such as motorcycles, trips abroad, and a certain amount of prestige.

Thus a federal commission investigating unions in Nigeria as late as 1977 reported that the unions were ridden with personal rivalries, that union constitutions were flouted, that illegal elections were common and that smaller unions were bribed to join union centrals; in short, that internal union democracy was a sham.[24] This view of unions in Nigeria is also substantiated by a case study conducted by Lubeck, who described the union he encountered as a 'management-sanctioned extortion agency whereby supervisors forced workers . . . to pay initiation fees and monthly dues'[25], and officials used overseas training programmes to further careerist ambitions to enter government, politics, or the employ of transnational corporations.

Sandbrook concluded from his review of the trade union literature that 'in contemporary Africa, national union officials can more often be found stifling rank and file initiatives than articulating common grievances or co-ordinating industrial action.'[26] Part of this is undoubtedly due to the weak internal organization of trade unions mentioned above. Workers who are new to industrial employment and urban life, who may still consider themselves to be quasi-peasants or have aspirations to enter petty commodity production, and who may well be semi-literate at best, are in a weak position to demand accountability from careerist trade union officials. But of more importance in explaining the behaviour of trade union officials is the control of unions, and cooptation of their leaders, increasingly practised by corporatist governments in Africa.

The mechanisms employed to control trade unions in the various Commonwealth African countries tend to be very similar, regardless of the alleged pro-capitalist or pro-socialist tendency of particular regimes. The task of the state in Commonwealth Africa is to transform trade unions which originally did constitute competing bases of power into neutralized, sycophantic bodies.[27] The mechanisms which the state uses to achieve these ends include, according to Sandbrook, the registration of all trade unions and the imposition of restrictive conditions upon them, the abolition of the right to strike, compulsory membership of all trade unions in state sponsored federations, the cooptation of leadership through inducements of finance or office, and finally, when all else fails, repression.[28]

In Nigeria and Kenya, the state has obtained a measure of control over trade unions without co-opting them directly into the governing party (an option not available in any case in Nigeria, which to date has had either a military government or a multi-party system). The purpose of the 1977

Tribunal of Inquiry into Trade Unions in Nigeria was to eliminate the small, feuding unions and join them together in one common central, thus consolidating the control already achieved by the periodic (but not entirely successful) banning of strikes, for example in 1968-9 during an official national emergency which lasted well into the 1970s.[29] In Kenya, the government has made a number of tripartite agreements with business and labour to ban strikes and freeze wages, at the same time effecting a 10% increase in employment.[30] The many small unions which existed in Kenya shortly after independence were brought together by the government into the Central Organization of Trade Unions; labour leaders acquiesced in this arrangement in return for union check-off privileges (and consequently stable financing) for the new central.[31]

While the measures taken by the Nigerian and Kenyan governments might seem organizationally rational, especially given the internal problems demonstrated during their earlier union history, they allow the government to decide which unions will be registered, and contain the threat that check-off privileges will be revoked if unions do not adhere to government wishes. Such control and threats do not, however, constitute the outright cooptation of unions practised especially in one-party states in Commonwealth Africa.

The most completely corporatist models of integration of trade unions into the ruling party in Commonwealth Africa are those of Nkrumah's Ghana and post-Arusha Tanzania. Kraus argues that the largest wage increases for unskilled labour in Ghana occurred when union-government ties were strongest.[32] In the 1950s, the Trades Union Congress and the ruling Convention People's Party made an alliance; in return for a £25,000 grant and the right to dues check-off, the government passed a bill which, among other highly restrictive measures, gave it the right to approve intra-union rules and procedures, to decide which unions could join the central TUC, and to control the right to strike.[33]

In Tanzania, a National Union of Tanganyika Workers (NUTA) was established in 1964. Trade unionists were no longer permitted to engage in political activity except through the ruling party, TANU. In return, however, they were constitutionally granted the right to nominate a national trade union member to parliament, subject to vetting by the Party.[34] The purpose of the union was explicitly stated to be to 'foster loyalty [of workers] to TANU and government in mobilizing wage-earners for development'.[35] The Secretary-General of NUTA is directly appointed by the President and until 1982 was also the Minister of Labour.[36] Originally, the union structure permitted workers' committees in the factories separate from the bureaucratic NUTA hierarchy, but these were abolished in 1976 and replaced by NUTA branches whose primary aim was to be 'education in production' and political and military training.[37] One reason for the abolition of independent workers' committees was undoubtedly that some of them took seriously the socialist ideology of workers' control of factories, elaborated in the Mwongozo guidelines of 1971. Workers at the

Mount Carmel rubber factory, for example, indulged in go-slows and strikes, with the result that they were fired, fingerprinted and repatriated to the countryside.[38]

How is it possible for governments so easily to co-opt trade unions in Africa? It is notable, first of all, that one-party states, which are buttressed by general repressive measures such as Preventive Detention Acts, are the most successful in such corporatist cooptation, although the one-party government in Zambia has not been able to co-opt the Mineworkers' Union. One-party states are generally also quite cavalier about the rule of law[39]; so that trade unions are not able to appeal to the courts for protections which they might have in principle, if not in practice, for their independence. Union shop and check-off privileges and promises of steady financing are powerful inducements to unions officials who, like officials in any type of organization, can easily become more interested in the continuation of the organization than in the achievement of its stated purposes.[40] These inducements to official position are of course far more powerful in the extremely poor economies of Commonwealth Africa than they might be in countries in which union officials are routinely well paid, or have a variety of professional opportunities available to them in the event that they are removed from office.

The ideology of development is also a powerful weapon in the hands of corporatist governments. Both nationalism and anti-imperialism are conveniently perverted to draw attention away from class rule and to argue for a spurious pulling together by all ranks of society. The Tanzanian government, for example, argued when it created NUTA that it had to do so in order to stop unionized workers' wages from pulling far ahead of the incomes of the peasants. 'NUTA's wages policy should be based primarily on the needs of the national economy . . . NUTA officials should concern themselves less with the fear of exploitation and more with the sacrifice needed for Nation-building.'[41] 'Socialism and Self-Reliance' are, in the anti-capitalist rhetorical milieu of corporatist one-party states, strong rallying slogans against which one argues at one's peril, even if the objective consequences of such slogans are obviously discordant with their aims.[42]

Repression of trade unions in the name of 'sacrifice' or of a general levelling of wages to that of peasant's incomes has two detrimental human rights consequences. In the first place, as Sandbrook has documented,[43] the standard of living of urban wage workers is not substantially higher than those of people working in the informal sector, or of peasants, given the higher costs of urban living, extended family obligations and remittances to home villages. In fact, Tanzania recently became one of the few countries in Africa in which peasants' incomes now appear to be higher than those of urban wage workers.[44] In a country suffering from climatic disasters, insecure reliance on the world economy, and a history of poor economic policies and premature socialist centralization, workers who are denied union rights undoubtedly suffer more than they otherwise would.

But even more important than this undermining of workers' substantive rights (to material welfare) in Tanzania is the long-term undermining of their right to have rights; that is, of those civil and political rights which are both preconditions for, and consequences of, successful long-term trade union struggle. As Ananaba points out the trade-offs which the state offers to unionists in the form of more stable working conditions, closed shop and union check-off cannot substitute for the 'fundamental human rights of the workers to choose their leaders freely and to remove them from office when they forfeit their confidence.'[45] Those who are in power do not voluntarily give up the power they have. The allegedly developmentalist model of trade unionism denies trade unionists the right to establish a principle which in the long run, will benefit all those who are powerless; the right to demand rights.

In this sorry tale of state cooptation of trade unions in Commonwealth Africa, however, it must be kept in mind that not all trade union leaders are corruptible, nor do all bend to the government's will. The creation of NUTA in Tanzania was accompanied by the arrest and preventive detention of over two hundred trade unionists; many were kept in prison for over two years and blacklisted from all formal employment when they were released.[46] In Zambia, although the state has also created one union central, the government has not been able to bring the Mine Workers' Union under its control.[47] The reasons for the Mine Workers' success are essentially structural. They are a large, concentrated labour force occupying a central location in the Zambian economy; copper mining in 1980 accounted for 91% of Zambia's export earnings. Because of its crucial location, the union has been able to maintain its independence of the ruling party and its responsiveness, through a branch system, to the rank and file. It is a policy of the union not to be involved in ruling party politics.[48] The Mine Workers' Union exists in one of the few developed capitalist (albeit extractive, rather than productive) sectors in Commonwealth Africa. Thus even since the world downturn in the price of copper in the mid-1970s, it still has considerable power. In 1981, for example, President Kaunda detained a number of prominent union leaders in a dispute over abolition of autonomous mining townships and the unionists' refusal to engage in party politics, but he was obliged to release and re-instate them after a short while.[49]

The case of the Zambian mine workers illustrates the strength which trade unions can have in developed capitalist sectors. But most of Commonwealth Africa is extremely underdeveloped, both economically and in class structure, and in the long economic recession of the late twentieth century, likely to sink even further into economic crisis. Thus one can predict that increased state repression and corporatism will be applied in the foreseeable future to trade unions, as to all other oppositional bodies. In such a situation, can one make any positive predictions about the role of trade unions and their ability to promote human rights in Africa?

Corporatism, Trade Unions and Human Rights

It is clear that at present, trade unions in Commonwealth Africa are neither revolutionary organizations nor organizations dedicated to preserving other than a very narrow, but nevertheless absolutely essential, band of human rights. Trade unions do not yet represent the entire wage labour force. They do not appear, for example, to be penetrating the growing capitalist agricultural sector[50] which employs female[51] and child[52] as well as adult male labour. Nor do they take it upon themselves to represent the entire urban underclass of sub-proletarians and the working poor, let alone to forge alliances with the peasantry. In some human rights issues they are more likely to favour than to oppose violations. For example, mass expulsions such as that of non-citizen and citizen Asians from Uganda in 1972, and those of West African aliens from Ghana in 1969 and Nigeria in 1983 and 1985, are likely to be perceived as Africanization measures, opening up job opportunities for indigenous citizen workers.[53] In cases of extremely severe violations of human rights, as in Uganda since 1971, trade unionists are simply too weak, whatever their views, to put up even the mildest resistance.

Thus just as academic socialist revolutionaries may be disappointed in the revolutionary potential of African trade unions, so academic human rights advocates might be disappointed in their potential as promoters of human rights. Both, however, would miss the point. In the realm of human rights, which are very fragile and constantly subject to assault by the state, trade unions are a very necessary buttress. Even the most economistic, conservative union advocates and defends two fundamental human rights; the right to a decent living (an economic right), and the right to assemble, associate, speak out and strike in order to acquire that decent living (political rights).

Without, therefore, necessarily accepting that socialist revolution is either desirable or likely in Commonwealth Africa at the present time, or that socialism is the best route to human rights, or that trade unions are the route to socialism, I maintain nevertheless that it is important for an advocate of human rights in Africa to analyse the future of trade unionism there. I believe that the immediate future is bleak. Given the current economic and political crisis of Africa, corporatism, and perhaps even a variant of fascism, are the likely modes of political organization and repression (whether civilian or military) in the foreseeable future.

Classically, corporatism is taken to mean the division of society into three basic groups, namely state, employers and employees. Under the definition, corporatism as a political phenomenon can apply only to societies in which private ownership of the means of production is permitted. Thus the periodic tripartite agreements among state, employers and trade unions in Kenya, can be interpreted as a form of corporatism, but the all encompassing politics of socialist states such as Tanzania, in which there is no independent private sector, cannot be considered corporatist.

But in the underdeveloped economies of Africa, it is perhaps more useful to use corporatism to describe any attempt by the state to bring all possible interest/oppositional groupings under its control.[54]

Tanzania is a quintessential example of such corporatism. Along with trade unions, a central women's group and a central youth group are incorporated into the ruling party, with constitutional representation in the parliament. Nkrumah's Ghana was another such example of incorporation of workers', women's and youth organizations into the ruling party. Other governments in Commonwealth Africa have had varying degrees of success in controlling trade union activities through corporatist methods. So far, with the atypical exception of Amin's Uganda, governments have not resorted to large scale state terrorist methods to control trade unions or other interest group based centres of opposition, although preventive detention is frequently used, along with selective political murder.

Claude Ake goes beyond analyses of African corporatism to suggest that fascism is the political future of Africa.

> The present state of economic stagnation will continue, deepening class contradictions and causing governmental instability but not necessarily sparking off revolution . . . [T]he politics of anxiety will become institutionalised; increasingly, the ruling class will display signs of paranoia while the subordinate classes become frustrated, demoralised and available for induction into extremist . . . movements . . . [T]he ruling class will increasingly appeal to loyalty, patriotism, discipline and dislike for outsiders. Enemies of society will be found all too ubiquitously and will be dealt with summarily. Fascism – that is the reality staring us in the face in most of Africa.[55]

If fascism does develop in Commonwealth Africa, how will it differ from corporatism, of which it could be argued it is an extreme variant? I believe that it will differ in two significant respects. Firstly, the use of repression will intensify. There will be more preventive detention, more political murder, more spurious treason trials. As the national bowl of stew becomes ever shallower, there will be fewer pay-offs to offer recalcitrant union leaders and fewer funds with which to raise the minimum wages of unionized workers. Moreover, repression has a threshold effect; once ideological legitmacy is seriously undermined by the visible use of state terrorism, there is no longer any point in restraint; widespread terrorism becomes an option.

The second change will be the increased use of political scapegoatism; the identifying of more and more of what Ake calls 'enemies of society'. Non-negro minorities will become increasingly vulnerable to attack, both by the state and by the enraged poor. A possible outcome in Sierra Leone, for example, will be the sudden expulsion of the stateless ethnic Lebanese on populist grounds of economic exploitation. Ghana has already witnessed a new variant of populist scapegoatism, namely the destruction of large markets, run by women, in Accra. These are not measures which trade unions, even the most independent, will necessarily oppose; unions are more likely to be carriers of the populist 'tendency to hold an allegedly corrupt and supercilious elite personally responsible for an inegalitarian and oppressive social order.'[56] Given the underdeveloped, politically unsophisticated, and co-opted nature of most African trade unions, a liberal human rights stance in favour of protecting their visible (if not real) exploiters is highly unlikely.

One can, however, accept that in the middle-range future African trade unions may be effectively prohibited from action by state terror, and co-opted by racist, nationalistic and possibly even misogynistic forms of rhetoric, without being persuaded that they have no future at all as human rights organizations. Regardless of the possible existence of a moral sense among ordinary Africans which will result in the overthrow of any extremely unfair system in the long run, Africa lacks the basic physical infrastructure for totalitarian fascism; the repressive apparatus of transportation, communication, and more importantly, control of the military, simply does not exist. It is possible that Commonwealth Africa is in for a long period of coup and counter-coup, as populist young officers, for example, overthrow repressive corporatist civilian regimes (as almost occurred in Kenya in 1982) and are themselves overthrown in turn.

In the interstices of such political chaos, trade unions will be, as Southall suggests they already are, 'the only remaining mass organization of the labouring poor.'[57] The Nigerian Labour Congress, for example, has continued its activities in the wake of severe repression since the 1983 military coup. As Van Hear notes, 'That the NLC has survived and remained relatively independent in such parlous circumstances is no mean achievement.'[58] Trade unionists in many countries have shown enormous courage in the face of political terror, either from the right or from the left. We do not need to romanticize either the revolutionary consciousness of trade unions, nor their commitment to social justice as a whole, to recognize their long-term historical importance in attaining both economic and political rights for ordinary people worldwide. Short-term seduction by populist rhetoric and scapegoatism may well give way to a more advanced understanding of the nature of class society, albeit in circumstances which will border on the tragic.

Human Rights and the Responsibilities of Marxist Intellectuals

Cohen mentions that he has encountered the criticism that international labour studies is the wrong object of focus 'because . . . it does not raise the significant political and social questions.'[59] While I do not agree wholeheartedly with this criticism, I think that there is a measure of truth in it. The erroneous (and unarticulated) assumptions which I examined above, namely that social justice can be realized without regard to individual human rights; that socialist revolution is the only true road to social justice; and that trade unions can promote human rights/social justice only by revolutionary activity, focus academics' interests in social justice on only one human rights actor, and ignore the others. Yet human rights are attained only by the constant political involvement of a large number of groups, most of which are concerned only with particular human rights pertinent to their own situations.

At the moment the range of non-trade unionist human rights actors in Commonwealth Africa is limited. They include students, professors, and professionals, such as the Ghanaian Association of Professional Bodies which was partly responsible for bringing down the Acheampong government in 1978. They also include judges and lawyers, including those brave enough to challenge government decisions in one-party states and risk detention for representing known political dissenters. They include organized church groups and fundamentalist sects who courageously resist the sanctification of the state.

Many of these human rights actors are concerned with rights which uncritical socialists might easily dismiss as bourgeois. Elsewhere I have argued that even the most socialist (material) rights are predicated upon bourgeois civil and political rights such as the right not to be tortured, and the right to freedom of speech.[60] It is true that these groups, like trade unions, do not concern themselves with the entire range of human rights. But human rights are obtained and protected in an interactive and dialectical fashion; each right feeds into and protects the other. Alliances between working-class actors (trade unions) and bourgeois actors (e.g. professionals and judges) are acknowledged by many Marxist analysts to be tactically useful in the struggle against capitalist ruling classes. What is not so readily acknowledged is the necessity to retain bourgeois rights after successful revolutionary action has resulted in new socialist societies with new ruling classes.

I believe that the intellectual who is truly committed to human rights has a responsibility not to hide behind prevailing ideologies which limit his or her perception of what constitutes justice. This is as true of socialist intellectuals as it is of liberals who ignore the realities of class structure as long as a purely formal equal opportunity is observed. It is also the responsibility of the intellectual not to be seduced into accepting that entire categories of people are not entitled to human rights. It is now the habit of male radical intellectuals to make routine bows in the direction of Marxist feminism when reviewing the state of justice or injustice in African countries. This is an improvement over previous decades. But Marxist intellectuals, male and female, have been singularly unconcerned about other aspects of oppression in Africa, for example, religious and racial oppression. You may or may not like fundamentalist Christians or Muslims; you may equally like or not like the Asian or Lebanese petty bourgeoisie. But all of these people are human beings, and quite a few of them are likely to experience severe repression, torture, and murder if the predictions of fascism in the near future in Africa are realized.

Moreover, it is time now to face the reality of socialist repression.

Socialist regimes in the 20th Century have created a new type of crime, namely mass murder on the basis of class origin or position (alleged or real). Such crimes extend from the deportations and starvation of alleged kulaks in the Soviet Union in the 1930s to the more recent mass murders in Kampuchea. As they have happened elsewhere, so too these crimes could happen in Africa. Such crimes provoke new questions, which in turn require critical reconsideration of old answers.

Some work is now being done by socialist or Marxist intellectuals to analyse the bases of power of new ruling classes in socialist societies. Bureaucratic collectivism[61] is recognized as a fact of practice. It is acknowledged that through the control of nomination and succession to positions of power in party, bureaucracy and government, new ruling classes with inherited membership can be created.[62] But while Marxist intellectuals are adept at finding the seeds of capitalist injustice in capitalist theory, they are not so adept at finding the seeds of socialist injustice in Marxist theory. Yet it is as possible to find the roots of socialist class structure in the guiding ideology of socialism, as it is to find the roots of capitalist class structure in its guiding ideology. For example, Marxist theory permits hegemonic control of society, economy and ideology by the socialist ruling class. Gramsci's[63] notion of ideological hegemony applies much more forcefully to socialist than to capitalist societies, as one lone critic in Tanzania has discovered.[64]

Liberal criticisms of socialist social structures must also be taken seriously. In societies with very little separation of power between the political and the economic sector, there is little room for competing classes or class fractions. In such hegemonic societies, the rule of law, so fragile in all societies, disappears completely; there is no basis in practice for the subordination of government to its own law. Finally, as I noted earlier, the Marxist theory of class based justice contains within it the seeds of the notion of dispensability of entire groups of people, regardless of individual guilt or innocence;[65] those who are perceived to be a threat to the ruling class can be labelled as having the wrong class origin or position, and disposed of accordingly.

Thus, to repeat, I am suggesting that it is time to analyse the practice of socialism with the same tools, and with the same realism and scepticism, as Marxists have always analysed capitalism. Karl Marx's dream has been supplanted by almost seventy years of reality. It is irresponsible to continue advocating socialist revolution, in Africa or elsewhere, without considering the possibility that such gross violation of human rights as have happened in the Soviet Union or Kampuchea could be repeated for lack of understanding of their causes. To leave the violation of human rights in socialist regimes to analysis by the political right, or to attribute any such structural analysis to right-wing or conservative tendencies, is both an intellectual and a moral error. Similarly, it is both an intellectual and a moral error to dismiss concern with human rights by reference to an outdated eighteenth-century liberalism, without taking into account both contemporary changes in the idea of human rights (the acceptance both of a second generation of economic, social and cultural rights and a third generation of rights to peace and development), and the massive violation of all categories of rights by governments/ruling classes in both capitalist and socialist societies in the late 20th Century.

Why make this statement in a paper on trade unions and human rights in Africa? Because it is true, whatever your views about the efficacy of socialism and revolution, that trade unions are extremely important human rights actors whose rights to act must be protected. But it is equally true that they are not the only human rights actors; indeed, like the state, they must be pressured from below by women, ethnic minority groups and the very poor before they will truly represent the interests of the entire proletariat. In the long run, human rights are indivisible. An attack on one right is an actual or potential attack on all. Scholars interested in trade unions both in their own right, and as the potential leaders of the African masses to a better life, should not permit ideological blinkers or an unwillingness to face unpleasant truths to deter them from the rigorous discovery of those social structures which, in socialism as well as in capitalism or fascism, prevent the proletariat, the peasantry, the poor, women, and religious and ethnic pariah groups (as well as many other groups) from enjoying basic human rights.

Notes

1. F. Frobel, J. Heinrichs and O. Kreye, *The New International Division of Labour* (Cambridge University Press, London, 1980), p. 6.
2. Ibid., p. 7.
3. Rhoda E. Howard, *Human Rights in Commonwealth Africa* (Rowman and Allanheld, Totowa, N.J., 1986).
4. Walter Laquer and Barry Rubin, *The Human Rights Reader* (New American Library, New York, 1979), pp. 208-24.
5. Henry Shue, *Basic Rights* (Princeton University Press, Princeton, N.J., 1980), p.127.
6. Elaine Pagels, 'The Roots and Origins of Human Rights', in Alice H. Henkin (ed.), *Human Dignity: the Internationalization of Human Rights* (Oceana Publications, Dobbs Ferry, N.Y., 1979). p. 4.
7. Howard, *Human Rights.*
8. Claude E. Welch Jr and Robert I. Meltzer (eds), *Human Rights and Development in Africa* (State University of New York Press, Albany, 1984), Appendix One.
9. Richard Sklar, 'Democracy in Africa', *African Studies Review*, vol. 26, nos. 3/4, 1983, p. 11.
10. Roger Southall, 'Third World Trade Unionism: Equity and Democratization in the Changing International Division of Labour', *Canadian Journal of Development Studies*, vol. 5, no. 1, 1984, pp. 147-56.
11. John Saul, 'The "Labour Aristocracy" Thesis Reconsidered', in Richard

Sandbrook and Robin Cohen (eds) *The Development of an African Working Class* (University of Toronto Press, Toronto, 1975), p. 303.

12. Robin Cohen, 'The "New" International Labour Studies: A Definition', McGill University Centre for Developing-Area Studies, Montreal, Working Paper No. 27, 1979, p. 14.

13. Robert Justin Goldstein, 'Political Repression and Political Development: The "Human Rights" Issue in Nineteenth Century Europe', in Richard F. Tomasson (ed.) *Comparative Social Research*, vol. 4, (Jai Press, Greenwich, Conn, 1981), pp. 161-98.

14. Richard Sandbrook, *The Politics of Basic Needs* (University of Toronto Press, Toronto, 1982), p. 130.

15. Claude Ake, *A Political Economy of Africa* (Longman, Harlow, Essex, 1981), p. 188.

16. On this distinction see Shue, *Basic Rights*, pp. 75-6.

17. Peter Waterman, 'Third World Workers: an Overview', McGill University Centre for Developing-Areas Studies, Montreal, Working Paper No. 9, 1975, p. 7.

18. Nicholas Van Hear, paper in this volume.

19. Frobel *et al.*, *New International Division of Labour*, p.15.

20. Southall, 'Third World Trade Unionism', p.151.

21. Julius O. Ihonvbere and Timothy M. Shaw, 'Petroleum Proletariat: Nigerian Oil Workers in Contextual and Comparative Perspectives', paper presented at a conference on 'Third World Trade Unionism: Equity and Democratization in the Changing International Division of Labour' Ottawa, Canada, 25-27 October 1984, p.23.

22. Timothy M. Shaw, 'Beyond Neo-Colonialism: Varieties of Corporatism in Africa', *Journal of Modern African Studies*, vol. 20, no. 2, 1982, p.256.

23. Jon Kraus, 'African Trade Unions: Progress or Poverty?', *African Studies Review*, vol. 19, no. 3, 1976, p.103.

24. Federal Republic of Nigeria, *Report of the Tribunal of Inquiry into the Activities of the Trade Unions* (Federal Ministry of Information, Lagos, 1977), p. 25 and elsewhere; but for a different view, see Van Hear, in this volume.

25. Paul Lubeck, 'Unions, Workers and Consciousness in Kano, Nigeria: a View from Below', in Richard Sandbrook and Robin Cohen (eds), *The Development of an African Working Class* (University of Toronto Press, Toronto, 1975), p.147.

26. Sandbrook, *Politics of Basic Needs*, p.138.

27. Claude E. Welch Jr, 'The Right of Association in Ghana and Tanzania', *Journal of Modern African Studies*, vol. 16, no. 4, 1978, p.651.

28. Sandbrook, *Politics of Basic Needs*, p.203.

29. Federal Republic of Nigeria, *Tribunal Report*, p.87.

30. Kraus, 'African Trade Unions', p.99 and Colin Legum (ed.), *Africa Contemporary Record*, vol. XI, 1978-9, p.B275.

31. Wogu Ananaba, *The Trade Union Movement in Africa: Promise and Performance* (C. Hurst, London, 1979), p.40.

32. Kraus, 'African Trade Unions', p.102.

33. Ananaba, *The Trade Union Movement*, p.10.

34. United Republic of Tanzania, *Constitution*, in Albert P. Blaustein and Richard F. Flantz (eds.), *Constitutions of the Countries of the World* (Oceana, Dobbs Ferry, NY, 1971-), Article 29, 1.

35. United Republic of Tanzania, 'Report of the Presidential Commission on the National Union of Tanganyika Workers' (Government Printer, Dar es Salaam,

1967), p.5.

36. Theo Mushi, 'Tanzania: New Role for Labour Union,' *Weekly Review*, 28 June 1976, p.5 and I. Bavu, 'Transformation of Trade Union Movement in East Africa', paper presented at the Ottawa conference on 'Third World Trade Unionism'.

37. Mushi, 'Tanzania'.

38. Paschal Mihyo, 'The Struggle for Workers' Control on Tanzania', *Review of African Political Economy*, no. 4, 1975, pp.82-3.

39. Rhoda E. Howard, 'Legitimacy and Class Rule in Commonwealth Africa: Constitutionalism and the rule of law', *Third World Quarterly*, vol. 7, no. 2, 1985, pp.323-47.

40. Welch, 'The Right of Association', p.651.

41. United Republic of Tanzania, Government Paper No. 2, 'Proposals of the Tanzania Government on the Recommendations of the Presidential Commission of Inquiry into the National Union of Tanganyika Workers', (Government Printer, Dar es Salaam, 1967), p.14.

42. Ibid., preface.

43. Sandbrook, *Politics of Basic Needs*, p.130.

44. Legum, *Africa Contemporary Record*, p.B278.

45. Ananaba, *The Trade Union Movement*, p.36.

46. Ibid., p.35.

47. S.D Sacika, 'Trade Union Rights in a One-Party State', in International Commission of Jurists, *Human Rights in a One-Party State*, (Search Press, London, 1978), p.83.

48. Nsolo N. Mijere, 'Zambian Decentralization and Integration Policy: the Case of the Mineworkers' Union', paper presented at the Ottawa conference.

49. Ibid.

50. See for example Andrew Shepherd, 'Agrarian Change in Northern Ghana: Public Investment, Capitalist Farming and Famine', in Judith Heyer *et al.* (eds.), *Rural Development in Tropical Africa* (Macmillan, London, 1981), pp.168-92.

51. Sam Jackson, 'Hausa Women on Strike', *Review of African Political Economy*, no. 13, 1978, pp.21-36.

52. Nicholas Van Hear, 'Child Labour and the Development of Capitalist Agriculture in Ghana', *Development and Change*, vol. 13, no. 4, 1982, pp.499-514.

53. Van Hear, paper in this volume.

54. David Collier, Glossary, in David Collier (ed.), *The New Authoritarianism in Latin America* (Princeton University Press, Princeton, NJ, 1979), p.400.

55. Ake, *Political Economy*, p.189.

56. Sandbrook, *Politics of Basic Needs*, p.139.

57. Southall, 'Third World Trade Unionism', p.153.

58. Van Hear, paper in this volume.

59. Cohen, 'The "New" International Labour Studies', p.3.

60. Rhoda E. Howard, 'The Full-Belly Thesis: Should Economic Rights Take Priority over Civil and Political Rights? Evidence from Sub-Saharan Africa', *Human Rights Quarterly*, vol. 5, no. 4, 1983, pp.467-90.

61. Milovan Djilas, *The New Class* (Praeger, New York, 1957) and Umberto Melotti, *Marx and The Third World* (Macmillan, London, 1977).

62. Zygmunt Bauman, 'Officialdom and Class: Bases of Inequality in Socialist Society', in Frank Parkin (ed.), *The Social Analysis of Class Structure* (Tavistock, London, 1974), pp.129-48.

63. Antonio Gramsci, *The Modern Prince and Other Writings* (International Publishers, New York, 1957).

64. Ludovic A. Ngatara, 'Free Indoctrination in Tanzania', Journalist's Organization of Tanzania, mimeo, 25 September 1978 (available through Human Rights Internet, Washington, DC).

65. Leo Kuper, *Genocide* (Penguin, Harmondsworth, Middlesex, 1981), pp.99-100.

Part 3 Comrades or Competitors? Capital Restructuring and the Prospects for Labour Internationalism

Introduction

Critical studies of trade unions' international activities, potential and limitations in the post-1945 world have been very largely conducted within two major traditions. The first is that of the trade union imperialism school, which has subjected the internationalism of the world's major international labour actors (the ICFTU, WFTU, ITSs and western national bodies) to searching examination and a resulting largely negative critique, focusing principally upon their domination and manipulation of third world unions and the subordination of international solidarity to Cold War and domestic labour protectionist concerns. The second is that body of literature which (for lack of a better term) we might call the global unionism school, whose thrust has been that the internationalisation of capital carried forth by the transnational corporations has provided an objective basis for a new and historically advanced level of international trade union activity, for whose attainment only the 'subjective' (political and organizational) conditions of labour must and likely will catch up.

The first tradition was represented at the Ottawa conference by Hobart Spalding whose paper,[1] in an extension of previous work detailing how closely the foreign policy objectives of American labour have matched those of US government and business, presents a damning account of how the American Institute for Free Labor Development (AIFLD – the AFL–CIO's operational arm for Latin America) has systematically supported right-wing anti-labour regimes and has sought to counter progressive and/or nationalist working class offensives. The AFL–CIO, he argues, apart from having become incorporated into the US intelligence gathering network, has actively worked to expand the global market for US capital in order to preserve and create jobs for labour at home, whilst simultaneously seeking to deter companies from moving plants abroad by encouraging wage raising unionism (albeit after its own highly conservative and pro-capitalist image) at sites competing for US investment overseas.

The second tradition was embodied in the presence of Charles Levinson, who in his writings and his practice has done more than anybody to promote the notion that the rise of the transnational corporation provides the necessary basis for the development of an international trade union counter-force. The global power of the TNCs must accordingly be matched by an international trade union challenge for integrated bargaining and democratic workplace rights which the very internationalization of production allows, providing thereby the basis for the socialization of advanced industry, economy and society.

The detailed exposure of labour imperialism remains a vital and continuing task; yet such analysis must move beyond any implication that third world workers are merely acted upon and do not play an active role in shaping their own fate, just as it must also recognize the competing tendencies–ideological, political, national, motivational and institutional–which render the machinery of trade union internationalism oft times. complex, contradictory and cumbersome. From this perspective, the paper by Arne Wangel offers an instructive examination of how the International Labour Organization–established in the wake of the Bolshevik Revolution to pre-empt similar uprisings throughout the West whilst simultaneously embodying a social-democratic belief in the efficacy of international legislation for protecting workers against unfair labour standards–provides an arena wherein determined and well organized third world workers may effectively confront denial of minimal rights, yet only within severely defined political and legal limits which simultaneously offer the right denying agencies (governments and employers) legitimacy as 'partners in development'.

The ILO, as Robert Cox has observed elsewhere, has historically been 'the expression of a global hegemony in production relations' offering 'organised labor participation in social and industrial reform within an accepted framework of capitalism . . . yet ever heedful of the practical limits imposed by dominant conservative forces.'[2] What Wangel does, in a detailed study of the struggle of the Electrical Industry Workers' Union in Malaysia to secure the right to organize workers in the electronics industry in the teeth of the government's determination to fragment the union movement (as described by Wad above), is to illustrate the inherent contradiction between the idea of universalizing labour standards within a world market context wherein governments are competing for internationally mobile capital and TNCs' strategy is precisely to exploit the unequal development between different regions in their global sourcing. But what is particularly apposite to the question of whether first and third world workers are 'comrades or competitors' is his observation that, within the world order which the ILO strives to harmonize, history demonstrates that workers have only gained their 'universal' rights once they have come into direct competition with working classes under advanced capitalism.

Clearly, the internationalization of production must by this token serve as a foundation upon which dramatic advances in international worker solidarity may be laid. However, that this does not amount to an endorsement of Charles Levinson's position is made clear by the contribution of Nigel Haworth and Harvie Ramsey, who argue against what they label the complacency of the established labour movement which, 'in country after country', assumes that the spread of TNCs will inevitably generate effective international unionism in response.

Basing their argument upon the work of Olle and Schoeller, who have argued that any internationalism which is economically based works to reproduce competition between nationally different conditions of production in the form of a latent fractionalization within the trade union movement,[3] Haworth and Ramsey maintain that the TNCs have extended the asymmetry of labour and capital. Thus whereas the identity of workers as workers is concrete in that it revolves around the workplace (extending outward to the community and nation but dissipating the further away it moves), transnational employers view workers as abstract labour, subject to global financial calculations whose concern is to achieve an infinitely flexible international workforce. TNCs therefore continuously enjoy the initiative over their trade union opponents, who–apart from having to overcome enormous obstacles to unity (not least of which are national and political divisions as well as those revolving around gender)–as a result consistently react to management and are forced to fight on capital's terrain in response to decisions made beyond their control. Attempts by labour to redress the balance by calling upon the state for assistance fall victim to capital's much greater influence with governments.

Haworth and Ramsey conclude that the prospects for international labour solidarity–if based on the internationalization of capital–are decidedly grim, even if these are mitigated by the facts that: the shared interests of workers subject to a global system of exploitation may provide some basis for unity; TNCs, although powerful, are not omnipotent and make mistakes; and contradictions within and between them may be exploited to advantage by labour. The major hope for a new labour internationalism therefore lies in the development of a political consciousness that transcends workplace relations–although the authors suggest no substantive basis on which such a transformation might come about.

The issues addressed so far–dilemmas of trade unions internationally concerning the equalization of conditions of labour in high and low wage countries, the reproduction of national conditions of production if internationalism is constrictively economically based, and the need to build worker solidarity across nations upon shared political concerns–are all taken up in the highly provocative paper by Manfred Bienefeld, who argues in favour of an enlightened nationalism as a basis for a more genuine internationalism than either exists currently or is proposed by what he regards as flights of fancy on the left.

For Bienefeld, the internationalization of production and the world's capital markets pose a fundamental threat to trade unions, for the transition to an unregulated labour market would–in the absence of global full employment–erode the protection which workers enjoy by virtue of some element of scarcity. Such protection has been offered, historically, by nationally defined labour markets and market economies whose domestic and international regulation has provided the framework for unequalled rates of accumulation, growth and change, and have been associated with the emergence of liberal democracy. What is required, therefore, if such historical achievements are not to be lost in the wake of the collapse of Bretton Woods, is a restoration of global market stability (the absence of which undermines labour globally whilst increasing the likelihood of conflict and war) via a new system of international regulation of trade and capital flows, within which context national economies would be enabled to restructure their economies in accordance with technical change, geared to the international market yet not merely appendages to it. Trade unions should therefore respond to present contradictions, not by shifting their operations to an international level (where they face insuperable obstacles), but by safeguarding domestic growth and moderating the rate of adjustment without doing so at the expense of other societies and economies.

Bienefeld's is a challenging argument, not least because he demands that we confront the issue of how trade unions should respond to global inequities in the conditions of labour without suggesting either that they compose an uncomplicated zero-sum relationship between first and third world workers, or that the competitive relation which does obtain can be rendered unproblematic by the development of a common political consciousness. By this account, trade union internationalism will ever be a messy business, yet distinguished by a genuine commitment to workers' rights and conditions which extends beyond the confines and the concerns of the nation. None the less, Bienefeld's formulation raises as many problems as it sets out to solve. *Inter alia*, in its concern to eschew utopianism it argues for a social market economy which, in essence, is welfare capitalism (give or take a dose of social democracy), directed by economic planners from the command posts of society; in its call for a return to Keynesianism and a new Bretton Woods it may well be ahistoric in that capital, more internationalized than ever before, seems less and less susceptible to the required level of international regulation; and finally, apart from rendering unions an appendage of the state, it rests upon a notion of trade unionism so calculatedly nationalistic and defensive that it offers little prospect of providing a basis for new developments in labour internationalism.

All this is too unremittingly pessimistic, focusing as it does upon the limitations and difficulties of international labour solidarity, for there are contrary indications not only of what Haworth and Ramsey term the 'enduring potentialities' of labour internationalism but also evidence of the development of a new working class internationalism over recent years. Not least of these is the groundswell of revolt – noted by Spalding in relation to the machinations of the AIFLD – at home and abroad against politically regressive trade union international policies and programmes. Similarly, for all the emphasis upon the asymmetry of capital and labour, it may be argued that there remains some life in Charles Levinson's thesis yet, for if we look, for instance, at the South African case, then account must be rendered of why it is that emergent unions there have set considerable store (and apparently to some avail) on contacting counterpart unions in Europe and US to bring pressure upon locally operative TNCs at home.[4] Likewise, the traditional, western-based and controlled international union bodies have been increasingly bundled into responding to the needs of Black workers by an amalgam of the latter's militance, shop-floor internationalism and a variety of other pressures.[5]

It is by now no more than a commonplace to observe that a new internationalism must go beyond workplace concerns to link up with other campaigns–against racism, sexism, sectionalism and nationalism (if unenlightened, doubtless!)–which seek to encourage unity amongst labour.[6] It is more difficult to analyse how these developments are (or are not) taking place, why they are occurring in the present era, and how they may be extended. It is thus fitting to conclude with the contribution by Peter Waterman, not only because it sounds a positive (and perhaps practical) note, but also because it offers an as yet isolated attempt to map out new ground upon which a new working class internationalism might be built.[7]

Waterman's intent is to sketch out and analyse the variety of the communications media 'whose dramatic expansion has accompanied the re-birth of working class militancy and working class internationalism in recent years' and to contrast it with traditional forms. In brief, he characterizes the latter (which emanate from the dominant, established labour, union and socialist bodies) as dependent on and subordinate to capital and state, politically elitist, hierarchical, inaccessible to most workers and uncritical and/or authoritarian; in contrast, the new media (flowing from solidarity and worker-oriented service groups, democratic single issue movements and radical christians, academics and tendencies within the traditional labour organizations) are autonomous, non-statist, grassroots and shop-floor internationalist, discursive and compose an international, horizontal network. What he argues is that this network of alternative movements (alternative in the sense that they are subversive of the global institutions of exploitation and oppression) have been fostered by new communications technologies, which offer yet greater potentialities. However, this new communications network remains unevenly developed, controlled rather more by professionals and intellectuals than by rank and file labour, is concentrated in the industrialized capitalist world and so on, to overcome which deficiencies Waterman makes a number of initial proposals.

It may be that there is an element of ideal typing (caricature) in Waterman's analysis of the traditional and new media flows,[8] and it is at least debatable whether or not the alternative networking he depicts is in fact the offspring of a particularly *working-class* internationalism. Perhaps, too, he is over optimistic concerning the inadvertently democratic nature of communications technology, whose advantages, many would say, are not unlikely to accrue overwhelmingly (perhaps exponentially) to capital and the state rather than to those subversive of them. None the less, in that the transformation of the international division of labour has in recent years centred around advances in computer and telecommunications technology, Waterman has performed a valuable service in pointing to new strategies and techniques of international labour communication. However, further work needs to be done to examine how effectively third world workers and unions are plugged into the new network, how much they contribute to it and what benefit they derive from it.

The changes in the international division of labour which have been sketched out in this book and elsewhere clearly imply a reduction in the rewards and power of labour on a global scale. The five papers in this concluding section all contribute to a greater understanding of the obstacles to, and potential for, international labour solidarity–spanning ideological, national and North–South lines–in support of workers everywhere in the struggle against economic exploitation and political repression.

Notes

1. Previously published in a more extended form in *Labour, Capital and Society,* vol. 17, no. 2, 1984, pp. 136–73.
2. Robert Cox, 'Labour and Hegemony', *International Organization*, 31, 3 1977, pp. 385–424 (citation from p. 387).
3. Werner Olle and Wolfgang Schoeller, 'World Market Competition and Restrictions upon International Trade Union Policies', *Capital and Class*, No. 2, 1977, pp. 56–75; reprinted in Peter Waterman (ed.), *For a New Labour Internationalism: a set of reprints and working papers* (International Labour Education, Research and Information Foundation (Ileri) The Hague, 1984), pp. 39–56.
4. Roger Southall, 'Monopoly Capital and Industrial Unionism in the South African Motor Industry', *Labour, Capital and Society,* vol. 18, no. 2, 1985.
5. Eddie Webster, 'The International Metalworkers' Federation in South Africa (1974–80)', *South African Labour Bulletin*, vol. 9, no. 6, 1984, pp. 77–94; reprinted in Waterman, *For a New Labour Internationalism*, pp. 213–30.
6. An earlier version of this paper is offered in Waterman's 1984 collection, pp. 232–55.
7. Mike Press, 'The Lost Vision: Trade Unions and Internationalism', in Waterman, *For a New Labour Internationalism*, pp. 87–105.
8. One international trade union official certainly thought so. In a letter to the editor he described Waterman as 'a former WFTU official unable to disguise his Trotskyist tendencies writing about the ICFTU' and opined that the paper was 'pretentious crap'. If nothing else, this may serve as a base from which reviewers may choose to judge the entire book!

10. US Labour Intervention in Latin America: The Case of the American Institute for Free Labor Development

Hobart A. Spalding, Jr.

At a meeting of the California Labor Federation's International Affairs Committee on 2 December 1982 not one participant came out in support of the AFL–CIO's position on third world countries. The National Federation had brought in top experts such as Irving Brown, Director of its International Affairs Department, but delegates remained unconvinced. Resolutions specifically called for an end to Reagan's foreign policy of support for and aid to union-busting regimes such as those in El Salvador and the Philippines.[1]

At the same meeting William C. Doherty Jr, Executive Director of the AIFLD, spoke about the situation in El Salvador. Among other things, he claimed that not a single union was affiliated with the opposition Frente Democrático Revolucionario. An AIFLD agrarian specialist flown in from Salvador admitted that probably the number of peasants thrown off the land by the new government fully equalled the number of those who had returned to the land. Yet the AIFLD and the US government claimed great success for the land reform programme.

Solid opposition to AFL–CIO foreign policy and to the AIFLD – the Federation's main foreign policy operational arm – represents a growing trend. Increasingly rank and file or local labour councils have come to question AFL–CIO foreign policy and to voice their opposition to specific actions taken by the Federation and the AIFLD. Several calls for the AIFLD's withdrawal from El Salvador have been approved by regional bodies. To date, however, these efforts have met limited success. AFL–CIO foreign policy is not subject to open discussion or approval by rank and file. Policy is formulated by the International Affairs Department and implemented by organs such as the AIFLD. General planks on foreign policy are voted at national conventions, but executive boards of each union name most delegates allowing the entrenched bureaucracy to dominate the floor. Thus, foreign policy positions receive approval with little or no discussion. The AFL–CIO, although the largest national labour body, represents fewer than 20% of all workers. It has weak representation also among women and minority workers, those most likely to object to pro-capitalist and imperialist policies.[2]

The involvement of the US labour movement in foreign affairs dates from the early 20th Century. Not surprisingly, Latin America and the Caribbean have been areas of particular interest. Since 1962 the principal organization representing the official US labour movement embodied by the AFL–CIO has been the AIFLD. The AIFLD has become the foreign policy arm of the AFL–CIO and the US government's principal labour foreign policy vehicle. Thus at the international level government and the big labour bureaucracy increasingly work together. An examination of the AIFLD can lead to an understanding of AFL–CIO (and US government) labour foreign policy in general.[3]

AFL–CIO Ideology and Foreign Policy

AFL–CIO foreign policy flows directly from its ideology and analysis of US society. It holds that labour is just another pressure group in a pluralistic society that should seek to reform the system in its favour. Unions, therefore, exist primarily to gain economic benefits through collective bargaining. Strikes should only come into play when all other recourse fails. The long range goal is a constantly rising material standard but always within the context of the system. As the late long-time head of the AFL–CIO, George Meany, said

> We believe in the capitalist system and we are members of the capitalist society. We are dedicated to the preservation of this system, which rewards the workers. . . . We are not about to trade in our system for any other.[4]

Abroad, the AFL–CIO combats anti-capitalist ideologies and organizations and it aids and encourages pro-capitalist unions. It attempts to influence existing unions and to form new ones in its own image. Where interests overlap, it works with US corporations in close cooperation with their representative, the US government. Disagreements between business, government, and the labour bureaucracy in foreign policy matters, as in internal affairs, stem from tactical questions, not from basic philosophical antagonisms. As a part of the US foreign policy team, labour's role in Latin America (as elsewhere) is highly political despite protestations to the contrary. It openly uses financial and cultural means to influence Latin American labour organizations and workers. It also participates in less visible activities such as intelligence gathering and often is used as a cover to disguise other kinds of US involvement. In short, US labour's foreign policy credo is: What is good for the US government abroad (and therefore

US capitalism) is almost always good for US labour, and therefore for labour everywhere.

The advantages of these positions to the AFL–CIO are several. The more widely influential capitalism is, the larger the market for US goods produced by union members. Foreign investment generates profits that help maintain salaries and fringe benefits at home. Friendly unions abroad can help assure a steady flow of strategic materials and natural resources at hopefully cheap prices. This then, in turn, keeps US workers employed. By aiding US capitalism in its struggles with the working class overseas, the labour bureaucracy helps preserve the system which maintains it. Moreover, the growth of a union movement outside the United States may deter companies from moving plants and shedding jobs in the United States.

Reality, however, does not always match theory. US corporations do consistently move production to Latin America, even in areas where the AIFLD operates and often as a direct result of the AIFLD's policy of weakening unions not 100% friendly to free market capitalism. As one commentator wrote: 'Instead of leading to greater democracy and a strong native trade union movement in Latin America, however, in most cases AIFLD has had a record of support for dictatorial regimes.'[5] In truth, the AFL–CIO and AIFLD have consistently supported right-wing and fiercely anti-left-wing administrations and military governments no matter what their policy toward labour. Local US supported labour organizations and US operatives have worked against all unfriendly labour entities (Catholic, Communist, or Social Democratic), even at the cost of losing working-class unity and strength. The AIFLD's ideology is mirrored in its education programmes for Latin American trade unionists. In all cases a predominant place is reserved for 'democracy versus totalitarianism' sessions, which preach the AFL–CIO doctrine. These courses so dominated the AIFLD curriculum that a Congressional Investigating Committee wondered 'if for trade unionists to be brought to this country to be given training in political and social structure' was not 'a little unusual'.[6] In 1978 the AIFLD's Board of Trustees noted that 'there was an increase in the groups against democratic trade unionism' (reflecting the AIFLD's lack of success?) and that 'therefore emphasis should be given to political orientation courses'.[7] As a result, the AIFLD held these courses in Colombia, Costa Rica, the Dominican Republic, and Honduras. In addition, political orientation became a central feature of education programs at the George Meany Labor Center in Silver Spring, Maryland.

By 1981, the AIFLD ran sixteen political orientation courses in Central and South America. Its US classes, in turn, often included the formation of 'political trainers'. At that time, the AIFLD noted its increasingly open political stances saying that,

> labor education programs of Latin American unions are beginning to cover political ideas in addition to the traditional 'tool courses' on negotiating,

> organizing, and finances. This shift reflects the increasing influence of many national labor movements in politics, on the one hand, plus the growing competition democratic labor faces in many countries from the dictatorial Left.[8]

In short, the AIFLD acts as an ideological arm of the US government and therefore of US business in the labour field. Representative of its attitude are the remarks of Lane Kirkland (current AFL–CIO President and top officer of the AIFLD). He claimed that Latin America's problem today was that 'extremists seek to debase trade unionism by linking it to the question of who owns the means of production'; these concerns he continued, are only 'esoteric theories about social organization'.[9]

The Historical Background

The AFL moved into the foreign policy mainstream under the leadership of Samuel Gompers during the early 20th Century, a stance that coincided with its acceptance of capitalism as a system. US interest in hemispheric labour matters heated up markedly during World War II as it sought to combat the influence of the left-wing *Confederación de Trabajadores de América Latina* (CTAL). Once the war ended and the anti-fascist front which united progressive and capitalist forces lost its importance, the AFL took the offensive. In 1948 it created a confederation which two years later became the *Organización Regional Inter-Americana de Trabajadores* (ORIT).[10]

The ORIT by and large adopted similar positions to those of the AFL, preaching reform within the capitalist system, denying class antagonisms, promoting 'democratic trade unions' and fighting all Communist influences. The ORIT consistently worked closely with US agencies such as USAID or the State Department and it supported such actions as the Bay of Pigs invasion of Cuba, the ousting of President João Goulart of Brazil in 1964 and the 1965 intervention in the Dominican Republic. At the same time it approved the 1973 right-wing military coup in Chile and the Brazilian military regimes after 1964 despite their supression of all trade union liberties, only changing its line on Chile in the late 1970s. In short, the ORIT's criteria for approval or censure seems to depend upon a government's relationship to the United States. Only recently has the organization shown any tendencies to a more independent existence.[11]

The ORIT, however, proved too bureaucratic and slow moving to satisfy the AFL–CIO and US government policy needs in Latin America. Despite basic agreement, too much diversity existed within its ranks and US labour still needed to justify or explain its actions. Further, increasingly the ORIT's constant support of US positions made it less credible as an independent entity. As a result, in 1960 AFL–CIO top bureaucrats decided to create a new organization with they could direct. This was the AIFLD.

The Creation of AIFLD

By creating the AIFLD, the AFL–CIO hoped to have at its disposal an organization totally under its control. Specifically AIFLD was formed 'primarily in response to the threat of Castroite infiltration and eventual control of major labor movements within Latin America'. It is dedicated to 'strengthening the democratic labor sectors in terms of institution building . . . in terms of technical assistance and social projects . . . primarily in the areas of education and training, manpower studies, cooperatives, and housing.[12]

Clearly the AIFLD's central functions are to combat non-capitalist tendencies within the ranks of Latin America labour and to strengthen US labour's influence and the US business image in order to develop pro-capitalist, reformist unions while maintaining Latin America as a field for investment. In addition to opposing all Communist, socialist, or Trotskyist unions, the AIFLD also often opposes those of Christian Democratic or social democratic origin. As AIFLD chief Doherty has said,

> The key question of our time is the future road of their [Latin America's] revolution: toward communist totalitarianism or towards democracy. For the American labour movement this is one of the paramount, pivotal issues; all other questions must remain secondary.[13]

In turn, J. Peter Grace, head of W.R. Grace and Company, a large conglomerate which once had extensive Latin American and Caribbean investments, and then Chairman of the AIFLD Board, echoed,

> The choice in Latin America is between democracy and communism. We . . . cannot allow communist propaganda to divide us between liberal and conservatives, as between business and labor, or between the American people and their government. Above all, we have to act together as Americans defending our interests abroad. The AIFLD is an outstanding example of a national consensus effectively at work for the best interests of the people of Latin America.[14]

Given the structure of the AIFLD it clearly represents US business and the big labour bureaucracy.[15]

AIFLD is but one part of the AFL–CIO effort in Latin America. The parent organization directly funds a variety of projects in the area and it also works through the International Trade Secretariats (ITSs) which are groupings of national industrial unions in a particular or related group of industries at the international level. Most ITSs rely heavily on US affiliates for funding, but they also receive funds from European members and even from private foundations. The AFL–CIO, as the most important architect of US labour foreign policy, spends millions abroad each year through its Foreign Affairs Department and the International Affairs Department of affiliate unions. Up to 23% of its budget has gone to international affairs in a single year. It pumps as much as $2 million annually into a special projects fund to complement the one million flowing into its international activities accounts.[16] How this money gets spent, however, is known only to AFL–CIO top officers as no process for accountability exists.

Business, government, and labour leaders provide the AIFLD's main resources, and they share common goals. The US government has given the bulk of the AIFLD's support. Between 1962 and 1967, for example, 89% of its funds derived from USAID and that source continues to provide the vast majority of funding. During that same period, labour contributed 6%, and over seventy business grants represented only 5%. Moreover, the government's share of overall funding increased steadily, from 64% in 1962 to 92% in 1967. By 1971, the AIFLD ranked as the fifteenth largest recipient of USAID contracts with a total of $7.6 million. Ten years later, AFL–CIO funds represented 5% of the AIFLD'S $7.7 million budget, and USAID monies the rest. At times, the organization gathered support from other sources. Between 1961 and 1963 one writer claims that it received nearly $1 million from CIA conduits. A complete financial picture of the AIFLD is impossible because it does not choose to make those figures public.[17]

From its inception, big business, private institutions, and labour all sat on the AIFLD's governing body along with sympathetic Latin American labour bureaucrats. In 1981, in response to continued criticism, the AIFLD limited positions on its Board to members of the US and Latin American trade union movements. Despite this change, Grace in his farewell speech pledged that the business community 'will continue to perform in a friendly and supportive capacity'.[18] Many of those who sat (and sit) on the AIFLD's Board also held (or hold) membership on the Council on Foreign Relations and the Trilateral Commission, each a high level working group with input into and/or influence over foreign policy decisions. The AIFLD also collaborates with the Council for Latin America, Inc. comprised of 225 companies and founded by David Rockefeller. In this arena the AIFLD sees its function in the following way: 'Our collaboration takes the form of trying to make the investment climate more attractive and more inviting to them'.[19] Since 77% of all US investment in the third world lies in either Latin America or the Caribbean (some $7 billion in all), business interest in labour's cooperation is clear.[20]

US Labour Abroad: Case Studies in the 1960s and 1970s

In Brazil during the presidency of João Goulart (1961-64), the AIFLD along with ORIT and the US Embassy, extended themselves to combat influences they thought harmful to pro-capitalist labour. This involved sabotaging unity at the 1962 Third National Labour Congress and aiding the *Movimento Democrático Sindical* under its motto 'God, private property, and free enterprise'. At this time, the *Instituto Cultural do Trabalho* (ICT), the AIFLD's Brazilian affiliate, and an institute for labour studies partially financed by US business increased its activities. The AIFLD also moved into the rural north-east with training and aid programmes for reformist groups and leaders. At home the AIFLD trained its first all-Brazilian class in 1963. The AIFLD and ICT trainees played a role in the coup that ousted Goulart helping to prevent a general strike against the military takeover and, among other things, keeping lines of communication open for the military. AIFLD officials later testified to this involvement before Congress.

After the Coup, the military severely repressed labour freedoms and union activities throughout the country, ousting – with the help of AIFLD members – the legitimate leaders of more than 450 labour organizations. It drove down working-class living standards, reducing real wages by over 20% in the following years. The AIFLD and the ICT, however, continued to operate with official blessing. Despite the obviously repressive nature of the regime and its markedly anti-labour and anti-working-class bias, as late as December 1965 the AIFLD still claimed that a 'democratic revolution' had taken place in Brazil.[21]

US agencies also intervened in the Dominican Republic. The AFL–CIO formed the *Confederación Nacional de Trabajadores Libres* (CONATRAL) under AFL–CIO and ORIT influence, which opposed attempts at unity within the Dominican labour movement. It opted for bread and butter unionism, summed up in the position that 'unions exist to obtain benefits for their members–period'. The CONATRAL organized against the populist Juan Bosch in 1963 even though he allowed labour relative freedom advocating profit sharing and prompting recognition of majority unions as legitimate bargaining agents in each sector. The CONATRAL justified its actions with declarations of non-involvement in politics.

Bosch's case shows big labour's foreign policy. Shortly before the 1963 US supported coup which ousted Bosch, the CONATRAL called for the military to save the country from Communism, a barely disguised invitation for the action that soon occurred. It also praised the 1965 US military invasion, echoing the AFL–CIO, State Department and ORIT line that the intrusion thwarted Communism and prevented another Cuba. In 1966 it clearly supported the reactionary candidate, Joaquin Balaguer, backed by the United States (and AFL–CIO, ORIT, etc.) even though he took anti-labour positions. These actions had a detrimental effect on the organization. After its support for the intervention, several unions resigned, and membership fell by over half. The AIFLD finally created the National Confederation of Dominican workers to replace the CONATRAL, but its membership consisted largely of company unions and tightly controlled pro-government organizations.

The AIFLD also trained peasant leaders in the Dominican Republic in conjunction with the ORIT and the AFL–CIO. Among its social projects, it initiated a housing development for sugar workers. Illegalities which favoured CONATRAL members at the work site and in access to the new housing in violation of Dominican law forced the project to halt. Finally completed through direct AID financing, the complex totalled 110 units rather than the 700-900 promised.

US investment doubled between 1965 and 1975 to nearly $400 million and labour strategy changed. In response to a growing anti-imperialist consciousness among Dominicans, the AIFLD reduced its programmes. It now worked more directly with transnationals to squash militant working-class activities and funelled activity through the ITSs. Several ITSs expanded their activities through funds from US affiliates which in turn got monies from the AIFLD. The government encouraged efforts to strengthen reformist unions by using force against progressive independents.[22]

US labour efforts in Argentina provide further insights into labour foreign policy. The AFL–CIO opposed the Peronist labour unions and Perón's continental labour policy. After his ousting in 1955, the AFL–CIO, attempted to exclude Peronists from a restructured movement. Despite its efforts, however, the democratic unions never dominated the CGT (the central labour confederation) and so divisions continued. After 1963, the AFL–CIO tried to split the Peronists, courting right-wing elements with material concessions. Gradually, a conciliatory labour bureaucracy emerged within several major unions. The deteriorating economic situation after 1955 made their economic programme more appealing. But at the same time, a number of militant leaders, backed by growing support within the rank and file, openly linked demands to an anti-imperialist, pro-socialist position. US labour's efforts thus came in reaction to a militant, left-wing, nationalist labour sector.

The AIFLD's Argentine activities increased markedly after 1963. Grants to labour leaders increased and now included selected CGT officials for the first time. Strong nationalist and anti-US sentiment within the labour movment prevented the AIFLD from operating as openly as in other countries. It therefore increasingly combined its programmes with those of the ITSs. By 1974, eight ITSs (incorporating 32 local unions) functioned and the Postal Telegraph and Telephone International (PTTI) maintained a sub-regional office in Argentina. These organizations co-sponsored seminars with the AIFLD, gradually extending their programmes into the interior.

As class struggle escalated, the AIFLD found itself on the defensive. It first closed down its Córdoba office and then, in 1974, shut down its entire Argentine operation under pressures from nationalist left-wingers in the labour movement. To offset these reverses, US labour increasingly relied on the ITSs using AIFLD graduates to give ITSs sponsored classes. Local unions also gave internal education courses modeled on US created programmes and taught by AIFLD trainees.[23]

In Chile, AIFLD and US agencies manoeuvred to split the progressive labour movement during Salvador Allende's presidency (1970-73). In particular port workers and the communications sector fell under AIFLD influence. AIFLD trained leaders and sponsored unions even aided the military coup against the democratically elected Unidad Popular government. The new junta outlawed all labour organizations and arrested thousands of activists. The AIFLD acted as an apologist for the junta at international gatherings and 'the AIFLD's National Workers'Confederation was the chief labour spokesman for Chile's Junta'.[24] Only in the last years have the AFL–CIO and AIFLD changed their tune, condemning the military for its repressive labour policies that threaten even AIFLD allies. While now opposing the junta, AIFLD oriented unions usually refuse to work with progressive forces, thus weakening the movement toward democracy.[25]

Several strands emerge from these examples. The scope and depth of the AIFLD's activities give it enormous resources to gain its ends. Although US labour cannot play a decisive role in countries such as Argentina where a mature and progressive labour movement exists, its presence gives pro-capitalist unions extra reserves in their struggle against nationalist and anti-imperialist forces. In countries with less mature labour movements, as we shall see, this type of aid can have an important impact. The AIFLD opposes anti-US or anti-capitalist governments no matter what labour policies a government pursues or a movement is likely to pursue once in power. Thus the interests of unions and of the working class are given second place or are not even considered in the formulation of the AIFLD's plans.

The AIFLD Network

The AIFLD's daily activities divide essentially into education and specific projects . The former covers education at the local, regional, national and international levels. The latter include social projects, 'impact' projects, and union-to-union programs. These activities also mask some of the AIFLD's less known operations.

The AIFLD runs courses and feeds into educational programmes run by the ITS and local or regional labour institutes such as those sponsored by the ORIT, the ICT, or the Central American Institute of Labor Studies (IESCA), the latter two set up and aided financially by the AIFLD. Local seminars instruct those attending in history and international activities of the labor movement, organization, structure, finances, collective bargaining, labour legislation, and 'democracy versus totalitarianism' (i.e. capitalism vs socialism). Selected students move to regional and national classes and a few ultimately go to the US for training.[26]

The AIFLD's *Centro de Estudios Laborales del Perú*, opened in Lima during 1962-3 and had an annual budget of about $200,000. The center ran a branch in Arequipa, giving night courses, short seminars in various provinces, and longer essential programmes for the best candidates from the seminars. During the 1960s about 11,800 Peruvians received AIFLD training, including almost all important labour leaders of the *confederación de Trabajadores del Perú*, the country's largest confederation, an exponent of AIFLD-style unionism, and backer of capitalist development.[27]

The AIFLD's April 1974-March 1975 regional contract with USAID, for example, indicates educational efforts in Bolivia. The programme would train approximately 400 national, departmental, and local union leaders and 30 campesino leaders in advanced trade union techniques as well as about 400 activists in basic and intermediate techniques in evening courses. Two hundred union leaders would get instruction in service fields such as technical aspects of union administration, cooperativism, or community services, along with 30 campesino leaders. Bolivian labour organizations under the AIFLD's technical supervision would help direct these courses. The AIFLD would send five leaders completing in-country training to the US, give an equal number the opportunity for advanced stuides in their country labour centers, send a person to the Inter-American Labor Economics Course at Mt Vernon College in Washington, DC, and sponsor eight others at international labour conferences. Lastly, it would assist social development projects for ten rural and urban unions. The budget for this amounted to $187,000. Similar programmes existed for more than a dozen other Latin American and Caribbean countries varying only in detail and numbers.[28]

The breadth of the AIFLD's educational efforts is impressive. At Front Royal in 1972, for example, a typical set of trainees included 110 men and 30 women, of which 80 came from Spanish-speaking countries, 20 from Brazil, and 40 from English-speaking areas. In 1981, an AIFLD programme took in the French-speaking Caribbean for the first time and four students from French-speaking Africa attended sponsored by the *Force Ouvrière*.[29]

In all, as many as 400,000 persons have graduated from AIFLD courses and it runs about 750 of these each year in some seventeen countries. Almost 4,000 unionists have taken an advanced course in the United States. The Institute also underwrites economics conferences. To complement its educational activities, the AIFLD publishes books and pamphlets like primers on democracy or a history of the world trade union movement in Spanish.[30]

The AIFLD's specific projects cover a number of activities. The most important of these are social projects, 'impact' projects, and union to union programmes. Social projects and impact projects most commonly involve donations for community centres, credit unions, consumer cooperatives, disaster relief, medical and dental clinics, primary schools and vocational training, or a gift of some specific item needed by a particular union or desired by its members. The AFL–CIO Impact Projects Fund, administered by the AIFLD, and the Regional Revolving Loan Fund (RRLF) composed of AID monies, finance these efforts. In 1979, for example, the AIFLD initiated 26 impact projects valued at $74,000 to go with 9 Loan Fund projects of much greater value. The Impact Fund provides capital costs of up to $5,000 in which labour is contributed by union members. This fund also gives smaller amounts for things like conferences or equipment. The Regional Revolving Loan Fund involves projects between $5,000 and $50,000.[31]

A single case example can provide an indication of the scope of the above activities. The Social Projects Department report from the AIFLD/Uruguay for September-October 1973 reported 15 ongoing impact projects including the following: office furniture for a transport federation: dental equipment for newspaper vendors; medical centres for sugar workers, public employees, and musicians; community centres for teachers and for maritime, brick, graphic arts and sugar workers. It also enumerated 30 small projects ranging from help for consumer or housing cooperatives, gifts of school materials, toys, administrative expenses, or life rafts for fishermen, to food, clothing, and shoes for sugar workers. Finally, it listed an RRLF item of $50,000 for a housing cooperative supermarket in Montevideo which had been approved but not yet disbursed.[32]

Housing is another major AIFLD endeavour. Projects exist in over half a dozen countries and by the mid-1970s the Insititute had spent over $77 million on 18,048 units. Housing funds almost invariably go to a staunchly anti-Communist unions facing competition from progressive rivals. Housing provides individual unions with an incentive to offer recruits and rewards for faithful members. In reality, cost factors often mean that mostly middle level bureaucrats can afford the units. But several major projects have stalled. In some instances the end product has been of an inferior quality. In all cases, the extensive questionnaires demanded by AIFLD for housing applications by local unions provides an opportunity to collect important information about unions and their members.[33]

The union-to-union programme involves the AIFLD's connections with the ITSs. The Institute co-ordinates and administers programmes of technical assistance through sub-grants between AIFLD and AFL–CIO member unions affiliated with those ITSs active in Latin America. Most of these grants or contracts have been given to four unions: the Brotherhood of Railway and Airline Clerks (BRAC), a member of the International Transportation Workers Federation (ITF); the Communications Workers of America (CWA–PTTI); the Oil, Chemical, and Atomic Workers (OCAW), International Federation of Petroleum and Chemical Workers (IFPCW); and the Retail Clerks International Association–International Federation of Commercial, Clerical and Technical Employees (FIET). In 1973-4, for example, each of these received over $100,000, and two small unions, one composed of textile workers and the American Federation of Musicians got less than $50,000 each under AIFLD grants. AID support for some ITS operations through the AIFLD really picked up after 1968 when funding from the International Confederation of Free Trade Unions diminished because the AFL–CIO pulled out of that body (it returned in 1982).[34]

The ITSs are seen as a complement to the AIFLD in offering specialized training in a particular industry or occupation that builds on the AIFLD's generalized worker education and social projects. Further, ITSs representatives normally maintain close liaison with AIFLD country programme directors, although problems of ITS autonomy obviously concern AIFLD and USAID officials. In some areas the ITSs have taken over AIFLD functions when the Institute has been forced to cut back or end its overt activities. The ITSs are considered to be more neutral organizations and thus can provide good cover for labour programmes written and funded by USAID and AIFLD. Yet the ITSs receive additional financing from the US government as well as from private US based foundations. The State, County and Municipal Employees ITS, the Public Services International and the International Federation of Journalists, for example, received grants from the Gotham and Granery Funds respectively, both proven CIA conduits.[35]

In all, the Institute's efforts have a considerable multiplier effect, mainly through labour education institutes in various countries. The ICT in Brazil, for example, 80% funded by the AIFLD, graduates up to 300 students annually and some 8,000-9,000 attend its regional seminars. Most of its staff are AIFLD trained and its Director is usually an AIFLD Board member. The Central American Institute for Trade Union Studies is a regional education body and the AIFLD financed the building of a labour college for the English speaking Caribbean in Barbados. In Peru, the Association for the Development of Labor Education and Economic and Social Research (AFELIES) opened in 1977 and held over 75 programmes by 1979 for 5,000 persons; AIFLD graduates played a key role in its operations. Similar facilities exist or existed, for example, in El Salvador and Honduras. Through these programmes the AIFLD can reach significant numbers; for example, about 5% of the union force in Colombia and Peru have passed through an AIFLD course. In Chile the figure stood at 3-4% in 1973, including 3,000 campesino leaders. When Ecuador struck oil, US labour programmes greatly expanded in line with the strategy of concentrating on industries or nations considered particularly vital to the US economy. As of 1975, over 10% of the entire labour force, including a heavy representation from the oil sector, had received some kind of AIFLD-related education.[34]

AIFLD training programmes not only peddle the AFL–CIO class collaborationist strategy, which benefits the transnational corporations and local capitalists, but they also create a substantial pool of unionists who can be used potentially for other purposes. Graduates from advanced training get nine months paid time as an intern upon their return home and this period may be extended. The AIFLD is sensitive about this, claiming that interns 'do not work for AIFLD–they get their assignments, their supervision, and their discipline from confederations or federations which are responsible for their activities.' Although the distinction between direct or indirect control or influence is a subtle one, interns have played an active role in the AIFLD's actions as a part of the larger labour apparatus. In Guyana, US efforts helped topple the legally elected government of Cheddi Jagan. There CIA agents worked as labour people, the AIFLD maintained anti-Jagan trade union leaders on its full-time payroll, and the American Federation of State, County and Municipal Employees supplied almost one million dollars in strike benefits to anti-Jagan forces through the Public Service International.[37]

The AIFLD holds a key position within the US foreign policy team because it alone directly treats labour and the working class. Richard T. Booth, Labour Advisor in the State Department's Latin American Bureau, clearly stated the AIFLD–government relationship. Referring to the AFL–CIO's three institutes for Asia, Africa, and Latin America, he said, 'Our government fully supports our labor movement in this effort,' and noted that the US government provides its labour assistance through these institutes because 'We believe labor movements abroad should be independent' [sic].[38]

Further, the AIFLD serves as a go-between for the government and international and national organizations. This importance becomes obvious upon examining the breadth and scope of the Institute's links with other entities. Typical AIFLD planning sessions or conferences draw representatives from several ITSs, the Inter-American Development Bank, the Organization of American States, the ILO, Histadrut (the Israeli labour confederation), and several transnational corporations. On the government side, officials from the Department of State, AID, the Peace Corps, or National Security Council regularly attend. More recently right-wing social democratic groups like the A. Phillip Randolph Institute, Freedom House, or the Social Democrats, USA, have appeared. Also seen are officials from the AFL–CIO, the Asian–American Free Labor Institute and the African–American Labor Center (to which Mr Booth referred above), these last two being the AIFLD's counterparts for their respective areas of the world. The AIFLD also works closely with a number of universities and colleges at given times, among others, the University of Florida at Miami, Florida International, the University of Pittsburgh, the University of Wisconsin through its School for Workers, Georgetown (DC) University, and the University of Chicago.[39]

The question of links between the AIFLD, the AFL–CIO, and the CIA is controversial. The AIFLD's obvious role as a quasi-official agency makes it doubly suspect of having functions other than its stated purposes, suspicions highlighted by its role in right-wing coups and anti-left activities. Philip Agee, an ex-CIA agent, has exposed some CIA–AIFLD connections. Another informed writer claims that 'today a CIA case officer is undercover in almost every AIFLD office abroad.'[40] Evidence of connections continuously surfaces. The US Solicitor-General, referring to the assassinations of AIFLD staff members Michael Hammer and Mark Perlman in January 1981 said: 'Just recently two Americans have been killed in Salvador. Apparently they were some kind of undercover persons working under the cover of a labor organization.'[41] Whatever the case, one labour spokesperson noted after the assassination, that 'Hammer and Pearlman . . . were not US trade unionists in any meaningful sense, their only connection to the labor movement being their employment by AIFLD.'[42] Although AFL–CIO officials steadfastly deny that they have CIA connections, under close scrutiny or Congressional investigation such links become clear.

The AIFLD's direct or indirect involvement in right-wing coups marks it as a suspicious agency. Immediately before the military takeovers. AIFLD training of Chileans and Brazilians rose by 400% and 600% respectively. It also massively trained Bolivians for the first time just prior to the conservative 1964 coup there. In both Brazil and Chile, AIFLD controlled unions helped the military by keeping open communications and port facilities. This is clearly one result of the AIFLD's past and present emphasis on communications and transport workers in its programmes and ITS contacts.[43]

AIFLD in the mid-1970s and 1980s

The AIFLD currently maintains stations in 13 countries and one in the Caribbean area. In the past decade it has been forced either to withdraw or lower its profile in more and more countries because of progressive and nationalist opposition. The AIFLD has re-ordered its priorities and training programmes recently concentrating its efforts mainly in the circum-Caribbean basin. At the same time, its efforts focus more on agricultural workers, rural dwellers, and women particularly in Central America and the Caribbean. This shift responds, in part, to the fact that the US government and labour officials saw the storm brewing in the area, a storm now breaking full force over Central America.[44]

The AIFLD has played an active role in the Caribbean Basin Initiative recently passed by the US Congress and it includes two million dollars for AIFLD activities. The Institute hoped to have a special labour clause included in the CBI banning funds for any nation where 'democratic' unions could not organize. This clause, however, proved too radical and it was excluded from the final text. In early 1983, USAID allotted funds for a Caribbean Basin Labor Fund administered by the AIFLD. So far, 42 projects have received loans or grants in 5 Central American and 9 English-speaking Caribbean countries. In addition, the AIFLD works closely with the Caribbean Congress of Labour (CCL)–the ORIT affiliate for the English-speaking Caribbean. The AIFLD and the CCL run many programmes together including education programmes at the Barbados, Guyana, and Trinidad and Tobago Labour Colleges. Recently the CCL's eighth biennial congress elected a two-time AIFLD graduate as its Secretary-General. Special AID monies also finance an Eastern Caribbean Development Fund. Among other things, this Fund has given grants or loans or new union and community development centers (as in St Vincent, St Lucia, Dominica, and Montserrat) to selected unions with pro-ORIT and pro-AIFLD records.[45]

The AIFLD Labor Program for the Caribbean for 1979-83 included an extensive program for trainees both at local labour colleges and in the United States.[46] In all, the AIFLD aimed to have 300 trade unionists in training, including at least 75 agricultural workers. The program also had high hopes for an AIFLD supported Caribbean Labour Economic Research Training Center (CLERT). The AIFLD hoped that CLERT would become the 'primary source of economic data available to the trade union movement, government bodies and private institutions' – a modest goal! In plainer language, the AIFLD sought to set up a propaganda centre to influence the whole area.

In addition, the AIFLD sought to strengthen the CCL and its affiliates, anticipating that by the end of 1984 CCL membership would increase by 25% over that of 1979; and that the CCL would be the 'chosen instrument' as the voice of Caribbean labour in regional, hemispheric and international bodies. The AIFLD sought additional ITS participation and urged more Caribbean unions to affiliate with the appropriate body. It also hoped that the ITS would expand their activities in the area and that ORIT would strengthen its ties. The total Caribbean area budget for 1979-80 amounted to $262,197. This figure, of course, does not include impact projects, RRLF monies or AID grants.

The Eastern Caribbean island of Grenada has drawn special attention. US trained unionists played an active role in the formation of the island's first unions. The head of the Seaman's and Waterfront Workers' Union (SWWU), for example, received training in Puerto Rico and elsewhere and its union cultivated friendly relations with the old plantocracy. During the Gairy dictatorship's (1967-79) later years, the working class began to move in response to the inflation that lowered real wages. The formation of the New Jewel Movement (NJM) in March 1973 crystallized opposition to Gairy which culminated in the declaration of an all-island general strike in January 1974. Just when the prolonged shutdown looked as if it would succeed, a section of the leadership of the SWWU (one associated with the AIFLD) agreed to mediate through the CCL after first abandoning the strike action. Once the dockers returned to work the movement petered out.

Tensions mounted between Gairy and the opposition headed by the NJM in subsequent years. NJM supporters formed unions (e.g., the Bankers' and General Workers' Union) and tried to occupy key positions in others. The regime in the meantime increased its repressive actions including passing a number of anti-labour laws. The Essential Services Act of 1978, for example, severely curbed the right to strike in the service sector. The Technical and Allied Worker's Union (TAWU – the union most effected) leadership, however, failed to challenge this act. The fact that the union's chief officer was at the time on the AIFLD payroll through the CCL may have influenced this attitude.

In March of 1979 the NJM took power, but labour troubles continued, mainly from those unions which had opposed militant action earlier. In late summer and early fall of 1979 the SWWU leadership attempted to initiate industrial actions, but without success because the rank and file would not follow. In December 1980, the SWWU refused to load a shipment of milk when the government ruled against it in a major jurisdictional dispute. Public opinion rallied against the strikers and the government got other workers to unload the milk. A similar incident occured with a shipment of Cuban sugar when the leaders convinced the dockers not to unload the cargo. In October 1979, the head of the TAWU told the electric power workers to turn off the current, apparently as a part of a larger plot against the government which may have included some SWWU officials as well. A few months later, under pressure from progressive elements within the union, the TAWU leader left the country. Earlier, the old time leader of the Commerical and Industrial Workers' Union had also been replaced by a more progressive person.

In March 1981, the leaders of several unions including the Public Workers' Union, the Grenada Union of Teachers, and the TAWU called a sick out to back demands for a 70% wage increase over a three year period. The government had offered 36%. Here too a majority in the unions and a large majority of the country opposed the action and eventually the dispute wound down through mediation. Later that same year, rank and file dissidents formed a committee which eventually won a majority on the executive committee of the Public Workers' Union. Common to all these incidents on the labour front was the presence of AIFLD and/or ORIT trained personnel. For this reason, Prime Minister Maurice Bishop denounced the 'corrupt, opportunist trade union leaders' as 'one of the most popular categories of the CIA for counter-revolution'. He accurately prophesied, 'We have not seen the end of them. We are going to see them in action again in the future of our country'.[47]

At this point there is no public direct evidence of the participation of AIFLD or AIFLD agents in the US invasion of Grenada on 15 October 1983 or the immediate events leading up to it. It is worthy of note, however, that in early October 1983, the AFL–CIO adopted a resolution condemning 'the dictatorship of Maurice Bishop in Grenada and Desi Bouterse in Suriname for their continuing repression and abuse of trade union organizations. Collaborators of Fidel Castro, they have trampled on human rights, press freedom and the right to strike.'[48] In fact, the People's Revolutionary Government issued Grenada's first labour legislation guaranteeing the right to organize based on elections with secret ballot (People's Law No. 29 of 1979). It also encouraged the formation of new unions, settled labour disputes by mediation, and intervened in not a single union.

After the invasion, US agencies and institutions wasted little time in moving into Grenada. A Report written by a US Government Inter-Agency Team in December of 1983 noted that 'organized labor is in disarray now that the dominant, highly radicalized portion of its leadership has been removed'. It explained that the Trade Union Congress leaders had been killed along with Bishop, and other radical (i.e. NJM) labour leaders rounded up after the invasion. It further mentioned that the 'AIFLD had maintained close contact' with the 'two, perhaps three of the unions that have in the past functioned in a manner that can be considered democratic' and that 'AIFLD is on the scene now' and 'is developing an extensive plan to reorient and train the labour leadership'. Finally, it recommended that: AIFLD should take the lead in restructuring and training the unions as quickly as possible, and that the Department of Labor CBI specialist should engage in discussing a new labour code that meets the proper criteria.[49] The implementation of these recommendations soon followed. From 16 to 27 January 1984, the AIFLD sponsored a seminar on Political Theories and Systems in Grenada. The seminar enrolled 17 union leaders from 5 unions and was held in the building of the SWWU which the AIFLD singled out as one of the unions remaining under democratic leadership and fighting the excesses of the Bishop regime. Indeed, eye witnesses after the invasion reported that the SWWU collaborated fully with the invaders, volunteering time, for example, to erase revolutionary slogans from buildings and walls.[50]

A typical AIFLD endeavour of the mid-1970s was Operation Solidarity, a programme designed to 'reaffirm solidarity and the commitment of the American labor movement to the task of helping our Latin brothers in their efforts to develop a free labor movement.' To this end the AIFLD arranged for three teams of AFL–CIO Executive Council members to visit Latin American and Caribbean countries for the purposes of meeting labour and government representatives and acquiring first hand knowledge of AIFLD programmes upon which they would be asked to vote support. While not unusual as a programme itself, some of the reports concerning the programme reveal important aspects about AIFLD.[51]

In all countries the delegations met with the US Ambassador, always on the most friendly and mutually laudatory terms. They also wined and dined with labour ministers and, in many cases, the Prime Minister or President of the country. The first team visited Guatemala, Honduras, Nicaragua and Panama during April 1975. One of its recommendations made after encouragement from the US Ambassadors to both Nicargua and Guatamala, was to ask AIFLD and AFL–CIO head George Meany to give serious attention to the matter of US taxpayers' resources being granted to the CLAT (Christian Democratic) affiliates in those countries through the Inter-American Foundation. Clearly, the ambassadors disapproved of this support and wanted it stopped. In Nicaragua, then under the iron hand of the Samoza dictatorship, no mention at all appeared of repression of unions or lack of trade union freedoms.[52]

The second team visited Brazil and Paraguay. It met with the Labour Minister in Brasilia and was 'pleased with the Minister's outright endorsement of AIFLD's program in Brazil'. 'He [the Minister] also made special mention of the meaningful work of the ICT which is sponsored by AIFLD.' The report went on to note the US Embassy's positive attitude toward the AIFLD's work. It then made passing reference to the fact that the government imposed some political restrictions on labour, but assured the reader that "the course content of labor education courses are similar to what our young labor leaders are exposed to in the US" and recommended that these programmes continue. The writer, Joseph D. Keenan, International Secretary of the International Brotherhood of Electrical Workers, sent a carbon copy to the US Ambassador in Brazil.[53]

Nor does the faith of the Labour Minister, the US Ambassador and the AIFLD in its programmes and the work of the ICT seem misplaced. Until the labour resurgence in the Spring of 1978, Brazilian workers remained for the most part subdued by government repression. The labour offensive which began that year, continued into 1979, centred around the metal workers in the province and city of São Paulo. At the height of the tension filled negotiations a government appointed labour bureaucrat and ICT and AIFLD trainee, Joachim dos Santos Andrade, head of the São Paulo metal workers, attempted to undermine the strike by accepting the government wage offer of a 45% increase which fell 32% below that demanded by the workers. He also pushed aside non-economic issues such as job security, a shorter work week, direct negotiations with employers, and recognition for shop floor union delegates. Although the workers rejected this betrayal, they later settled for a 63% increase and gained none of their demands. Clearly, although not decisive, the cooperative attitude of the AIFLD trained leader helped the government and employers gain a partial victory over the workers.[54]

US labour programmes and the AIFLD after 1962 had concentrated their efforts on agricultural and other workers on the payroll of transnational corporations like the United Fruit Company (later United Brands). In the 1970s, however, the AIFLD increased its efforts among non-urban workers both in response to rising militancy among these groups and to the realization that a majority of people in many Latin American countries still toiled on the land. In 1974, for example, 74 rural leaders, including persons representing unions of United Brands, graduated from AIFLD programmes. In the United States, the AIFLD gave a one semester course specifically for banana workers from Central and South America.[55]

The creation of the Agrarian Union Development Department (AUDD) testifies to the importance assigned to this new area of concentration. The AUDD now has programs in six countries designed to assist peasants' organizations. It divides these countries into two types. In nations where campesino organization is already established and under 'democratic' leadership such as El Salvador, the Dominican Republic, Honduras, and Venezuela, AUDD helps existing entities with funds, training, and technical assistance. By far the largest of these programmes is the one maintained in El Salvador discussed elsewhere in this article. The AUDD also operates in countries like Costa Rica, Ecuador, Guatemala and, until recently, Nicaragua where peasant organizations are less formed. In all, while AUDD projects do help specific rural workers they are mostly concerned with small farmers rather than the landless who compose the vast majority of rural workers. The AUDD set up a Regional Agrarian Coordinating Committee in 1976 composed of Central American rural unions and it organized a strategy meeting for English-speaking Caribbean unions implemented through the Caribbean Congress of Labour. By 1977, it had helped create over fifty new agrarian organizations in Colombia, the Dominican Republic, El Salvador and Panama. Most of these, however, seek to improve the lot of small farmers growing cash or export crops rather than organizing campesino unions. Thus, the development of small farmers with capitalist tendencies rather than unionization seems to be the AUDD's main goal.[56]

In addition to its agrarian ventures in El Salavador discussed later, the AIFLD has stepped up other programmes in the area. In all it has trained over 19,000 Central American workers either in local, regional, or US courses. Many of these have been educated at the IESCA located since 1964 in San Pedro Sula, Honduras. This Institute's courses, according to one critic,

> "have as their objective to corrupt and domesticate union leaders, inculcating them with a deadly hate toward the communists, championing the theory of 'class collaboration' and prejudicing them against all patriotic movements as well as those of popular origins."

In Honduras, the AIFLD seized the opportunity to unionize a previously unorganized workforce, collaborating frequently with the banana companies or with the government. Progressive elements managed to organize workers despite AIFLD efforts, but the Institute throught its policies of divisionism succeeded in preventing working class unity and upon more than one occasion AIFLD aligned unions attacked unfriendly unions or broke strikes (e.g. the 1977 Texaco strike) by left-wing workers.[57]

In Nicargua, the AIFLD supported the CUS (Confederation for Trade Union Unification), a confederation which, in operating, was relatively free from Somoza's repression. As the war against the dictatorship sharpened, the CUS took conservative positions proclaiming its political neutrality, and many workers perceived it as a pro-Somoza organization. After the triumph of the Sandinistas in mid-1979, the CUS quickly lost support to the Sandinista Workers' Confederation (CST) and by 1982 had only several thousand members. The AIFLD and its friends denounced the CST and declared 'the end of "free" trade unionism in Nicaragua,' but the CUS's loss of power was 'in fact a reflection of CUS' organizing ineffectiveness and of AIFLD's reactionary politics'. Interestingly enough, the AIFLD's budget in Nicaragua under Somoza varied between $100,000 and $150,000 per year. As soon as Somoza fell, it skyrocketed to over $500,000 annually and AID granted additional special funds too. By 1982 the AIFLD was financing some 44 projects mostly through the CUS.[58]

The AIFLD's heaviest involvement, however, is in El Salvador. In the mid-1960s the Institute helped to organize the Unión Comunal Salvadoreña (UCS), a peasant pressure group. By August 1973 the AIFLD had been expelled from the country for its designation of a known CIA agent as in-country director of its programme there and subsequent refusal to recall that officer upon the government's request. At this point the Inter-American Foundation, a private organization which receives substantial US government monies, picked up funding from UCS to the tune of $700,000 yearly. After futile attempts to convince the government of its utility, the AIFLD finally received permission to re-enter Salvador in mid-1979 just before the military coup of 29 October, now backed with $250,000 in USAID money but under embassy control. By the 1979/80 fiscal year, specific USAID labour contracts amounted to $2.7 million. After that, AIFLD influence increased and it actually designed the land reform decreed on 6 March 1980, an act which the government accepted without consulting the Minister of Agriculture, much less the rural population. To do this work, the AIFLD contracted Professor Roy Prosterman, a University of Washington law professor, despite the fact that he had no experience in Latin America. Prosterman, however, had planned agrarian counter-insurgency and resettlement programmes in Vietnam (Operation Phoenix), which resulted in the deaths of over 30,000 Vietnamese peasants. He brought with him Cleto Di Giovanni, a reputed CIA agent who also had served in Vietnam.[59]

Under the agrarian reform programme, landless peasants have not received land and, by some calculations, could not even if the reform were implemented. Currently it is bogged down in danger of total collapse. Indeed, its very intent has been questioned. One study called it 'just another US pacification program aimed at forcing some North American version of progress upon the Salvadorean people' while an AID official remarked that 'there is no one more conservative than a small farmer. We're going to breed capitalists like rabbits.'[60] An independent US labour delegation made several poignant observations. 'For our delegation' their report read, 'it was difficult to see how the (agrarian) reform, as currently structured, could ever significantly impact on El Salavador's campesinos.' Further, it noted, 'There is no trade union freedom in El Salvador, no semblance of the trade union rights we as North American trade unionists consider fundamental to democracy.' It then queried, 'Is United States involvement in El Salavador likely to extend the space for free trade union activity? We doubt that.' And it concluded, 'The US goal as explained by the Embassy was to give private investors confidence.'[61] These visitors went on to question the AIFLD's role in Salavador and US policy aims for that country. In truth, any observer may find it strange that a US labour organization is making agrarian reform policy for a right-wing Central American government as well as supporting a regime so decidedly anti-labour.

The AIFLD, however, does not operate in a vacuum. Opposition to overt (and covert) US labour activities has mounted in recent years both inside Latin America and in the United States. One such case is that of Trinidad and Tobago, where the People's National Movement (PNM), a pro-capitalist regime, felt forced to curtail the AIFLD's activities in 1972.

Trinidad and Tobago had long been a field of AIFLD interest by 1970, probably because of its strange value as an oil producer and because of its progressive union traditions. The majority position within most unions and the Trade Union Congress, however, hewed to a pro-CCL and ORIT line. In turn, many union members received AIFLD education and at least one union received an impact project grant to purchase printing equipment. Between 1967 and 1975, 33 people took courses at Front Royal and 7 others trained in special courses at Georgetown University or Mt Vernon College, not an inconsiderable total in a country with only a few thousand unionists. When these persons returned home many occupied key posts in unions and in official entities like the Industrial Court, National Insurance Board, and External Communications Branch and positions in the sugar industry. This list demonstrates yet another way in which AIFLD training can infiltrate beyond the labour structure.

In summer, 1971 a new local AIFLD Director for the Caribbean area set up his headquarters in Port of Spain. He initiated an active programme of seminars and recruitment for out-of-country training. In a little more than a year, however, the ruling PNM government had ordered the expulsion of this Director after a General Council meeting at which the question of foreign interference was raised. An official 'White Paper' discussed this expulsion, defending it in the face of complaints by the CCL and TUC. Only George Weekes of the relatively progressive Oilfield Workers' Trade Union supported the action. The CCL further called a boycott of Trinidad for its forthcoming congress and shifted the location.

The White Paper showed that the official in question maintained close contact with the US Embassy labour people, that he had subjected his staff of Trinidadian nationals to US security checks, and that he had collected systematically information from AIFLD trainees and others within the country. Reports from one intern included such items about local unions as 'political orientation (stated, known, suspected); new leaders (explain carefully), internal friction among leaders, between leaders and members.' It also asked for information on individuals such as political and financial data and motivation. This standard AIFLD intelligence gathering, however, was more than the government could publicly condone.[62]

In the United States, the rank and file was not consulted about AFL-CIO activities abroad nor informed of their intent and results. One study acknowledged that, 'no more than two out of 50 labor officials knew even the barest details about the organization . . . and not a single one of hundreds of union members canvassed had any idea at all of the existence of AIFLD'.[63] But after the 1973 right-wing military coup in Chile, in particular, and more publications dealing with the AIFLD's role in Latin America, US workers began to question the AIFLD's role. A Union Committee for an All-Labor AIFLD was formed; it sought to eliminate the influence of government, business, and the CIA from the organization. The Santa Clara County Labor Council confronted a high ranking AIFLD official and condemned the Institute's role in Chile. Unionists at the 1975 convention of the Communication Workers of America (CWA) expressed opposition to US unions engaging in covert activities in Latin America. More recently a progressive trade unionist noted that 'while AIFLD is ostensibly dedicated to providing technical assistance for development of democratic trade unions, its real impetus comes from anti-Communism' and that 'local union leader and rank-and-file members in California and New York have been forming labor committees for solidarity with the people of El Salvador, and adopting resolutions condemning US intervention and calling on the AFL–CIO to end its connection with AIFLD.'[64]

The AIFLD's record makes it clear that the foreign policy aims of US labour bureaucrats closely coincide with those of the US government and US business. Despite its rhetoric about apolitical unionism, the Institute purchases a highly political course based upon virulent anti-Communism and opposition to all forces which it deems as unfriendly to the United States or to US investments. From this flows its constant support for right-wing anti-labour regimes, as well as its frequent lack of support for social democratic governments.

Many of the AIFLD's specific programmes do generate goodwill and may materially help individual unions and union members. With these incentives, however, comes ideological influence. Basic educational programmes on running a union, collective bargaining, or social security may seem apolitical in and of themselves; but they are taught within a highly political context. The labour movement, moreover, as even the AIFLD has acknowledged recently, is political. Economic questions and organizational themes therefore reflect the AIFLD's positions.

The results of the AIFLD's efforts have varied. In numerical terms it helped form over 1,000 unions with more than 100,000 members, but this is an inconsequential percentage of Latin America's working class. On the other hand, it has influenced existing unions and confederations which at times may exercise power at the national level. Further, the AIFLD's concentration on communications and transport workers give it a potential impact far beyond its numbers. Lastly, its educational programmes reach significant numbers of people, particularly at the upper and middle leadership levels. Without doubt it has helped to check the growth of progressive and nationalist organizations in some cases and to blunt progressive working-class offensives in others. The Institute's greatest impact seems to have occurred in nations with the smallest labour movements or where the AIFLD has been the prime organizer of the working class in recent years. Not surprisingly, when allowed to operate under repressive right-wing regimes, the AIFLD has fared best because the competition is severely hampered or non-existent.

Despite all its efforts, nowhere has the AIFLD prevented progressive elements within the labour movement from expanding or maintaining positions. In Argentina, US efforts could not contain left-wing Peronist influence in the unions until the right-wing military coup. Chilean workers voted solidly for a Marxist president in 1970 and increased their support for the left-wing government thereafter, despite considerable expenditure of funds and energies by US labour and the US government to prevent it. More recently, in Brazil the growth of new labour militancy has not been 'made in USA.' Even in Honduras or tiny Grenada, workers not in accord with the AIFLD's aims and assumptions built new unions or received electoral support from fellow unionists despite the Institute's efforts.

Finally, the AIFLD carried out non-labour related activities acting as a government agency in, for example, land reform programmes. It also serves as a cover for intelligence gathering. The AIFLD tries to hide this latter agenda both from Latin American workers and from its own constituency. As these activities have become common knowledge along with the AIFLD's conservative indentification, they have resulted in a growing groundswell of questioning and protest from US unionists. The AIFLD's future, however, ultimately depends upon two things: the ability of US workers to influence AFL–CIO and US government labour foreign policy, and upon the tolerance of Latin American workers for interference in their affairs.

Notes

1. An earlier version of this article, which was prepared for the Ottowa Conference, was published in *Labour, Capital and Society*, vol. 17, no. 2, 1984, pp. 136–72. A yet earlier version, written for the Centro de Estudios y Documentación Latinoamericano (CEDLA) in Amsterdam Holland, was published as 'La politica exterior de los sindicatos norteamericanos y el papel de AIFLD'. *Cuadernos Semestrales* (Institutio de Estudios de Estados Unidos, Mexico, numero 11 (1 semestre, 1982), pp. 261-86. On the California Labor Federation meeting, see Richard Hobbs, 'Rank and File Challenges AFL–CIO Hierarchy on Foreign Policy', *Counter-Spy* vol. 7, no. 3, 1983, pp. 21-2.

2. See George Morris, *CIA and American Labor* (International Publishers, New York, 1967), p. 131; Carl Gershman, a right-wing social democrat and aide to former US Ambassador to the UN Jeane Kirkpatrick has written, 'Thousands of American trade unionists have engaged in international activities, but the architects of American labor's foreign policy have been a handful of individuals' in Gershman, *The Foreign Policy of American Labor* (Sage Publications, Beverly Hills, 1975), p. 7.

3. The history of US–Latin American labour relations and the AIFLD up to the 1970s can be found in Hobart A. Spalding Jr, *Organized Labour in Latin America* (New York Univ. Press/Harper & Row, New York, 1977); on the AIFLD, see also William Bollinger, (ed.), *The AFL–CIO in Latin America: Documents and Analysis on the American Institute for Free Labor Development (AIFLD)*, revised edition (Interamerican Center/Centro Interamericano, Los Angeles, 1983).

4. Meany, 2 April 1966, quoted in David Langley, 'The Colonization of the International Trade Union Movement', Burton H. Hall (ed.) *Autocracy and Insurgency in Organized Labor*, (Rutgers Univ. Press, New Brunswick, NJ, 1972), p. 299.

5. Michael J. Sussman, *El caballo de troya norteamericano. La historia del Instituto Americano para el Desarrollo del Sindicalismo Libre* (Ecumenical Program for Inter-American Communication and Action [EPICA], Washington, DC, 1983), pp. 43-4.

6. Ibid., p. 33.

7. On Political Theories Seminars as they are called, see AIFLD, *Report* [hereafer *AR*] vol. 17, no. 2, 1979, p. 2 and *AR* vol. 18, no. 2, 1980, p. 2; AIFLD, *Annual Progress Report, 1962–1982*, (AIFLD, Washington, DC, 1983).

8. *AR*, vol. 19, no. 2, 1981, p. 2.

9. *The Guardian* (N.Y.), 24 March 1982, quoted in Tom Barry, Beth Wood and Deb Preusch, *Dollars and Dictators* (The Resource Center, Albuquerque, New Mexico, 1982), p. 110.

10. Spalding, *Organized Labour*, ch. 6.

11. See Spalding, *Organized Labour*, pp. 256-8 and on ORIT today, see Julio Godio, *Sindicalismo y politica en América Latina* (Instituto Latino-Americano de Investigaciones Sociales [ILDIS], Caracas, n.d.) pp. 210-26.

12. Quoted in US Congress, Senate, Committee on Foreign Relations, Subcommittee on American Republics Affairs, *Survey of the Alliance for Progress, Labour Politics and Program*, 90th Congress, 2nd Session, July 15 1968 (USGPO, Washington, DC, 1968), pp. 9 and 5. On the AIFLD's origins see Sidney Lens, 'Labor Lieutenants and the Cold War,' in Hall (ed.),*Autocracy and Insurgency in Organized Labour* (Rutgers University Press, New Brunswick N.J., 1972) p. 319; for Meany's version see '16 Years of AIFLD,' *AR*, vol. 16, no. 3, 1978, p. 3; for Serafino Romualdi's version, see his *Presidents and Peons: Recollections of a Labour Ambassador in Latin America* (Funk and Wagnalls, New York, 1967), ch. 24. An opposing view is given in Jack Scott, *Yankee Unions, Go Home: How the AFL Helped the US Build an Empire in Latin America* (New Star Books, Vancouver, 1978), chs. 16-17.

13. Quoted in 'AIFLD: Order of Battle', *Counter-Spy* vol. 2, no. 2, 1975, p. 39.

14. Quoted in US Congress, Senate, *Survey of the Alliance for Progress*, p. 15; on W.R. Grace, the AIFLD, and labour see North American Congress on Latin America (hereafter NACLA), 'Amazing Grace: The W.R. Grace Corporation', *Latin America and Empire Report* [hereafter *NACLA Report*] vol. 10, no. 3, 1976, pp. 12-14.

15. Lists of AIFLD directors and policy statements can be found in its *Report*; also see US Congress, Senate, *Survey of the Alliance for Progress.*

16. Morris, *CIA and American Labour*, p. 79; and Jeffrey Harrod, *Trade Union Foreign Policy: A Study of British and American Trade Union Activities in Jamaica* (Anchor Books, Garden City, 1972), p. 125.

17. For discussion of funding see US Congress, Senate, *Survey of the Alliance for Progress*, p. 11. AID figures are taken from Michael Locker 'AID for the Domestic Economy', *NACLA Report* vol. 6, no. 2, 1962, p. 20; re. 1981 funds AIFLD official Jack Heberly is quoted in Barry, *et al.*, *Dollars and Dictators*, p. 107; re. CIA support, see Jim Mellen, 'Leaders for Labor – Made in America', in NACLA, *New Chile*, (NACLA, Berkeley, CA, 1972), p. 55.

18. *AR*, vol. 19, no. 3, 1981, p. 3.

19. US Congress, Senate, Committee on Foreign Relations, *Foreign Assistance Act of 1967*, 90th Congress, 1st Session (Gov. Printing Office, Washington, DC, 1967), p. 1096.

20. See Susanne Bodenheimer, 'The AFL–CIO in Latin America: The Dominican Republic: A Case Study', *Viet Report*, September-October 1967, p. 19; *AR* vol. 11, no. 5, 1973, p. 5; Liana Chin, 'The Foreign Policy of the AFL–CIO', unpublished BA thesis, University of California, Santa Cruz, 1980, pp. 106–9.

21. An excellent analysis of pre- and post-coup Brazilian labour is Kenneth Paul Erickson's *The Brazilian Corporative State and Working Class Politics* (Univ. of California Press, Berkeley, CA, 1977), real wages from p. 165; also Kenneth Paul Erickson and Patrick V. Peppe, 'Dependent Capitalist Development, US Foreign Policy and Repression of the Working class in Chile and Brazil', *Latin American Perspectives* vol. 3, no. 1, 1976, pp. 19–44, esp. pp. 36–41; Timothy F. Harding, 'The Political History of Organized Labor in Brazil' (unpublished PhD dissertation, Hispanic American Studies, Stanford University, 1973), esp. p. 330, pp. 415-16, p. 425, p. 436, p. 550, pp. 565-6, p. 575 and p. 603; Jan Knippers Black, *The United States' Penetration of Brazil* (Univ. of Pennsylvania Press, Pennsylvania, 1977), Ch. 6. By the early 1970s the ICT had trained over 28,000 unionists and the AIFLD another 24,000. See *AR* vol. 10. no. 5, 1972, p. 5; William J. McIntire, 'US Labor Policy' in Daniel A. Sharp, (ed.) *US Foreign Policy and Peru*, (Univ. of Texas Press, Austin, Tex., 1972), p. 301, who says that within days of the coup the AFL–CIO was already bargaining for expanding activities within Brazil.

22. On the Dominican Republic see Bodenheimer, 'The AFL–CIO in Latin America', pp. 19-28; Susanne Jonas, 'Trade Union Imperialism in the Dominican Republic,' in *NACLA Report* vol. 9, no. 3, 1975, pp. 16-28; Carroll Hawkins, *Two Democratic Labor Leaders in Conflict* (Arlington Books, Lexington, Mass., 1973), pp. 52-53. On housing elsewhere see Susanne Bodenheimer, (US Labor's Conservative Role in Latin America', *The Progressive* vol. 31, no. 1, 1967, p. 25.

23. On Argentina see Romualdi, *Presidents and Peons*, pp. 140-53 and 156-67; Samuel L. Bailey, *Labor, Nationalism, and Politics in Argentina* (Rutgers Univ. Press, New Brunswick, NJ, 1967), pp. 121-2, 149-52; Santiago Senén González, *El syndicalismo después de Perón* (Editorial Galerna, Buenos Aires, 1971); Spalding, *Organized Labour*, Ch. 4; NACLA, *Argentina in the Hour of the Furnaces* (NACLA, New York, 1975), pp. 20-41, 65-72.

24. Penny Lernoux, *Cry of the People* (Penguin Books, NY, 1982), pp. 211–12.

25. On Chile, see among others NACLA, *New Chile*; Fred Hirsch, *An Analysis of Our AFL–CIO Role in Latin America* (1974, San Jose, Calif.), pp. 30-42; Erickson and Peppe, 'Dependent Capitalist Development', pp. 30–36; James Petras and Morris Morley, *The United States and Chile* (Monthly Review Press, New York, 1975); US Congress, Senate, Senate Select Committee to Study Governmental Operations with Respect to Intelligence Activities, *Covert Action in Chile, 1963-1973*, 94th Congress, 1st Session, 1975 (Government Printing Office, Washington DC, 1975); recent AIFLD activities in Chile in *AR* vol. 19. no. 3, 1981, p. 1; *AR* vol. 2. no. 2, 1982, p. 1; *AR* vol. 21. no. 3, 1983, p. 4.

26. Every issue of *AR* contains information on courses, topics, etc.

27. William A. Douglas, 'US Labor Policy in Peru – Past and Future', in Daniel A. Sharp, (ed.) *US Foreign Policy and Peru*, p. 320; and McIntire, 'US Labour Policy', p. 304.

28. Bolivian Annex to AIFLD Regional Contract covering 1 April 1974 to 31 March 1975, pp. 1-5 (NACLA library).

29. Re. 1972 trainees, see *AR* vol. 11, no. 1, 1973, pp. 2-3; on francophone programmes see *AR* vol. 19, no. 3, 1981, p. 7.

30. *AR* vol. 16, no. 3, 1978, p. 2 gives current figures; final total is extrapolated from subsequent annual figures in the *Report*. The courses were moved in 1979 from Front Royal, Virginia to the George Meany Center for Labor Studies in Silver Spring, Maryland. See *AR* vol. 15, no. 3, 1977, p. 4 for education totals; and *AR* vol. 18, no. 2, 1980, p. 2, Re. US programmes, see *AR* vol. 20, no. 2, 1982, p. 2. The ORIT and the AFL–CIO now sponsor the Labor Economics Conference. On publishing see, for example, the AIFLD, summary of Education Department Activities for period 1 July–30 September 1973, dated 15 October 1973, p. 2; the primer is *Fundamentos de Democracia* published in two volumes in Buenos Aires, document in the NACLA library.

31. *AR*, vol. 18, no. 2, 1980, p. 2, and vol. 15, no.3, 1977, p. 4.

32. Data from the AIFLD/Uruguay, Quarterly Program Progress Report, Oct. 10, 1973 and Report of Activities, 16 September–15 October, 1973, 18 October 1973 and enclosures, in NACLA library.

33. Bodenheimer, 'US Labor's Conservative Role', p. 27; Mellen, 'Leaders for Labour', p. 55; AIFLD, *Annual Progress Report, 1962–1975*: NACLA, *Argentina*, p. 28.

34. Terms of Contract for Union-to-Union Program (AID to AIFLD) – 1973-4, Appendix A., 15 pages. On specific grants see the document marked "AIFLD–ITS Grant (Union-to-Union Program)," undated but obviously from early 1974, 4 pages (NACLA library).

35. For a complete listing of ITSs, see US Department of Labor, Bureau of International Labor Affairs, *The Shape of International Unionism: International Trade Secretariats*, Monograph No. 3, (Gov. Printing Office, Washington, DC, 1979). See also Langley, 'The Colonization of the International Trade Union Movement,' pp. 303–6 on ITSs and the CIA; and *Counter-Spy: Special Issue on the CIA* vol. 2, no. 2, 1974, p. 33.

36. On the ICT, see Black, *United States Penetration*, pp. 122–3; re. Central America, see *AR* vol. 14, no. 4, 1976, pp. 2, 8; for Perus see *AR* vol. 17, no. 3, 1979, p. 5; for numbers see Don Thompson and Rodney Larson, *Where Were You Brother?* (War On Want, London, 1978), p. 43; Spalding, *Organized Labor*, p. 266; and NACLA, 'Labor Coming of Age', in *Report*, vol. 9, no. 8, 1978, pp. 20-24.

37. Chin, 'Foreign Policy', p. 100; *AR* vol. 15, no. 3, 1977; on intern programmes; on Guyana, see Sidney Lens, 'Labor and the CIA', *Progressive*, vol. 31, no. 4, 1969, p. 26; Scott, *Yankee Unions*, p. 233; *New York Times*, 24 February 1967; Colin Henfrey, 'Foreign Influence in Guyana: the Struggle for Independence', in Emmanual de Kadt (ed.), *Patterns of Foreign Influence in the Caribbean*, (Oxford University Press, London, 1972), pp. 65-72; Cheddi Jagan, *The West on Trial* (International Publishers, New York, 1972), pp. 226-34.

38. *AR* vol. 19, no. 2, 1981, p. 2.

39. For lists of participating organizations see, for example, *AR* vol. 10, no. 1, 1972, pp. 1-2, and vol. 18, no. 1, 1980, p. 3, and vol. 20, no. 3, 1983, p. 6. Schools are discussed in 'Exporting Corporate Unionism: the Wisconsin School for Workers', CALA *Newsletter* vol. 6, no. 5, 1977, pp. 1-12.

40. See Philip Agee, *Inside the Company: CIA Diary* (Penguin, Harmondsworth, 1975), esp. pp. 74-8; for quotes see 'Clandestine Enforcement of US Foreign Labor Policy', *Counter-Spy* vol. 2, no. 1, 1974, p. 43; and anonymous, 'CIA Operations in Latin America', *Counter-Spy* vol. 2, no. 1, 1974, p. 33; Sussman, *El caballo*, p. 24.

41. This slip occurred at Agee's trial. See Philip Agee, *White Paper Whitewash*, (Deep Cover Publications, New York, 1981), p. 54.

42. Helen M. Kramer, International Affairs Department, International Association of Machinists and Aerospace Workers, AFL-CIO. Remarks at the First National Teach-in on El Salvador at Wayne State University, Detroit, Michigan, 3 April 1981, mimeo, p. 1.

43. Chin, 'Foreign Policy' pp. 71-2; Black, *United States Penetration*, p. 117.

44. For example, on rural workers, see *AR* vol. 12, no. 3, 1974, p. 1; vol. 12, no. 2, 1974, p. 4; also vol. 10, no. 1, 1972, p. 5; vol. 11. no. 2, 1973, p. 1. On women, see *AR* vol. 12, no. 1 1974 which cites two courses for women; also vol. 15, no. 3, 1977, p. 2, and vol. 16, no. 1, 1978, pp. 4-5 give examples of other activities. See vol. 20, no. 4, 1982, pp. 1 and 4.

45. On the CBI see *AR* vol. 20, no. 2, 1982, p. 2; vol. 20, no. 3, 1982, p. 2; vol. 21, no. 1, 1983, p. 2; on Labor Fund see *AR* vol. 22, no. 1, 1984, p. 4; re. CCL, for example, see *AR* vol. 15, no. 2, 1977, p. 3; CCL elections, *AR* vol. 21, no. 4, 1983, pp. 1 and 4; re. Development Funds see *AR* vol. 20, no. 6, 1982, p. 2; re. community centres, see *AR* vol. 19, no. 2, 1981, p. 5 and vol. 21, no. 4, 1983, pp. 4-5.

46. A copy of the Caribbean Area Proposal is found in Trade Union Committee of the People's Popular Movement, *The CIA and Local Trade Unionism*–An Analysis of the Role of the AIFLD (The Committee, Trinidad and Tobago, 1982), appendix 1.

47. Grenada Section is based on EPICA, *Grenada: The Peaceful Revolution* (Washington, DC, 1982), pp. 42-50, and 62-6; anonymous, *In The Spirit of Butler: Trade Unionism in Free Grenada* (Fedon Publishers, St. Georges, 1982), esp. pp. 86-91 and 71-5; anonymous, *Focus on the Eastern Caribbean* (The Resource Center, Albuquerque, NB, 1984), pp. 23-4; Chris Searle, *Grenada: The Struggle Against Destabilization* (Readers and Writers, London, 1983), pp. 421-45; quote from *Forward Ever! Three Years of Maurice Bishop* [collected speeches of Bishop] (Pathfinder Press, Sydney, Australia, 1982), p. 197.

48. *AR* vol. 21, no. 3, 1983, p. 4.

49. US Government Interagency Team on Commercial and Private Sector Initiatives, 'Prospects for Growth in Grenada: The Role of the Private Sector' (Washington, DC, 5 December 1983, pp. iii-iv and 20-21).

50. *AR* vol. 22, no. 1, 1984, p. 3; interview with the US Health Workers Delegation, 25 May 1984.

51. William C. Doherty, Jr, 'Operation Solidarity, 1975 Report,' unpublished, NACLA library.

52. Memorandum from AFL–CIO team to George Meany, 5 May 1975, NACLA library.

53. Keenan to Meany, 27 May 1975, letter in NACLA library.

54. Latin American Working Group, 'Workers' Movement and Economic Crisis in Brazil,' *LAWG Letter* vol. 8, no. 2/3, 1984, pp. 11-12.

55. See note 44 on rural workers and *AR passim* for subsequent efforts.

56. *AR* vol. 15, no. 2, 1977, pp. 2-3; vol. 20, no. 4, 1982, pp. 1, 4; Barry, *et al.*, *Dollars and Dictators*, p. 107.

57. Quoted in Mario Pozas, 'Tendencies ideológicas actuales en el movimiento obrero hondureño,' *Anuario de Estudios Centro-americanos* (Costa Rica), no. 6, 1980, p. 31; on Honduras see Pozas and Steve Volk, 'Honduras on the Border of War', NACLA *Report* vol. 15, no. 6, 1981, esp. pp. 8-11 and 24; graduates in AIFLD, *Progress Report*, 1962-1982 and on Central America in general see Barry *et al.*, *Dollars and Dictators*, pp. 105-10.

58. See EPICA, *Nicaragua: A People's Revolution* (EPICA, Washington, DC, 1980); also "Target Nicaragua," *NACLA Report* vol. 14, no. 1, 1982, pp. 21-2.

59. See Sussman, *El Caballo*, pp. 2, 40-41; also Carolyn Forché and Philip Wheaton, *History and Motivations of US Involvement in the Control of the Peasant Movement in El Salvador: The Role of AIFLD in the Agrarian Reform Process, 1970–1980* (EPICA, Washington, DC, 1980); Philip Wheaton, *Agrarian Reform in El Salvador: A Program of Rural Pacification* (EPICA, Washington, DC, 1980). Almost every issue of *AR* carries material on El Salvador.

60. Quoted in Frank Arnold, "Ban AIFLD in El Salvador," *Counter-Spy* vol. 4, no. 1, 1980–1, p. 50; second quote from Wheaton, *Agrarian Reform*, p. 16.

61. Quotes from, National Labor Committee in Support of Democracy and Human Rights in El Salvador, *El Salvador: Labour, Terror ad Peace: A Special Fact Finding Report* (The Committee, New York, 1983), pp. 7, 10, 11.

62. Trinidad and Tobago section is based on Trade Union Committee of the People's Popular Movement, *The CIA*.

63. Hirsch, *An Analysis*, p. 51.

64. Quote from Kramer, Remarks, pp. 2, 3; see Timothy F. Harding and Hobart A. Spalding Jr, 'The Struggle Sharpens', *Latin American Perspectives* vol. 3, no. 1, 1976, p. 6; Arnold, 'Ban AIFLD', pp. 45–46; Richard Hobbs, 'Open Letter to the Labor Movement,' *Counter-Spy* vol. 4, no. 1, 1981, pp. 47-51.

11. The ILO and Protection of Trade Union Rights: The Electronics Industry in Malaysia

Arne Wangel

The transition in a number of third world countries to a strategy of industrialization, in which production for export organized by transnational capital plays the major part, has led to severe set backs for trade unionism. Most significantly, this kind of integration into the world market has weakened the bargaining power of the trade unions, as changes in the labour legislation have been introduced to contribute to a favourable investment climate.[1] This paper will discuss the extent to which the ILO labour standards machinery offers protection for workers' basic trade union rights in the export-oriented manufacturing industries in the Third World.[2]

The production and assembly of electronic components is one of the major sectors in which the relatively high proportion of labour to capital has motivated transnational capital to relocate production to low cost labour countries in South-East Asia. This change in the division of labour between western industrialized and South-East Asian countries has created a specific labour process characterized as 'bloody Taylorism'.[3] The term refers to the combined relocation of monotonous segments of production and the exploitation of a female labour force whose most important qualification is a centuries-long subordination to patriarchy in a traditional society.[4] Control and discipline are exercised through the Taylorist method of fragmenting the production process into little or no skill operations. The capital–labour relation is 'bloody' because the continuous influx of young women to the labour market allows a complete disregard for the reproduction of the labour force beyond the age of 25 – a situation only comparable to that in the period of early industrialization in Europe.

Although 'bloody Taylorism' may turn out to be a temporary form of accumulation detrimental to the long-term, dynamic development of the national economy, the impact on the power relations between the trade union movement, management and government authorities is decisive.

This paper starts out by criticizing the demand for a social clause – based upon a set of fair labour standards selected from the ILO conventions – to be introduced in trade agreements. This early policy response from the international labour movement to changes in the division of labour between industrialized countries and a number of third world countries is characterized as inefficient and as basically first world protectionist in its mode of operation.[5] The discussion then proceeds to look at the strongest part of the ILO machinery itself–the complaint procedures concerning violations of the freedom of association–which is reviewed through an example from Malaysia.

The case discussed is that of the electronic industry. Unlike the garments industry, which constituted another major thrust of labour-intensive production to low cost labour countries in the late sixties, the production and assembly of electronic components will continue to be a first priority in the strategy of export-oriented industrialization. Based upon a kind of technological determinism, governments of the newly industrialized countries in South-East Asia tend to view the high tech industries as the most reliable path to economic and political power. The transnational electronic corporations, for their part, seek to maintain their production facilities while introducing computerized automation systems. The low cost of labour is still an important incentive, while the climate of industrial relations in third world countries is expected to produce less resistance from the workers to the necessary experimenting with new forms of organizing the production process.[6]

In the first half of the 1970s a number of export processing zones were established in Malaysia.[7] Since then, the Electrical Industry Workers' Union (EIWU) has struggled to organize about two-thirds of the 72,720 workers (1979) employed in the manufacture of electrical machinery apparatus, appliances and supplies by transnational electronic companies. However, the Malaysian government has effectively denied these workers their right to organize, although Malaysia ratified the ILO Convention No. 98 on the Right to Organize in 1961. EIWU has not been allowed to unionize this major membership potential, nor have the workers been in a position to form a union of their own.

What contribution has the ILO made towards changing this no union condition offered to transnational capital by a third world government? From the description of the struggle for unionization of the electronic workers in Malaysia it is concluded here that the ILO has offered marginal support. Its recommendations to the Malaysian government were based upon strictly legal argument; the ideal of universal harmonization of labour standards it proposed provoked bitter opposition from the government side. In the latter's replies to the ILO Committee on the Freedom of Association of the Governing Body, the real complexity of the problem was revealed, and the western concept of trade unionism and of the role of trade unions in the development of the national economy were challenged.

The overall conclusion argues that although the ILO may provide useful instruments in the defence of the rights of individual trade union activists, its system of labour standards does not cope adequately with labour problems of a structural nature as produced by changes in the international division of labour.

The ILO System of Labour Standards in the Stategy of the International Labour Movement

The International Labour Organization (ILO) was established in 1919 as a result of the Treaty of Versailles. Formally based on the idea that peace can only exist when social justice prevails, the new organization reflected a widespread concern about low labour standards as source of social conflict. On one side there were bourgeois fears stimulated by the Russian revolution and the uprising in Berlin in 1918; on the other there were forces within the international trade union movement of a social-democratic orientation which for years had pushed for international legislation on social policy and the protection of workers.

Such fears apart, two developments were important for the creation of the ILO. Firstly, the unionization of major proportions of the labour force in advanced capitalist countries, together with technological progress in the production process, produced a shift in the general orientation of labour control and social policy. The simple effort to discipline the reserve army of the marginalized and the poor for wage labour was developed into a system of collective agreements and social security provided by the state. Some of the important issues in this process were the recognition of the right to organize, one day of weekly rest, a maximum of eight hours' working day as a goal, a ban on child labour, and equal pay for work of the same kind.

Secondly, the change of the dominant political orientation within western trade union movements, in short the growing integration on a national level of organized labour into the institutions of bourgeois society, implied that the safeguard of workers' living standards was seen to a large extent as conditioned by the reproduction of national capital in the context of world market competition.

Hence it was that any lingering momentum towards labour internationalism across borders was weakened and the basic rationale of the new tripartite international labour organization became one of promoting ILO labour standards in the name of social justice and peace, thereby initiating a process of harmonization in the advanced capitalist countries which would make it possble for the individual nation state to embark on labour legislation and social policies without undermining the competitive strength of diverse capitals in their production for the world market. The clearly Eurocentric goals of the universal ILO standards illustrate that the concern to transfer collective bargaining and social policy to the national level in all advanced capitalist countries arose from the situation of direct competition between the diverse capitals which employed workers within discrete national boundaries wherein wage levels and conditions of employment differed markedly. Meanwhile, provision was made for adapting international labour standards to local circumstances. Protective standards were not to be extended to the colonies in more than rhetoric alone.[8] Accordingly, a worker gained his universal right only when he entered into direct competition with the working class in the advanced capitalist countries, be it as an immigrant or a worker employed in the manufacturing of industrial goods for the world market.

Such differentiation in application of standards was maintained after decolonization when third world countries became members of the ILO and the emphasis of the organization shifted from standard setting activities to operative technical assistance programmes.[9] The ILO World Employment Programme of 1969 and the Basic Needs Strategy of 1976 mark a change of priorities away from poverty primarily conceived as unemployment (the right to work) to an integrated strategy of structural reform (redistribution of income and more equal access to resources) in which the fulfilment of the basic needs of the rural poor was a central goal. Now the option was to develop the material preconditions for achieving the social goals defined in the ILO conventions. The rationale of the basic needs strategy is comparable to the social policy orientation of the welfare state, which emerged in industrialized countries during the 1960s; it was a question of investing in human capital in order to develop it as a productive force. Thus a successful basic needs strategy may contribute to political integration on the national level and reduce any labour related barriers for the expansion of capitalist relations of production by transforming the underemployed, the poor and workers into a potential labour force.[10]

During the 1970s a group of 'newly industrialized countries' penetrated the world market for a number of manufactured products with considerable competitive strength. This change in the structure of the world economy placed sections of the industrial labour force in third world countries in direct competition with workers in industrialized countries, all pooled in a new expanded world market of labour.

The significant differentiation in wage levels and bargaining strength presented a serious challenge to large sections of the working class in the industrialized countries employed in traditional and now declining industries, often located in provincial regions already experiencing a process of de-industrialization. This challenge added to the difficulties confronting the trade union movement in a time of economic crisis.

It is well known that the trade union movement in most third world countries survives in an unfavourable environment. Apart from outright state repression, the structural heterogeneity of dependent capitalism and the highly segmented labour market are fundamental restraints upon the unionization of workers. Even in industrial centres trade unions are hard pushed to establish strongholds, given management's ability either to recruit a new workforce from the vast reservoir of surplus labour or to introduce automation into the production process.

Given this background, ILO standards have been assigned an important part in the strategy of the international trade union movement, (or more particularly that section of it which has a welfarist and social democratic orientation). This implies the optimistic belief that supra-national bodies like the ILO have the power through internationally negotiated agreements in a tripartite forum to influence working conditions and trade union rights in member countries. This position, however, fails to take account of the fact that the scope of direct co-operation between trade unions in countries differentiated by pattern or level of development is inevitably very limited.[11]

The contradiction between the intensity with which labour standards are promoted and the practical results can be illustrated by discussing the early policy response to the changing international division of labour: the demand for a social clause in the GATT Treaty.

The First Policy Response to the Changing International Division of Labour: the Demand for a Social Clause in the GATT Treaty

Throughout the 1970s the introduction of a social clause in international agreements granting access to the markets of the industrialized countries for manufactured goods produced in third world countries has been discussed in several international fora.

Within the General Agreement of Tariffs and Trade (GATT) Scandinavian governments, in particular backed by the Swedish Federation of Trade Unions and the International Metalworkers' Federation (IMF), have been active in promoting a proposal for a social clause. They argue that the concept of fair labour standards should be inserted in article XIX of the GATT Treaty. This article deals with general exceptions from the main provisions of the treaty, and the proposed amendment would allow a restricton of imports in the case where fair labour standards are violated. The proposal includes the establishment of a tripartite commission to monitor the application of the social clause.

The concept of fair labour standards has never been formally defined, but in the discussions the following areas have been touched on:

I Fundamental human rights
Right to Organize (Convention nos 87, 98, 141)
Non-discrimination (Convention no. 111)
Forced Labour (Convention nos 29, 105)

II Working conditions
Health and Safety (Convention nos 115, 119, 127, 136, 139, 148)
Labour Inspection (Convention nos 81, 129)

III Women and children
Equal Remuneration (Convention no. 100)
Child Labour (Convention nos 5, 79, 90, 138)

In the ILO the social clause was discussed in 1972–4, but the employers' representatives and third world governments opposed the idea, while the workers' representatives did not support it with any significant enthusiasm.

In 1978 the EEC Commission put forward a document very much in line with the proposal for a social clause; it had no effect, however, on the outcome of the second Lomé Convention in 1979. The EEC and ACP countries seemed to agree not to introduce a conflict on human rights and labour standards. In 1980 the Economic and Social Council presented a new version of the introduction of labour standards in EEC third world policy in the form of a so-called 'social agreement'. Although the provisions of this proposal reflected the severe opposition of third world countries, it has not been discussed in practical terms.

The basic political criticism from third world governments against the proposal for a social clause is that the relations between the industrialized and the developing countries should remain purely economic without interference in the internal matters of sovereign states. The social clause is regarded as a hidden form of protectionism and reference is made to the fact that many industrialized countries have not ratified or do not apply important ILO conventions, in particular with regard to migrant workers and their relations with the apartheid regime in South Africa.[12]

The argument that a social clause basically serves the purpose of protection of production in industrialized countries is supported by the possible functioning of such a clause. First of all, the GATT rules indicate that import restrictions can only be imposed on exports that lead to market disruptions. Accordingly, to implement the social clause within the GATT Treaty implies that it has to be proved that the low wages or bad working conditions in a particular country are the *decisive* cause of improved competitiveness on the world market. If this kind of evidence is established, it will support the point of view held by a number of labour ministers, particularly in South-East Asia, that priority at this stage in the development of their national economies cannot be given to the improvement of labour standards. To this end, they cite the very bad conditions under which the workforce laboured during the early period of industrialization in advanced capitalist countries and the Soviet Union.

Secondly, the clause affects only industries, disregarding the fact that the worst examples of exploitation and suppression of workers are often found in other sectors. Thirdly, even in the hypothetical case that an effective clause might lead to increased wages in the export sector, a government would be inclined to impose higher taxes on these workers in order not to introduce imbalances in the economy.[13]

Generally speaking, it is difficult to imagine that a negative sanction against a proven occurrence of exploitation would produce an improvement of bad working conditions and low wage levels. What remains in the mode of operation of a social clause is a basically protectionist justification.

From this perspective, a social clause can only be justified as a unilateral measure of foreign policy towards countries flagrantly violating human rights and thereby also basic trade union rights. In such cases of 'social dumping', a trade embargo against the country in question could be a relevant instrument in weakening its government and pressurizing it into changing its policies.

According to officials of the ILO the debate on the social clause has created political difficulties in the normal operation of the ILO system of labour standards. The Director-General of the ILO concluded in his report to the 70th session of the International Labour Conference, June 1984 (of which Part One discusses international labour standards), that

> it is a complex issue which requires detailed discussion as a distinct problem, on the basis of a detailed analysis of all relevant elements. In these circumstances it has been considered preferable not to take it up in the context of the present report.[14]

Although a social clause in trade agreements is not likely to be realized, the mere existence of this policy concept as an expression of western protectionism reinforces a nationalist point of view from the third world.

But since 1950 the ILO itself has operated a complaint procedure in cases where the right to organize (Convention no. 87, Freedom of Association and Protection of the Right to Organize, 1948; Convention no. 98, Right to Organize and Collective Bargaining, 1949) is violated. In the period 1973–82 more than 400 cases of complaints from trade unions–often supported by organizations of the international trade union movement–have been put before the ILO Committee on Freedom of Association of the Governing Body.[15]

The Struggle for Unionization of Workers in the Electronic Industries of Malaysia

The Electrical Industry Workers' Union (EIWU) was registered in 1971 and since 1974 EIWU has campaigned to unionize the about 48,500 workers (1979) in the electronic industries. By the end of March 1984 the union had a total membership of 8,142, and since 1972 has been an affiliate of the International Metalworkers' Federation (IMF). It is outspoken in its criticism of the government's development and labour policies, in particular the Look East option, and of the largest national trade union centre Malaysian Trade Union Congress (MTUC), which is blamed for presenting a too soft opposition. EIWU is well organized and has proved effective in concluding collective agreements with substantial wage increases and other benefits. At present (1985) it is campaigning for a 40-hour week, for an agreement in the unionized factories on the introduction of new technologies and basic conditions for employment creation, as well as giving high priority to improve conditions of health and safety in the individual workplace.

The Free Trade Zone Act was passed in 1971 to provide incentives for attracting foreign investment. The shift to a strategy emphasizing export-oriented production proved successful, with many companies setting up manufacturing facilities (a substantial number being in the electronics sector). In 1979 Malaysia was the second largest supplier of electronic components to the USA; its exports there were valued at $594.4 million or 16.7% of the total exports produced by firms such as RCA, Motorola, Texas Instruments, Intel, National Semiconductor, Hewlett-Packard and others.

Among the ten free trade zones (FTZ) in Malaysia Bayan Lepas on the island of Penang has the largest concentration of electronic factories and its situated in close proximity to an international airport. The factories under discussion here are located in this area.

One of the most important incentives offered by the Malaysian government is the provision in the Industrial Relations Act (1967) Section 15, which gives 'protection of pioneer industries during the initial years of its establishment against any unreasonable demands from a trade union'. When this law was amended in 1980, the three-year restriction on unionization amongst workers in pioneer industries was lengthened to an indefinite period. However, in 1961 Malaysia had ratified ILO Convention no. 98 on the Right to Organize and Collective Bargaining (although no. 87 has never been ratified).

On this basis the case of the struggle for unionization of electronic workers in Malaysia was filed with the ILO. The first phase of the struggle, which will be discussed here, covers the period from 1977 to 1982, during which the Malaysian government flatly turned down every attempt to unionize workers by the EIWU. Let us look at the basic argument of the government by following the treatment of the problem by the ILO Committee on the Freedom of Association of the Governing Body.

Case no. 879

On 3 June 1977 the International Metalworkers' Federation (IMF) and the Malaysian Trade Union Congress (MTUC) complained to the ILO that the metal workers in Malaysia were divided between seven different unions. The complainants claimed that this fragmentation of a total membership of 13,000 workers was not a result of the free choice of the metal-workers, but due to arbitrary government decisions, which were in contradiction with the principles of the ILO.

The EIWU had likewise been restricted in organizing workers engaged in the manufacture of electrical home appliances. Since the 30,000 workers engaged in the manufacture of electronic components and semi-conductors had no union of their own, the EIWU had appealed several times, but unsuccessfully, to the Minister of Labour.

The government of Malaysia explained to the ILO Committee that trade unions generally enjoyed freedom of association but that such freedom could not over-ride other national considerations. The Registrar of Trade Unions (RTU) had made the decision that the EIWU was not eligible to organize the electronic workers because of the disparity between electrical and electronic industries.

The conclusion of the Committee recalled that the right of workers to establish and join organizations of their own choosing was one of the basic tenets of freedom of association. The Committee noted that the difficulties were not of recent origin and that attention had already been drawn to them during a survey of the trade union situation in the Federation of Malaya carried out by the ILO in 1961.[16]

At this stage the EIWU applied to the RTU for a change in the name of the union to Electrical and Electronic Workers' Union and for an amendment in its membership scope in order to make it possible for workers engaged in the manufacturing of articles, components and parts related to the manufacture of electrical appliances to become members of the union. Both proposals were turned down despite the fact that in the application reference was made to major trade unions in other countries which organize electrical and electronic workers together (for example Denki Roren (Japan), IG Metall (West Germany), IUE (USA), ETU (Australia), Svenska Metall (Sweden)).[17]

A major conflict between MTUC and EIWU broke out, as the MTUC, against protests made by EIWU, set up a temporary committee to draft the constitution for the information of a national union for electrical workers. However, EIWU returned to the MTUC in 1980, when the government amended the labour legislation in line with the Committee's recommendations.

Case no. 911

On 3 July 1978 the IMF filed a new complaint saying that the Malaysian government had taken no steps to implement the recommendations made by the Committee in Case no. 879. The complaint was accompanied by a copy of a memorandum of appeal to the Prime Minister dated 1 May 1978 from the EIWU.

The union had lost a case at the Federal Court against the RTU and drew the attention of the Prime Minister to the official recognition of the similarity between electrical and electronic industries. It pointed out that the Malaysia Industrial Classification of 1972 classified the electrical industry as a major one and electronics as a branch within it. Likewise in the Third Malaysia Plan it is stated that electronics is a branch of electrical engineering. Similarly, the Dictionary of Occupational Classification of 1973 also classified electrical and electronic workers under the same group.

By April 1978, in line with this apparent official acceptance of the close connections between the two industries, the EIWU had succeeded in organizing workers at Mitsumi Electrical Company and served a claim for recognition. However, although it was demonstrated to the RTU that various electrical components made at the Matsushita company – where the workers had been permitted to join the EIWU – were similar to the products manufactured at Mitsumi, he decided to classify Mitsumi as an electronic factory and accordingly the EIWU was not allowed to organize its employees.

The government again explained that at this stage of its development

Malaysia needed to maintain industrial peace in order to accelerate economic growth and social progress. Because of the workers' low level of education, it argued, they were not able to exercise wisely and logically their right to choice of unions and would be too easily influenced into changing union membership at the whim of union leaders without regard to their own interests or the interest of the industries in which they worked.

The Committee recalled its previous observation that the restrictive interpretation of the word similar was inconsistent with the freedom of association, in particular as it was applied on the level of national federations and confederations and thus constituted an obstacle to the establishment of strong and effective organizations able to defend the occupational interests of the workers.[18]

In July 1979 the IMF and MTUC gave further evidence to the ILO Committee on the fragmentation of Malaysian unions and unnecessary delays in recognition procedures. The complaint also referred to the refusal of the RTU to approve an amendment to the membership scope of the EIWU.

In the government's reply the reasons for rejecting the various EIWU appeals were clearly stated. It was said

> (a) that the electronic industry plays an important socio-economic role (in attracting foreign investment and in reducing unemployment) and that the question of unionisation of its workers should be dealt with in a cautious manner in the present stage of the country's economic development, where foreign investments are greatly needed;
> (b) that allowing the electronic workers to be unionised by an established union, the EIWU, would create a disincentive for foreign investors in this field, who might leave the country, and would make the EIWU too unwieldy, (electronic workers number around 42,000 in 46 establishments);
> (c) that the membership scope of the EIWU is confined in its membership clause to companies manufacturing complete and finished goods, whereas the electronic industry manufactures components which may be found also in products of other industries. It was for this latter reason that the Registrar of Trade Unions had rejected applications for changes in the EIWU's membership clause.[19]

The Committee could only note with regret that the administrative authority in Malaysia did not appear to have taken into account the previous comments of the Committee.

In spring 1980 major changes in the labour legislation were introduced by the Malaysian government in the wake of a conflict with the employees in the national carrier Malaysia Airline System (MAS). When negotiations between MAS and the Airlines Employees Union (AEU) broke down in the beginning of 1979 this led to the deregistration of AEU, arrest of several trade union leaders including the representative in Asia of the International Transport Workers' Federation (ITF), Donald Uren. Co-ordinated by ITF, boycott actions in Sydney and London inflicted severe losses on MAS, and the international pressure subsequently led to the release of the arrested AEU members and trade union officials. AEU was replaced by two separate organizations, one for the MAS employees and one for employees in foreign airlines.

One of the amendments implied that unions might be deprived of their right to join international trade union organizations. Another serious amendment was the introduction of a new provision in the Trade Unions Act, which expanded the authority of the RTU so that he was given powers to suspend a trade union branch; and a provision which gave the Minister of Labour the power to suspend a trade union up to six months, if the union in his opinion was being used for a purpose prejudical to or incompatible with the interests and the security of or public order in Malaysia or any part thereof.

Case no. 1022

On 26 January 1981 the IMF again filed a complaint, this time concerning the unionization of the workers employed at a specific factory, RUF Electronics in Bayan Lepas FTZ.

After a spontaneous strike the EIWU succeeded in organizing 600 out of a total of 800 employees and managed to persuade the workers to return to their work. But again the RTU refused the claim for recognition referring to the argument about the lack of similarity.[20]

The EIWU appealed against the decision to the High Court. On 7 April 1982 the government informed the ILO Committee that the High Court had not yet reached a decision about the appeal of the EIWU. Accordingly, the question about the right to collective bargaining had not yet arisen. However, noted the government, RUF employees had set up joint meetings with the management of the company from time to time. It concluded its reply by saying that a cordial relationship existed between the two parties.[21]

But it was another factory in Penang which was to be the touchstone in the second phase of the struggle for unionization of the electronic workers – ITT Transelectronics Bhd, which is owned by Standard Elektrik Lorenz AG, a West German unit of an International Telephone and Telegraph subsidiary. It makes audio products and – according to EIWU – also electronic components, such as printed circuit boards, to go into its finished products.

During 1981 the EIWU had succeeded in recruiting a number of ITT workers as union members. On 12 February 1982, 200 workers were sent on vacation until 5 April and the working week was reduced from five to three days. A number of the workers left the factory for other employment during this period.

In August the EIWU asked for a meeting with the authorities about their refusal to recognize unionization of ITT Transelectronics. But it was not until November that the RTU announced that workers employed at ITT, Philips-Audio, Granek, Clarion and Atlas – all located in the Bayan Lepas FTZ – would be allowed to join the EIWU.[22] The reason given for this decision by the RTU was that these companies manufactured 'complete electrical goods'.

In December 1982 the Minister for Labour and Manpower, Datuk Mak Hon Kam, welcomed the statement of the Malaysian Trade Union Congress (MTUC), that the government, the unions and the employers should co-operate during the recession to maintain employment levels and workers' welfare.[23] Then, in a later announcement, the government expressed concern about worker retrenchment especially in textiles and electronics and requested management to consult trade unions or worker representatives.[24]

In January 1983 a decision about whether the EIWU would be allowed to recruit ITT workers had not yet been announced, even though the union now claimed that some 68% of the workers had joined. However, Datuk Mak Hon Kam argued that outsiders (i.e. the EIWU) should not champion the cause of electronic workers, and stated that a separate union could be formed at ITT only if it was satisfactorily proved that a majority of workers were in favour.[25] Meanwhile, Dan Nelson, the Managing Director of Hewlett-Packard, an American owned electronic factory in Bayan Lepas, said that trade unions were 'an unwelcome third party. It is hard to imagine what the union can offer or contribute to the employees. Besides being redundant, it may even work against the good relationship between the management and the employees.'[26] It was also reported that management staff at the electronic factories stayed on duty during the night shift because they feared that workers would discuss the formation of a union.[27] Other reports stated that 400 workers employed in electrical manufacturing had been retrenched during the past month.

By the end of January Acting Prime Minister Datuk Musa Hitam warned against the 'possible exploitation of the economic recession by certain elements which would cause maximum damage to the country's economy'.[28] He concluded that the type of trade union should be specifically tailored to the nature of any particular industry; Information Minister Adib Adam commended quasi-Japanese, in-house trade unions as an appropriate model.

Despite these pressures, the EIWU's campaign to secure recognition intensified, and by 23 February 1983, the MTUC had collected 10,000 signatures in a campaign to support the unionization of the electronic workers. Meanwhile, although ITT Transelectronics Management attempted to set up an in-house union and threatened workers with dismissal if they refused to join it, EIWU managed to recruit some 450 workers (in contrast to the 100 who became members of the stooge union).

The struggle culminated on 14 April when the EIWU committee at ITT was recognized by the RTU and management was given two weeks to consider recognition. Despite the concern registered by Hewlett-Packard that this development at ITT would disturb foreign investors, the RTU went on to refuse to recognize the in-house union and to indicate that, in principle, a process of collective bargaining between the EIWU and the ITT management could begin. The recognition of the RTU came at the same time as the EIWU was in the process of filing an order of *mandamus* at the chambers of the Attorney-General against the Minister of Labour.

Nonetheless, ITT continued to resist the EIWU's intervention. At first, union officials were not allowed to meet the workers' factory committee during working hours, and it was only after the police and the press had been informed that EIWU finally gained official access to ITT premises. Even then, management threatened to close the factory during the first meeting with EIWU, whilst the beginning of the second meeting was delayed by some three hours until the personnel office could be prevailed on to appear. However, continuing EIWU activity, together with pressure exerted by IMF headquarters in Geneva against the ITT head office in Stuttgart and contact with IG Metall at ITT plant, (as well as a meeting by the executive secretary of the EIWU with ITT in Stuttgart), resulted in an acceptance in January to start negotiations for a collective agreement. After a number of intensive negotiation sessions during a period of two months an agreement was signed on 16 March. For 800 employees covered by the 1st collective agreement the minimum wage was increased by approximately 40% and the average wage increase was 17%.

A Minor Contribution of the ILO

What made the government authorities refuse to recognize the in-house union established at the ITT and eventually intervene on behalf of the EIWU? A number of factors are important. From early on in the 1980s the international recession was making its influence felt in the export-oriented sectors; for example, 18 companies unionized by the EIWU laid off approximately 2,300 workers during 1982–3. The practice mentioned in the ITT case of cutting down weekly working hours and forcing the workers to take their annual leave at a given time has also been introduced in many factories. Given the prospect of major industrial unrest the government seems to be motivated to give serious consideration of some kind of organized workers' representation *vis-a-vis* management decisions.

The Malaysian government is presently in a position to take a strong stand in its relations with foreign investors. Applications for the extension of the pioneer period have been turned down and new investments have been directed to development areas on the east coast. Most electronic companies are planning to stay in Bayan Lepas, although there is an upward trend in the wage level due to the high concentration of industries in the Penang area; the contracting pool of surplus labour is shown by 'job hopping'. This may develop into a serious problem for investors when changes in the production process require a higher level of qualification of the labour force, though electronic factories generally prefer automation as a cost reducing strategy to moving to lower cost labour countries like Sri Lanka and the Philippines which are regarded as much more politically unstable than Malaysia. There is therefore a possibility that some factories may expand their production by adding more segments or products, and it is expected that such a process will be supported by the establishment of state initiated plants for the production of chemicals.

However, the intention of the government to fragment and limit the scope of trade union activities still stands. When the EIWU sought recognition for the union in the Accuron (M)Sdn BHd Company, which manufactures electronic calculators, the RTU surmised that the workers were engaged in the manufacture and assembly of office equipment since calculators were basically used in offices. By this logic, the workers should have joined the Machinery Manufacturing Employees' Union. Thus the permission given by the RTU for workers at the five factories at Bayan Lepas to join the EIWU cannot be regarded as the final breakthrough. There is no indication that factories which produce only electronic components such as semi-conductors will be open for unionization in the near future, and in-house unions have been encouraged in a number of instances when the EIWU has been in the process of recruiting members from a particular factory. This is one of the features of the general orientation towards Japanese management style and industrial policies which is frequently proclaimed by Cabinet members.[29]

Under these circumstances the progress made by the EIWU in the struggle for unionization must be ascribed to the combination of an effective mobilization on the grassroots level, a protracted legal battle against government authorities, and the publicizing in a very concrete way of the flagrant violations of the right to organize both in Malaysia and in the international context. By employing its practice of campaigning at one factory at a time the EIWU managed to recruit the majority of the workers at ITT as members against the odds of management imposed control and discipline. The legalistic approach, which was made at substantial financial cost, included an optimum of efforts to overcome the intricate labour laws.

On the international level the support of the IMF has clearly been of value to the progress in unionization via general seminars on the problems in the electronic industry regionally, specific advocacy in the ILO complaint cases and in the difficult negotiations for a collective agreement with the ITT management. However, the EIWU leadership does not give much credit to the ILO involvement, and, in general, the value of international solidarity orally expressed at international conferences is regarded with considerable scepticism, particularly in the light of the growing protectionism in western countries. The main reason of the EIWU for filing the complaint cases to the ILO was to publicly embarrass the Malaysian government.

The progress of the EIWU in Bayan Lepas was not achieved on the basis of a fundamental change of the power relations, but through a process which ended up questioning the legitimacy of state authority at a time of emerging disharmony when no such question should be put; in that respect the ILO contribution has been a supportive one. The crucial question is whether the progress made can form the beginning of a process in the dense industrial area of Bayan Lepas which can develop a dynamic of its own creating more awareness among the workers about the significance of unionism for better wages and working conditions. But the continued struggle will face a major challenge when dealing with the American semi-conductor factories in which unionization seems irreconcilable with a management strategy based upon a family ideology and which are accustomed to a no union situation in their operations in the United States. This touches upon the second kind of contribution of the ILO.

The ILO intervention is limited by the strictly legal point of view which the ILO Committee of Freedom of Association of the Governing Body is forced to employ in its conclusions. But the ILO process has forced the Malaysian government to enter into a dialogue on the reasons behind their industrial relations policy. In order to bypass the legal condemnations of the ILO forum, the government has opened a discussion on the nature of trade unionism in Asia and on the relationship between trade unionism and economic development.[30]

The Asian 'Dialogue' on the Relationship between Trade Union Rights and Export-oriented Industrialization

The fundamental disagreement between the Malaysian government and western trade union organizations can be elaborated by looking at the dialogue between the International Confederation of Free Trade Unions (ICFTU/Asia Regional Organization (ARO), the International Trade Secretariats (ITSs) and the Asian Labour Ministers with the Secretary-General of the ILO as a mediator. These talks were triggered off by the earlier mentioned confict between the Malaysian Airlines System (MAS) and the Airlines Employees' Union (AEU) in 1980. In particular, the active participation of the International Transport Workers' Federation (ITF) has provoked a severe confrontation and elevated the dialogue to the regional level.

The basic argument from the side of Asian Labour Ministers has been expressed very precisely in a statement from the Malaysian government:

> The concept of freedom and rights held by developed countries, especially European countries, is different from the one held by developing countries . . . Conventions belonging to this category invite resentment and resistance from developing countries, including Malaysia, because they are not practical to their political systems and the security of their countries . . . improving the wage earning population through implementing international standards would only increase the disparities between the 'haves' and 'have nots' in these economies and thus create social and political instability'.[31]

The Minister of Labour and Employment of the Philippines, Blas F. Ople, has elaborated these views by saying that the re-appraisals of industrial relations in Malaysia, Singapore and India were not accidental:

> they were a part of an emerging trend towards a search for new modes and approaches with a view to relating industrial relations policies more closely to the national cultural traits and certain indispensable requirements of development.

In other words, there should be a rethinking of the industrial relations system in terms of indigenous features, harmonizing the recognition of employers' and workers' rights with the promotion of industrial peace, harmony and productivity. Mr. Ople further stated that a protectionist attitude of western trade unions was sometimes cleverly dressed up as 'international altruism'; 'the abundance of labour was surely a comparative advantage of developing countries in world trade and labour surplus must be accepted as a regulating force in wagefixing.'[32]

However, the trade union side in the dialogue, ICFTU/ARO, does not seem to question the strategy of export-oriented industrialization;

> any discouragement or inhibition of this flow of industrial investment capital can only serve to damage or detract from the fundamental commitment of international free labour to narrow the development gap between the developed and the developing worlds.[33]

What is important is to clear up the misunderstandings about trade unions and to stress their supportive role in the development process, in particular conceived as social change;

> if it comes through violent upheaval, it is not merely disruptive but devastating . . . That is why for peaceful development, the leadership in the developing countries must belong to governments who draw their main support from those who stand to gain from development.[34]

What the ICFTU/ARO has to offer at this stage in the discussion about trade union rights in the context of rapid economic development is a belief in the possibility of convincing the Asian governments that an autonomous and institutionally guaranteed scope for independent trade unions is also more rational from the point of view of the political rulers than the present authoritarian system.

Conclusion

For the international trade union movement of a welfarist and social–democratic orientation the ILO system of international labour standards represents an approach to internationalism which is consistent with the movement's basic point of view on the relationship between union and government. Improvements in labour standards can successfully be negotiated on the basis of a common interest in the reproduction of the national economy within the context of world market competition.

But the idea of universal harmonization of labour legislation as a measure to counter the differentiation between different sections of the world market of labour ignores the fact that the strategy of export-oriented industrialization of the seventies directly contradicts this goal.[35] The option

But the idea of universal harmonization of labour legislation as a of the transnational corporations is exactly to exploit the unequal development between different regions in their worldwide sourcing. The foreign investments oriented towards exports reinforce the structural heterogeneity of dependent capitalism and strengthen the focus of the economic policy on the integration into the world market, both developments narrowing the scope for the articulation of trade union interests.

The authority and legitimacy of the ILO is closely related to the independent and objective functioning of procedures which imply that only a strictly legal point of view can be applied. The system does not allow for a discussion of individual difficulties of implementing the conventions. However, the continuous process of monitoring the labour market situation and industrial relations in the member countries and of presenting recommendations when complaints are brought before ILO committees makes this contradiction between universal standards and unequal development continuously evident.

It is argued here that, instead of responding to the labour market situation in third world countries on a largely case by case basis, the ILO should examine more thoroughly all the aspects of protecting trade union rights in an environment of export-oriented industrialization. Studies of systems of industrial relations and labour processes could thereby contribute to a more far-reaching analysis on the relationship between economic development and political participation. Both the international trade union movement and the ILO need to formulate alternative strategies for third world industrial development giving priority to fundamental trade union rights in a way comparable to that of the basic needs strategy conceived for third world rural development.

Meanwhile, the fact that officials in the ILO and the EEC Commission have begun to discuss using labour standards as indicators and catalysts for aid programmes directly aimed at improving specific working conditions (notably in the spheres of occupational health and safety) suggests a move in the right direction, even though the present trend towards commercialization of development aid implies that close link between the monitoring of labour standards and aid priorities is not politically viable. The major use of the ILO to third world unions is therefore likely to be in dispensing knowledge about the ever more complex technologies with which workers have to contend.

Finally, although it can be concluded that the ILO's definition of minimum employment standards offers third world unions only marginal support (especially in conditions where exploitative labour conditions are the result, in part at least, of deeply rooted structural problems within a peripheral economy), the ILO does none the less provide an ideological reference point for the promotion of associative rights. As these are central to the democratization of the development process throughout the third world, the role of the ILO all its limitations not be ignored in the presently unequal struggle between labour and capital at the periphery of the world economy.

Notes

1. Johannes Schregle: *Negotiating Development: Labour Relations in Southern Asia* (Geneva ILO, 1982), highlights the current re-assessing of the labour relations systems in the region.

2. The protection of trade union rights in general are analysed in two studies published by the ILO: H.G. Bartolomei de la Cruz, *Protection against anti-Union Discrimination* (ILO, Geneva, 1976), Jay A. Erstling, *The Right to Organize* (ILO, Geneva, 1977). A number of specific cases are described in James Avery Joyce, *World Labour Rights and their Protection* (ILO, New York, 1980).

3. Alain Lipietz, 'Towards Global Fordism?', *New Left Review*, no. 132, 1982.

4. Diane Elson and Ruth Pearson, 'The Subordination of Women and the Internationalization of Factory Production', in Kate Young *et al.*, *Of Marriage and the Market* (London, CSE Books, 1981); Christina Tse, *The Invisible Control–Management Control of Workers in a US Electronic Company (with reference to Hong Kong and Korea)*, (Hong Kong Center for the Progress of Peoples, 1981); L.H. Chan, M.L. Young and K. Salih, 'Women Workers in Malaysia: TNCs and Social Conditions', in Irene Nørlund, Peter Wad and Viago Brun (eds), *Industrialization and the Labour Process in SouthEast Asia*, Institute of Cultural Sociology, University of Copenhagen, Repro-serie, 1984, no. 6.

5. Göte Hansson, *Social Clauses and International Trade: An Economic Analysis of Labour Standards in Trade Policy*, Lund Economic Studies no 25. (Lund, 1981).

6. Dieter Ernst, *The Global Race in Microelectronics: Innovation and Corporate Strategies in a Period of Crisis* (Frankfurt, Campus, 1983).

7. Mrinal-Datta Chanduhri, *The Role of Free Trade Zones in the Creation of Employment and Industrial Growth in Malaysia* (ILO/ARTEP, Bangkok, 1982).

8. Eva Senghaas-Knobloch, *Reproduktion von Arbeitskraft in der Weltgesellschaft. Zur Programmatik der Internationalen Arbeitsorganisation* (Campus Verlag, Frankfurt/New York, 1979), Kapitel I.3.

9. Ibid., Kapitel II.

10. Richard Sandbrook, *The Politics of Basic Needs: Urban Aspects of Assaulting Poverty in Africa* (Heinemann, London 1982), p. 9.

11. Werner Olle and Wolfgang Schoeller, 'World Market Competition and Restrictions upon International Trade Union Policies', in *Capital and Class*, no. 2, 1977.

12. In the Lomé III Convention of 1984 reference is made to the promotion of human rights and the elimination of every kind of discriminatory policy.

13. Gus Edgren, *Spearheads of Industrialization or Sweatshops in the Sun? A Critical Appraisal of Labour Conditions in Asian Export Processing Zones* (ILO/ARTEP, Bangkok, 1982).

14. International Labour Conference 70th Session 1984, *Report of the Director-General*, (ILO, Geneva 1984), p.6.

15. ILO, *Freedom of Association and Collective Bargaining: General Survey by*

the Committee of Experts on the Application of Conventions and Recommendations (ILO, Geneva, 1983).

16. ILO, *Official Bulletin Series B*, vol. 61, no. 2, Geneva 1978, pp. 22 ff.

17. EIWU, *Secretariat Report to the 3rd Biennal General Meeting*, 24 September 1978, Dewan Hamzah, Klang.

18. ILO, *Optical Bulletin Series B*, vol. 62, no. 1, Geneva 1979. pp. 112 ff.

19. ILO, *Official Bulletin Series B*, vol. 63, no. 2, Geneva 1980, pp. 26 ff.

20. ILO, *Official Bulletin Series B*, vol. 64, no. 3, Geneva 1981, pp. 133 ff.

21. ILO, *Official Bulletin Series B*, vol. 65, no. 2, Geneva 1982, pp. 80 ff.

22. *The Star*, Kuala Lumpur, 24 November 1982.

23. *The Star*, Kuala Lumpur, 24 December 1982.

24. *New Straits Times*, Kuala Lumpur, 30 December 1982.

25. *New Straits Times*, Kuala Lumpur, 13 January 1983.

26. *The Star*, Kuala Lumpur, 4 January 1983.

27. *New Straits Times*, Kuala Lumpur, 7 January 1983.

28. *The Star*, Kuala Lumpur, 26 January 1983.

29. See Peter Wad, 'The Japanization of the Malaysian Labour Market System', in this volume.

30. Guy Caire, *Freedom of Association and Economic Development* (ILO, Geneva 1977) gives a review of the literature on this topic.

31. ILO/Asian and Pacific Project for Labour Administration (ARPLA), *Developing countries and ILO Standards: Proceedings of the Regional Seminar on Practice and Procedures in Formulating Labour Standards,* Bangkok, Thailand 26–30 April 1982, p. 97.

32. Summary Notes of the Meeting between the Asian and the Pacific Labour Ministers and ICFTU/ITS Representatives, Geneva, 7 June 1982, p. 2.

33. ICFTU/ARO, *Report on Activities Jan 1973–Dec 1975* (New Delhi), p. 99.

34. Memorandum submitted at the time of an informal meeting between leaders of Asian Governments and the Free Trade Union Movements of Asia, Bandung, Indonesia, September 1970.

35. See Eva Senghass-Knobloch, 'The New International Division of Labour and International Labour Standards: Do Levels of Technology of Socio-economic Structures Matter?', in Dieter Ernst (ed.), *The New International Division of Labour, Technology and Underdevelopment* (Main, Frankfurt, pp. 162–4.

12. Workers of the World Untied: International Capital and Some Dilemmas in Industrial Democracy

Nigel Haworth and Harvie Ramsey

> Developing a truly international force has become a condition for national trade union survival.[1]

Charles Levinson, erstwhile Secretary-General of the International Chemical Workers' Federation, is the most articulate spokesperson of a line accepted in most public statements by union leaders in the advanced capitalist countries. In his view, multinational corporations (MNCs) have developed from a national base through early cautious forms of foreign investment to global operations; in response unions must and will develop national unity, simultaneous company bargaining in different countries, and finally integrated international bargaining coordination.[2] Unions are the potential but secure democratic counter-force to capital. The creation of objective conditions for international cooperation has preceded but must result in the subjective conditions.[3] Later, Levinson presents this as a global challenge for democratic rights in industry, with all countries conceding to workers by statute or collective agreement by 1976 or 1977.

> At that point the first important phase of the modern industrial revolution will have been reached and the process of restructuring industrial society into a social and democratic system based upon socialized enterprise and a more democratic work environment will have truly begun.[4]

Unfortunately for Levinson, his specific forecast, though still very much the official line, looks exceedingly threadbare with hindsight. This paper seeks to challenge that prognosis, at least in its proclamation of inevitability, and to indicate the problems which Levinson's assumptions led him to underplay or ignore. It seeks to pull together a number of themes and recent research to provide an overview of the obstacles confronting labour in its efforts to match the power of capital. Inevitably, it does not detail all the obstacles which might be raised. In particular, the paper's central interest in issues relating to industrial democracy takes the discussion away from a focus on one of the major weaknesses of the internationalism debate; that is, the impact of gender on the structure and practices of union action. Nor does the paper discuss the international dimensions of the relationships between bureaucratic and rank and file union practices. We mention these omissions to highlight the directions which further analysis of international union action might take.

The Visible Challenge

There is little disagreement in labour movement circles on the nature of the problems which are posed by transnational capital. Countless books and pamphlets detail the capacity of multinational corporations to create problems for employees and governments, including an exemplary contribution from the British Labour Party.[5] Transfer pricing, currency speculation, profit repatriation and remote control over investment decisions can damage balance of payments, regional and other nation state policies. Governments and workers can be blackmailed by threats to invest elsewhere. Economic autonomy can be lost when no one country has full production facilities, relying on supplies from and/or sending partly finished products to another susidiary. Control over technology, and research and development is also commonly lost as companies centralize some activities, often in the country of origin. Ownership of patents, trademarks and even particular skills compounds MNC control of research and development. On the industrial democracy front, the difficulties created by working only for a subsididary directed from outside the country are obvious, creating dilemmas for national unions or plant based employee organization, and also for statutory prescriptions for worker participation.

Discussions of multinationals also dramatically present the scale of the problem. A decade ago we heard that by the mid-1980s, 300 corporations would control two-thirds or more of world production outside the socialist countries, and that a thousand top executives would between them control the core of the capitalist economy globally. Exxon and General Motors were bigger economies than Sweden, Yugoslavia, Greece, New Zealand, Austria – indeed of the hundred largest economic entities in the world, more than half were corporations.[6] This was widely viewed as more than just a matter of MNCs *per se*: the dominance of American based corporations in the size league led to their spread being seen as surrogate US imperialism.[7]

It seems clear that the 1970s recession also saw a sharp brake on the startling post-war rate of MNC growth. Indeed many MNCs began to cut back the scale of their operations,[8] and this in turn has shifted the focus of much fear and criticism onto the resulting processes of rationalization and cutback. Yet just because MNCs have not matched the expectations of earlier observers does not mean that their magnitude is of little significance. By the mid-1970s they accounted for perhaps one-fifth of world output, and were still growing at nearly twice the rate of overall world expansion. In 1976, there were 11,000 MNCs with 82,600 affiliates between them, and 371 companies were each operating in over twenty countries. By the end of the 1970s, the liquid assets amassed by MNCs amounted to three times world gold and foreign exchange reserves.[9] Between 1971 and 1980 the top 50 companies increased their share of total sales from 12% of GDP in the developed market economies to 16%.[10] In 1977, of the largest 483 MNCs, the greatest number were in the growth-oriented sectors of metal manufacturing products, chemicals and pharmaceuticals, petroleum, food, and electronics and electrical appliances (in that order).[11]

While this kind of informed analysis of the extent of MNC penetration in the UK is not uncommon, the data are often left to speak for themselves. Yet if MNC power were directly proportional to the presence of the companies according to these measures, it would make no sense to see a decline in that presence as an expression of that power, for instance. In short, the usual appreciation of MNC power is static and superficial. This is evident, too, in discussions of responses such as those described below. Here MNCs are treated as sitting targets to be fired at by codes of conduct, inter-union contacts, government legislation and intervention, and so forth; they respond, if at all, in a purely reactive manner. This patently invites a serious underestimate of the conscious and usually calculated manoeuvres of MNCs, which are far more likely to take the initiative than their labour movement opponents.

The Pluralist Response

When it comes to coping with the power of capital, for which it is accepted internationalization of corporate activity is a qualitative step upwards, the reaction of both unions and liberal academics can be characterized as pluralist. The image into which they strive to fit reality is one of rule governed conflict, in which formal institutions develop to restrain and channel confrontation into compromise. Neither side in the pluralist model wishes to annihilate the other, and even if such an outcome were threatening, the state exists as an overseeing mediator and referee, intervening to correct the balance as necessary.

This is also standard industrial relations theory. More implicit and less often discussed is the presumption of evolutionary progress built into such views. Yet the notion that compromise is facilitated by the prospect of long-term shared advance for all, so that all parties have a vested interest in the status quo, is a crucial binding force in the argument. The area of institutional representation of worker interests, and so influence on decision-making, is one key facet of the supposed advance – and hence the various components of a supposed evolution towards industrial democracy are essential to pluralism.[12]

It will be evident that the 1970s and the 1980s offer ominous challenges to the viability of the pluralist prognosis. This interpretation arises not only from the growth of international capital, but also from the rise of monetarist state policies which embody von Hayek's hostility to trade unionism and industrial opposition of any sort.[13] Since both are aspects of the restructuring of capital, the concerted nature of the offensive is unsurprising. None the less, it is the former to which this paper restricts its attention. If the varied proponents of pluralism cannot demonstrate a progressive response from labour, if necessary with benevolent state support, to redress the balance of power, the entire political order of which industrial pluralism is a pillar must totter and fall. This might be expected to produce similar reactions to those displayed by the revolutionary left seeking vindication of their hopes – constant emphasis on the hopeful signs, de-emphasis on the setbacks, discussion in generalities only, clutching at each straw and a refusal to acknowledge the possibility of ultimate failure.

The literature on developments in international trade unionism is extensive, but somewhat repetitively and hollowly rhetorical in its reporting of advance and recommendations for the future.[14] Lists of innovations and areas for further advance are plentiful, but can be exemplified by a typical inventory from the TUC's education department.[15] This notes 14 methods of meeting the needs of international organisation, 6 involving government support, 4 efforts within British subsidiaries, and 4 international union cooperation. The state is to play its part by using its own potential economic and statutory controls and sanctions, and by encouraging other governments to co-operate. Inter-state cooperation is to operate through supra-national bodies – thc UN, the ECC, the OECD and the ILO in particular. These bodies are to produce agreed codes on investment and other MNC behaviour to ensure information disclosure, and to pressurize any companies stepping out of line.

Locally unions are to collate information, seek facilities (including overseas liaison with employees elsewhere) and develop member education. Internationally the banner is to be carried in a number of organizations, international union federations (such as the International Confederation of Free Trade Unions (ICFTU) or the European Trade Union Congress (ETUC)); international trade secretariats (e.g. the International Metalworkers' Federation (IMF)); joint trade union councils covering an MNC (e.g. in Michelin – an official union body organized by the International Chemical Workers' Federation); international shop steward combines (less formal, via plant representative contacts, as in the much publicized Dunlop-Pirelli case); and international work councils. The TUC account does observe some persistent weaknesses in this crucial area, but a tone of eventual advance understandably remains uppermost.

The justification for such strategies is typically provided in a list of advances – World Auto Councils for this or that firm; exchanges of information and solidarity agreements between shop stewards in various plants of another; legislative proposals from this or that government or inter-governmental organization (IGO). Progress is presented as cumulative, and initiatives are described for this success, as recipes for others to follow.

The broad, underlying presumption was noted earlier: that objective conditions exist, and this not only must but will (the two are often blurred, as if need wills success into being) create the necessary unification of labour. This is raw economic determinism in thin disguise – a conviction that because it seems logical that only cooperation between workers across frontiers can achieve their collective interests, it will turn out that they see it thus and act effectively thereon. Yet this fallacy is daily challenged by sectionalism within the labour movement that defeats the achievement of supposed unified purposes even within a country, a firm, or a plant for that matter. The causal model is at fault, not least because it ignores the problems of the way the real world presents itself and is experienced by those who sell labour power.

Two other presumptions need to be made explicit and broadly questioned here, so that subsequent discussion can take them up. One is that the state is a neutral agency, or even tends to favour its own workers against foreign capital. This leans heavily on the crutch of nationalism, which is a treacherous enough support when international resistance is the objective even without the additional questions raised by considering the nature of the state itself. Unless the state is indeed a neutral referee redressing balances, or is amenable to capture by a sympathetic political party, then reliance on its intervention as a progressive force for labour is dangerously naive. If alternative analyses of the pivotal role of the state in sustaining capitalism, or at least of the structural constraints and limits on government action in a capitalist society, have any plausibility, dependence on state backing for labour loses its remaining credibility.

The second addendum is that the heralds of progress are inclined to see the erosion of capital's power as a matter of nibbling away at a tough but immobile obstacle. Capital is sitting still, waiting to be fired at and offering the chance for reloading or weapon development without fear of any counter-blow. David Coates[16] makes this criticism of the Alternative Economic Strategy in general, and its view on MNCs in particular, borrowing the analogy supplied by Tawney: capital is a tiger, not an onion; it is not peeled unresistingly, but reacts in deadly fashion to those who would skin it. In other words, notwithstanding the awed recounting of the capacities of MNCs noted above, and indeed of the co-ordinated and highly deliberate orchestration of their development, orthodox views tend to underestimate grossly the power and adaptability of huge corporations. The search for the right formula for opposing MNCs, as if it were just a formula (and usually an organizational one at that), is severely misplaced if this criticism is correct.

In the critique of the orthodoxy which follows we have drawn on our knowledge of, and in one case involvement in, examples of labour struggles in multinationals, and it is from experience of these rather than merely an abstracted conceptual exercise that our analysis is derived.

Labour and International Capital: A Different Departure

There seems no good reason for presupposing that the universe of action and associated organizational principles for a MNC management, and those for collective labour, are the same or even similar. This point is well argued in part by Olle and Schoeller[17] although their conclusions appear to have attracted little attention. The supposed linkage between and equalization of wages and other conditions and other actions of MNCs in making consistent their policy towards their workforces, are in themselves questionable as steady developments. But more important is the mechanical reliance on a narrow view of material causality, whereby all previous efforts at international solidarity are consigned to the dustbin of history as idealist efforts made too early. This analysis is a crude and unconvincing attempt to tailor history to prejudice. If there is a development following from MNC policies, say Olle and Scheoller, it is probably a depoliticization of union action, limiting challenges to economic issues.

Olle and Schoeller argue that international union cooperation has been contingent on a coincidence of different national union interests. Not only is this an insecure, shifting basis, but it is all the more so for its economistic limits – as exemplified by growing national union campaigns for protectionism (particularly in the USA and UK, countries subject to jobs export more than most) in recent years. Nothing displays this more clearly, they remark, than the lack of genuine solidarity with third world unions, who are on the contrary often seen as rivals for jobs by workers in developed countries. What Olle and Schoeller have begun to do needs extending analytically and examining more closely empirically. The following are some initial steps in this process.

A useful way of conceptualizing the fundamental dilemmas facing labour's response to capital is provided by Marx's analysis of abstract and concrete labour. When something is made, Marx argues that in all societies it embodies the specific labour of an individual or group oriented to fashioning something for use – in his terms, use values are produced by useful or concrete labour. However, use values are not comparable since the labour embodied in them is not comparable. In order that capitalist exchange can take place, products must be expressed in some common form, their exchange value, which in turn must rest in Marx's analysis upon the one common property all goods have, the labour expended on them. Since concrete labour is not a comparable currency, then labour must instead be translated into some form with shared characteristics. Commodity producing labour thus takes the form of abstracted labour, and the distinction between this and concrete labour is, for Marx, 'the pivot on which a clear comprehension of Political Economy turns'. Abstract labour is a concept necessary to explain the specific historical form of production and exchange under the capitalist mode of production, i.e. it describes one integral aspect of social relations within that mode. As such it is not merely a theoretical construction, but an expression of reality.[18] The social character of such labour is concealed by its expenditure in an employment relationship, the returns from which are only generated in the exchange of resulting commodities in the market place; hence it is expressed in the mystified form of prices and so exchange value.[19] It is only this arrangement which makes possible the reduction of all labour to a physiological equivalence, i.e. abstract labour is labour reduced by and for exchange to an homogeneous unit.

This unit is effectively what shapes calculations of labour as a resource–humanpower–by capital, as well as being the basis of fair exchange between buyers and sellers. In other words, the capitalist must calculate the best use of available labour power considered thus, as abstract labour, in order to maximize surplus. The action of abstract labour thus describes also the strategic concept of employers, a concept likely to become prevalent once a firm gets beyond the minimal scale of the small workshop. At the same time, each worker experiences his or her activity as concrete labour, alongside that of others. In other words, it may be suggested that there is a close relationship between Marx's concepts of labour and the actual perception of labour by social actors. Indeed, Marx's analysis of the ideological representation of surplus value as profit on sales, on labour concealed as prices, and so on the obscured appearance of the employment relationship (commodity fetishism), stresses throughout that we are not dealing merely with economic concepts but with ideas and so attitudes.

Having argued in a highly truncated manner the connection between abstract and concrete labour and ideologies, it remains to test the significance of this connection and to consider any particular implications for MNC–union relations. The universe of labour revolves around the individual and collective expenditure of concrete labour, mediated by the fact that that labour is sold as labour power to employers. This engenders both oppositional attitudes over the control of work and the rewards received, and also an appreciation of the need for cooperation in production, which for most will manifest itself as a need, however constricted, to co-operate with management and make an enterprise profitable. There are multiple implications of these perceptions (including their ambivalence); but we wish to discuss here only selected and simplified aspects. Shared experience and visible links between those performing concrete labour will be the chief source of identity, perceived interests, and collective organization and action. In short, the focus of solidarity is the workplace, which may be defined normally as the workshop or even workgroup and may not easily extend beyond a simple site or plant. This will tend to be reinforced by direct contacts through the local community, socially and culturally. A sense of national identity may be reinforced by nationalist ideology to broaden this sense of community–but probably at the expense of sharpening the distinction from outsiders, who may be employers or workers in other nations.

It will be apparent that much of what has been argued applies equally to multi-plant firms in one country as to MNCs, and this is witnessed by the problems of creating and sustaining collective organization and unified action in non-multinational conglomerates. The last point does suggest one major further obstacle to the creation of labour solidarity, however; and others relate to the particular nature of MNC operations considered in the light of the employer view of labour.

The employer's view, it has been suggested involves a far closer approximation to seeing labour in its abstract form. For management purposes, the task is to arrange and secure the input of labour as a resource, adjusting sourcing and control strategies to minimize the cost per unit of production. This view of labour as calculative, objectified, impersonal aggregates is likely to become more dominant as the enterprise grows, and even more so as it progresses beyond national boundaries. Any illusion that there will be an enduring sentimental attachment to company origins is likely to be rudely shattered – as those at Fort Dunlop or Massey-Ferguson in Toronto could testify. For US employees of MNCs, the chief fear has always been what they experience as the export of jobs, and workers in Europe and Japan (as with the recent union resistance to Nissan plans to invest in Britain) are increasingly becoming aware of the same threat. The very manner of the perception of that threat by labour bears witness to the formation of attitudes discussed above.

MNCs are thus essentially rational in seeking to enable themselves to substitute labour in one location for that in another, compelling different groups of workers towards conformity to the lowest common denominator in unit costs by also ensuring flexibility in increasing or reducing output without immovable, fixed labour costs that cannot be disposed of in periods of low demand. This process is accelerated by the shift of control to finance capital internationally, which both reinforces the detached, calculative approach to operations, and also emphasizes cash flows, rates of return, currency movements and so forth rather than the labour process *simpliciter*. This entails a further distancing of the logic of MNC activity designed to maximize its return from the traditional terrain comprehended by labour in terms of the wages, conditions, productivity or profitability of a single plant. Financial flows and the effects on production levels in other sites may make it appropriate to capital to close a profitable plant, a logic which employees will be hard put to understand at all, let alone knowing how to oppose or suggest alternative conclusions.

In this sense, labour and capital in MNCs are not even fighting in the same dimension – but since the initiative is capital's, labour's counter-blows simply find no tangible opponent on which to land. If this account misses something out, then if anything the inclusion of that something makes labour's response more difficult still. Clearly MNCs' managements do not ignore local, concrete conditions; they are well aware that labour is not merely a passive resource, but a potentially intractable one. In order to homogenize labour as an input, and to make different sources of labour interchangeable, specific circumstances in different locations have to be assessed and exploited, not ignored. If cultural and other conditions make all workers, or workers from particular social groups, or workers of one gender and/or age group, or workers in particular areas, (such as the special economic zones springing up in the Far East, including China, and now in the West also) more susceptible to MNC demands of them, even if only temporarily, they will be made use of. If the plant-level logic of worker perceptions can be used to limit wage demands or facilitate rationalization, then this will be done: plant will be set against plant, with any strike or wage demand provoking mangement warnings that the plant's viability is threatened, while companies with quiescent and highly productive workers elsewhere will be stressed. The recent manoeuvrings of the Hyster Corporation, persuading employees in Irvine, Ayrshire to accept wage cuts in order to secure investment and jobs by undercutting the company's Dutch factory is a good example. The Dutch unions sought legal redress without success. Meanwhile, early in 1984 the company still managed to announce redundancies at Irvine, having achieved the desired wage cut and production transfer. Ford has used the doom message against strikes across their British operations, to browbeat employees and try to ensure behind the scenes government pressure on the unions. The image of the loyal, energetic committed Japanese worker is a persistent device employed in Britain and the USA, though in Japan itself Hanami reports that the public image in the media is of constantly strained, and irrational labour–management relations.[20]

The conceptualization of labour as abstract and concrete may speculatively be thought of as dealt with by senior and local management respectively. It is likely that top management will take the former view, expecting industrial relations and personnel specialists to advise on the labour related factors in locational decisions and to handle problems. In contrast local management will have the task of proving themselves by meeting or exceeding not only production but industrial relations targets (such as wage rises or stoppage levels), with their jobs hence being as vulnerable to restructuring as those of other employees. This division of managerial tasks should not obscure the corporate ability to detect, analyse in its own terms, and respond to specific labour resistance strategies, however, as will be discussed later.

The above description is a caricature which needs to be filled out with an empirical investigation and analysis of how far and in what different ways MNCs conform to the stereotype. Industrial, country of origin and other possible sources of diversity may be considerable, though we would expect them to be variations around a theme, and perhaps to lessen as finance capital becomes the common orchestrator. For the general purposes of this paper, however, the characterization seems valid. The combination of the different universe of capital decisions from labour responses, and the ability of capital to appreciate and manipulate labour's view and specific conditions, constitutes a formidable barrier to effective worker resistance.

This discussion suggests that protestations of the need for international solidarity have little relevance in answering the question: is it likely to be achieved? In what follows, a number of aspects of labour's international experience and response will be considered. The emphasis throughout will be on the capacity of organized labour to cope, not because the trade union movement is seen as the sole source of reaction or the only hope for effective resistance (as will become clear), but because the conventional wisdom suggests that this is so and needs to be confronted as such.

Reactive Conservatism

Trade unions have always been most comfortable fulfilling the task which brought them into existence: defending employees against employer initiatives. All the emphasis of unionism has reflected a Maginot line consciousness – what we have we hold. To venture beyond the line is to do battle in unknown territory, with a sense that the union does not belong. Any advance must be a matter of creeping encroachment, with meticulous consolidation at each step, in accordance with the principle of extending the defences, not striking at the enemy HQ. Quite reasonably, invitations to participate in enemy HQ decisions are seen as an attempt to lure out and ambush key battalions; experience often confirms this suspicion, and reinforces defensive posture. All of this becomes still more comprehensible given the limits on outlook considered in the previous section.

But this stance has a number of serious flaws which have been remarked upon by a variety of critics in recent years. Most importantly, it means the unions always react to management and are never in a position to take the initiative.[21] Their responses to minor management tactics may appear quite successful while their plant remains viable in management's strategy; but the impulse to build international defences is weak and perceived as of marginal importance relative to traditional sources of strength. Confronted by a major restructuring or closure proposals from management, the union strategy is exposed since, particularly in an MNC, it is likely to find its line of defence utterly outflanked. It is too late to build an offensive strategy to divert the enemy, or to seek alliances where others may see short-term benefits from the management plan, or resent lack of earlier support when they were in need in turn. Meanwhile the union reaction to management is likely to be hasty and confused, often retreating still further into the false security of traditional forms of defence.

If the contingencies which dictate reactive positions have been correctly identified, the building of links between existing union organizations is likely to be more a matter of lip-service than real commitment to a new internationalism. There would need to be a major revolution in official union attitudes before a more positive outlook on developments is likely through existing channels on any significant scale. Even if such a revolution were possible, it too would tend to be a reaction to circumstances so dire as to make the chances of success against capital poor.

The Phases of Internationalism

The arguments in the previous section can be augmented by reconsidering the pattern of development of international labour links since World War II, without the interference of evolutionist Messianism. An awareness of the material (experiential) basis for innovations indicates both the extent and limitations of those innovations.

The period of post-war MNC rapid growth, right through to the early 1970s, was also characterized by relatively tight labour markets in the developed economies. Although full employment policies had come under attack and been effectively defeated long before,[22] conditions remained relatively favourable for labour to exert bargaining pressure on national and multi-national capital from a local level. Political accommodation continued in a Keynesian mould, securing the conditions of expanded reproduction for capital and various rights and state policies for labour; this in turn tying labour first and foremost to national coordination and liaison. International links were rudimentary, once the anti fascist unity of 1945 disintegrated into cold war unionism. The TUC and its member unions were slow to recognize the growing threat of MNCs, being encapsulated in a comfortable complacency; it was 1970 before the TUC produced a major policy statement on the issue. None the less, the conditions for advance were favourable, in that in many industries workers had the power to challenge management and make gains, not merely to minimize losses. At the same time, realization of plant level strength, even *vis-á-vis* MNCs, developed only slowly in Britain and elsewhere.

Analyses of the development and impact of the recession vary considerably and we have no intention of entangling ourselves in their complexities here. However, notionally we can view the 1960s as a period of emerging crisis for capital in which expansion none the less continued, while the 1970s, only slowly and in unsteady jerks (such as the oil crisis), began to see the squeeze on growth. By the late 1970s and early 1980s, however, contraction was widespread, and a very much starker set of monetarist, social as well as economic, policies became extant. The employers' efforts to begin restructuring and productivity improvements in the 1970s met a reaction from workers who felt pressured and were able and willing to fight it. The upsurge of militancy of the late 1960s and early 1970s spread right across and beyond western Europe.[23] The conditions for international contacts were extremely good, whether through union channels or between shop steward committees, for each plant could draw on others' experience and benefit by giving and receiving information and promises of support. How far such links went, and how far they became etched in the rank and file worker's outlook, is another matter to which we shall turn in a moment.

Once the recession began to bite, and plant closures began on a significant scale, the need for international solidarity became particularly great. Yet this served chiefly to expose the inadequacies of what had been built, and to make many groups of workers far less willing to act on an international basis than before. Efforts to standardize pay and conditions, and to co-ordinate bargaining to this end, were overshadowed by the threat to plant survival, and this threat seems to have driven local reactions back to their roots, and to an every plant for itself mentality. To strike to save the jobs of workers in a climate where closure seemed inevitable through necessity (as claimed by management) or because no one could force a multinational company to stay open for long, became a most unappealing option.

Particular industries and/or regions have faced secular restructuring in response to technological, market or other variations, which puts them out of step with this broad phasing (fuller discussion would need to consider the pattern in far more detail to explain specific events).[24] While the account we have given remains extremely rough and ready, however, it does seem to make more sense than the orthodox view of the rapid developments in the 1960s and early 1970s, and the stagnation or retreat of the late 1970s and the 1980s so far. It suggests that international solidarity is often economistic in nature and generated largely between organizations with compatible interest, not something welling up from rank and file demands or initiatives. So far from being given ground in which to flourish by the exigencies of the recession, it retreats, since local economic interests no longer appear so mutual.

Combines, Councils and Contacts

The argument thus far suggests that the various standard union based strategies for building countervailing organization to match international capital are likely to be fragile under any conceivable circumstances, and far from strengthening may well fracture precisely when the need is greatest. It remains to confront this prediction with the usual description of a gradual accretion of international labour solidarity, advancing on a ratchet basis in which gains, once made, are securely there to be built upon. Although we have acknowledged that there are important differences between various types of organization based on shop steward or formal union channels, the general points being developed here can be applied more or less equally to existing variants.

In the past, we have dwelt on the Massey-Ferguson, Kilmarnock example at length because it provides a concrete illustration of standard union based strategies, documented in depth.[25] Studies by Warner and Peccei[26] and at far greater length by Northrup and Rowan[27] provide poorly theorised but nonetheless useful confirmation of the problems of developing a coherent multinational bargaining force to counter MNCs. The latter account highlights four causes: management opposition, union reluctance, obstacles arising from variation in laws and procedures, and lack of employee interest. These problems can readily be confirmed and extended from the analysis developed in this paper.

In particular, our previous accounts of the Massey-Ferguson case led us to the following conclusions. Contacts, while they are exhilarating and impressive in some of their manifestations, are merely verbal or paper ties. Of themselves, they are not a resource to challenge the power over capital and jobs of MNCs. Information, similarly, is of little use *per se*. Unless an organization exists to use it, or unless it embarrasses an MNC in some way, it carries little threat. Management can always deny or reformulate figures on its own terms if it is important enough to do so, and unions are left asserting suspicion and little else. Even links for the above purposes do not emerge easily, let alone Rebhan's 'putting together pressure at the industrial base'. Those involved must keep running flat out merely to stand still. The nature of labour organization means that if we can speak of a natural tendency, it is for such links to fade when events are not dramatic (or plant interests conflict within the drama). There is no rising floor, no ratchet which sustains the international movement at some level once reached, ready for a further step onwards. The effects of recession have only served to confirm the fragility of substantial international collaboration. The use of experts – pro-union consultants brought in to do research and resource work for MNC subsidiary workforces – carries its own problems, and these are exacerbated when they are brought in under crisis conditions, as our own experience illustrates.[28] Experts not only tend to be trapped into reacting to management in such circumstances, but may also focus labour's effort more on management's ground of reasoned argument and debate, thus potentially dissipating their only real counter weapon, militant action, and the growth in identity that usually goes with its use. Longer term and two-way relationships have rather better educative and organizational push beyond local levels to date. Suggesting alternatives provides a good example of a practice readily capturable by management. In our analyses of the Massey-Ferguson case we describe how management turned the alternative products banner back on workers in a suitably modified form. We are aware of a similar management strategy in several other corporations, such as International Harvester and Singers (where PA Management Consultants, hired by the unions, were the source of the notion).

Politics, Nationalism and Unions

It was noted earlier that Olle and Schoeller view what unity has been forged between unions in developed countries as directed against the employment of cheap labour in LDCs. It is now generally accepted that MNCs have sought, particularly since the mid-1970s, to create a new international division of labour.[29] This process seeks to exploit the cheapest sources of labour in LDCs, often trying to make them cheaper still by company and government efforts to squash local union organization and suspend hindering legislation protecting workers. While this scarcely constitutes a great benefit for those exploited under appalling conditions in the Philippines, Mexico or Singapore, it does manifest itself to many workers in developed countries as a matter of a battle for investment and jobs between themselves and those who are undercutting them. This is just what MNCs would wish them to see, of course.

However, while Olle and Schoeller's analysis is broadly accurate, it is too narrowly economistic. There is another dimension to the activity of unions in MDCs which is at least as significant, and well documented though rarely discussed. The problem for international labour solidarity is a political one which is most starkly but only partly manifested in the third world itself. It already appears above, in fact, in the problems of links between the CGT and CFDT in France, and probably also between IG Metall in Germany and FLM in Italy.

The issue is nationalism, largely but not exclusively in the form of cold war unionism. In the years following the Second World War[30] an anti-fascist front was established in the international labour movement under the tutelage of the British TUC. The next few years saw the division of this World Federation of Trade Unions (WFTU) into two camps, with unions east and west alike falling largely into line with the political stance of their governments. The TUC led the unions in the capitalist nations to form the ICFTU (1949) (with the cold war emphasis on the 'Free'). Communist Party influenced unions such as the French CGT and the Italian CGIL remained with WFTU, whose HQ was established in Prague, and as a result were frozen out of ICFTU. Despite ICFTU's stand, it failed to be sufficiently anti-communist for the American AFL–CIO, which for long periods has been at odds even with this western confederation. A third body, the World Confederation of Labour, has continued to organize largely Catholic unions, though these unions have been less at odds with ICFTU over time (which is not to say the division is not still important in many countries). Despite the formation of the European TUC in 1973, with the French CFDT and Italian CGIL forming cautious links thereto, the obstacles to cooperation remain severe even without the nationalistic divisions within the ICFTU.

The effect of the conformity of unions to the diplomatic political lines of capitalist (or state socialist) governments is to make them more or less conscious agents of these governments in the third world. If this seems too harsh, consider the following passage from a British Cabinet Paper written in 1959.

> Since it is difficult to accuse unions of serving colonialism, with their aid it should be possible to establish harmonious relations with the new social and political institutions of Africa . . . Trade union help will be needed to check

> irresponsible nationalisation and to maintain control of the key sectors of the economy in the newly created African states.[31]

The only limitation was that British unions would wish to see themselves as building genuine unions. The unfair advantage of the Americans, whose unions had no labourist commitment and would simply execute CIA policy, is bemoaned in the same paper.[32] In Africa, the history of trade unionism is predominantly one of post-colonial societies where each imperialist grouping seeks to promote itself and encourage local unions to follow their line.[33] Inducements of aid, trade union education, and other advantages are held out as persuasion. In countries such as Nigeria the union movement has been split and rendered far less effective against authoritarian governments and foreign capital by this outside interference. The efforts of TUC educators to persuade unions to be non-political and strictly pluralistic in their stance, avoiding any fierce militancy, is a harrowing one to those who believe in international solidarity. Both the struggle for union rights and the political role of the TUC in sponsoring the founding organization of the Labour Party appear to be conveniently forgotten in the effort to deny the Soviet Union or USA political leverage and protect the interests of British company subsidiaries. The battle between ICFTU, AFL–CIO and WFTU influence, with local labour often seeking desperately for independence but hampered by the power of outside forces to corrupt or remove their leadership, is the African reality.

International labour solidarity is even less evident in Latin America.[34] Here the AFL–CIO holds almost exclusive sway, battling to repress 'communism' in all its forms and advance the interests of American MNCs. As the then head of the AFL–CIO, George Meany, put it in a statement to the House of Representatives Committee on Foreign Affairs in 1963, 'You can't dictate to a country . . . unless you control the means of production . . . Whether you control them through ideological methods or control them by brute force, you must control them.'[35]

The AFL–CIO's international department is heavily financed by American corporations, and staffed in many cases by known or suspected CIA agents. The *Organisacion Regional Interamericano de Trabajadores* (ORIT) was set up in 1951, with the support of the AFL and the CIO, which, after their unification in 1955, jointly directed Latin American interventions. The organization receives sizeable sums of money and is said to have gained affiliation from national labour organizations totalling up to 30 million members. It is hard to accept many of these as free or democratic given the countries where they are based and their patron–client relations with American or local authoritarian interests. In 1962 to ORIT was added an education body, American Institute for Free Labour Development (AIFLD), which trains union officials. A large proportion of all officials and active unionists in Latin America have been trained in this institute – 260,000 by the end of 1974.

Several case studies exist of the active collaboration between Americn labour and capital to crush or marginalize independent and troublesome local unions.[36] In one example, Harrod describes how the United Steelworkers of America co-operated with American bauxite companies in Jamaica to freeze out a local, independent union.[37] He quotes another source, which reports that the MNC management valued the Steel workers' 'police function' in support of corporate objectives.[38] In short, the problem of politics and of nationalistic support for capital rather than genuine international class awareness is anything but a side issue. It is as material as the organizational and economistic barriers discussed earlier, and in some ways more difficult to combat, since it is largely subterranean and yet to confront it is to invite opprobrium in influential official union circles.

Calling on the State

If international labour itself is unable to match and contain within a pluralist balance the power of international capital, it was suggested earlier that orthodox theory will turn to the state to redress the balance. There is a cheap and easy way to reject the potency of this option, by invoking analyses of the capitalist state which suggest that governments are either active agents of or at least constrained to operate in accordance with the logic of the survival and prosperity of capital. Since reformist or gradualist revolutionary (if such a thing can exist) postures must rely on the idea that the state can either be persuaded by its own workers to resist foreign capital or can be captured and turned like a machine to serve different interests under the control of different guiding hands, they are as vulnerable as pluralist accounts to arguments that the state is a reflection of economic structures or (less mechanically and more convincingly) that it is itself an internal relation of capitalism, untransformable in isolation.[39] While we may be predisposed to this argument, it seems as useful at least to consider what has been proposed for state action at national and IGO levels without overmuch prejudice, not least in order to avoid reliance on what may appear a priori grounds for scepticism alone.

Worker participation

Within Britain, the labour movement has repeatedly affirmed the magnitude of the MNC threat and called for controls to support the rights of employees facing such powerful employers. While part of the strategy calls for international common action, there have also been demands for national action, altough these rely as a first step in the not inconsiderable task of getting a radical Labour Party government elected. Under the last Labour government, one channel for control was considered to be worker representation in the boardroom. The Bullock Report did address itself to the question of multinationals, and proposed that MNCs should not escape the obligation to allow the representatives of the workforce to sit in the boardroom of the British subsidiary (if it qualified in terms of number of employees), or of a British company with overseas operations (in contrast to Dutch law).[40] It recognized the impossibility of compelling representation outside the British state's jurisdiction, however, and the general tone of the chapter which includes discussion of MNCs is that the best has been made of an impossible task. The 2x + y formula of Bullock was to allow for considerable influence amounting almost to a right of veto for the parent company in appointing the y element of a subsidiary's board in foreign based MNCs. The alternative of treating the subsidiary as an entirely independent operation was rejected on the grounds that it would be inequitable and because it 'would disturb foreign governments and foreign capital, and have a deleterious effect on inward investment'.[41]

Other more obviously problematical factors in the proposals for worker directors in general swamped any debate over the specific issue of MNCs in the aftermath of Bullock, and ended in the effective abandonment of the entire strategy. The White Paper on *Industrial Democracy* already a dead letter before it appeared, devoted only fleeting attention to the question of MNCs proposing once more to treat subsidiaries as the appropriate target, noting the inability to impress change on company headquarters overseas, and limiting itself to the wistful hope that the 'will seek to operate within the spirit of its proposals'.[42]

Proposals for worker participation have also been in the air for well over a decade within the EEC.[43] The fate of these proposals over the years is also instructive. Essentially there are two elements–the Fifth Directive on company law and boardroom structure, and the Eurocompany Statute. The 1972 draft of the Fifth would have required all member countries to harmonize their company law to have, *inter alia*, workers on supervisory boards in line with the then existing Dutch or German arrangements.[44] The draft then sank into periodic discussion by the Council of Industrial Ministers, emerging with promises of a prolonged transition in 1975. In 1980 the proposals were defeated by a right-wing coalition in the newly elected European Parliament led by the British Conservatives. The drafters returned to the drawing board and in 1983 came up with a fresh elaboration which finally removed the compulsory element of boardroom representation, allowing some variants of souped up works' councils or forms of collective agreements as alternatives as well as the Danish single tier arrangement for the board.[45] Despite this dilution into almost an anything goes set of options, the recession has removed any urgency to process the proposals, and they were still officially under consideration by ministerial working parties (with no sign of any priority being given to discussing them) in early 1985.

The Eurocompany Statute proposes a regulation which would become binding on all member countries once passed (unlike a Directive, which requires countries to legislate internally to harmonize law over a subsequent period). The statute would apply to all large companies registered in Europe and operating in more than one EEC country. It dates back even further, to 1970, and in its original form proposed one-third worker representation on a supervisory board, together with a European works council with rights akin to those provided by German law. The potential of these proposals for creating at least regular contacts between employees within a company in different countries is at least worthy of consideration. But the Eurocompany Statute seems to have been buried even deeper than the Fifth Directive, with far less attention being given to it in recent years. As of early 1985, the problem of co-ordinating legislation with arrangements in different member states meant that the working party on the topic had effectively ceased to meet, with little or no discussion for two years.

Planning Agreements

The other main weapon targeted at increasing the democratic rights of labour in national and international undertakings in this period was the planning agreement. Although the Labour government passed legislation designed to encourage the signing of long-term agreements on the development strategy of companies, in the end only one company did so: the Chrysler Corporation, so obliged by the receipt of rescue funds for their British operation from the government. The Agreement was always a nebulous sham of little significance to management and disbelieved by the unions,[46] but it was only finally discredited when Chrysler sold their British operation to Peugeot without bothering to consult on the terms of the agreement or any other of the participation channels much publicized by the enthusiasts for such things in the 1970s. If the planning agreements had any net effect, it was the weakening, not strengthening, of shop floor organization.[47]

The Labour Party and TUC have sought to learn the lessons of the bruising defeats of the 1970s by putting forward a far broader brush strategy in the early 1980s. This has drawn in turn on a variety of expositions from different shades of opinion within the party of the Alternative Economic Strategy. It might be expected that these, particularly on the left of the party, would involve a far more searching appraisal of means to contain and counter the power of MNCs, particularly given the full acknowledgment of the scope of its power noted at the start of this paper. If so, the anticipation is misplaced. The TUC–Labour Party Liaison Committee's proposals published in 1982 genuflect accurately to the threat posed by MNCs to a planning and industrial democracy framework, yet provide no concrete proposals for dealing with this problem or building any form of internationalism at all. Even the Conference of Socialist Economists' London Working Group offers little more. The MNC problem is given a more centre stage billing, and while ITS and ICFTU information gathering is praised it is acknowledged to be patchy and hampered by its covert and piecemeal basis. The answer is pronounced to be Planning Agreements, enforced through the readiness of government to 'mobilise all the sanctions and incentives available', though just what these might be is left unspecified. In addition, 'the trade union movement can be expected to continue to develop its organisation and cooperation at the international level' in which connection the 'growing practical solidarity' in the Commonwealth Trades Union Congress (CTUC) is pronounced and lauded. At the same time nationally based struggles are represented as the main route to countering capital. The entire discussion seems nebulous and naive in the light of the discussion elsewhere in this paper, being matched by the authors' preparedness to turn to workers' control more generally as the universal solvent for dangers of capital's resistance, for corporatism or bureaucracy.

Codes of Conduct

Somewhat more extensive consideration of the means to control MNCs appears to have been given by those bodies, mostly IGOs such as the ILO, OECD, EEC and UN, which have published codes of conduct for agreed acceptance by affiliated nations as a means to regulating MNCs within the bounds of responsible behaviour. These codes all bear a marked resemblance to each other, with near identical proposals and often almost indistinguishable wording. Particular emphasis is placed on information disclosure, consultation and bargaining procedures in these codes. Although some of the codes attempt to detail the kind of information to be included in this process, including investment plans, employment policy, profitability and so on, they inevitably remain somewhat vague in formulation. The ILO, for instance, calls for 'regular consultation on matters of mutual concern' and argues that MNCs 'should provide workers' representatives with information required for meaningful negotiations . . . to enable them to obtain a true and fair view of the performance of the entity'.[48]

More recently, the much debated Vredeling directive of the European Commission has sought to turn such proposals into a statutory form with greater bite to apply throughout the EEC. The proposals raised a storm of protest from MNCs, backed *inter alia* by the British government, although as will be argued below their real impact would almost certainly be negligible. In 1983 a number of modifications were accepted by the Commission as a result of reactions in the European Parliament. Disclosure was restricted to once rather than twice yearly, the requirement that regular information be given on rationalization plans, and on production methods (including work systems), was dropped, and a let out was provided for secret information, i.e. that which would damage the company's interests, to give a few examples of the changes. None the less, the Directive continued to be opposed, particularly by the British government, and so in June 1984 a working group of EEC member nations' Labour Ministers was set up to seek a new approach. The resulting proposals, which had received cautious informal support by early 1985 from most countries, suggested further changes.[49] Firstly, the Directive would cover all companies, not just MNCs, with over 1000 companies. Secondly, a new emphasis on mutual cooperation rather than conflict was proposed to appease the employer lobby. Thirdly, the option of a collectively bargained alternative to legislation is considered (despite which the British government continues to oppose the existence of any Directive on this subject). In effect, these proposals would further weaken the Directive, which in any case would be still more at the mercy of national governments' willingness to implement and police it, while the original specific focus on international operations becomes blurred and faded.

It is hard to see how such codes may significantly influence matters. First of all, the let out clauses may cover almost anything the company wishes to conceal. But the problems only begin here. Who is to judge, and on what basis, whether information provided by MNCs is fair, sufficient, accurate, timely and so forth? If an MNC were adjudged at fault, what redress would there be to impose a fair bargain, stop a closure or rundown, put right an authoritarian stance? The revised Vredeling proposals leave this to the member states to find and apply sanctions. Then there is the still more difficult question of how we are to ascertain the criteria for evaluation of information, or bargaining in good faith. Information itself is far from neutral, as research on disclosure in Britain revealed starkly some time ago,[50] and in some forms it can undermine the resistance of workers by its concealed embodiment and so confirmation of the rationality of capital. This takes us back to the question of competing rationalities raised earlier in this paper, but in a far more specific context. Even if it were possible to penetrate the logic of information provided and invert or neutralize (an improbable process this last) its rationality, there would remain the problem of turning knowledge into the power to change MNC actions. Again the ground is well trodden above.

It seems likely that almost all MNCs, unless they chose an unusually unsophisticated style of industrial relations management, could readily give the appearance of conforming to the conditions laid down in any conceivable code with little effort and scant danger of provoking sanctions.[51] Elsewhere the ability of Massey-Ferguson management to present their actions satisfactorily in the case of the Kilmarnock closure, even though behind the scenes they simply refused to acknowledge contrary union arguments and used a variety of other devices to undermine union opposition to their plans, has been laid out at some length.[52] In short, the prospects for an effective intervention by the state (other than in an unofficial and coercive way well behind the scenes, and usually on a highly nationalistic basis) which will bolster the strength of labour against MNCs are poor to non-existent.

The line of argument developed in this paper leads to an unequivocal prognostication for the future of industrial democracy in the era of the MNC and the drastic restructuring of capital and the division of labour. The outlook seems grim, at least as far as the standard channels for countering the power of the corporations is concerned: the internationalization of the labour movement from its existing bases and the backing of the state. While the outward forms of participation machinery may wax and wane, they too hold out little prospect for the democratic control of management actions.

None the less, in this final section we want at least to raise the possible lacunae of the foregoing, partly in an attempt to be less determinedly gloomy and partly in response to recent debates on the subject.[53] In particular, it may be argued that by reacting to the optimistic orthodoxy which focuses on the extension of the traditional collective bargaining model within the rubric of economistic trade unionism, this paper has harped entirely on the limitations and not at all on the nonetheless enduring potentialities of international labour solidarity.[54] A number of themes may be taken up in this connection.

First, it may be argued that even in terms of trade union outlooks, the analysis presented here is one sided. It ignores the shared interests of workers created by their common subjection to a global system of exploitation, which may surely be reinforced by the pressure for homogenization of labour by MNCs. This contention is rather weaker than it seems, though, since the abstract labour calculus of capital remains consistent with the survival of (and MNC manipulation of) phenomenal or experienced divisions within the workforce – as illustrated by the persistence of sectionalism at any level from the workshop or office upwards. The main modification to this paper's argument which emerges here is probably that it takes a too determinist, too automatic, too absolute form. Perceptions of reality convey both division from those elsewhere, but also unity, and the latter is exhibited by the constant moves to establish or consolidate international links just as the former is demonstrated by their continual capacity to decay or fade. The question of attitudes becomes a more empirical and potentially more variable one than is allowed in much of the paper – though it must be added that our own observations still stress the fragility which has been discussed above.

Secondly, and going beyond the previous point, a far more hopeful perspective may become possible if consideration goes beyond narrow trade union solidarity and consciousness, to allow for political and social awareness which in turn transcends the institutionalized barriers of pluralist industrial relations. It is this which fuels hopes of a new working-class internationalism on the left, or raises the prospect of community and/or women's mobilization rather than the restrictive workerism of most Marxist utopias. It is political consciousnesss which has always been the life blood of internationalism, and which may readily bridge the gaps even of gender, race, or between more and less developed countries. The Lucas example is the most obvious popular illustration of how an attempt to take the initiative from management in fairly limited union terms led logically to a questioning of the entire structure and relations of production. Moreover, the greater visibility of politics in labour relations in LDCs such as Brazil undoubtedly tends to generate a far sharper sensitivity to the political and international nature of struggles with capital. Again, however, it is necessary to issue caveats. For a start we have already seen that politics can be as divisive as it is unifying for international labour. It also may generate politicism, in which the goal of capturing the state becomes the self-appointed task of union and working class party leaders, and the role of local mass resistance is officially marginalized. Politics is a minefield as dangerous as economism. Even the Lucas example cited a moment ago has been re-read by some critics as the political brainchild of a few leaders, divorced from most of their membership and received coolly with partly political suspicion by union leaders, perhaps doing more to emphasize than break down the division amongst labour between head and hand.

A third issue concerns the power attributed to capital in the account above. It may be thought that in emphasizing the dynamic and deliberative quality of MNC power, there has been a tendency to lend it an aura of mysterious omnipotence, able to detect or predict all of labour's responses and effortlessly outmanoeuvre them. In practice, it could be suggested, capital is liable to make or be pushed by labour pressure into committing mistakes, while there are also important contradictions within managerial structures (hierarchical, functional and locational) and between capitals. All of these open up opportunities, spaces for struggle, for labour. This is obviously true, and capital is not without its worries, although we have suggested some ways in which these may be handled in the course of the paper. There remains good reason to keep the capacity for conspiracy by MNCs well to the fore, though, and it also seems to these writers that the gaps which the contradictions or errors of management open up are almost all very limited in their scope for labour, and often very easy for the controllers of the enterprise to block off or eliminate. This should become another matter for empirical investigation, since such disputed interpretations cannot be settled by assertion and a priori theorizing.

While some of the above ground should be ceded to those involved in and experiencing some results from efforts to establish, sustain and service with strategic information the international solidarity of labour in its traditional and broader, more liberating sense, this does not deplete the central purpose of the arguments presented here, which is to call into question the pervasive complacency in other circles concerning the prospects for industrial democracy to be achieved through the internationalization of the evolutionary, pluralistic collective bargaining model, particularly at a time when that model seems singularly unable to cope with born again free market philosophies even at a national level in many countries.

Notes

1. See C. Levinson, *International Trade Unionism* (Allen and Unwin, London, 1972), p. 141.
2. Ibid., p. 110–11.
3. Ibid., p. 141.
4. See C. Levinson, *Industry's Democratic Revolution* (Allen and Unwin, London, 0000), p. 72.
5. The Labour Party, *International Big Business: Labour's Policy on the Multinationals*, (Labour Party, London, 1977).
6. See e.g. Bob Edwards, *Multinational Companies and the Trade Unions*, (Spokesman, Nottingham, 1977), who offers one summary of the predictions. H.V. Perlmutter, 'Super-Giant Firms in the Future', *Wharton Quarterly*, Winter 1968 and others have estimated the likely engulfing of world capitalist production by MNCs, while the control by executives was predicted in the magazine *Fortune*.
7. The classic statement is by J. Servan-Screiber, *The American Challenge*, (Penguin, Harmondsworth, 1969). N. Hood and S. Young, *The Economics of Multinational Enterprise* (Longman, London, 1979) cite figures which suggest that of the 260 largest MNCs in 1973, 126 were of US origin and 105 from the EEC. The US position was in relative decline, though, while by 1977 the UK had lost second place to Japan (Trades Union Congress, *Trade Union Rights in Multinational Companies* (TUC, London, mimeo, 1983).
8. See H. Rose, 'Multinationals in retreat', *Fortune*, August 1977; N. Hood and S. Young, *Multinationals in Retreat: The Scottish Experience* (Edinburgh University Press, Edinburgh, 1982).
9. See J.H. Dunning, *International Production and the Multinational Enterprise* (George Allen and Unwin, London, 1981).
10. TUC, *Trade Union Rights*.
11. Ibid.
12. See H. Ramsay, 'An international participation cycle: variations on a recurring theme', in S. Clegg, G. Dow & P. Boreham (eds), *The State, Class and the Recession* (Croom Helm, London, 1983) pp. 257–317 and H. Ramsay, 'Evolution or cycle? Worker participation in the 1970s and 1980s', in C. Crouch and F. Heller (eds) *International Yearbook of Organisational Democracy and Political Processes*, Wiley, London, 1983), pp. 203–225, for critical assessments of the worker participation model of evoluton to industrial democracy. This paper forms a parallel critical assessment to those.
13. The challenge of monetarism to pluralism is argued in J. Roddick and N. Haworth, 'Labour relations in the new orthodoxy: The Chilean and British cases compared', mimeo, Glasgow 1982; N. Haworth, 'Monetarism and the challenge to industrial relations theory', seminar paper, Dept. of Industrial Relations, University of Strathclyde, 1983.
14. For example, the overall outlook in volumes such as R.J. Flannagan and A.R. Weber, *Bargaining without Boundaries: The Multi-Corporation and International Labour Relations* (Chicago University Press, Chicago, 1974); D. Kujawa (ed.), *International Labor and the Multinational Enterprise* (Praeger, New York, 1975); H. Gunter (ed.), *Transnational Industrial Relations*, Proceedings of a symposium held at Geneva by the International Institute for Labour Studies (Macmillan, London, 1972), or in Levinson's efforts cited earlier, give the flavour.
15. See Trades Union Congress, *Trade Union Studies: Book Two. Trade Unions*

and the Economy (BBC, London, 1976).

16. See D. Coates, 'Labourism and the transition to Socialism', *New Left Review*, no. 129, 1981.

17. See W. Olle and W. Schoeller, 'World market competition and restrictions upon international trade union policies', *Capital and Class*, no. 2, 1977.

18. See D. Sayer, *Marx's Method: Ideology, Science and Critique in Capital* (Harvester, Hassocks, 1979).

19. Ibid.

20. See J. Hanami, *Labor Relations in Japan Today* (John Martin, New York, 1980.

21. See N. Haworth, 'The trade union response to multinationals', in S. Maxwell (ed.), *Scotland, Multinationals and the Third World* (Mainstream Publishing, Edinburgh, 1982).

22. See N. Apple, 'The historical foundations of class struggle in late capitalist democracies', in S. Clegg, G. Dow and P. Boreham (eds), *State Class and the Recession* (Croom Helm, London, 1983).

23. See C. Crouch and A. Pizzorno (eds), *The Resurgence of Class Conflict in Western Europe*, 2 vols, (Macmillan, London, 1978).

24. The growth of combines in BMC or Ford in the 1950s and 1960s illustrate one process responsive to the particular conditions of the car industry. Similarly the early restructuring of production planned by Dunlop-Pirelli resulted in one of the best known shop steward level initiatives, though the general climate of labour optimism probably did much to promote the combine. On the other hand, technological change in electronics has outpaced the union movement almost entirely, it would seem, in some areas such as the displacement of clockwork by digital watches.

25. See C. Baldry, N. Haworth, S. Henderson and H. Ramsay, 'Fighting Multinational Power: Possibilities, limitations and contradictions', *Capital and Class*, nos 20 and 21, 1983; C. Baldry *et al.*, Multinational closure and the boundaries of resistance–implications of the case of Massey-Ferguson, Kilmarnock', *Industrial Relations Journal*, vol.15, no. 4, 1984.

26. See M. Warner and R. Peccei, 'Management decentralization and worker participation in a multinational company context', in B. Wilpert *et al.* (eds), *Workers' Participation in an Internationalized Economy* (Ohio Comparative Administration Research Institute Kent State University, Kent, 1978), pp. 66–83.

27. H.R. Northrup and R.L. Rowan, *Multinational Collective Bargaining Attempts: The Record, the Cases and the Prospects* (Industrial Research Unit, The Wharton School, University of Pennsylvania, Philadelphia, 1979).

28. See especially the afternote to Baldry *et al.*, *Fighting Multinational Power.*

29. See F. Froebel *et al.*, *The New International Division of Labour* (Cambridge University Press, Cambridge, 1980).

30. For an account of the split outlined here, see B. Bye and M. Doyle, *European Trade Union Co-operation*, Workers in Europe Study booklets in European Trade Unionism no. 1 (WEA, London, 1976); G. Busch, *The Political Role of International Trades Unions* (Macmillan, London, 1983); D. Thomson and R. Larson, *Where Were You, Brother? An Account of Trade Union Imperialism* (War on Want, London, 1978).

31. Quoted in A. and N. Seidman, *US Multinationals in Southern Africa* (Tanzania Publishing House, Dar Es Salaam, 1977).

32. Ibid.

33. On Africa see Thomson and Larson, *Where were you, Brother?*; Busch, *The*

Political Role of International Trade Unions; I. Davies, *African Trades Unions* (London, Penguin, 1966).

34. On Latin America see Thomson and Larson, *Where were you, Brother?*; Busch, *The Political Role of International Trades Unions*; H. Spalding, *Organised Labor in Latin America* (Harper Row, New York, 1977).

35. Quoted in Thomson and Larson, *Where were you, Brother?*

36. Spalding, *Organised Labour in Latin America*, summarizes several of these.

37. See J. Harrod, 'Multinational corporations, trade unions and industrial relations: A case study of Jamaica', in Gunter (ed.), *Transnational Industrial Relations*.

38. Ibid., p. 188.

39. See P.R.D. Corrigan, H. Ramsay and D. Sayer, 'The State as a Relation of Production' in Corrigan (ed.), *Capitalism, State Formation and Marxist Theory* (Quartet, London, 1980).

40. See Bullock Report, *Report of the Committee of Inquiry on Industrial Democracy* (under the Chairmanship of Lord Bullock), (HMSO, London, 1977).

41. Ibid., p. 147.

42. See *Industrial Democracy*, Cmnd 7231, (HMSO, London, 1978).

43. See Commission on Industrial Relations, *Worker Participation and Collective Bargaining in Europe* (HMSO, London, 1974); J. Elliot, *Conflict or Co-operation? The Growth of Industrial Democracy* (Kogan Page, London 1984); *European Industrial Relations Review*, Oct, 1983; J. Pipkorn, 'Employee participation in the European Community: Progress and Pitfalls' in B. Wilpert and A. Sorge (eds), *International Yearbook of Organisational Democracy*, vol. II (Wiley, London, 1984).

44. The German model at that time involved one-third of the supervisory board being workers or their representatives; the Dutch system involved co-option of members of the supervisory board subject to workers' representatives' (or shareholder) veto.

45. The Danish system involves worker representatives in a minority on a single board, but in a non-executive role; the board appoints a management committee to carry out its instructions, and determines the powers exercised by that committee, which consists of professional managers.

46. See C. Lockyer, L. Baddon and T. Oliver, *Management, Participation and the Search for Control. A Forty-year Case Study*, paper for BSA Conference on Work, Employment and Unemployment, Bradford, April 1984.

47. Ibid.

48. See International Labour Office, *Multinational Enterprises annd Social Policy* (ILO, Geneva, 1973).

49. See *European Industrial Relations Review*, February 1985, pp. 10–14.

50. M. Gold, H. Levie and R. Moore, *The Shop Stewards' Guide to the Use of Company Information* (Spokesman, Nottingham, 1979).

51. An analysis by B. McSweeney shows that in Britain the provisions for disclosure under the Employment Protection Act have been almost totally unenforcible and ineffectual. Of 11 appeals to the Central Arbitration Committee between 1978 and 1983, where unions were seeking financial information, not one claim was judged 'well founded' (*Guardian*, 26 October 1983). See also H. Gospel and P. Willman, 'The Role of Codes in Labour Relations: The case of disclosure', *Industrial Relations Journal* vol. 14, no. 4, 1983.

52. See Baldry *et al.*, *Fighting Multinational Power*.

53. In particular, these arise from two sets of discussions in the Netherlands,

since most of the above was drafted, one of these (at the ISS in The Hague) being organized specifically to discuss N. Haworth and H. Ramsay, *Grasping the Nettle: Problems in the Theory of Labour Internationalism*, mimeo, 1983, and a partially responding set of recommendations from Peter Waterman (ed.), *For a New Labour Internationalism*. This discussion also brought us into contact with parallel but more positive work by M. Press, 'The Lost Vision: Trade unions and Internationalism', in ibid. (Press, incidentally, offers a telling critique of Northrup and Rowan's work cited earlier in this paper).

54. Waterman, *For a New Labour Internationalism.*

13. In Defence of Nationalism as a Trade Union Perspective

Manfred Bienefeld

> This paradox was topped by another. While laissez-faire economy was the product of deliberate state action, subsequent restrictions on laissez-faire started in a spontaneous way. Laissez-faire was planned; planning was not.
>
> Liberal writers . . . offer an account of the double movement . . . but put an entirely different interpretation on it. While in our view the concept of a self-regulating market was utopian, and its progress was stopped by the realistic self-protection of society, in their view all protectionism was a mistake due to impatience, greed, and shortsightedness, but for which the market would have resolved its difficulties. The question as to which of these two views is correct is perhaps the most important problem of recent social history.
> (Karl Polanyi, 1944).[1]

Current international developments constitute a fundamental threat to those forced to sell their labour in the world's labour markets. With capital markets becoming more international and with their existing institutional defences under attack, all working people face the prospect of being cast in into the maelstrom of an effectively unregulated global labour market that will long be characterized by a large labour surplus. Such a market tends to destroy any systematic connection between the average product and the wage, so that their historically high productivity will not protect today's workers from a potentially unlimited erosion of their living and working conditions. Moreover, the alternative availability of subsistence incomes, which provides the only effective lower limit to this pressure in large parts of the world, is being steadily eroded by the continuous alienation and commercialization of land. If present trends continue, only those protected by skill, technological or institutional barriers will escape the threat of destitution, and their numbers will fall, in so far as technical change redefines and simplifies skills, as the growing international mobility of capital equalizes access to technology and the key institutions – i.e. the trade unions and the nation state – are undermined, both ideologically and economically.

This paper is concerned with the institutional barriers that still impede the establishment of an unregulated, global labour market. It contends that the emergence of such a market would undermine those delicate social, political and economic balances which are essential if the market economy is to combine long-term economic efficiency with social harmony and liberal democracy. Since the nation state constitutes the main framework within which those balances are established and maintained, the ability to formulate social and economic policy from a national perspective is of vital importance. Moreover, as representatives of society's working people, the trade unions must take a lead in creating the enlightened nationalism that this implies.

This argument conflicts directly with the view that nationalism is the main threat to peace and prosperity and that it must be rejected in all its manifestations, in favour of an international perspective in economics, in politics and in trade union matters. This view is strongly represented on both the left and the right of the political spectrum, but it is neither theoretically nor historically defensible.

The trade unions must take a lead in the struggle for an enlightened nationalism; but they will not succeed unless other sections of the community also recognize its vital importance. Unfortunately, such support has become less likely because international economic imbalances have already been allowed to undermine the social and political cohesion of many nations, reducing the chance of such a response and leaving only two inter-related and disastrous alternatives: an aggressive and militaristic nationalism that seeks to resolve internal contradictions by manipulating the international economy to its advantage; or the continued, dogmatic adherence to a free trade internationalism that insists on treating the social and political consequences of a volatile, unbalanced and highly politicized international market simply as the necessary consequence of policies whose alleged long-term benefits justify their enforcement at any cost. These alternatives are related in that the latter, pursued dogmatically enough, will inevitably lead to the former.

Despite the disastrous implications of these alternatives, large sections of capital have historically preferred them to an enlightened nationalism in times of crisis, because, at such times, the latter imposes restrictions on the mobility of capital and forces it to operate within an incomes policy framework at a time when this necessarily implies a lower rate of return. Until recently, those who represent the interests of financial capital have clung to the free trade dogma in the belief that present global contradictions could be resolved and their interests fully protected so long as the international institutions were sufficiently resolute in insisting that national governments implement whatever cuts in the social costs of production were required. However, it is now becoming clear that there are political limits to this adjustment process and that these make a substantial liquidation of existing assets unavoidable. As a result, some powerful national concentrations of capital have already become much more aggressive in solving their problem at the expense of other national capitals. This process has led to war in the past and could do so again. All that is required is a massive programme of militarization and a public acceptance that a war may be necessary and that such a war can be won. Ominously, both of these requirements are well on the way to being satisfied.

In espousing an enlightened nationalism that would allow current tensions to be defused gradually, the trade unions and their allies will have the greatest difficulty in distinguishing themselves from these militaristic and predatory forms of nationalism. They must, however, accept that challenge, since no alternative can now lead to a socially, politically or economically defensible outcome.

The Theoretical Case Against Nationalism

The most general case against nationalism argues that all political units, bound together by some politically defined common interest, are dangerous and divisive: dangerous because of the virtually infinite malleability of such concepts as the national interest; divisive because they breed antagonism and enmity between political units and inevitably generate a destructive tension between the individual and society. These fears, amply reinforced by the apparent historical association between nationalism, war and depression, have led many to espouse a form of internationalism which implies that these dangers can be avoided simply by dispensing with such political units.

This form of internationalism receives strong support both from those who shape western public opinion and from a wide range of radicals and idealists. Both groups believe that it would foster peace and prosperity to remove artificial and dangerous divisions between people and allow the world's resources to be better utilized. Unfortunately, the beguiling beauty of this argument is merely a mirage of utopia. Indeed, under present conditions, this approach could actually increase the risk of depression and war, because it would leave social and political conditions, everywhere, at the mercy of volatile and effectively unregulated global market forces.

In effect, an internationalism that consists primarily of a rejection of all things national is merely a euphemism for global laissez-faire, so long as there are no effective global political mechanisms to contain, channel and stabilize the global market. Moreover, so long as that remains true, global laissez-faire is not likely to be desirable or efficient, since even the most ardent defender of the market must acknowledge that there are simply too many important issues that cannot be left to it, including: the setting of long-term social and political priorities; the creation of money and credit; determination of the social conditions to be tolerated in the search for efficiency; the fixing of the social discount rate, at which current consumption is to be sacrificed for, possible, future growth; the management of the conflict over income and asset distribution; the allocation of the costs and benefits of exogenous disturbances; and the evaluation and acceptance of the risks associated with various policy options.

In practice, such issues can only be resolved within the context of some political unit capable of inducing people to take account of their common interest as members of that unit. Those who would dispense with such political units must either indicate an alternative arena to which they would displace this political process, or deny the value or significance of such units altogether. Moreover, since the scale of the political unit that constitutes a nation state is not fixed, the general argument against the nation state must be based on a denial of their value.

In right-wing circles, the value of such political units is often denied on the grounds that capitalism works best when it is free from the interference and distortion of arbitrary and normative social, political and moral pressures. Even so, many who hold this view also extol the virtues of a strong state because they view it as an administrative and not a political unit; a view that derives from their basic premise that national interests are best served, along with individual, group and global interests, by allowing the global market to function freely. From this perspective, it is no longer the state's function to define the national interest, but merely to protect this interest, thus defined, against distortion from the narrow, sectional and indefensible political demands of local interest groups. The state thus becomes the executive agency of international capital and there is no longer any reason why it should not be closely and explicitly controlled by the international financial institutions.[2] From this perspective the possibility of a global state appears very real; but it is a state with the politics removed.

Left-wing internationalists are equally enthusiastic in their denunciation of nationalism, sometimes referring to it as one of 'the twentieth-century's deepest scourges'. A recent contribution follows the thought to its logical conclusion and denounces all 'social organisation to combat scarcity [i.e. our political units] as self-defeating and divisive'.[3] Unfortunately, this confuses the promised land of perfect, harmonious freedom with the totally fragmented and individualized society ultimately implied by the logic of capital. This confusion stems from a marriage of socialism and individualism, a union that inevitably yields some form of anarchism and that provides no plausible account of how the interests of the world's countless individuals are to be reconciled.

Within the Marxist tradition the conflict between individual freedom and the requirements of social harmony and welfare has remained largely unresolved. It has been argued that, after the revolution, the problem disappears because a classless proletariat will sustain that unity which was forged in its revolutionary struggle against capital. Unfortunately this is not a solution, but an evasion of the problem. Although the contradictions of capitalism could unite the proletariat in a revolutionary struggle, it is contrary to any defensible version of Marxist analysis to suggest that this revolution would mean the end of contradiction, the end of class struggle and the end of history.

Meanwhile, as regards the time before the revolution, Marxists can argue that capitalism already reconciles the individual interests of all workers in so far as their common interest in revolution transcends any differences between them. Moreover, given the international logic of capital, it has often been argued that only an international proletarian revolution could alter the long-term consequences of capitalist accumulation for the working classes.

More than a century later, Marx's prescient focus on the essentially global logic of capital is more pertinent than ever. However, the political judgment as to the best means by which effective political control could be exercised over capital must be derived from the experience of the past and from a judgment regarding the political possibilities of the present. This judgement may well differ from that of Marx: partly because the international revolution has proven rather more elusive than had been envisaged; partly because, under present circumstances, the proletarian struggle could not be organized directly on a global scale, without smaller constituent political units; and partly because, in some national economies, it has proven possible to impose extensive social and political controls over the process of capitalist accumulation and to ensure that, over extended periods, the market has delivered the goods, bringing relative material affluence, greatly improved working conditions and liberal democracy to the great majority of workers in those countries. In this sense it could be said that history has demonstrated the importance of the nation state as the one arena within which it has occasionally been possible to harness and channel the explosive but volatile and potentially destructive power of the market. Even though these national situations have been unstable and have often been undermined by the activities of international capital, the absence of a plausible global alternative implies that national controls over capital must remain the most important immediate object of struggle.

Whether such controls can go beyond those associated with post-war social democracy towards some form of democratic socialism, is a matter for political struggle and judgment, and not for *a priori* assertion. In any case, the distinction must ultimately be a fine one given that, even in a democratic socialist system, private enterprise should undoubtedly have a considerable role to play. Certainly, it is analytically and politically unhelpful to treat the struggle for greater political control over capital as a discrete either/or choice between capitalism and socialism. The real world is not so simple nor the choices so clear. Moreover, what is feasible and desirable in this regard can be defined only in relation to the historically specific circumstances of a particular society, as emerges very clearly in the conclusions of a recent Marxist analysis of the US economy.

> With the threat of a highly authoritarian form of capitalism looming, and in the context of current political realities, the best that progressive forces in the United States may be able to hope and work for in the 1980s is a program based on the

> social-democratic strategy for economic revitalization. Perhaps some elements of democratic socialism may be attainable in the next few decades
>
> Historical experience suggests that the power and the privileges of the capitalist class have been gradually circumscribed from one capitalist institutional structure to the next. Each successive crisis has made possible institutional innovations that previously seemed infeasible and that opened up new opportunities for non-capitalist classes. From a more equitable sharing of income and wealth under a social-democratic form of capitalism, the logic of history would suggest a move toward a more equitable sharing of economic decision-making under an embryonic form of democratic socialism.[4]

From an entirely different perspective, the fundamental importance of the contribution made by the nation state to the relative success and longevity of the capitalist economy was also eloquently acknowledged by Sir John Hicks, when he wrote,

> If there were no nations – if everyone could go where he liked, was just as acceptable wherever he went, and was willing to go wherever he was wanted – the absorption of the whole human race in the ranks of the developed would be relatively simple. Even so, it would take time; and it may well be that even in the century, or century and a half, that may be held to have elapsed since the beginning of the process we were considering, not enough time has been allowed. We have seen that until the absorption was completed, or within sight of completion, there would – on this assumption – be no general rise in real wages; so even to the liberal and to the internationally minded, it is perhaps not so very agreeable an assumption after all.[5]

As travel, transport and communication become cheaper, investors more mobile and technologies less skill dependent, the situation assumed by Hicks has become a genuine possibility. However, trade unions or governments tempted to espouse an unrestrained internationalism under these circumstances must carefully consider his conclusions and decide whether the market is now likely to complete that global absorption of labour within a reasonable time. They should also remember that Hicks' conclusions also apply in reverse, so that if such a global economy were established before labour had been fully absorbed, the market would tend to reverse the wage increases achieved in the meantime.

This not only raises the question of how any one generation of trade union representatives or of government leaders could obtain a legitimate mandate to sacrifice the material interests of their own (and following) generations, for a pay-off that is neither certain, nor foreseeable; it also raises the more fundamental question of whether, on such assumptions, the market economy would be socially desirable, politically viable or economically efficient in any meaningful sense.

Had there been no increase in real wages in the first 150 years after the industrial revolution, as in Hicks' hypothetical case, would the market economy have survived? Would it have been associated with the simultaneous emergence of liberal democracy? Would it have been morally or politically defensible as a system to serve the general interest of societies? The answers to each of these questions must be a resounding no!

But the question needs to be further sharpened. Not only would wages not have risen, they could hardly have been kept from falling, under conditions where the market held absolute sway and where labour was persistently in excess supply. After all, the cost of reproduction of labour is no clearly defined magnitude that can be relied upon to provide a socially acceptable or even a subsistence floor to the wage structure. To believe that it does is to mistake a long-run tendency for a short-term certainty and to forget Polanyi's reminder that a pure, unrestricted market for labour 'would result in the demolition of society'.[6] Those who today press their ideological faith, or their self-interest, to the point where they lose sight of this historic fact do so at their peril. Unfortunately, in doing so they imperil all of us in turn.

To conclude this section, the genuine difficulties and dangers that are associated with the management of political units such as the nation state cannot be evaded by wishful thinking about self-regulating markets or international proletarian solidarity. Those who argue that those political dangers are excessive and espouse internationalism as an antidote to the scourge of nationalism are simply pushing people more directly and more firmly into the clutches of an international market that is not constrained by any effective political process. For those who have an unwarranted faith in the unregulated market, this choice is at least consistent; for those who have no such faith, it is merely an indication of naive and fuzzy thinking.

Nationalism and the Lessons of History

Given the above theoretical perspectives, it is hardly surprising that nationalism is often treated as the root of all evil. Time and again it is held responsible for some wonderful model's failure to fulfil its hypothetical promise, simply because the social and political tensions of the real world find organized expression through the state. Those who would do away with the state are merely seeking an escape from the problems of that real world.

The current liberal consensus argues that depression and war are fostered by economic nationalism and points to the clear and close historical association between strident nationalism and economic and military conflict to support its claim. However, although the association is undeniable, the direction of causation will frequently be in the opposite direction since excessive liberalization will undermine existing social and political controls over capital, foster social and economic instability, inhibit productive investment and eventually foster aggressive forms of nationalism.

The current consensus persists because it suits those who have material reasons for arguing that liberalization is the all-purpose remedy for the world's economic problems. They cling to this view despite the fact that historical studies of past depressions have generally emphasized the dangers of excessive instability, as illustrated by Arthur Lewis' classic study of the 1930s depression, which concluded that

> The analysis of bilateralism leads to the same conclusion as the analysis of currency experience and of tariff policy, namely, that the importance of obstacles to the free flow of trade will depend on the degree of stability in the economic system. If international trade is stable it will be freed of obstacles, and will correspondingly be increased.[7]

Such insights have often been obscured by the fact that classical and neo-classical trade theory 'has always turned primarily on adaptability of resources' and especially on the 'adaptability of the internal economy to external changes'.[8] Moreover, the desirability of adapting to changes in the international economy has generally been too directly derived from the theory of comparative advantage, with little regard for the problems raised when its conclusions are applied to a dynamic, imperfect world, far from full employment equilibrium. Problems concerned with the adjustment path, its delays or its costs have generally been repressed, exorcised by the view that all obstacles to instantaneous, perfect flexibility constitute mere imperfections that should be identified, denounced and, wherever possible, removed by people with the necessary political will. Such a frame of reference excludes the possibility that the adjustment in question may not be feasible or even desirable and this danger increases in a depression when economics often becomes a zero-sum game and mutuality of interests yields to direct conflicts of interest.

This is why it was in 1933 that Keynes came to recognize the limitations of the theory of free trade as a guide to practical policy. Writing that, as he

> was brought up, like most Englishmen to respect Free Trade not only as an economic doctrine which a rational and instructed person could not doubt . . . (he) . . . regarded departures from it as being at the same time an imbecility and an outrage.

However, now he was 'not content with it as a working political theory', if only because it did not appear to be the most obvious way of ensuring peace. In fact he concluded

> it does not now seem obvious that a great concentration of national effort on the capture of foreign trade, that the penetration of a country's economic structure by the resources and the influence of foreign capitalists, that a close dependence of our own economic life on the fluctuating economic policies of foreign countries, are safeguards and assurances of international peace. It is easier, in the light of experience and foresight, to argue quite the contrary. The protection of a country's existing foreign interests, the capture of new markets, the progress of economic imperialism – these are a scarcely avoidable part of a scheme of

> things which aims at the maximum of international specialisation and at the maximum geographical diffusion of capital wherever its seat of ownership.[9]

In other words, under such conditions, it becomes potentially disastrous to continue to liberalize the international economy. Indeed, in the absence of any reasonable prospect of global full employment, this would amount to a foolhardy and dangerous policy which would increase social and political instability. Writing of the 1930s Polanyi summarized the inability of the liberal perspective to come to grips with reality in terms that are reminiscent of the present.

> Liberal economists, as usual, saw only a romantic aberration induced by unsound economic doctrines, where in reality towering political events were awakening even the simplest minds to the irrelevance of economic considerations in the face of the approaching dissolution of the international system. Geneva continued its futile attempts to convince the peoples that they were hoarding against imaginary perils, and that if only all acted in unison free trade could be restored and would benefit all . . . The nation-state was deemed a parochial prejudice by A.J. Toynbee, sovereignty a ridiculous illusion by Ludwig von Mises.
>
> To expect that a community would remain indifferent to the scourge of unemployment, to the shifting of industries and occupations and to the moral and psychological torture accompanying them, merely because economic effects, in the long run, might be negligible, was to assume an absurdity.[10]

Nationalism and Current Global Economic Problems

Since the mid 1970s, the world economy has once again entered a prolonged phase of slow growth, high unemployment and unstable prices, interest rates and exchange rates; once again, an increase in social and economic conflict has been the inevitable result. Within many national economies, social and political strains have reached dangerous levels and there is little sign that economic pressures are about to ease. Once again, predatory and aggressive national economic policies have been accompanied by an unprecedented build up of armaments, which has itself increased economic imbalances in the global economy as much as it has increased political tension. The result is an explosive situation that will not be easily defused.

At the heart of the current crisis lies an excessive, accumulated mass of capital assets, whose demand for a high real rate of return is, under present circumstances, not compatible with the simultaneous need to generate sufficient effective consumer demand to maintain production and to stimulate additional productive investment. The result has been a prolonged and intensifying struggle over income shares that has pitted specific capitals against each other and capital in general against all other income and welfare recipients.

In theory such an excessive creation of capital assets should have been eliminated, as it first appeared, by a fall in the rate of profit or interest (and hence of savings) and/or an increase in bankruptcy or default. However, in practice, there is much scope for evading, delaying or diverting these judgments of the market, especially as capital markets become more internationalized and hence less subject to effective regulation. Capital gains from property, commodities or currencies can ease the pressure for a time, though only at the cost of higher prices or the periodic bursting of speculative bubbles; a rapid expansion of consumer credit or of government deficits can bring temporary relief, though only by mortgaging future incomes; the running of export surpluses can improve the investment climate in particular economies, without the need to create additional internal demand, though only at the expense of other economies forced to accept the consequent deficits; and investment can be diverted to newly industrializing countries, although this may provide only a temporary respite, if the terms of the transfers force the recipients to sell the bulk of the resulting output in the same metropolitan markets where sluggish demand projections were already inhibiting investment.

All of these mechanisms have now been widely used for more than a decade. Indeed, since 1979, the US has pushed them to the limit, conjuring a cynical and irresponsible boom out of foreign capital inflows and an astronomical government deficit, both stimulated by historically unprecedented and economically unsupportable interest rates. On the ephemeral froth of this false prosperity the Reaganite political revival has been launched, complete with the greatest peacetime build up of armaments in history.

By now the world's underlying economic imbalances have reached desperate proportions; but it seems these are to be encouraged to widen even further. Thus, when the developing world is staggering under an unsupportable debt burden, the Seoul financial summit of 1985 has produced a scheme to allow the developing world to take on yet more debt at the same high rates of interest.[11] This is a sign of desperation; but it no more constitutes a solution than the monetarism that has been so fashionable over the past six years. In fact, while monetarism was sold to people as the painful, but necessary, radical cure for deep seated problems, it has actually sharply intensified those problems as rentier capital has enriched itself beyond its wildest dreams on the basis of historically unprecedented interest rates suddenly and quite arbitrarily levied on the mountain of assets that had been generated and off-loaded on to many countries at deceptively low, even negative, interest rates during the 1970s. The largest confidence trick in history might be an apt description. Apart from being regressive and immoral, these policies were particularly damaging to the world economy as a whole because they further restricted real production, so that the task of feeding this insatiable and ever expanding army of rentiers became ever more unmanageable.

By now, many nations, including most of those of Africa and Latin America, are so tightly shackled by their accumulated debts that their future is inexorably mortgaged, leaving no scope, even on optimistic assumptions, for any significant expansion of domestic demand by the end of the century. Even in most of the industrial countries, those same forces are rapidly eroding the conditions on which their social harmony and consensus politics were based. The resulting pressures will not be defused until effective social control is re-asserted over the creation, mobility and remuneration of international financial assets. So long as their creation remains unregulated, the demands made on other income earners will continue to be effectively unlimited. Any reductions accepted by other income earners will merely allow a few more assets to survive at current interest rates, allow a few additional assets to be created, or provide a few asset holders with windfall capital gains.

Under these conditions, no trade union can hope to secure the interests of its members simply by seeking the best deal available, given the facts of economic life thus defined; and this would remain true, even if it were to engage in this economistic struggle at an international level. Trade unions would always remain the prisoners of a volatile and manipulated international market. Instead, the unions must take a lead in securing a return to full employment within their national economies and to do that they need to secure an increased degree of political control over capital. This would create new possibilities, as Keynes pointed out when he argued, in 1933, that the then existing institutions were

> incompatible with that degree of material well-being to which our technical advancement entitles us, unless the rate of profit falls to a much lower figure than is likely to come about by natural forces working . . . under a system by which the rate of interest finds, under the operation of normal financial forces, a uniform level throughout the world.[12]

Keynes did not mean that capital should not move across boundaries, but that its movement should occur only within the context of coherent, nationally defined and socially acceptable economic policies; such policies constitute the enlightened nationalism of this paper and their objectives would include: the achievement of a mutually acceptable compromise between profit, rent and wages; the maintenance of effective control over the creation and international movement of capital assets; and the maintenance of a sufficiently high level of employment to ensure that the operation of the market remained simultaneously conducive to economic efficiency, social harmony and political stability.

Enlightened Nationalism and International Rules

The precise specification of such enlightened nationalist policies cannot be attempted in this brief paper. However, they would necessarily involve some controls over the international movement of capital, goods and people since, without such controls, the facts of economic life, as defined in an unregulated and politically irresponsible international market, would become the only effective arbiters of social, moral or political acceptability. Unfortunately, today, countries are systematically forced to abandon the means by which they might protect themselves from these judgments of the international economy and those who resist often find themselves the victims of economic reprisals or even of active subversion.

This means that life is a choice of evils, particularly for the trade unions of the developing world. Acceptance of the facts of economic life promises a bleak future; challenging them ensures a difficult and painful struggle, with only a modest prosperity as the best possible outcome in most cases. Moreover, in the struggle for an enlightened nationalism, they can expect little support from those with a chance of entering the ranks of the transnational bourgeoisie as managers, academics, military officers, bureaucrats or even trade union officials. Only occasionally, when depression threatens or repression spills over into their secluded lives, do such groups become widely receptive to appeals for a nationalist alternative and even then their commitment to it may be short lived.

Under these circumstances it would be arrogant and foolish to assert that all trade unionists should commit themselves fully to the struggle for a nationalist alternative. The uncertainties, the dangers and the difficulties of such a project are so great that the choice can only be made by those directly involved in a particular struggle. Even so, over the next decade, unless there is a radical change of policy at the centre, a growing number of people will embark on this road, despite its dangers and uncertainties, simply because the social and political pressures transmitted by the international economy will prove unbearable.

The urgent need for a change of policy at the centre gives working people and their allies in the industrialized world a special responsibility, since it is their governments that currently enforce the global logic of capital in such an unfair, aggressive and uncompromising way. The first task of those in the industrialized world is not, therefore, to prescribe blueprints for others to follow, but to induce their own governments to resolve present international contradictions in ways that will defuse current tensions by curbing the power of the rentier.

Unfortunately, many separate national struggles are not likely to yield a desirable collective outcome, in the absence of international rules and institutions that discourage the pursuit of destabilizing, aggressive national economic policies and encourage full employment and consensus politics. At present these institutions exert their influence in the opposite direction, forcing economies to liberalize and to deflate, even in response to balance of payments deficits that have resulted from the wilful manipulation of interest rates at the centre. The burden has fallen primarily on working people who have paid the usurers with the food of their children. Moreover, most of those workers in the industrial countries who may still believe that they are immune from these pressures will soon discover their mistake, unless their trade unions can secure a return to full employment policies in their economies.

Unfortunately the unions are confronted by the widespread argument that progressive workers should support the continued liberalization of the international economy as that is said to be the only policy compatible with the interests of workers in the developing world. All other strategies, and especially those based on nationalist perspectives, are decried as selfish attempts to protect the richer workers of the industrial countries at the expense of those in the developing world. This claim is derived from the free trade argument and is merely another way of saying that the market yields universal benefits and that any interference with it reduces total welfare and provides benefits to some only at the expense of others. While this explains why those with faith in the market should accept this view, it does not explain why it is shared by many radicals.

Trade unions that accept this view have three options open to them. They may attempt to organize international unions on a sectoral (petroleum workers) or a firm (Ford workers) basis, seeking a share of the oligopoly rents available in certain privileged parts of the market; they may seek such rents on a national basis, by fighting for protection but without seeking increased influence over capital; or, finally, they may simply agree to compete with workers abroad, by accepting (or even promoting) pay restraint or the intensification of work, again without seeking to gain influence over investment or capital flows. Unfortunately, under present disequilibrium conditions, none of these three strategies could do more than protect particular groups for some unspecified period and, ironically, even this could be achieved only at the expense of other groups. In every case labour effectively remains at the mercy of an unregulated market in a surplus labour world. Moreover, in supporting economic liberalization in the current world, where capital's claims can be multiplied virtually at will, the workers of the industrialized world both undermine their own position *and* intensify the plight of those in the developing world who are now suffering so badly at the hands of those applying the global logic of the market so ruthlessly.

The truth is that the only policy that would serve the interests of workers in both industrial and developing countries is an enlightened nationalist policy combining lower interest rates, reflation, protection and full employment and that, on this more secure basis, financed Marshall Aid type capital flows from the industrial to the developed countries. In fact, the real tragedy of the last decade has been the destruction of the post-war consensus that capitalism is only viable and desirable when it operates at something approaching full employment and that that is neither the automatic, nor even the normal outcome of an unregulated market. In a world where unemployment is again endemic, it is timely to recall Keynes' judgment that

> the decadent international but individualistic capitalism, in the hand of which we find ourselves after the war, is not a success. It is not intelligent, it is not beautiful, it is not just, it is not virtuous – and it doesn't deliver the goods.[13]

It must be emphasized that the return to full employment is not primarily a technical or economic question but a political one and that, unless it can be achieved through an enlightened nationalism, established with trade union support, it will probably appear in its fascist form when social and political instability has so undermined production and investment that growing sections of capital join in the clamour for a return to stability. Kalecki described this process in the 1940s.

> One of the important functions of fascism, as typified by the Nazi system, was to remove the capitalist objection to full employment.
>
> The dislike of government spending, whether on public investment or consumption, is overcome by concentrating government expenditure on armaments.
>
> The fascist system starts from the overcoming of unemployment, develops into an 'armament economy' of scarcity and ends inevitably in war.[14]

Such solutions will be averted only if it proves possible to introduce and enforce new international rules that support and encourage enlightened nationalist policies – and here the unions must also play an active role. The sorts of rules required should build on the foundations laid by the Bretton Woods system, which served the world so well until the 1970s.

Because that system was primarily intended to avert the problems of the 1930s it encouraged multilateralism, currency convertibility and international trade, but not without establishing clear safeguards against the potentially destructive and irrational instability of an unregulated international market. In other words, the so-called rigidities of this system did not reflect ignorance of the hypothetical benefits associated with resource flexibility but an awareness of the fact that, in the real world, the costs of instability can easily destroy those hypothetical gains.[15]

The experience of the last twenty years suggests that these fears were well founded, especially when we consider that the rigid Bretton Woods system was associated with the greatest economic boom in history; a boom that was built on a dangerously fragmented and unstable post-war world and that was not primarily a consequence of reconstruction, as shown by the very different experience after World War One. Moreover, the foundations of this boom were laid in the first fifteen years after the war, when the European economies began their recovery, protected by a range of national controls on international trade and capital flows that far exceeded those allowed under Bretton Woods.[16] In fact, once full convertibility of the world's major currencies had been established and capital and trade flows began to be substantially liberalized in the latter half of the 1960s, it was not long before the strains on the system grew unmanageable, so that by 1971 it had effectively broken down. Some argue that the system failed because its excessive rigidity prevented it from responding to economic changes in the real world; this view was largely responsible for the misguided attempt to combat increasing instability by further dismantling the system's controls for the sake of greater flexibility. In fact, this merely made the problem worse because it allowed a rising flood of short-term capital to distort those economic parameters that might have identified the genuine need for structural adjustment in certain economies; as instability grew this was taken to justify yet more liberalization. Under these circumstances, it may not be incorrect to say that the system proved too rigid, but it would be far more sensible to say that the flexibility required of it was excessive. In Professor Crockett's words,

> With the benefit of hindsight it is not difficult to see the contradictions in the Bretton Woods system. A fixed exchange system could not operate *where there was a large volume of mobile capital ready to flow in response to expectations of exchange rate change.*
>
> *In the end the system was brought down by overwhelming speculative flows,* (emphasis added) prompted by a basic disequilibrium in the balance of payments position of major countries.[17]

The demise of Bretton Woods represented a major victory for an unregulated global capitalism and a defeat for the earlier, successful capitalism of sovereign nations. That defeat needs to be reversed. The economic sovereignty of nations must be strengthened within a set of international rules and institutions that strike a sustainable balance between stability and flexibility; and that encourage adjustment to real economic change, while containing volatile short-term capital flows, managing the creation of international liquidity and mitigating the effects of sudden, unforeseen and exogenous changes in the conditions of international production. This is a tall order; but there is no other way forward and if the trade unions and their allies do not join the struggle for such an alternative, then it will not be realized.

Getting from Here to There

The scale of present global contradictions is now so great that it will be very difficult for them to be defused gradually. Since any solution must involve the imposition of some controls over capital, any move in that direction will be punished severely by the very capital flows that have to be contained, as the French experience under Mitterrand has shown. In addition, an attempt to implement a solution along the lines proposed in this paper could have serious short-term consequences for others ensnared in the present web of contradictions, so that one country's attempt to return to full employment through policies that included increased protection and capital controls would face the threat of retaliation even though these policies might eventually enlarge its import market. Such threats of retaliation are today reinforced by the sanctions of the International Monetary Fund and this has tended to make current global imbalances self-perpetuating by blocking the only policies that could begin to resolve present problems. In fact, as the need for change has become more urgent, the threat of retaliation has also escalated.

Even so, a beginning must be made. Current conflicts of interest can only begin to be resolved once the world's main capital markets are brought under effective control, returns to capital are brought into an incomes policy framework and the present global stock of financial assets is substantially reduced. So long as these issues remain unresolved, the unacceptable face of capitalism will rule and will eventually destroy peace, stability and prosperity, as the present unregulated competitive struggle allows rentier capital to continue to gain at the expense of productive capital, to everyone's ultimate detriment.

While the task of regaining such control will be difficult, it is not impossible, even within the capitalist world. Thus Japan has been able to maintain full employment through the current crisis, at least in part because it has maintained a sufficient degree of control over its capital markets to allow interest rates to remain stable, to sustain a relatively high level of investment and to allocate these resources with the long time horizons needed to capture vital dynamic economies. Moreover, although the Japanese trade surplus has been a major problem for its industrial trading partners, its experience also shows clearly that relatively nationalist policies are not always contrary to the interests of the developing world, since Japan's imports from these sources have increased rapidly and steadily under this regime. Indeed, it is noteworthy that most of the developing countries that have weathered the debt crisis reasonably well to date are closely linked to this stable and dynamic economy.

The general conclusion suggested by this discussion is that a sufficient degree of social and political control must now be re-established over capital to allow a return to full employment within national economies. Once established and consolidated in a sufficient number of countries, the resulting increase in economic growth and political stability in the advanced economies could then become the basis for a more mutually beneficial pattern of trade and capital flow because it would reduce instability and the conflicts of interest that are fuelled by the existence and the threat of unemployment. Although at first growth in the less developed countries might be somewhat lower than it was in the best years of the 1960s and 1970s, it would be steadier and less volatile and it should allow a steadily increasing number of countries to bring their markets to function under conditions of labour scarcity, at which point they would begin to encourage income diffusion, technical change and improving social conditions. While trade would grow in such a world, it would not be the central point around which all other parameters were adjusted. Moreover, structural change would be easier to achieve and more permanent, hence providing a more secure basis for those building up new areas of production that are complementary to those in the industrialized economies.

Within each economy growth would depend more heavily on domestic savings, although in the developing world this would be supplemented by whatever volume of concessional capital flows could be generated. These would allow the developing countries to orient their growth more to their domestic markets, thereby inducing trade but reducing the scope for conflict, because an accumulating debt burden would not force them into exporting at any cost. Such policies would steadily improve the position of workers and trade unions both across space and time. All other strategies constitute diversions that are doomed to failure under present conditions.

In the final analysis, the nation state constitutes the political and social context within which economic life is organized and, while the market has an important role to play within such units, it must not be allowed to dominate them. Moreover, it is important to emphasize that this need not always refer to the existing nation states, immutably handed down through history. As regions are drawn together culturally and economically, the possibility of federations to form new nations will arise. Indeed if the European Community could now make that transition, this would represent a major advance if it allowed a larger unified market to be effectively controlled by a single, consensus based political process. Whether, in the very long run, such developments could lead to a unified, global political process, capable of controlling a unified global market cannot be known; that this is a remote possibility with no current practical significance cannot be doubted.

In the meantime, the trade union struggle must focus on the national, or regional level, and must aim at more effective political control of capital and the market at that level. Success in this endeavour, in some of the larger industrial countries, could transform the pressures bearing down on the developing countries. It is also possible that this could happen only in the context of more cohesive regional blocs strong enough to implement such controls and to resist the inevitable external opposition.[18] With specific reference to Europe, this possibility was recently described by Michel Aglietta.

> Only a fracturing into regions, combined with a system of inter-regional monetary relations managed by the states of the dominant poles could give European capitalism the necessary freedom to pioneer a new model of growth. Yet it is highly doubtful that the capitalist parties themselves could undertake this stupendous project; what might be imaginable instead would be an original synthesis of social democracy and decentralised, contractual planning that transformed the very content of growth . . . But – needless to say – the obstacles to this project are immense.[19]

This is the primary task to which the trade union movement must address itself. It will not succeed on its own, but neither will the struggle succeed without its active support. Moreover, if the achievement of these objectives poses many problems, the price of failure is also very high; and especially so for the trade unions, whose position around the world will be steadily eroded if they do not help to realize such an alternative. In that case, they will survive either as vestigial employee associations, organizing those workers still able to exploit some transient advantage in the labour market; or they will find themselves called up as the storm troopers of some fascist regime protecting the freedom of its capital.

The final irony is that today's new technology undoubtedly creates the possibility of major advances in the leisure and the wealth enjoyed by all working people; but it will deliver these only if competitive forces are channelled and controlled to positive purpose. Those who put their faith in the anarchy of the uncontrolled market have been proven wrong before.

Notes

1. Polanyi, *Origins of our Time: The Great Transformation* (Gollancz, London, 1945).

2. This view is repeatedly expressed in international agency documents which simply exclude the possibility that the global rationality on which their advice and procedures are based could conflict with the national interest of those whom they are advising. This is so in spite of the fact that they often acknowledge, in passing, that their advice assumes that national development objectives have been previously determined in some unspecified way. The issue was brought out very clearly in the World Bank's recent reviews of the problems of Sub-Saharan Africa, the latest of which was the 'Please Report' (IBRD, 1984).

3. R. Aronson 'Historical Materialism, Answer to Marxism's Crisis', *New Left Review*, no. 152, 1985.

4. Weisskopf, T. "The Current Economic Crisis in Historical Perspective", *Socialist Review*, Vol 11/No. 3, May–June 1981.

5. J. Hicks, *A Theory of Economic History* (Clarendon Press, Oxford, 1969).

6. Polanyi, *The Great Transformation*, p. 73.

7. A.W. Lewis, *Economic Survey 1919–1939* (Allen and Unwin, 1949, London).

8. J.H. Williams, 'International Trade Theory and Policy—Some Current Issues', *American Economic Review, Papers and Proceedings*, 1951, XLI, 2, 1951.

9. J.M. Keynes, 'National Self-Sufficiency', *New Statesman*, 8 and 15 July 1933.

10. Polanyi, *The Great Transformation*, p. 189.

11. These proposals, also referred to as the Baker 8 and 9 Initiative, were widely reported in the *Guardian* on 8 and 9 October 1985 and again on 28 and 29 October 1985. The *Financial Times* described them in two articles on 12 October. In essence they amounted to proposals to put pressure on the commercial banks to increase their lending to the high debt middle income countries, at unchanged interest rates. However, the question of government guarantees was left open so that the banks have proved rather reluctant. The idea of a $5 billion concessional fund for the least developed countries, which might actually have had some positive impact, was not

accepted at Seoul.

12. J.M. Keynes, 'National Self-Sufficiency', p. 65.

13. Ibid.

14. M. Kalecki, 'Political Aspects of Full Employment', in E.K. Hunt and J.G. Schwartz (eds) *A Critique of Economic Theory*, (Penguin, Middlesex, 1972).

15. The main source of this alleged rigidity derived from the system's espousal of fixed exchange rates, which were to be altered only by agreement and only in the face of genuine structural imbalances. In addition the system allowed a limited range of capital controls and provided for sanctions to be imposed on countries that did not keep their balance of payments in approximate balance. Unfortuntely the sanctions on the deficit countries were strong and effective; while those on the surplus countries were weak and ineffective. The best dicussion of the issues involved in the establishment of the system is to be found in R.N. Gardner, *Sterling-Dollar Diplomacy in Current Perspective* University Press, New York 1980.

16. A.S. Milward, *The Reconstruction of Western Europe: 1945–1951* (Methuen, 1984).

17. A. Crockett, *International Money: Issues and Analysis* (Thomas Nelson, Sunbury-on-Thames 1977).

18. M.A. Bienefeld, 'The International Context for National Development Strategies: Constraints and Opportunities in a Changing World', in M.A. Bienefeld and E.M. Godfrey (eds), *The Struggle for Development* (Wiley, Chichester, 1982).

19. M. Aglietta, 'World Capitalism in the Eighties', *New Left Review*, no. 36 1982.

14. Needed: A New Communications Model for a New Working-Class Internationalism

Peter Waterman

The purpose of this paper is to examine both the extent and the variety of the communications media whose dramatic expansion has accompanied the rebirth of working-class militancy and working-class internationalism in recent years. The new forms and contents will be contrasted with the traditional ones. An attempt will be made to consider the emerging pattern more generally and theoretically and to consider problems and suggest strategies.[1]

The paper is largely descriptive and classificatory. Given the absence of even *lists* of organizations and publications concerned with international labour studies/education/action, such a sketch of the field should itself provide both information and a stimulus to further work. It may also indicate major communications gaps and suggest areas for cooperation.

The paper is, however, more than an inventory. Even the more descriptive parts are intended to be informed by democratic, socialist and internationalist attitudes. Given, indeed, the limited length of the paper, such attitudes may come out more strongly than the information they are intended to convey. The piece, therefore, presents a clear political critique and policy proposal.

Once again, however, I feel the necessity to go further, and not simply in order to provide the theoretical underpinnings for my political position. The problem is that the very principles of a new working-class internationalism or of the alternative media are unclear. This is because there is little if any theoretical writing on these subjects.[2] And this can mean that we remain prisoners of old theories or models (often unconscious or absorbed via the mass media), trying to break out of the prison but without having appropriate tools for the job. I have therefore sought for relevant literature on working-class internationalism and alternative media and will consider to what extent this provides us with new tools for the new task.

The exploratory nature of the paper means that no systematic methodology is used. Space limitations also prevent a comprehensive treatment of the media or media sources listed. Examples are taken sometimes from personal research or experience (thus particularly from India, Nigeria, Western Europe, and international communism or social reformism).[3] If there is a stress on the International Confederation of Free

Trade Unions this is because of its power and influence in both capitalist core and periphery, its claim to be free and democratic, and its comparative sensitivity to pressures from below and outside. And if there is a stress on English-language literature this is because – for better or worse – it remains the major language for the new internationalism.

Traditional Media

This section attempts to survey the major different types of traditional media that interested activists (in the non-communist world) have access to for information and ideas on the foreign national or international labour movements.

Source and Nature

National and international media: Labour news must not only pass the criteria for newsworthiness quasi-universal in the bourgeois press. It is also subject to systematic anti-labour bias, to a hostile interpretative framework, to handling with delegitimizing vocabulary, and to stress on its activities primarily in terms of disruption and negation. This has been convincingly demonstrated in the work of the Glasgow University Media Group and others.[4] It might be thought that the mass media would be less partisan in their handling of international than national labour news. This is not so. If the image the international mass media provide of third world nation states is 'partial at best and patently false at worst', then we can hardly expect it to do better by the world's workers.[5] An analysis of foreign news topics covered by the three main American news agencies in the 1970s showed the following percentages devoted to labour: Western Europe 3%, Middle East 0%, Asia 0.9%, Latin America 0%, Africa 0%. By way of contrast, crime and terror got respectively 13%, 11%, 3%, 26%, 6%.[6] This refers to quantity, not orientation or quality. Even if, however, the BBC World Service or *Time* do give a comparatively detailed, objective and sympathetic account of – say – Solidarnosc in Poland, we obviously cannot depend on them to do so for cases that do not confirm their worldview and/or commercial criteria, to handle even this case in a manner stressing collective worker capacity nor to organize and mobilize workers internationally for solidarity. For such purposes the working-class movement evidently requires other media.

The International Labour Organisation (ILO): This is a major source of information and ideas amongst trade union professionals. Its publication and education activities ensure that these reach rank and file activists too. It is, however, in no sense an international labour organization. Class compromise and classless social development are built into the very structure of this tripartite inter governmental organization. Like most inter-state bodies, it is financed, staffed and politically dominated by the most powerful capitalist states. Although ILO decisions, norms and publications may reflect the outcome of class struggles, these reflections are so mediated and formalized as to be deprived of much consciousness raising or liberating effect. In international labour matters it is a major source of legalistic, technocratic, managerial and developmentalist attitudes.

The international trade union organizations: Here we must concentrate on the major producers of information, the communist controlled World Federation of Trade Unions (WFTU) and the reformist International Confederation of Free Trade Unions (ICFTU). To these there must, however, be added the business–unionist American Federation of Labour–Congress of Industrial Organizations (AFL–CIO). Whether in, out, or again in the ICFTU, this has long operated its own international union agencies and is a major international source of ideas and information. Whilst there are significant differences in origin, membership, ideology and structure, certain generalizations about these bodies and their publications are possible. They tend to reflect or reproduce inter-state or inter-bloc relations, so that even where the ICFTU has dropped its crusading free worldism this has been largely to adopt the attitudes of an international non-governmental development agency. (According to a Scandinavian document in my possession the ICFTU is dependent on state development funding for 42% of its total income). The internationals tend to encourage factionalism within their world countries by seeking loyal members, and such member organizations exercise a virtual veto on criticism of their own nation state. It follows from the above that their publications tend to respond to new waves of worker protest (Poland, South Africa, Brazil, Philippines) in a selective and partisan fashion. In India both the Emergency (1975–7) and the 15-month strike of over 200,000 textile workers (1981–3) were ignored by most if not all the publications of all the trade union internationals.

National union and socialist publications: The amount, type and interpretation of international labour news in these will, of course, be coloured by the nature of the organizations behind them, their interest in the working class internationally, and their international allegiances. In the 1960s and 1970s the Nigerian communists produced, successively, two professional and attractive periodicals, the newspaper *Advance* and the magazine *New Horizon*. Most of their foreign news was dependent upon the inter-national communist movement and that on the communist countries on state news agencies or local embassy propaganda handouts. *New Horizon* even reproduced whole sections of the international communist publication, *World Marxist Review*. It would be reasonable to assume that it was receiving a financial subsidy for this, covering all or part of the total publication costs. *Indian Worker*, the weekly of the government supported

Indian National Trade Union Congress (INTUC) is largely dependent for foreign reports on the orientation and information of the ILO and the ICFTU. The occasional neutral or friendly reference to some communist state's unions only reflects INTUC's endorsement of Indian diplomacy. *Marxism Today* is the attractive and non-sectarian monthly of the British Communist Party. It publishes original and controversial articles on British labour and the labour movement and has indicated its independence of Moscow by its lengthy and generally sympathetic analyses of Solidarnosc. In the three-year period 1980–83, however, whilst it carried 20–25 features on foreign *politics* (of which five or ten mentioned workers or unions), it had but two concentrating on *unions* abroad (France, Poland) and none on the third world or on the international restructuring of labour or on the international working-class movement generally.

International socialist publications: Such publications as *World Marxist Review* (Moscow-line communist), *Socialist Affairs* (social-democratic Socialist International) and *International Viewpoint* (Trotskyist Fourth International) have the international labour and socialist movement as their stock in trade. Given the absence of any Trotskyist government or state, we could expect a Trotskyist publication to be the most internationalist and to be the most open to new movements that question the institutionalized socialism of the others. So it is, and the 40 issues published in 1982–3 show an impressive international spread, attention to grassroots worker protest, specific treatment of the world economic crisis and the international (or inter-*European*) workers' movement, and consideration of such new social movements as those of women, for human rights and against nuclear war. *International Viewpoint* may have been the only such publication to give prominence (several articles) to the Bombay strike. The limitations of this publication (and by implication of similar ones) would seem to be that it represents, above all, a specific socialist ideology and organization, and therefore has a tendency to exaggerate the role of its supporters; the distinct ideological/organizational orientation means a similarly high ideological profile, encouraging the reader to believe or identify rather than make his/her own analysis on the basis of less processed information or conflicting alternative interpretations; whilst the long historical existence gives such bodies experience and authority, they tend to either respond negatively or defensively to new ideas or movements that fundamentally question them.

General Characteristics of the Traditional International Labour Media

Dependence on capital or state: Here we mean direct economic or political dependence, in whole or part. The ILO is the most obvious case of state dependence. The WFTU has never published anything unacceptable to the communist states and is dependent for all its income on state controlled unions.[7] I have pointed out that the ICFTU is heavily dependent on state funding, (even if its *membership* fees come from reformist unions in western liberal democracies that are not so subordinated). In India, *Indian Worker* accepts advertisements not only from state enterprises but also from at least one of India's largest monopolies – and multinationals – the Tata group. The international operations of the AFL–CIO were earlier financed by US multinationals, as well as being used and sometimes controlled by the Central Intelligence Agency. They are currently dependent upon state funding.

Subordination to capital or state: Here we refer to ideological and political subordination even where financial or structural political dependence cannot be demonstrated and may not even exist. (We include *statism* – an acceptance of the state in terms of its own claims to be representative and have legitimacy and authority.) The clearest case for such an optional subordination is of reformist unions in industrialized liberal capitalist societies. It is not because the ICFTU is *paid by* the TNCs that it exports the notion that these can have a positive impact on developing countries. Nor is it because its *leading members* are state controlled that it believes in 'strengthening the capacities of host governments in developing countries' to maximize this positive impact.[8] It is because the ICFTU and its leading member organizations still believe that the state in both core and peripheral capitalist countries *can* serve these societies. Thus, after the state approved closure of the Ford plant in Amsterdam, a Dutch union leader still declared that the authorities 'are mainly there to protect the weaker members of society'.[9] Subordination to the state also has its revolutionary form, as when western communists failed to support workers and unions being repressed during the Emergency in India. This was presumably because the *regime* was supposed to be of such an anti-imperialist, non-aligned, or national-democratic character as to justify its repression of opposition. Subordination to bourgeois liberal *ideology* (assuming the neutrality of the press and the value of good industrial relations) is revealed in the very terms of this complaint by a union leader during a strike in the UK.

> I am sick and tired of press and TV reports based on information which is wrong and false . . . The organs of publicity do not contribute to better relations in industry . . . [They] damaged the name of the union and made things worse for us.[10]

Politicism: This is the general tendency of traditional socialists and unionists to privilege struggle carried out by the leadership of national unions or political parties with the aim of influencing the state or taking over state power. It is a characteristic shared by the social-democratic and communist traditions, however much they differ in other ways. It is evidently related to the previous characteristic, even where such socialists as Trotskyists are opposed to all *existing* states. Associated with a privileging of the national political party or union form goes an unavoidable devaluation of everyday mass resistance and protest which, as Robin Cohen has pointed out for worker protest in Africa, are often covert in form.[11] Equally associated with such politicism is either a generalized elitism (of the professional politicians or union leaders) or the vanguardism specific to Leninist parties claiming to bring class consciousness to the masses. There is also an inevitable sectarianism, since each claim to leadership of the working class by a political party implies a condemnation of the claims of others. It is politicism that explains the concentration of *Marxism Today* on foreign 'politics' (i.e. national level struggles over the state) rather than working-class struggle even in its conventional sense. And, whilst we must not ignore the local roots of sectarianism and factionalism amongst workers, we are forced to recognize the way the traditional international union and socialist tendencies have brought ideological divisions to third world workers that have no relationship to everyday worker needs and capacities.

Hierarchical structures on a world scale: The structures of the traditional international communications media for workers reproduce those of the international media more generally. This means: control in the hands of an elite, professional or political, whether appointed or elected; vertical flow of communication from base to peak to base (an A-shaped flow); following from the above, a flow of information *up* and of ideology or interpretation *down*; iv) the inevitable manipulation of data at any political or bureaucratic level up or down the hierarchy. A graphic description of this structure in relation to the Ford Amsterdam close down is given by Cartier.[12]

Domination by the printed word and 'world' languages: If the 'medium is the message', what are we to make of the fact that even *national* forms of supposedly worker-oriented information are inaccessible to illiterate or semi-literate workers–or even to literate workers who cannot read a 'world' language? If the medium is *Indian Worker*, then the message would seem to be that only union officers literate in English should concern themselves with international (or, for that matter, national) union issues. This is not a problem exclusive to INTUC or India; it is a general problem in international labour communication. But this problem represents a political orientation or choice. At an earlier historical period the international socialist movement (particularly the communist tendency between the world wars) stimulated worker photography or worker film movements. There was also a worker Esperanto movement concerned with overcoming the national language obstacle to international worker communication. These activities seem to have been wiped out by capitalist consumerism or communist state media control after World War II. They had a pallid post-war echo in the international film festivals sponsored by first the WFTU and then the ICFTU. These were discontinued presumably because both tendencies were primarily concerned with influencing and controlling labour *leaderships*, not with mobilizing the masses.

Absence of debate: Here the labour-oriented international media are *worse* than many of their bourgeois competitors, which liberal tradition requires to provide space for, or reports on, important controversies or policy conflicts. There is no place for this in the magazines of the trade union internationals, the ILO (except on more technical issues), or the Trotskyist *International Viewpoint.* In part this could be seen as a structural problem of international organizations based on official national representatives. But it also reveals a certain attitude: that the formal position taken is authoritative, and that formal official positions are more important than the processes that lead to them. Crucial information is thus concealed from view, and the capacity and power to discuss is reserved for top officials with privileged access. This is true even for the 'free' ICFTU. There is nothing in any of its publications from which we can learn of the debate which must have taken place concerning the re-entry of the AFL–CIO in 1981–2. (Nor is this revealed in the press of its affiliates. I know of it only from confidential documents of the British TUC and the earlier mentioned Scandinavian document, which reveals concern about ICFTU dependence on the AFL–CIO for over one-quarter of its general funds). The effect on readers must be to discourage critical thought and action and encourage faith and subordination.

New Media

Sources

Geographically-oriented solidarity groups: Solidarity groups with specific foreign countries or regions have long been a feature of industrialized capitalist democracies. Since World War II anti-imperialist groups identifying with national liberation struggles or with post-independence struggles against imperialism have been the most common. Increasingly these have been paying attention to worker movements and stressing connections between worker (and other mass) struggles in such countries and within the core capitalist ones. Examples include: Japan's Pacific–Asia Resource Centre, the North American Congress on Latin America, Holland's *Comite Indonesie.* To these we can add the organizations or publications in solidarity with people in communist countries, some of which have from the beginning had a special interest in workers and worker protest. Examples include *Solidarite avec Solidarite* and *Labour Focus on Eastern Europe.*[13]

General worker, community or union service centres: Whilst nationally focused labour research centres have also long existed in core capitalist countries, the notion of the multi-faceted local or national resource centre as a major focus of democratic or socialist intellectual activity seems to have developed in the 1970s, alongside growing shop-floor protest and disillusion with traditional forms of organization. Examples include the Community Workshops in the UK, KOR (Workers' Defence Committee) in Poland and the Association *Trabajo y Cultura* (Work and Culture Association) in Lima, Peru. Some such are themselves internationally oriented, others are linked with bodies concerned with providing international services on or for a particular region, e.g. Australia–Asia Worker Links, Asian Worker Solidarity Links.[14] Yet others are concerned with the world more generally e.g. the International Labour Research and Information Group in South Africa.

Specialized worker service groups: Alongside, or as a development from, the above we find specialized worker service groups with an international orientation. These may be concerned with a particular problem, such as the multinationals, e.g. the Transnationals Information Exchange in Amsterdam[15], or IBASE, a Brazilian body additionally concerned with the relations between Brazilian MNC workers and other popular classes and categories locally.[16] They may be concerned with a particular industry, such as sugar or electrical/electronics, covered respectively by GATT-Fly in Canada[17] and SOBE in the Netherlands. They may even be concerned with a specific company, SOBE having a special interest in Philips.[18] They may, finally, be concerned with a particular type of worker, as with women wage earners, e.g. Women Working Worldwide, in the UK.

Democratic single issue movements: Organizations concerned with peace, consumer issues, the environment, human rights and women's liberation have increasingly been paying specific attention to workers and unions internationally. The clearest case is Amnesty, which has a union officer at its international office and which carries out active work with the unions in at least North America, the Netherlands and the UK. National and international women's resource centres have also been paying specific attention to women wage workers, e.g. ISIS Women's International Resource and Documentation Centre in Rome/Geneva.[19] The US consumer movement provided the basis for the first news magazine devoted to MNCs, *Multinational Monitor*, which inevitably deals with worker issues.[20]

Radical christian groups: Whilst many independent socialists or radicalized party socialists may be found amongst the categories above or below, it is uncommon to find them active as members of a particular party or tendency. And whilst christians may be contributing as individuals, they have also been doing so within specific international or national churches or christian organizations. Such an interest descends in part from the nineteenth-century tradition of urban missions, and the post-World War II worker priest movement; but they evidently find their major stimulus in the theology of liberation that developed in Latin America in the 1960s and 1970s. Amongst those who have been active on international worker issues or information we can identify the World Council of Churches Programme on Transnational Corporations in Geneva, the church supported Asian Cultural Forum on Development in Bangkok which has assisted Asian Workers Solidarity Links,[21] and the Christian Centre for Labour Concerns in Bangalore, India.

Radicalized academics: Again, many academics and professionals will be found in the above groups; but others may not be politically engaged and yet provide significant contributions to new information and ideas about workers internationally. In any case it is essential to identify the base that the universities have provided for the new international labour studies that has been developing over the last decade or so.[22] Universities, or university based groups, have provided the base for collective research projects. The Labour in Development, Subordination and Resistance project of AKUT in Sweden represented a distinct shift from a dependency focus to a labour focus.[23] The Centre of Developing Area Studies at McGill, Montreal, provides the base for the journal *LABOUR, Capital and Society*, with a specific focus on third world labour. And the Conference of Socialist Economists, a British association of socialist social scientists, publishes *Capital and Class*, a policy oriented journal which has given particular attention to foreign and international labour issues. The Social Science Programme of the Catholic University in Peru has long been the base of labour oriented research on workers and unions. In South Africa we find similar activities based in the Sociology Department of Witwatersrand University and the Economic History and Sociology Departments of the University of Cape Town.[24]

The radicalization of traditional labour and socialist organizations: The old/new opposition not only demonstrates itself between organizations or tendencies but also within them – at least in some cases. Thus we must recognize the extent to which the traditional sources have been not only responding to the new problems, new needs and the challenge of the new organizations, but even taking the initiative. Thus the Swedish labour movement has for some years had its own international magazine, *AIC Bulletin*, and the major Dutch trade union centre, the FNV, usually devotes one page of its fortnightly paper to international articles (which do not always support its official foreign allies). The ICFTU's *Free Labour World* has itself paid attention to the need for computerized data to aid international union struggles.[25] The WFTU's *World Trade Union Movement* has recently published some fresh and relevant analyses of the MNCs and the current world crisis, though it is significant that these are written by an American ex-union leader, based in New York. Trotskyist organizations have responded not only to the dramatic Bombay textile strike, as reported above, but also to the more problematic (for orthodox

Marxists) movements of rural labourers, outcastes and tribals.[26] *Nueva Sociedad*, produced in Caracas with the help of the West German social-democratic Friedrich Ebert Stiftung, seems to have provided a significant platform for Latin American discussion on the new social movements there. The World Confederation of Labour, whose European base is as much amongst christian aid agencies and intellectuals as in the small and shrinking christian unions, has none the less produced a number of documents dealing in an original and critical manner with the MNCs, the state, human rights and other general world social problems, (although whether in Latin America it practises what it preaches from Europe is a matter vigorously debated in both continents).

Forms

Academic journals: These are evidently a traditional form, often less accessible to motivated labour activists than the ILO's *International Labour Review*. However, we must note the increasing development of radical and socialist area studies journals, e.g. *Review of African Politial Economy, Journal of Contemporary Asia, Latin American Perspectives, Critique* (communist studies). We should also note the increased attention these are tending to pay to workers and unions, particularly the *Journal of Contemporary Asia.* We must also be aware of the development of strategy relevant socialist journals, such as the earlier mentioned *Capital and Class.* The gradual transformation of *Manpower and Unemployment Research in Africa* into *LABOUR, Capital and Society* was both the effect of and a contribution to the radicalization of third world labour studies in the 1970s.

Newsletters: These seem to be the favoured vehicle for the new international labour communication. Newsletters in this area tend to be low cost productions, to have a low ideological profile, to have a consequently high information content, to give much information on information. Some are confined to news items or solidarity appeals, e.g. *Global Electronics, Labour Communication* (Centre for Progress of Peoples, Hong Kong). Others, whilst equally aimed at or accessible to rank and file activists, are clearly intended to provide orientation as well as information, e.g. *Brazil Labour Report, Rodo Joho.* The *Newsletter of International Labour Studies*, which attempts to serve as a 'network of networks' for the new working-class internationalism and the new international labour studies, is explicitly aimed at worker support groups internationally, hoping thus to reach both research-minded activists and action-oriented researchers.

Popular researched reports and periodicals: These represent an attempt to overcome the serious popular opposition by combining systematic research or investigative journalism with an attractive illustrated product aimed at non-specialist audiences. One of the pioneers here is *NACLA Report on the Americas*, one of whose early products was on class struggle and trade unions in Argentina. *Multinational Monitor* adopts a news magazine style. *TIE Report* has been progressively popularizing both headlining and illustration. It has clearly been able to draw on the experience of Counter Information Services, which pioneered the worker-oriented popular report in the UK and has produced outstanding reports on multinationals and on labour in South Africa. TIE has used one of its issues for a CIS-type popular report on labour relations and unions in industrialized capitalist countries that is also the first of its kind.[27] The women's movement has also been a front runner here, with a Hong Kong produced, cartoon-style book on exploitation and struggle in the Asian electronics industry.[28]

Teaching aids: Whilst some of the above are evidently also suitable for teaching (and even research) purposes, others are meant *primarily* for this purpose. One of the longest lived is *IBON Facts and Figures* from the Philippines, which, whilst concentrating on that country, comes out in English as well as Philipino (and other local languages) and is thus available for international worker education.[29] IBON also produces other teaching aids.

Book publication, distribution and library services: At national level these are developing in a number of countries, Britain being perhaps one of the best served. But the systematic coverage of and supply to labour movements internationally is only beginning. In the UK, Zed Press has started an International Labour Studies book series;[30] the Trade Union Book Service includes a short international list in its occasional catalogues.[31]

Audiovisuals: At national level there are increasing numbers of unions or worker support groups both using and producing audio-visuals. Given the variety of the media (photo, film, cassette, slide, video, poster, mural, cartoon – to mention some of the two dimensional forms), and the variety of sources (commercial or state film and TV, 'alternative' producers, union or worker-oriented producers, workers themselves), it is best to give just a few examples most of which are unrecorded. In India a 1983 conference on mine labour and struggles in tribal areas ended with the showing of the British film, *Tin Mountain*, on the Siglo Veinte tin mine in Bolivia; in South Africa, the International Labour Research and Information Group reports showings of films by Polish director Andrzej Wajda,[32] and a tape-slide on Nigerian workers.[33] The Pakistan Institute of Labour Education and Research reports video shows for workers on the impact of the World Bank and western education in the third world; in 1983 an Argentinian exile produced a short video film on workers in Sao Paulo, Brazil, specifically aimed at European audiences; both British and Dutch groups supporting shop-floor internationalism have been taking video cameras on union study trips or to worker conferences; and *New Technology: Whose Progress?*, a 16mm and video production made on a shoestring in London, has 50 copies circulating in the UK and has been translated into 15 languages.[34]

Bibliographical, documentation and research services: The first serial bibliography on third world labour to give special attention to radical items is that still running in *LABOUR, Capital and Society*. The first to concentrate on the new international labour studies is that produced at the Institute of Social Studies in The Hague.[35] IDOC International, in Rome, is not only providing systematic documentation on multinationals for TIE,[36] and publishing some in its bulletin, but has also been developing information retrieval techniques–manual and computerized–for grass-roots documentation centres.[37] In Brazil, IBASE has pioneered activist computing for workers and other grassroots groups.[38] *Asia Labour Monitor* is an attempt to provide a systematic news service to labour in that continent and internationally. SOMO, in Amsterdam, is a documentation and research centre on multinationals that provides services, amongst others, to Dutch unions and worker groups. SOBE (Foundation for Research on The Electrical and Electronics Industry), in Eindhoven, also in the Netherlands, is more internationally–and action–oriented, and has organized conferences for Philips workers internationally.[39] It is interesting to note that one of the few regular coverages of international labour periodicals is given not by a labour documentation centre but a human rights one, *Human Rights Internet Reporter*.

Character

Autonomy from capital and state and traditional labour organizations: The new media have developed from a recognition of the danger represented by the MNCs internationally, of the inability of the nation state or inter-state structures to combat these (even where they are controlled by socialists or communists), and of the ideological, structural and strategic shortcomings of traditional labour organizations.

Rejection of statism: It follows from the above that such media reject not only the claims of their own nation state or bloc, but adopt a sceptical position toward the state as a form. They tend to see themselves engaged in consciousness raising and mobilizing work, and often present themselves as involved in movements of social transformation. They tend to reject the state-like behaviour of traditional labour organizations, stressing democratization, united action regardless of ideology or faith, and the necessary inter-connection between workplace and non-workplace struggle, between class and democratic movements.

The shop-floor, the grassroots and internationalism: Against the focus on the nation state level, we find the combination of daily life problems on the shop-floor *and* internationalism. The daily life focus has two major implications: a rejection of hierarchical structures and elitist definitions of the political, and a concern to build up from workers' experiences, perceptions and capacities for autonomous activity. The internationalism is not simply a rejection of ideological or political chauvinism, it is a recognition that the problems are international, the enemy is international, and the solution must be sought and fought internationally. The contrast of the new with the old here is clear when we compare the differing coverage and interpretation of the Ford plant closure in Amsterdam given by *Free Labour World*[40] with that of *TIE Bulletin*.[41]

Networking internationally: In place of hierarchical structure and political competition what we seem to have is the network structure and the principle of cooperation. Many of the organizations or publications are themselves run on non-hierarchical lines, or are networks of co-operating organizations. But even where this is not so, they tend to require and stimulate non-hierarchical relations of information and cooperation. If the traditional organization and communication flow is A-shaped, then we must think of these as grid patterned. And if the traditional communication flow exists primarily on a vertical plane, here it lies more on a horizontal one; ideas and information are here flowing across rather than up and down, inevitably undermining the control in the A-shaped flow. The horizontal plane is only exceptionally at shop-floor, grassroots or community level: we can conceive of it as the bar across the A. But, in any case, the producers of the new media are closer to ground level than those of the old and motivated toward facilitating shop-floor contacts and information flows internationally.

Stimulation of audiovisual forms: Whilst it cannot be said that the traditional international labour organizations ignore audiovisuals, and whilst we cannot pretend that the new reject the written word (and world languages), the latter are clearly favourable to audiovisual form.

Encouragement of debate: Again, we cannot say that the new media themselves necessarily *provide* debating platforms. Many seem shy of engaging in ideological conflict with the old organizations, or of taking any kind of explicit ideological position. This is not only because of desire to avoid involvement in traditional politics, but also because they tend to adopt towards workers a service rather than a leadership role. The very existence of the new media, however, undermines the power/information monopoly (or oligopoly), presents an alternative, and therefore provides a stimulus to discussion of international labour issues.

Some Theoretical Reflections

It is now necessary to look a little more systematically at the problem area we have so far been simply describing, ordering and politically characterizing. So far we have been treating the new working-class internationalism and the alternative media as if these terms were self-explanatory. They are, in fact, both problematic terms, and terms that – to my knowledge – have not been widely theorized, at least by socialists. And, again to the best of my knowledge, no socialist has dealt theoretically with alternative media for working-class internationalism – or alternative media for any other kind of internationalism. This section pretends to do no more than to consider the relevance of the limited literature I have been able to find on this problem area.

Towards a New Working-Class Internationalism

The latest contribution to recent debate on labour internationalism is that of Haworth and Ramsey.[42] Basing themselves both on Marxist theory and on practical experience in union struggle against a multinational, they seem to me to raise doubts about not only traditional union struggles but also the radical and democratic efforts of those attempting to create a new kind of worker internationalism. For this reason they need to be taken seriously. Since their argument is presented in detail in this volume, it is not necessary to repeat it here. It is, however, worth reiterating their conclusion, where they posit

> the need to go beyond analysis of workers at the point of production to comprehend the possibilities for and obstacles to resistance against capital. If a new approach to local, national and international solidarity against capital is to be forged, then it surely must start from an awareness of the strengths and weaknesses understood beyond the factory gates or the doors of the union office.[43]

Much of Haworth and Ramsey's argument is compatible with what we have said or implied abour the old or new internationalism. The radical critique they make of past internationalism confirms what has been said here about the traditional international media; their denial of a natural or spontaneous base for a new internationalism is well taken. I have mentioned media concerned with interests and issues defined outside the MNCs. I have suggested that the new communications pattern is itself subversive of capital and state. Their stress on the practical significance of the new role of women internationally is here recognized in the existence of media concerned both with women wage workers and with women in general; the necessity they stress for a worker internationalism that goes not only beyond the MNC but beyond the factory gate and union door is allowed for here in the existence of the international single issue movements. The analogy between international and national divisions is being recognized by those national or local organizations and projects simultaneously engaged in local and international work on the same broad principles: mass self-activity against capital, state and all forms of oppression and discrimination.

If Haworth and Ramsay appear somewhat pessimistic about the new working-class internationalism, this may be because they are prisoners of their own enemy. This is so in a number of senses: exclusive concentration on multinationals and internationalisation rather than the restructuring of capital more generally; definition of *labour* solidarity solely in terms of *union* solidarity; definition of international solidarity in terms of West–West and West–South solidarity, thus excluding consideration of the significance of the 'solidarity with Solidarnosc' positions of both the traditional western labour movements and the new ones in Brazil and South Africa. Given these shortcomings, the final proposal of Haworth and Ramsay on the need to go beyond is bound to lack weight. On the other hand, however, none of the qualifications made here would seem incompatible with their general line of argument, suggesting, rather, elements necessary to an all round consideration of the old and new internationalism. The economic basis for such an extension is provided by Ruivenkamp, who not only reveals the extent to which concentration of MNC control is accompanied by the spread of small, co-operative and domestice enterprise production, but also how international capitalism dominates the nation state and every sphere of private life.[44] The new understanding of politics necessary for such an extension can be found in those Marxists and other radicals writing on non-party political formations in India[45] or new social movements in Latin America.[46] Here we see not only a rejection of the traditional political forms and forums, but new worker movements growing alongside those of women, ethnic minorities, squatters and youth. And we see this interest in the politics of the base as being combined with recognition of the *international* source of the common problems.[47]

Understanding an alternative communications model

Lipnack and Stamps are concerned with defining, identifying, classifying, stimulating and co-ordinating a new type of organizational structure or relationship which they see as challenging the dominant established one in the United States. This structure is the network. The structure of the network differs from the bureaucratic/hierarchical model in so far as the latter is composed of self-reliant and autonomous participants, rejects concentration of power and the classical division of labour and distributes power and responsibility;

> while bureaucracies function along vertical lines, with information flowing up and orders flowing down, networks function along horizontal lines with information and ideas passing from person to person and group to group.[48]

It is accepted that informal networks operate at both ends of the global power hierarchy, but Lipnack and Stamps recognize diametrically opposed ideologies here. They evidently do not consider the ideology of the 'old boy' network particularly liberatory. They thus consider that it is the ideology or concepts of those outside the dominant organizations that are crucial. Such alternative values and attitudes are those summarized in the quote above; the book classifies hundreds of American networks into the related categories: health, co-operatives and communities, ecology and energy, politics and economics, education and communications, personal and spiritual growth, and global and futures networks attempting to surpass notions of nationalism, of limitless economic growth and of political hegemony. The individual networks listed include a great variety of humanist, libertarian, spiritualist, and other alternative movements, including a small number of labour, socialist and Marxist ones – some listed in this paper.

Let us first consider the network as organizational principle. It is clear that in so far as it is consciously posed against it the network is subversive of the bureaucratic organization necessary for exploitation and oppression. The network is also compatible (indeed embodied in) computer technology. The first industrial revolution and the nation state required and fostered the hierarchical, technocratic, bureaucratic structure and process. But it has been argued that

> the use of the computer runs counter to the very principle of the one-directional bureaucratic hierarchy, and replaces it with the network of interdependence ... The bureaucratic, mechanical model of organisation, in which every decision comes from above and has repercussions at every level of execution, is now replaced by the cybernetic model that requires the 'feedback' of dialogue, coordination and participation.[49]

However, this cannot be taken to mean that the network principle is sufficient to overthrow or even undermine the existing structures. This is implicitly recognized by Lipnack and Stamps, when they stress the centrality of certain values to the creation of 'Another America'. These values are generally democratic, egalitarian and solidarian. They are thus implicitly, and sometimes explicitly, opposed to capitalism, the state, nationalism, militarism, racism, consumerism and so on. Although Lipnack and Stamps fail to recognize the centrality of capital accumulation of the multinational as its most dynamic and dangerous representative (and therefore ignore workers and working-class internationalism), the principles and values they stress are not incompatible with the needs of workers.

Indeed by showing the range of non- or anti-capitalist interests and movements, Lipnack and Stamps suggest a broad range of popular interests and forces that national and international worker networks could appeal to or draw upon. Much of the experience of the democratic and egalitarian international networks is there for the workers' movement to learn from.

The same is true for the technology Lipnack and Stamps deal with. Much of what they say about the nature and role of newsletters is, for example, recognizable and helpful to the present writer. And faced with the general ignorance and passivity of the left concerning the computer their recognition of its potential for democratic communication is salutary.[50]

> While the argument against computers has been sagely presented and sorely experienced by nearly everyone living in over-industrialised societies, the decentralised small computer is one of the most powerful tools ever to become available to networkers.[51]

If Lipnack and Stamps tend to ideological populism and political eclecticism, then it may also be that they provide us with inadequate tools for our specific social force (the working class) and our particular level of operation (the international). Contemporary American experience, moreover, has too many national peculiarities (low level of worker organization, high technology used by both capitalism and its critics or opponents) to provide a sufficient base for an appropriate communications model. An avowedly Marxist model, drawing on Latin American and international experience – historical and contemporary – and concerned explicitly with the struggle against transnationalization should be more relevant. Fred Stangelaar entitles his study 'Alternative Communication.'[52] What follows is a translation and selective presentation of certain relevant passages.

For Stangelaar, alternative means opposed to both capital and bureaucracy. Opposition is primarily to the multinationals, their concentration of control, and their spreading of uniform western bourgeois values through a multiplicity of media channels and products. The alternative society is not an existing or projected model but something to be worked out in struggle by the mass movements and tendencies involved. Although such an alternative may be conceived and proposed by intellectuals and professionals, its construction depends not on their knowledge or theories (and certainly not in their grasping the media for themselves) but in the practical revolutionary work implied by the communication process itself.

The major source for alternative communication is the practical resistance to international capitalism in general, implying also struggle against racism, sexism, propaganda for the state and war. Stangelaar wishes to distinguish alternative communication from other forms of non-dominant communication such as marginal communication – not allied to the masses or social and political movements; horizontal communication – information exchange between dominated groups; anti-information and communication – which whilst subverting either the content or form of dominant communication does not (or not yet) connect with mass needs and struggles.

The four fundamental and interdependent characteristics of alternative communication are content, language, imagery and symbolism that comes directly from the people, their daily life and struggles, and that confronts those of the oppressors; an orientation towards a total social transformation; a mobilizing and organizing role, surpassing both vertical and horizontal information flows with a spiral communication model and the active role in both production and distribution of the relevant sector of the population and/or social organizations.

Such active participation implies, amongst other things, interaction between sender and receiver; messages that further interaction of both the population and the professional communicators; accessibility of both form and content to the population, at a minimum educational level, this education being part of the communication task; public access to both production and distribution channels; participation in the communication education structures and organization of a public capable of criticizing and eventually correcting the media.

Stangelaar sees the necessity of networking between different alternative communication projects as essential not simply for an integration of the different national and international projects, but similarly for the protection of a certain financial and technical autonomy *vis-a-vis* the dominant media. Such networking is also essential for the development of an international alternative.

If Lipnack and Stamps are strong on examples but eclectic in orientation and organizational principles, Stangelaar is strong on the latter even whilst giving few examples. His identification of the multinationals as the main enemy, of the alternative as implying struggle against capital and all forms of oppression and being formed precisely by and in the struggle against these, give the concept a cutting edge and strategic orientation lacking in Lipnack and Stamps.

His distinction of alternative from other forms of non-dominant communication is crucial for our subject. Most of what I have described above should probably be characterized as anti-information and communication. This becomes even clearer when we consider his four characteristics of alternative communication. For, even where the new international media could claim to conform to some criteria (social transformation orientation, mobilizing and organizing), few would claim to conform to the criteria of popular content and form, involvement of masses or mass organizations. None the less, the recognition of such standards – as well as those concerning participation – enable us to judge the products or projects, or to make explicit our reasons for not meeting the criteria.

Stangelaar stresses the central importance of networking between communications nationally and internationally. It seems to me that most of the examples in this paper are of such international networks of communicators – providing we define communicators to cover teachers, organizers, journalists and researchers. Thus, these new communications' forms mostly amount to international networking between those involved nationally in either subverting the existing structures, or building the alternative according to the criteria of mass participation and mobilization

Stangelaar suggests. In so far as we recognize that we are involved in international networking between organizers/mediators/catalysers or whatever, two interconnected questions remain for those working toward a new communications model for a new working class internationalism: are we not simply networking internationally between marginal or anti-communicators, giving ourselves self-satisfaction whilst failing to relate to mass struggles? To what extent are we creating an autonomous structure capable of both supporting local projects and synthesizing them internationally?

Problems and Proposals

The theoretical section may be of help in providing conceptual tools or suggesting aims and norms. It does not seem to be of much direct use in identifying practical problems or suggesting practical solutions to them. This is understandable given that the theory has not addressed our specific area. The problems and proposals identified are thus drawn rather from my experiences in international networking and reflection upon it. I hope my thoughts will be at least informed or inspired by the foregoing theoretical discussion.

Problems

Uneven development: We have within international labour communication both dynamic growth and considerable creativity; but this is combined with the kind of atomisation and instability suggested by Stangelaar above. There are also numerous gaps in geographical or problem coverage, duplication of effort and wasted effort. The world capitalist crisis does not avoid striking those who specialize in struggling against it. One community communicator in the US has suggested that we are at a critical turning point for issue-oriented organizations, which will either have to collaborate and share resources or die.[53]

Lack of labour control: Even where rank and file activists contribute to or supervise the new international media, these tend to remain in the effective control of professionals and intellectuals. The limitations and dangers of this have been spelled out above and are exemplified at the national level in the dramatic development of left media and research in Peru.

> Its extensive presence is matched by its inorganic structure and its lack of formal and sustained ties to the popular movements. The left-wing intellectual currents have in some cases developed working relations with trade unions, but more often such efforts are divorced from the real world. They also have a tendency to reify the separation: the first step towards the development of a professional caste within which careerist aspirations subordinate Marxist analysis to social mobility. The most pressing need today is for greater articulation between the flourishing intellectual and cultural centres and the mass movements.[54]

Such problems may be less in industrialized capitalist (and communist?) countries as the relative number of knowledge workers increases and the white collar blue collar distinction is replaced by the grey collar worker sharing characteristics of both. Herbert Schiller offers a scenario of increasing awareness on the part of such workers, shifting from classical wages and conditions demands to those concerning control.[55] Even today, those who have been refused, or lost, or reject, conventional employment for capital and state, and who are involved with the alternative media, can hardly be thought of in terms of the *Communist Manifesto* as 'a portion of the bourgeois ideologists, who have raised themselves to the level of comprehending theoretically the historical movement as whole'.[56] Nor is the model of the late nineteenth-century Russian Narodnik 'going to the people' relevant. Nonetheless, even the lesser separation existing can become reified and struggle against it must continue – from both sides.

Concentration in the industrial capitalist world: The reason for this is clear. It is at the capitalist core that consciousness of the problem, finance and technical capacities for responding to it – and political possibilities for doing so – best exist. Yet the existence of international communications projects in Hong Kong or Rio, and the nature of the new communications technology itself, suggest that there is no inevitability here.

Language problems: The first problem is the domination of English. This creates obvious linguistic and social barriers to international grasssroots, shop-floor or community communication. If we move from one predominant language to the use of several (or many) we may hypothetically overcome the linguistic problem, but would then be faced with that of the European Economic Community. Here each new member implies not an addition to but a multiplication of translation costs which have become a major constraint on EEC development. The third problem is the social one of illiteracy or semi-literacy, restricting the ability to even read the international publications.

Technology: Here we can only mention some issues. Even if we agree to employ user-friendly personal or microcomputers, to which users (workers, documentalists) are they to be friendly?[57] Problems and prospects with respect to at least computers and computer networking are raised in the last issue of IDOC's old publication and the first issue of its new trilingual one.[58] Microfiche documentation services are becoming increasingly cheap relative to printed ones, especially for international purposes; but printed matter is legible to the eye whilst microfiche has to be scanned by a (relatively cheap) viewer. Tape/slides are relatively cheap, allow for adaptation, editing and translation, but are limited in impact and reach; video equipment is expensive and complex, but gives access to almost infinite (pirated?) programmes, and can be hypothetically broadcast.

Domination: The new media are breaking the domination of the old oligopoly, but are themselves dominated by those with sufficient funds, by intellectuals and professionals, and by the core capitalist countries. There is, for example, a clear danger that those within, or deeply compromised with, old media or movements may make concessions to new needs or organized demands whilst restricting access to the new media or retaining control of them (a question relevant to the new international union computer network discussed by Graham).[59]

Proposals[60]

Coordination: It is obvious that we need an international inventory or register of those active in this area. We need to know both what exists and what as yet does not. This does not imply centralization or hierarchy but a network of networks based on the earlier identified technology and principles. An equivalent to the ISIS Women's International Information and Communication Centre of the Human Rights Internet would be the best solution. Alternatively, a series of specialised international worker networks (Latin America, Women, Health and Safety) with one co-ordinating centre to provide common services and encourage technological compatibility should be set up. We also urgently need national co-ordinating centres for internationalist labour information, education, research and action.

Training: It has already been suggested that alternative communication should imply communication training. Some of the techniques and principles necessary for international communication and documentation are taught and spread by IDOC in Rome. But these are not oriented directly to international labour communication, nor passed down to rank and file activists. In so far as international labour communication is recognized as crucial and specific, the necessary training will also need to be developed.

Spreading: Assisting and stimulating media centres outside the core capitalist countries is also necessary. In a number of national cases (Peru, South Africa) there may be more experience with worker-oriented media than in Britain or the USA. There are also advanced international or inter-regional projects, such as *Asia Labour Monitor* based in the third world. Simply publicizing the existence of such organizations, and how they support themselves, would assist their spread.

Solving the language problem: Various possibilities occur, but making systematic use of the language skills which–thanks to education and migration–exist amongst both activists and rank and file workers is the most obvious one.

Alternative technologies: A broad and experimental approach would seem necessary here. We also need systematic study and discussion, such as has begun with the use of computers. Whilst the cheapest and most widely accessible forms and capacities (street theatre, wall newspapers) should be employed, so should the latest capitalist technologies. Video is intended to be a means of privatized consumption of capitalist or state produced messages, images and values. But in industrialized liberal democracies 1 to 5% of TV material is potentially consciousness raising. Shown to the right audience in the right way it can be revolutionary. Making video can be even more so.

A research/action project. All the above suggests the necessity for research, ideally action research carried out according to the principles suggested above. The creation of a project to study and stimulate the development of international media for a new working-class internationalism should appeal to certain church bodies, as well as to advanced tendencies within social-democratic solidarity organizations or grassroots-oriented development aid agencies. Institutes or individual academics concerned with democratic communication should also be interested.

A declaration of principles: The above paper should provide sufficient ideas for a Declaration of Principles, an Action Plan or at least a short Discussion Document on new media for a new working-class internationalism. Indeed, this paper will have failed in its purpose if it does not lead to some such immediate and tangible political outcome. I fear that if the initiative for such a practical action is not taken now by those involved in the new media, either the impetus represented by its growth so far will fade, or the project will be realized by those compromised with the old internationalism or the old media. If not us, who? If not now, when?[61]

Afterthoughts

Here I want to at least mention some issues that are not explicitly treated in the body of the paper, but which are important in the context of this collection, and which will need to be dealt with later and more adequately. These issues are the relationship of the information and argument to i) the New International Division of Labour, ii) debates on the New International Information and Communication Order, (NIICO) and on labour and socialist struggles around information technology and the new media, iii) contemporary worker movements in the third world and iv) the balance of power between capital and state on the one hand and labour internationally on the other.

The New International Division of Labour

It has been theoretical work on the NIDL that has sensitized researchers to the dangers of the latest phase in world capitalist development for labour internationally. Whilst much of the theory and research on the NIDL has indeed been economistic and deterministic, stressing only what contemporary capital logic was doing to labour,[62] it has at least focused attention on the threat posed to employment, working conditions, union rights and powers by new products, new processes, new enterprise forms and a new national and international labour force composition. Work within this tradition–or criticizing and surpassing it–has also focused more specifically on the computer and telecommunication processes as central to the NIDL. Out of this tradition, finally, has sprung an awareness of the role of the communist world in the NIDL, and of processes analogous to those in the third world taking place between or within industrialized capitalist states. But even those rejecting the partial and one sided nature of NIDL theory, and dealing with the labour side of the equation have not dealt with a new kind of internationalism except in terms of principles, or cases. I am aware that in concentrating on the strategies and even techniques of international labour communication, I am dependent on just such cases or general principles. There is, in other words, a gap which needs filling if we are to be able to develop an internationalism grounded in the everyday experience of worker life under contemporary conditions in this capitalist-dominated world. One gap to be filled is precisely that of contradictions within the new products and processes. Informatization of economy, social, political, recreational and domestic life is not something confined to the first world. A few voices can be heard pointing out possibilities and necessities for labour struggle nationally opened out by computerization, satellite communication and new mass media.[63] I know of but one that has sketched this out for labour internationally.[64]

Contemporary debates

It is my strong impression, to start with, that debate on NIICO is obscuring or postponing debate and action in the issues raised in this paper.[65] There is an assumption, even amongst socialists writing on this topic, that national control over information is the priority, and an implication (in the best cases) that it is a precondition for democratic control. Writers are operating with the old centre–periphery model that obscures class contradictions around the media at the periphery and at the centre. It seems to me that whilst the NIICO debate may stimulate anti-imperialism, it also increases statism, since it is the third world state which acts for the nation. To me it is evident that third world state control of information and culture (and the possibilitiy for Rajiv Gandhi to communicate directly with General Pinochet without going via Washington) is a new and powerful obstacle to democratic communication within third world states and between the third world peoples. Such new linkages will be touted as being in the interests of the 'information poor'. But even where such new old boy networks are not used for police and army matters, they are going to be confidential, technically complex, expensive, and by these tokens inaccessible and inappropriate for popular communication internationally. The argument for the democratization of international communication implied by this paper articulates a powerful set of interests and values: labour, nationalism, internationalism, democracy. As for labour and socialist debate and action on communications, this has been bedevilled by the false dichtomy: subordination/opposition. Simple opposition to new technology and new media is a comprehensible response to a technological revolution dominated by capital and state, and largely directed against the traditional bastions of labour. Opposition is also an essential element of a counter-strategy. But my impression is that those who see this as the whole are forced either into repeated defensive positions on a terrain chosen by capital, or into a celebration of Luddism and sabotage which signally fails to equip workers to collectively empower themselves. Fortunately, I am not the only one who has been arguing for the possibility and necessity of a new worker communication activity taking advantage of the profound contradictions within the new technologies.[66] And my paper shows how many groups working with workers have been developing a new practice without necessarily theorizing about or arguing for it.

Third World Worker Movements

It would be possible, on the basis of developments in the one or two years since this paper was first drafted, to extend the list of alternative international labour communications projects in and from the third world. South Africa, admittedly an exceptional case, might be the best example. But there has been an increase in such activity from the Philippines and Brazil. This activty has involved not only publications in English from the new worker movements but exchange visits, including those of shop-floor activists (at least in the North–South direction). Third world labour communications specialists have also been active in international meetings on networking.[67] And it has been argued that it was third world groups that first began using the new information and communications technology. It is, however, doubtful whether this activity has as broad a base as that in the industrialized capitalist countries, for reasons suggested above. This poses before the new worker movements in the third world a special challenge in finding and developing appropriate media (new and old) for communication between workers at shop-floor level internationally. In overthrowing the Shah, Khomeini's communication strategy involved the use of the cassette and photocopier (new but widespread and comparatively cheap and simple technologies), the bazaar (as social base and space) and Islam (as popular ideology). Third world labour and democratic movements can learn from, and need to surpass, this model.

The Power of International Labour

The time that has passed since originally drafting this paper permits a tentative answer to the questions raised about the effectiveness or otherwise of the alternative international labour media. I say tentative because there is yet no research, and there is not yet even a research technology which we could propose to test for such effects. On relating to mass struggles, we might consider the British miners' strike and the Bhopal disaster. Given that the British TUC and the ICFTU were unable or unwilling to immediately and conditionally support the British miners, information and solidarity had inevitably to be carried by other channels. To an extent this was done by traditional oppositions within the western labour movements, but in the Netherlands it was also done by a dozen or more alternative groups and publications, resulting in visits and money collections long before the Dutch FNV did more than publish a post office savings account number (for charity, not solidarity). The Bhopal case saw fast, worldwide, informed and effective response in a possibly unparalleled way. Groups which have for many years been researching, protesting and warning about environmental threats to labour were able to launch national and international compaigns, using periodicals, pamphlets, postal services, video, film, and no doubt other means. They raised issues, particularly about the co-responsibility of the Indian state, which official labour publications – whether in India, the Netherlands or at the ICFTU – were unwilling or unable to do. Whilst the ICFTU was addressing itself to the Indian government or international agencies, the alternative groups in India and abroad were addressing themselves to the grassroots and the community. These cases demonstrate the contemporary potential for internationalist labour activity and the significance of the alternative media for mobilizing this. The rest depends on research and political activities by us.

Notes

1. Acknowledgements for sympathetic and helpful comments on earlier drafts of this paper are due most especially to Cees Hamelink but also to Tony Zurbrugg of Third World Publications, Vinnie Mosco of Queen's University, Canada, John Downing of Hunter College, New York, Robin Cohen of Warwick University, UK, Matty Klatter and Rachel Kurian of ISS, The Hague, Bertell Ollman of New York University and others.

2. On the first see Peter Waterman (ed.) *For a New Labour Internationalism: A Set of Reprints and Working Papers* (International Labour Education Research and Information Foundation, The Hague, 1984).

3. For more extensive bibliographies and resource lists see Peter Waterman and Matty Klatter, 'An Overview of Recent Studies and Current Serials', *International Labour Studies: A Third World and Labour-Oriented Bibliography*, no. 18 and Peter Waterman, 'International Labour and Communications', no. 22 in the same series,, ISS, The Hague. See further the *Newsletter of International Labour Studies* (NILS) from which many cited examples have been taken and in which many uncited ones may be found (for an index see NILS 20). Other continuing sources of relevant listings are *TIE Report* and *International Labour Reports*.

4. Glasgow University Media Group, *Bad News* and *More Bad News* (Routledge and Kegan Paul, London, 1980 and 1984).

5. NACLA, 'Toward a New Information Order', *NACLA Report*, vol. 16, no. 4, pp. 2-35.

6. A. Hester, 'The News from Latin America', *Gazette*, vol. 20, no. 2, 1974 and 'Five Years of Foreign News in US Evening Newscasts', *Gazette*, vol. 24, no. 1, 1978.

7. See the coverage of Poland in *World Trade Union Movement*, Monthly magazine of The World Federation of Trade Unions, 1980–83.
8. *ICFTU Economic and Social Bulletin*, nos. 5-6, 1983, p. 6.
9. Herman Lansink, 'Ford Won't Stay', *Free Labour World*, no. 6, 1981, pp. 30–31. 31.
10. *Financial Times*, 18 May 1970.
11. Robin Cohen, 'Resistence and Hidden Forms of Consciousness Among African Workers', *Review of African Political Economy*, no. 19, 1980, pp. 8-22.
12. Jan Cartier, 'Raising the Curtain', *TIE*–Europe Bulletin, no. 16, 1983, pp. 23-32.
13. *NILS*, no. 12, 1980, pp. 6-9.
14. *NILS*, no. 17, 1983, pp. 22-24.
15. *NILS*, no. 6, 1980, pp. 21-22.
16. *NILS*, no. 15, 1982, pp. 6-10.
17. *NILS*, no. 6, 1980, pp. 16-18.
18. *NILS*, no. 14, 1982, pp. 1-2.
19. *NILS*, no. 7, 1980, pp. 7-10, 19.
20. *NILS*, no. 9, 1981, p. 26.
21. *NILS*, no. 17, 1983, pp. 22-24.
22. Robin Cohen, 'The "New" International Labour Studies: a Definition', Working Paper No. 27, Centre for Developing Area Studies, McGill University, Montreal, 1980.
23. *NILS*, no. 19, 1983, p. 2.
24. *NILS*, no. 20, 1984.
25. *NILS*, no. 19, 1983, pp. 9-10.
26. Barry Pavier, 'Class Struggles in India', *International Socialism*, vol. 20, no. 2, 1983, pp. 55-81.
27. 'Industrial Relations: A Guide for Trade Unionists', *TIE–Europe Bulletin,* nos. 13-14, 1982-3.
28. *The Plight of Asian Workers in Electronics* (Christian Conference of Asia–Urban Rural Mission, Hong Kong), 1982.
29. *NILS*, no. 13, 1982, pp. 2-3.
30. *NILS*, no. 16, 1982, pp. 14-15.
31. *NILS*, no. 16, 1982, p. 6.
32. For which see *NILS*, no. 11, 1981, pp. 19-21.
33. *NILS*, no. 17, 1983, p. 25.
34. *NILS*, no. 16, 1982, p. 10.
35. Matty Klatter, *International Labour Studies: A Third World and Labour-oriented Bibliography* (ISS, The Hague, 22 issues 1979-1984).
36. *NILS*, no. 6, 1980, pp. 21-2.
37. *NILS*, no. 19, 1983, pp. 10-11, 20.
38. *Reset*, 1983. 'IBASE Pioneers Activist Computing in Brazil', *Reset*, no. 7, pp. 1–2.
39. *NILS*, 14, April 1982, 1982, pp. 1–2.
40. Herman Lansink, 'Ford Must Stay' and 'Ford Won't Stay', *Free Labour World*, no. 5, 1981, pp. 23-4 and no. 6, 1981, pp. 30-31.
41. Cartier, 'Raising the Curtain'.
42. See paper in this volume.
43. See p.
44. Guido Ruivenkamp, 'Multinational Cycles and Diffused Factory' in Waterman, *For a New Labour Internationalism*, pp. 146-171.

45. D.L. Sheth, 'Grass-Roots Stirrings and the Future of Politics', *Alternatives*, vol. 9, 1983, pp. 1-24.

46. Tilman Evers, 'Identity: The Hidden Side of New Social Movements in Latin America', in David Slater (ed.) *New Social Movements and the State in Latin America* (Favis Publications, Dordrecht, 1985). pp. 43–71.

47. Sheth, 'Grass-Roots Stirrings'.

48. Jessica Lipnack and Jeffrey Stamps, *Networking: The First Report and Directory* (Doubleday, New York, 1982), p. 8.

49. Roger Garaudy, *The Alternative Future: A Vision of Christian Marxism*, (Penguin, Middlesex, 1976), pp. 65-6.

50. Cees Hamelink, 'Appeal for a New Luddism: Why does the Left have no reply to the Computer Society?' (in Dutch), *De Groene Amsterdammer*, 13 July 1983, pp. 10-11.

51. Lipnack and Stamps, *Networking*, p. 139.

52. Fred Stangelaar, *Alternative Kommunikatie*, Master's dissertation, Institute of Political Science, Nijmegen. Netherlands.

53. Steve Johnson, 'Community Application of Information and Communication Technology', *IDOC Bulletin*, no. 7, 1983, pp. 15-17.

54. James Petras, M. Morely and A.E. Havens, 'Peru: Capitalist Democracy in Transition', *New Left Review*, no. 142, 1983, pp. 30-.

55. Herbert Schiller, *Communication and Cultural Domination* (M.E. Sharpe, White Plains, USA. (1976).

56. Karl Marx and Frederick Engels, *Selected Works in One Volume*, (Lawrence and Wishart, London, 1968).

57. Ian Graham, 'Programmed Solidarity: First Studies on a Union Computer Network', *NILS*, no. 19, 1983, pp. 9-10.

58. *IDOC Monthly Bulletin*, nos. 11-12, 1984, *IDOC Internazionale*, vol. 16, no. 1, 1985.

59. Graham, 'Programmed Solidarity'.

60. Since the first draft of this paper in February 1984 certain steps have been taken to translate the suggestions below into action. I have made a proposal ('The Mayday Project' ISS, The Hague, 1985) for a research action project on this area and have also been involved in the creation of the International Labour Education Research and Information Foundation (ILERI). This provides a potential vehicle for some of the activities indicated, although at present it has minimal human and financial resources. Its first activity has been the publication of Waterman, *For a New Labour Internationalism*, and its second should be the publication of a collection on international labour communication.

61. The answers seem to be i) a Spanish port workers network and ii) 1985 May 1. This document, submitted to an international alternative conference of port workers and port communities in Hamburg, deals primarily with written communication and computers. But in criticizing the information strategy of existing power holders and proposing a worker counter-strategy it produces the first ever international and internationalist declaration of principles on workers and information that I have come across. See 'Information and the Construction of Socialism: Document for the International Alternative Conference in Hamburg, May 1, 1985', (translation from Spanish), *Coordinadora*, 1985, ISS, The Hague.

62. Roger Southall, 'Reasserting the Import of Third World Union Struggles: Notes on the Ottawa Conference on Third World Unions', *NILS*, no. 25, 1985, pp. 1–10, 23.

63. Raymond Williams, *Towards 2000* (Chatto and Windus, London, 1983);

Michael Goldhaber, 'Microelectric Networks: A New Workers' Culture in Formation?', in V. Mosco and J. Wosko (eds), *The Critical Communications Review: Vol. 1, Labour, The Working Class and Media* (Ablex, Norwood, 1983), pp. 211-44.

64. 'Information and the Construction of Socialism'.

65. NACLA, 'Towards a New Information Order', *NACLA Report*, vol. 16, no. 4, 1982, pp. 2-35.

66. Goldhaber, 'Microelectronic Networks' and 'Information and the Construction of Socialism'.

67. *Monthly Bulletin*, 1984; *Internazionale*, 1985.

ICFTU Economic and Social Bulletin Bi-monthly bulletin of the International Confederation of Free Trade Unions, rue Montagne aux Herbes Potageres 37-41, 1000 Brussels, Belgium.

IDOC Internazionale Bio-monthly and trilingual quarterly, 'an instrument of communication for a non-dependent development'. *Address*: Via S. Maria dell' Anima 30, 00186 Rome, Italy. *Tel*: 06/6568332. *Subscription* (foreign airmail): L.35.000.

International Labour Reports Bi-monthly popular-style magazine concerned with creating a new working-class internationalism and oriented towards labour movement activists in Britain and abroad. *Address*: 300 Oxford Rd, Manchester M13 9NS, U.K. *Tel*: 061-273-8717. *Subscription*: (individual, abroad): £13.50.

Newsletter of International Labour Studies Quarterly on labour-oriented international labour studies and the new working-class internationalism. Frequent special issues on countries (India, Brazil, Indonesia) or themes (international labour migration, women's labour). Rubrics on research resources, audio-visuals, bibliography, etc. *Address*: Galileistr. 130, 2561 TK The Hague, Netherlands. *Tel*: 070-600791. *Subscription*: 10 issues air-mailed for US$ 14 (individual), US$ 31 (institutional).

Reset: News on Activist and Grass Roots Computing Appears approximately bimonthly. Deals with attempts to use computers and develop computer networks amongst anti-nuclear, environmental, social service and other such groupings. *Address*: Mike McCullogh, 90 E. 7th St., No. 3A, New York, NY 10009, USA. *Tel*: (212) 254-3582. *Subscription*: $0.50 per issue.

TIE Report Occasional (3-4 annually) publication of the Transnationals Information Exchange. Special issues on Ford, the motor industry, Brazil, industrial relations in West Europe, campaigning against corporations, etc. Regular resource lists. *Address*: Paulus Potterstr. 20, 1071 DA Amsterdam, Netherlands. *Tel:* 020-726608. *Subscription:* $15 for four issues (individual), $50 (institutions).